MAD LOVE CHASE

Kazusa Takashima

Volume 5

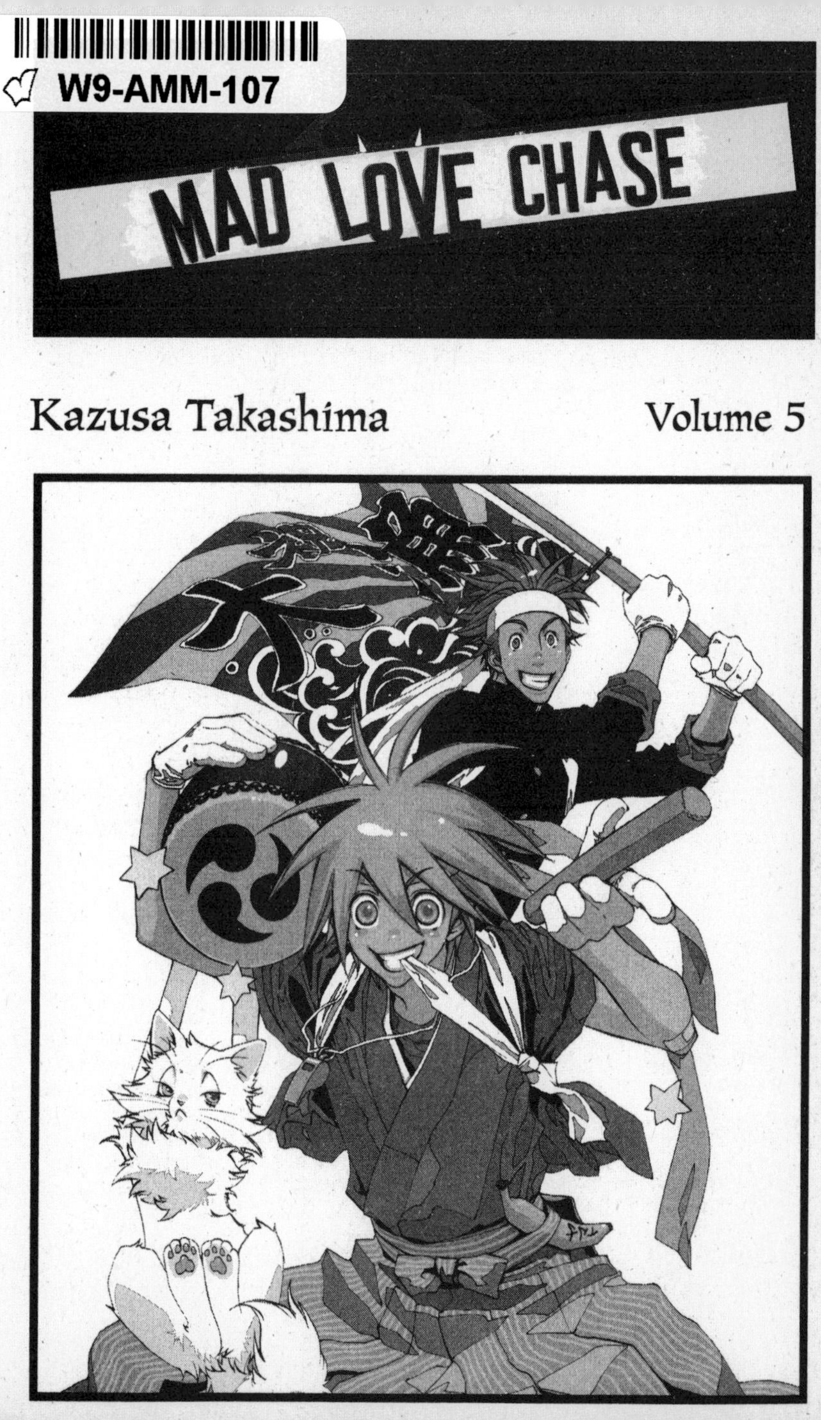

Harlem Beat Wa Yoakemade -Mad Love Chase- Volume 5
Created by Kazusa TAKASHIMA

Translation & Adaptation - Katherine Schilling
Retouch and Lettering - Star Print Brokers
Copy Editor - Daniella Orihuela-Gruber
Production Artist - Rui Kyo
Graphic Designer - Keiran O'Leary

Editor - Lillian Diaz-Przybyl
Print Production Manager - Lucas Rivera
Managing Editor - Vy Nguyen
Senior Designer - Louis Csontos
Art Director - Al-Insan Lashley
Director of Sales and Manufacturing - Allyson De Simone
Associate Publisher - Marco F. Pavia
President and C.O.O. - John Parker
C.E.O. and Chief Creative Officer - Stu Levy

A **TOKYOPOP** Manga

TOKYOPOP and are trademarks or registered trademarks of TOKYOPOP Inc.

TOKYOPOP Inc.
5900 Wilshire Blvd. Suite 2000
Los Angeles, CA 90036

E-mail: info@TOKYOPOP.com
Come visit us online at www.TOKYOPOP.com

HARLEM BEAT WA YOAKEMADE Volume 5
© Kazusa TAKASHIMA 2008
First published in Japan in 2008
by KADOKAWA SHOTEN PUBLISHING CO., LTD., Tokyo.
English translation rights arranged
with KADOKAWA SHOTEN PUBLISHING CO., LTD., Tokyo
through TUTTLE–MORI AGENCY, INC., Tokyo.
English text copyright © 2011 TOKYOPOP Inc.

ISBN: 978-1-4278-1645-0

First TOKYOPOP printing: February 2011
10 9 8 7 6 5 4 3 2 1
Printed in the USA

MAD LOVE CHASE

Volume.5

by Kazusa TAKASHIMA

HAMBURG // LONDON // LOS ANGELES // TOKYO

& STORY SUMMARY ♪

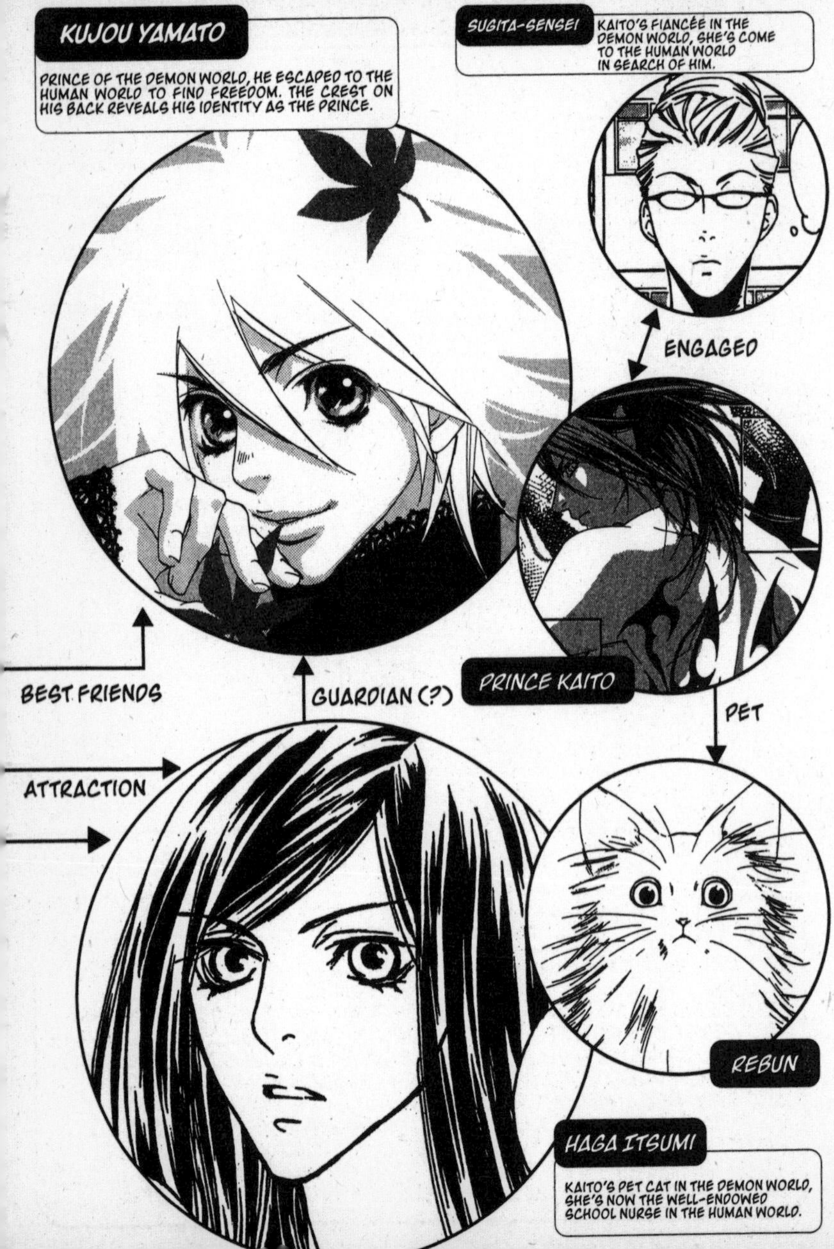

KUJOU YAMATO
PRINCE OF THE DEMON WORLD, HE ESCAPED TO THE HUMAN WORLD TO FIND FREEDOM. THE CREST ON HIS BACK REVEALS HIS IDENTITY AS THE PRINCE.
SUGITA-SENSEI
KAITO'S FIANCÉE IN THE DEMON WORLD, SHE'S COME TO THE HUMAN WORLD IN SEARCH OF HIM.
ENGAGED
BEST FRIENDS
GUARDIAN (?)
PRINCE KAITO
PET
ATTRACTION
REBUN
HAGA ITSUMI
KAITO'S PET CAT IN THE DEMON WORLD, SHE'S NOW THE WELL-ENDOWED SCHOOL NURSE IN THE HUMAN WORLD.

CHARACTER RELATIONS

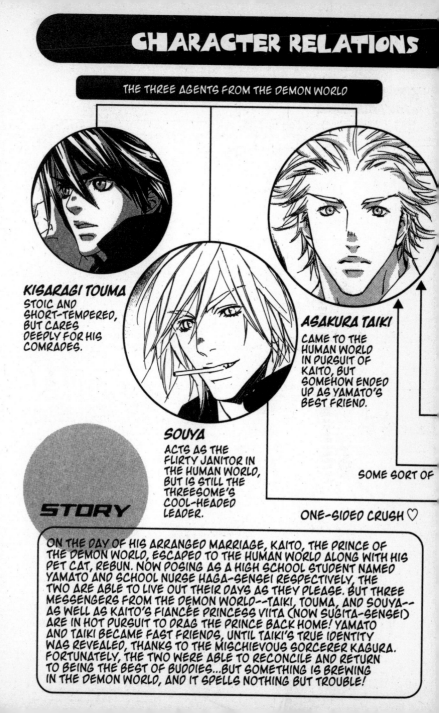

THE THREE AGENTS FROM THE DEMON WORLD

KISARAGI TOUMA
STOIC AND SHORT-TEMPERED, BUT CARES DEEPLY FOR HIS COMRADES.

SOUYA
ACTS AS THE FLIRTY JANITOR IN THE HUMAN WORLD, BUT IS STILL THE THREESOME'S COOL-HEADED LEADER.

ASAKURA TAIKI
CAME TO THE HUMAN WORLD IN PURSUIT OF KAITO, BUT SOMEHOW ENDED UP AS YAMATO'S BEST FRIEND.

SOME SORT OF ONE-SIDED CRUSH ♡

STORY

ON THE DAY OF HIS ARRANGED MARRIAGE, KAITO, THE PRINCE OF THE DEMON WORLD, ESCAPED TO THE HUMAN WORLD ALONG WITH HIS PET CAT, REBUN. NOW POSING AS A HIGH SCHOOL STUDENT NAMED YAMATO AND SCHOOL NURSE HAGA-SENSEI RESPECTIVELY, THE TWO ARE ABLE TO LIVE OUT THEIR DAYS AS THEY PLEASE. BUT THREE MESSENGERS FROM THE DEMON WORLD--TAIKI, TOUMA, AND SOUYA--AS WELL AS KAITO'S FIANCÉE PRINCESS VIITA (NOW SUGITA-SENSEI) ARE IN HOT PURSUIT TO DRAG THE PRINCE BACK HOME! YAMATO AND TAIKI BECAME FAST FRIENDS, UNTIL TAIKI'S TRUE IDENTITY WAS REVEALED, THANKS TO THE MISCHIEVOUS SORCERER KAGURA. FORTUNATELY, THE TWO WERE ABLE TO RECONCILE AND RETURN TO BEING THE BEST OF BUDDIES...BUT SOMETHING IS BREWING IN THE DEMON WORLD, AND IT SPELLS NOTHING BUT TROUBLE!

TABLE OF CONTENTS

Characters & Story 4

Special Short 7

Vol. 21 15

Vol. 22 41

Vol. 23 65

Vol. 24 89

Vol. 25 113

Vol. 26 127

Final Chapter 151

Postscript 175

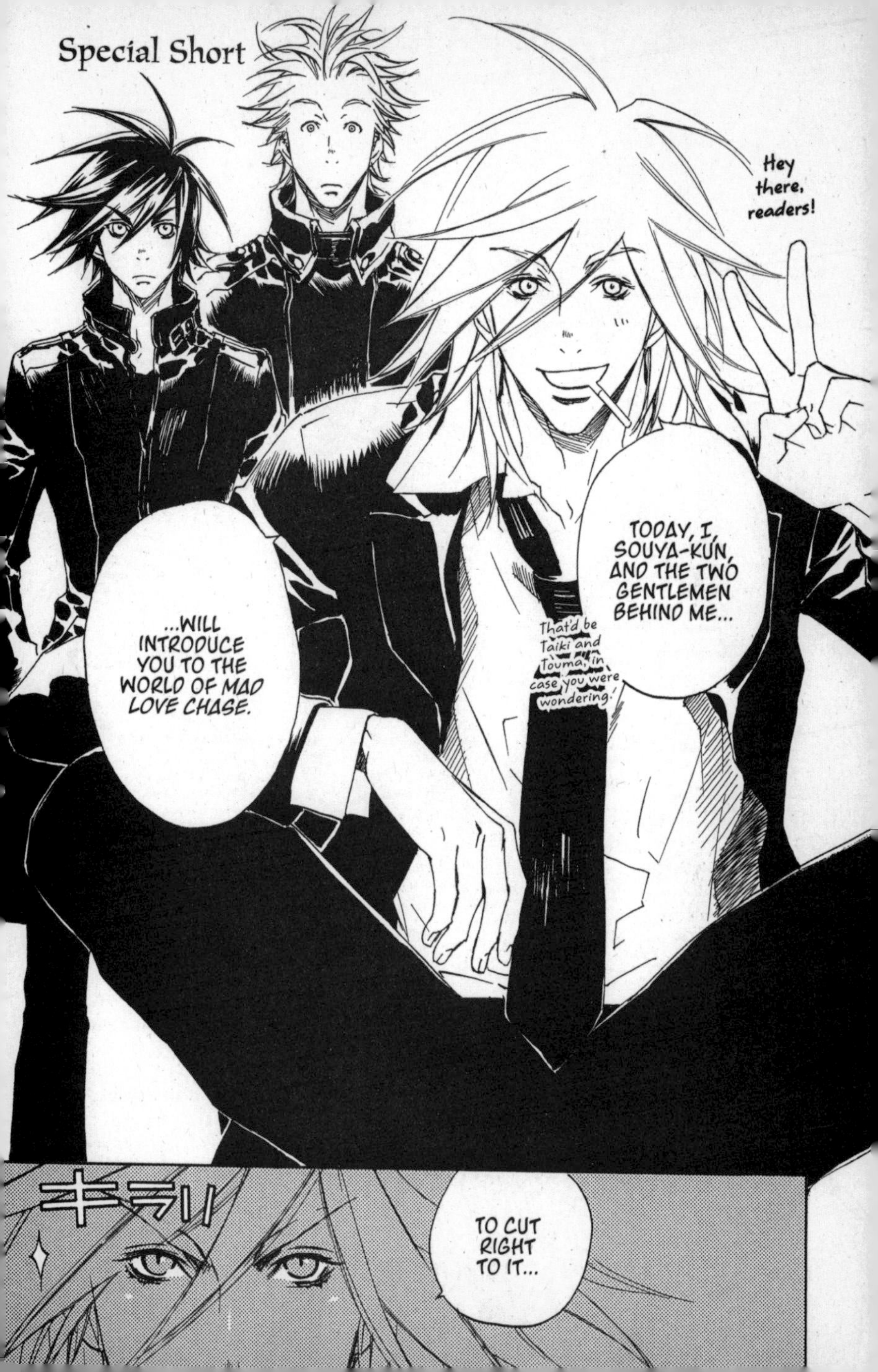
Special Short
Hey there, readers!
TODAY, I, SOUYA-KUN, AND THE TWO GENTLEMEN BEHIND ME...
That'd be Taiki and Touma, in case you were wondering!
...WILL INTRODUCE YOU TO THE WORLD OF MAD LOVE CHASE.
TO CUT RIGHT TO IT...
キラリ

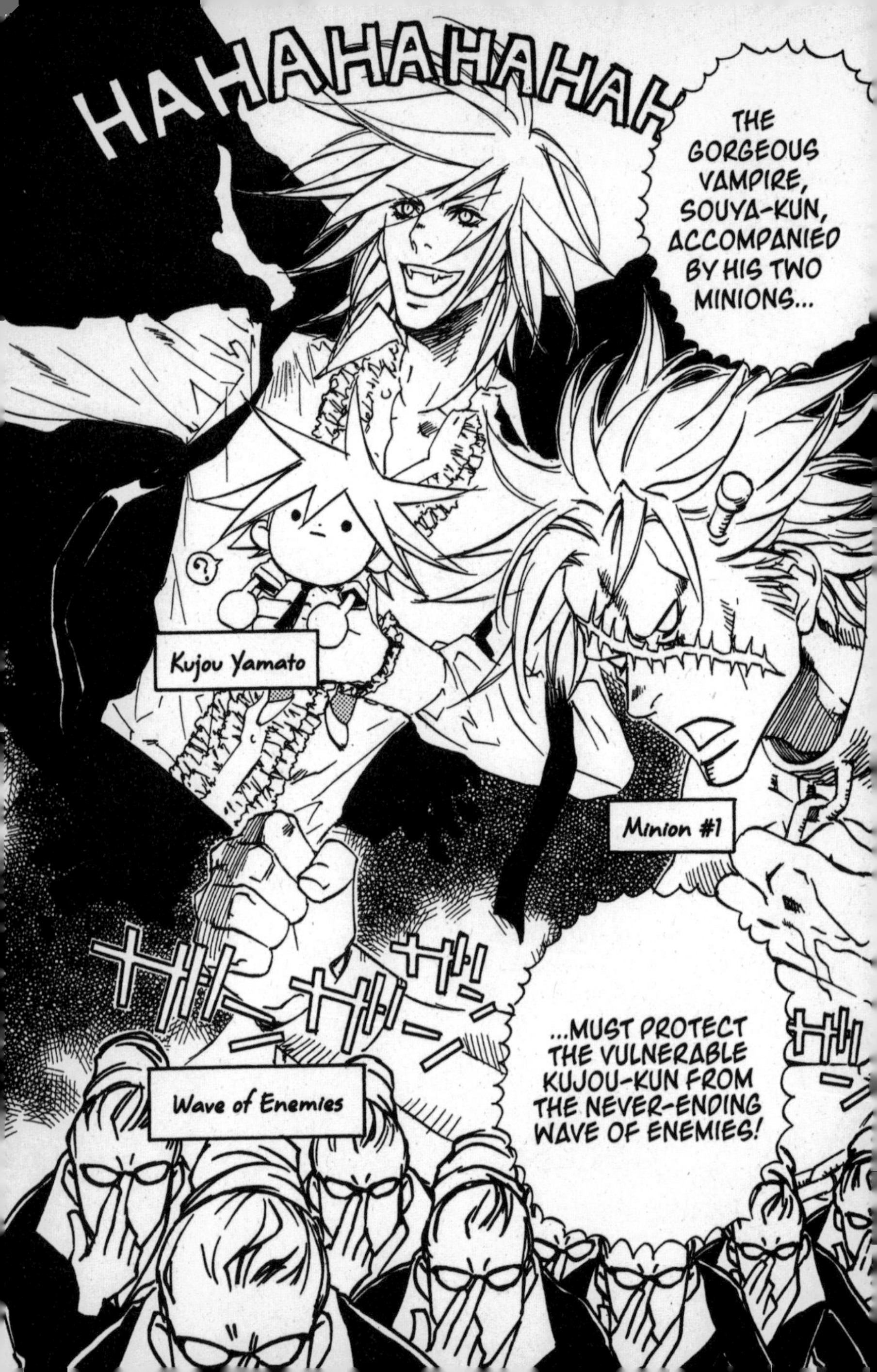
THE GORGEOUS VAMPIRE, SOUYA-KUN, ACCOMPANIED BY HIS TWO MINIONS...
HAHAHAHAHAHAH
Minion #1
Kujou Yamato
...MUST PROTECT THE VULNERABLE KUJOU-KUN FROM THE NEVER-ENDING WAVE OF ENEMIES!
Wave of Enemies

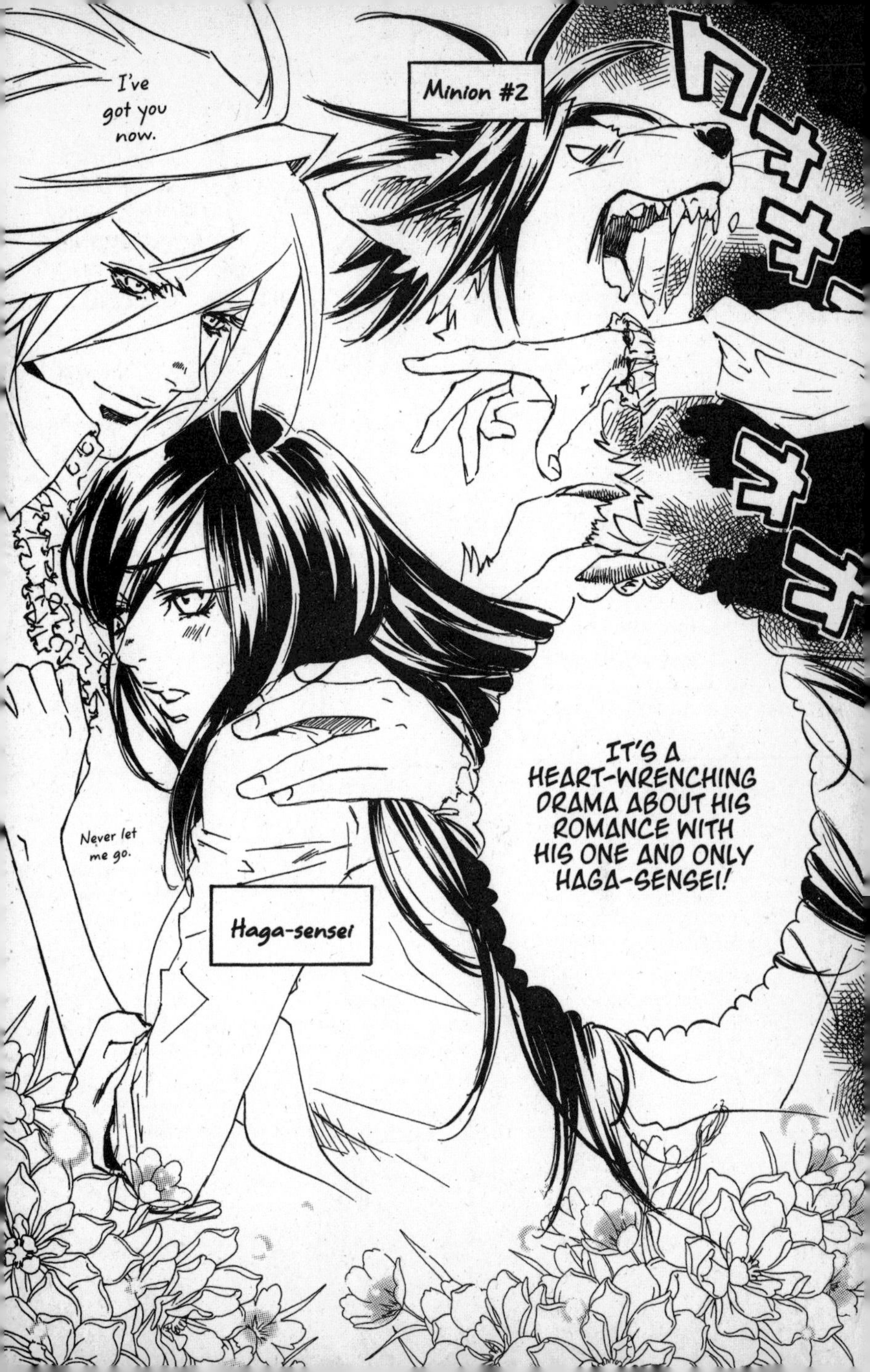
Minion #2
I've got you now.
IT'S A HEART-WRENCHING DRAMA ABOUT HIS ROMANCE WITH HIS ONE AND ONLY HAGA-SENSEI!
Haga-sensei
Never let me go.

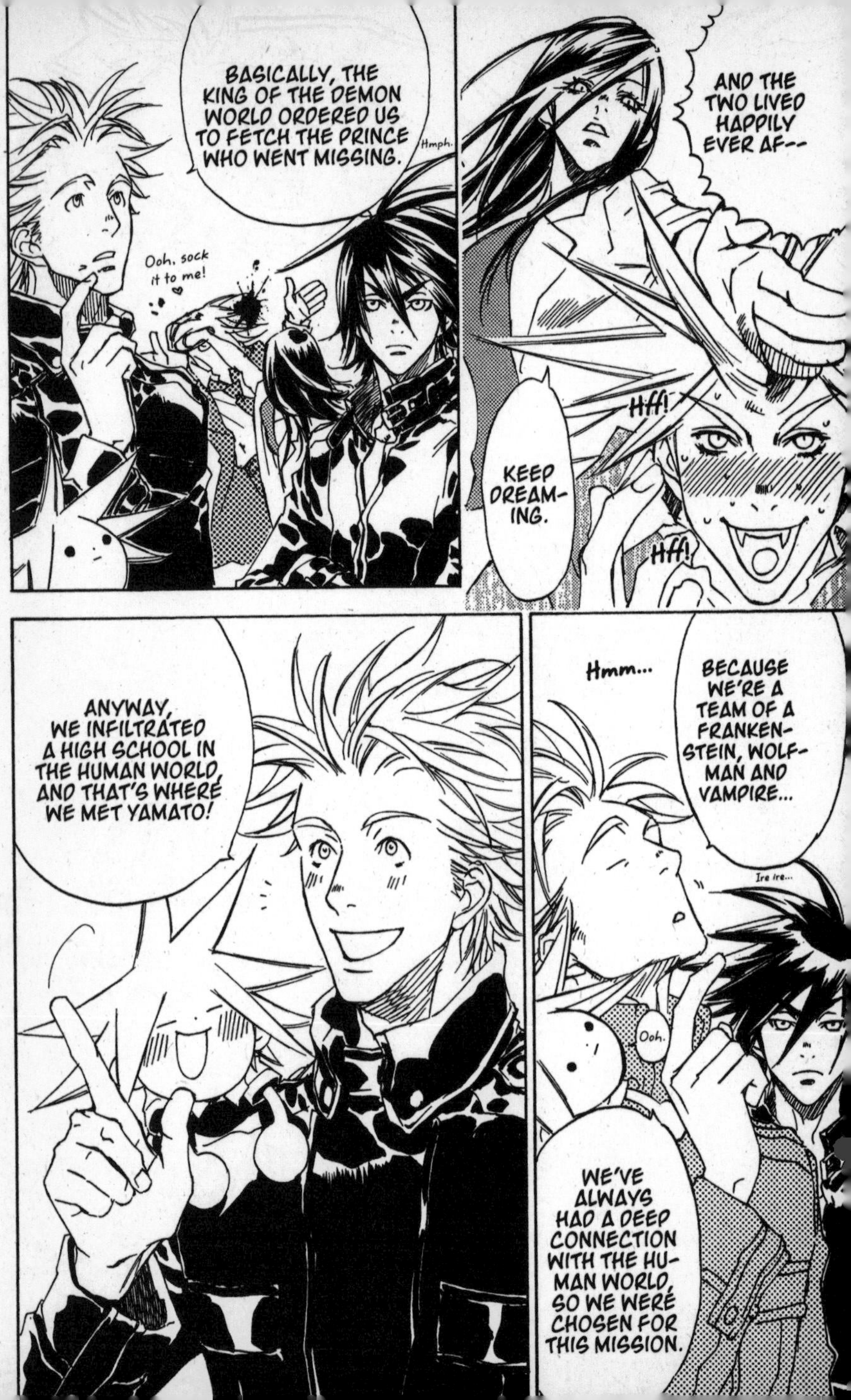
AND THE TWO LIVED HAPPILY EVER AF--
Hff!
KEEP DREAMING.
Hff!
BASICALLY, THE KING OF THE DEMON WORLD ORDERED US TO FETCH THE PRINCE WHO WENT MISSING.
Hmph.
Ooh, sock it to me!
Hmm...
BECAUSE WE'RE A TEAM OF A FRANKENSTEIN, WOLFMAN AND VAMPIRE...
Ire ire...
Ooh.
WE'VE ALWAYS HAD A DEEP CONNECTION WITH THE HUMAN WORLD, SO WE WERE CHOSEN FOR THIS MISSION.
ANYWAY, WE INFILTRATED A HIGH SCHOOL IN THE HUMAN WORLD, AND THAT'S WHERE WE MET YAMATO!

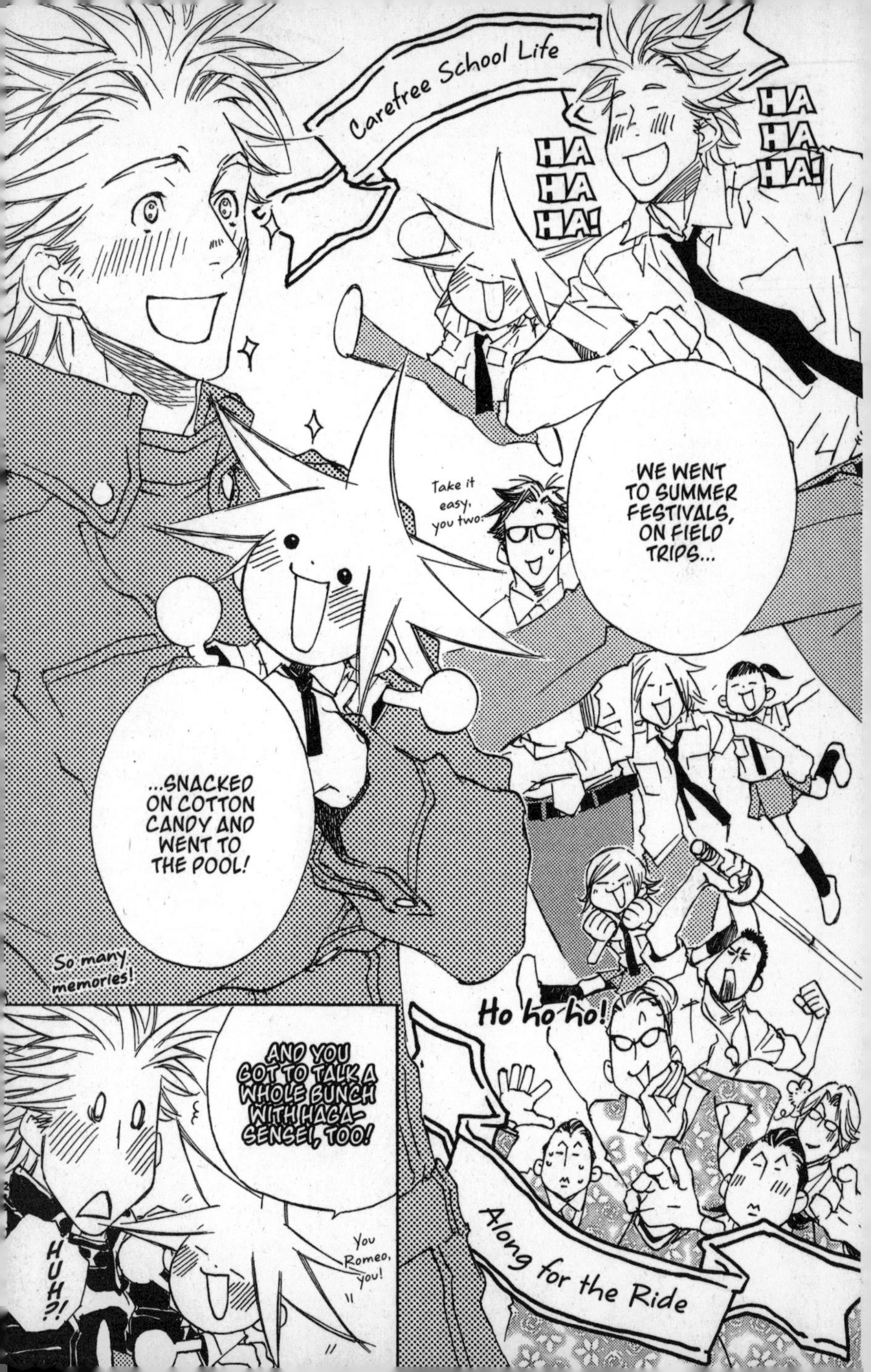
Carefree School Life
HA HA HA!
HA HA HA!
WE WENT TO SUMMER FESTIVALS, ON FIELD TRIPS...
Take it easy, you two.
...SNACKED ON COTTON CANDY AND WENT TO THE POOL!
So many memories!
Ho ho ho!
Along for the Ride
AND YOU GOT TO TALK A WHOLE BUNCH WITH HAGA-SENSEI, TOO!
You Romeo, you!
HUH?!

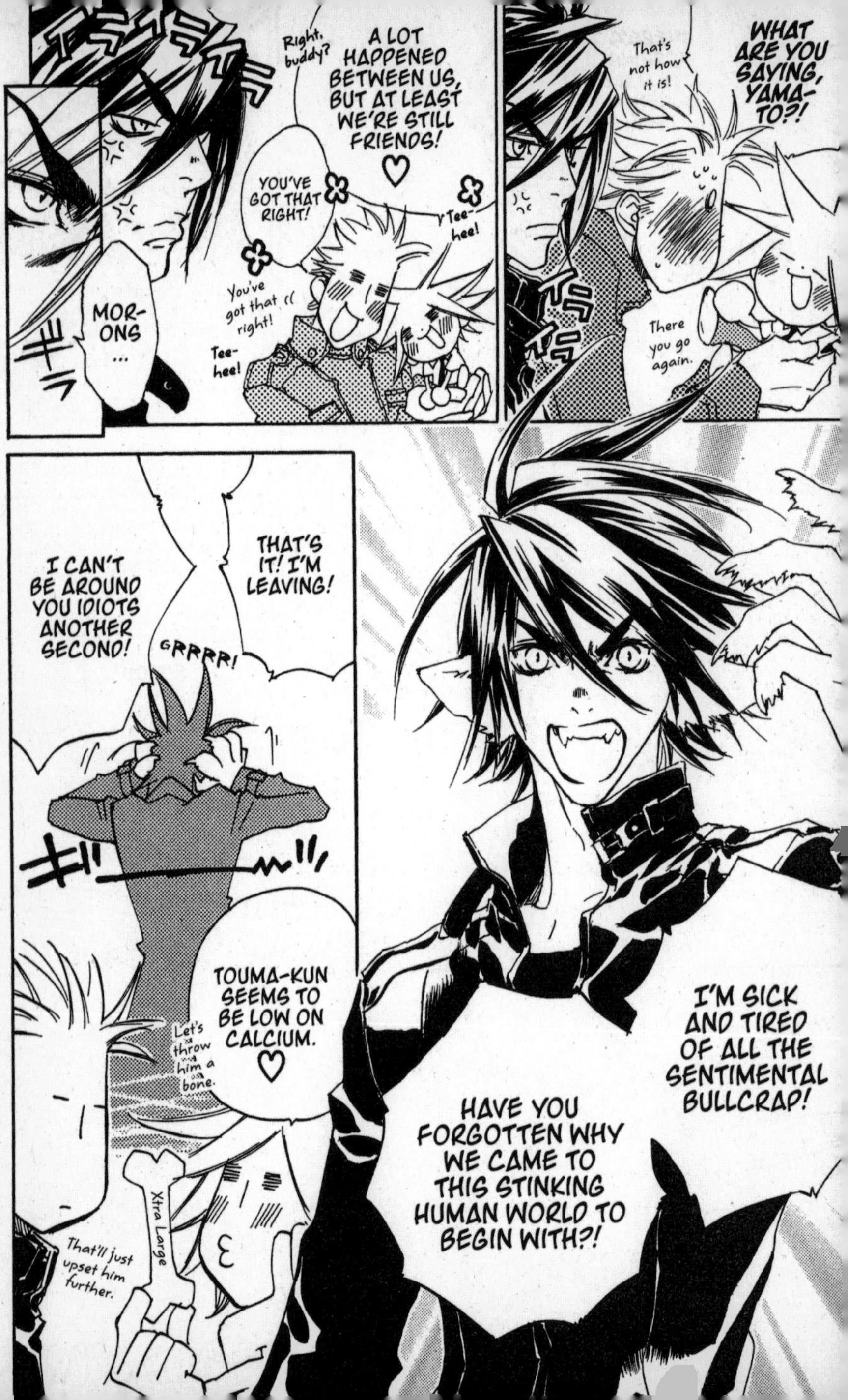

WHAT ARE YOU SAYING, YAMATO?!
That's not how it is!
There you go again.
A LOT HAPPENED BETWEEN US, BUT AT LEAST WE'RE STILL FRIENDS! ♡
Right, buddy?
YOU'VE GOT THAT RIGHT!
Tee-hee!
You've got that right!
Tee-hee!
MORONS...
I'M SICK AND TIRED OF ALL THE SENTIMENTAL BULLCRAP!
HAVE YOU FORGOTTEN WHY WE CAME TO THIS STINKING HUMAN WORLD TO BEGIN WITH?!
THAT'S IT! I'M LEAVING!
I CAN'T BE AROUND YOU IDIOTS ANOTHER SECOND!
GRRRR!
TOUMA-KUN SEEMS TO BE LOW ON CALCIUM. ♡
Let's throw him a bone.
Xtra Large
That'll just upset him further.

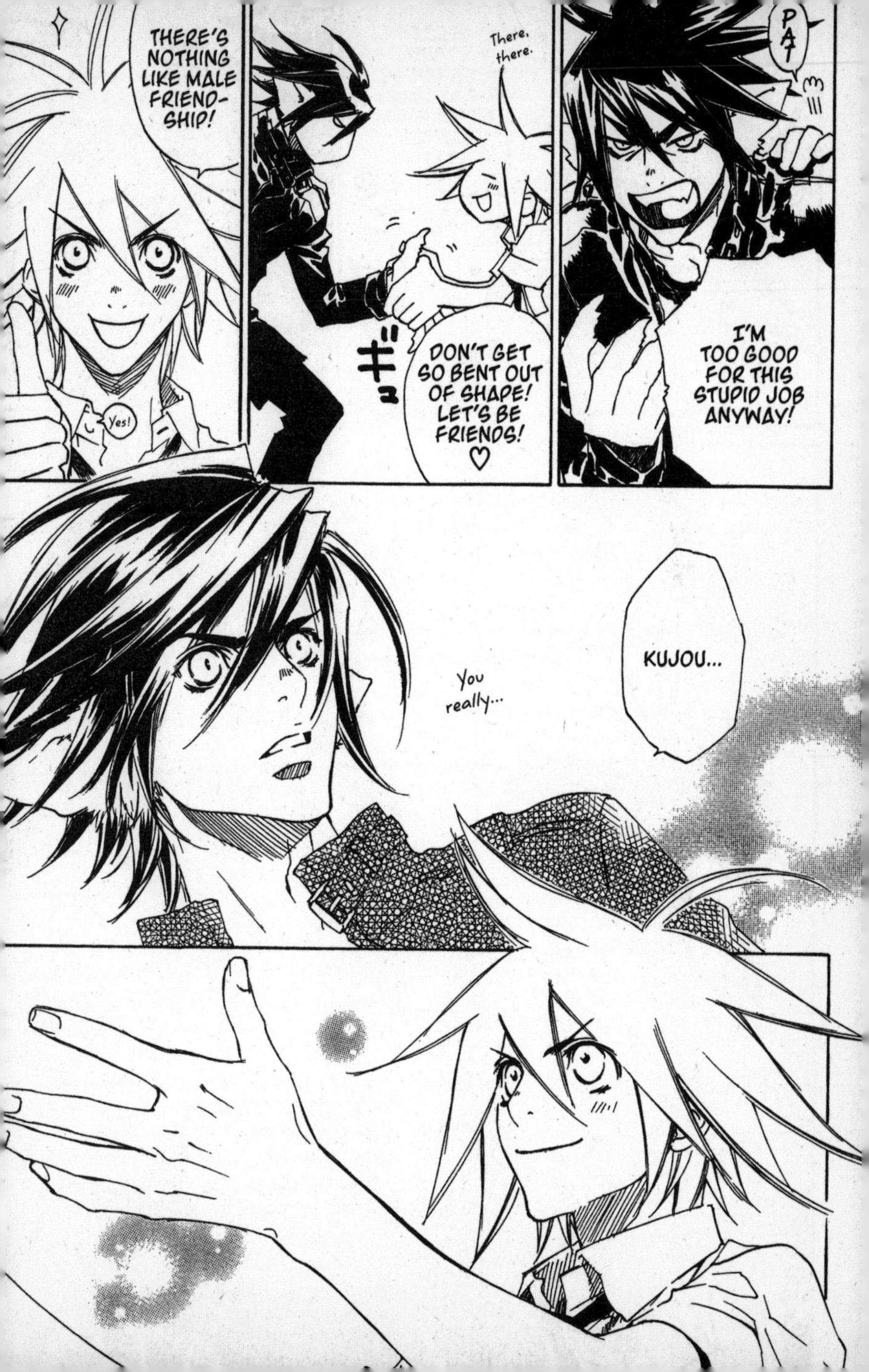
PAT
I'M TOO GOOD FOR THIS STUPID JOB ANYWAY!
There, there.
DON'T GET SO BENT OUT OF SHAPE! LET'S BE FRIENDS! ♡
ギュ
THERE'S NOTHING LIKE MALE FRIEND-SHIP!
Yes!
KUJOU...
You really...

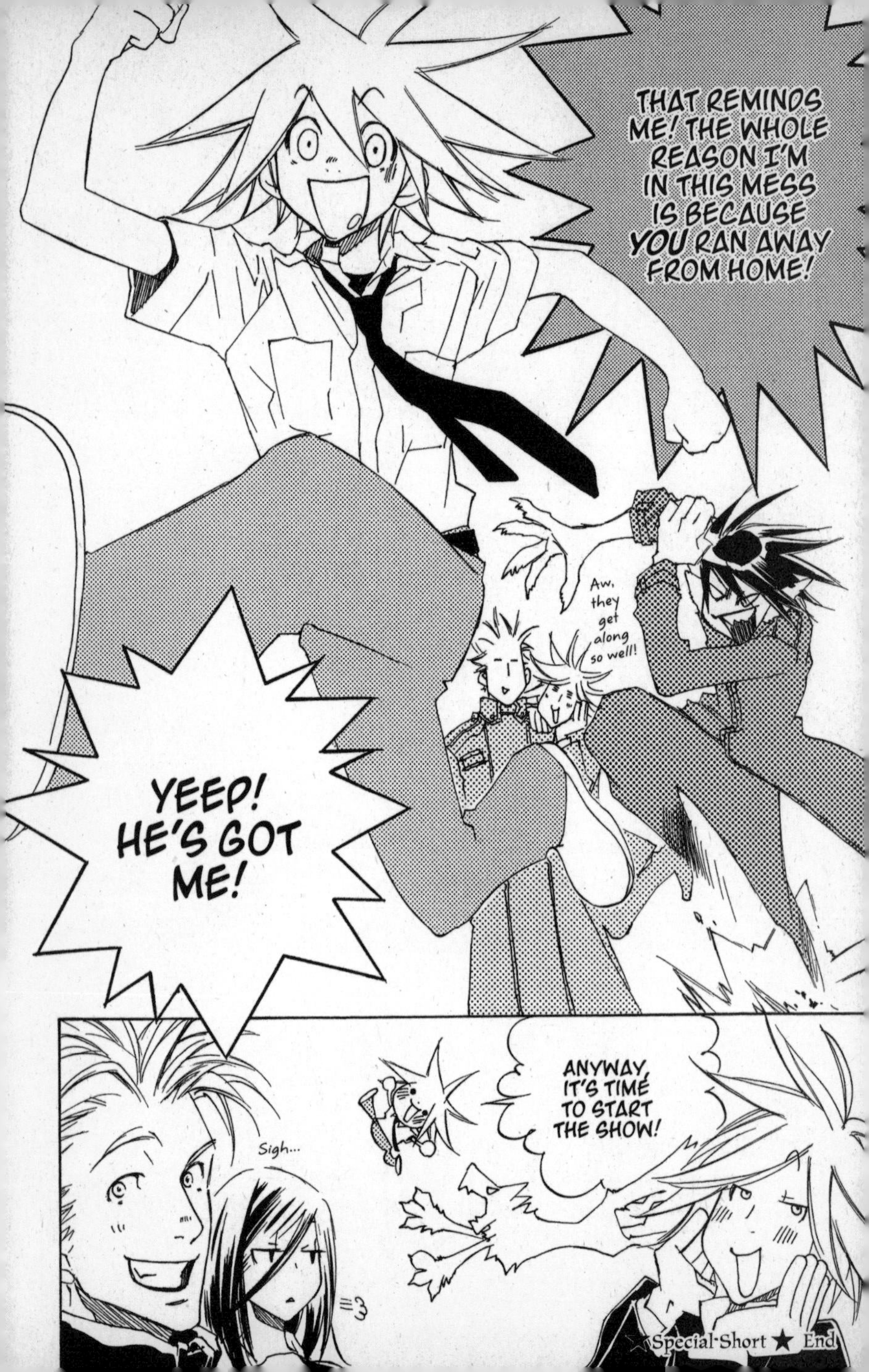
THAT REMINDS ME! THE WHOLE REASON I'M IN THIS MESS IS BECAUSE YOU RAN AWAY FROM HOME!
Aw, they get along so well!
YEEP! HE'S GOT ME!
ANYWAY, IT'S TIME TO START THE SHOW!
Sigh...
Special Short ★ End

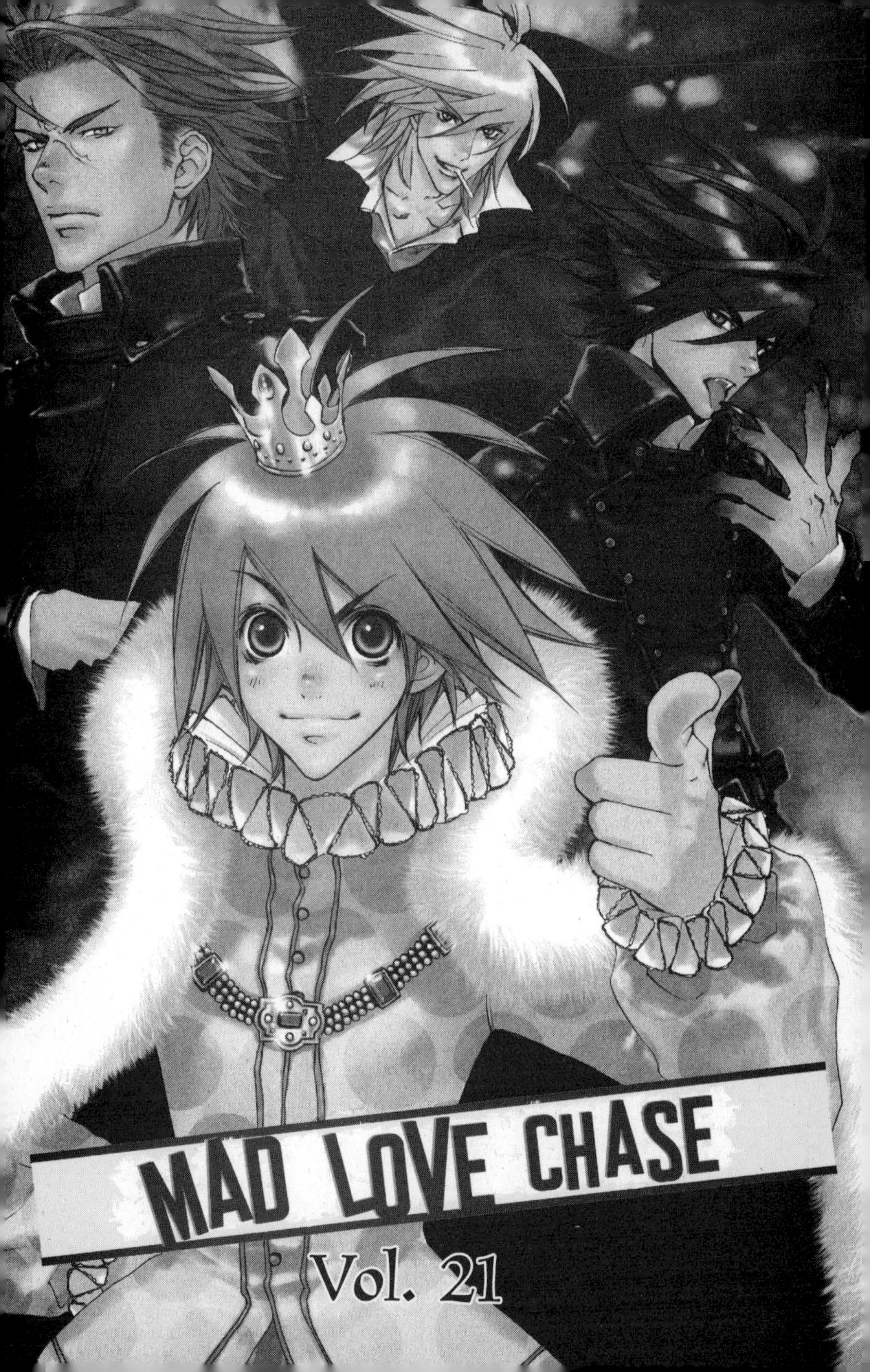
MAD LOVE CHASE
Vol. 21

MAD LOVE CHASE

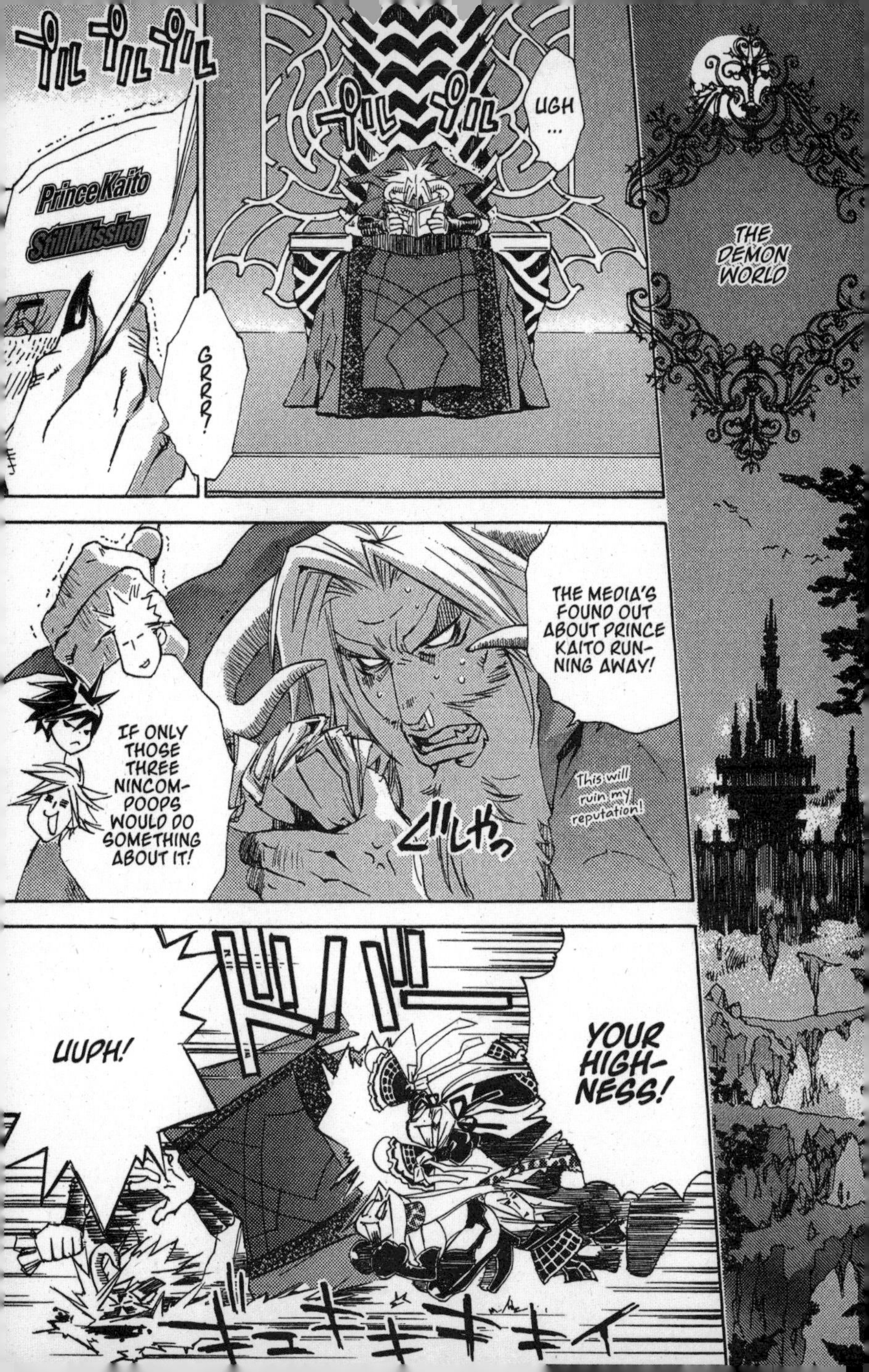
THE DEMON WORLD
UGH ...
Prince Kaito
Still Missing
GRRR!
THE MEDIA'S FOUND OUT ABOUT PRINCE KAITO RUNNING AWAY!
This will ruin my reputation!
IF ONLY THOSE THREE NINCOMPOOPS WOULD DO SOMETHING ABOUT IT!
YOUR HIGHNESS!
UUPH!

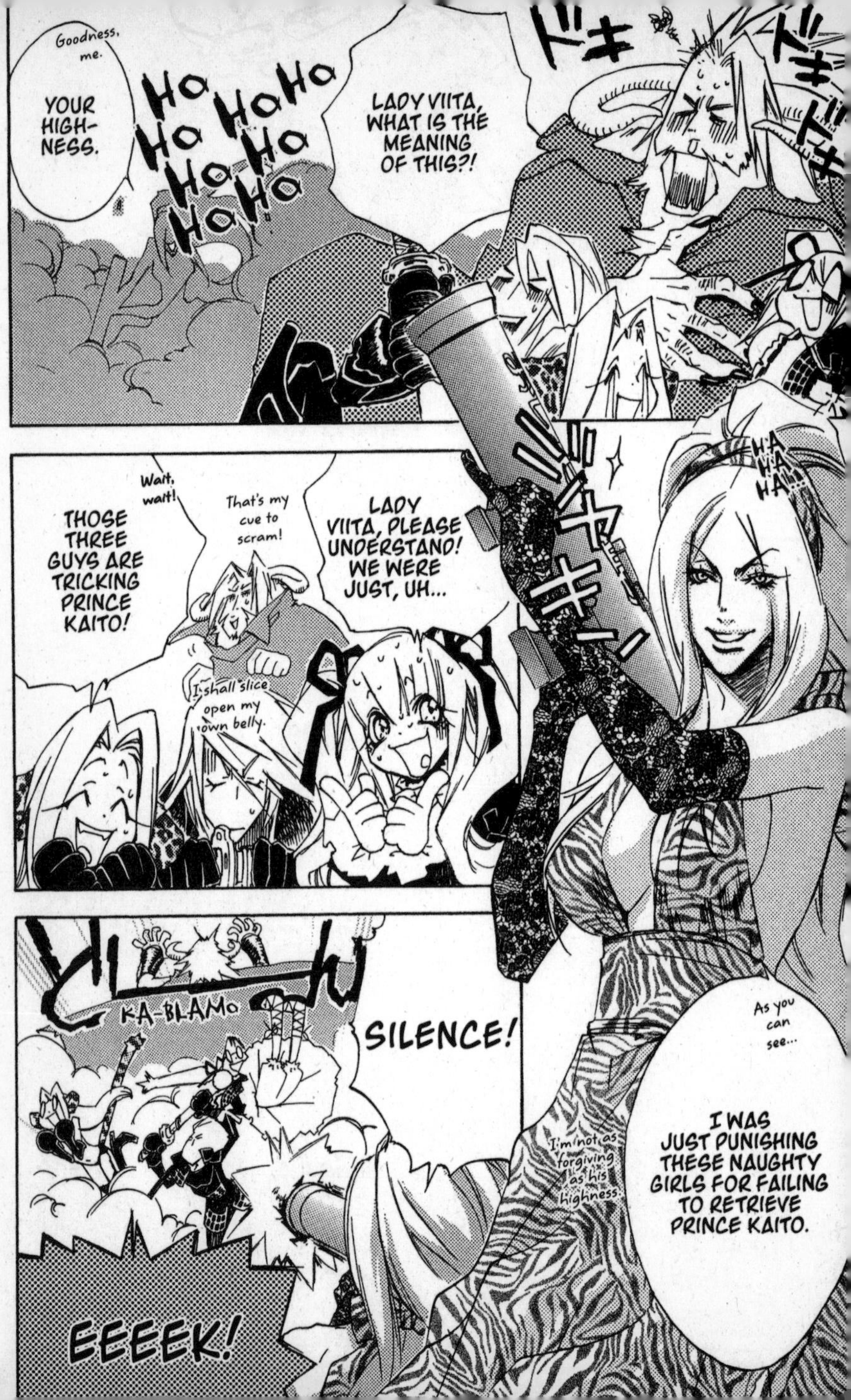
ドキ
ドキ ドキ
LADY VIITA, WHAT IS THE MEANING OF THIS?!
Ha Ha HaHa Ha Ha Ha Ha Ha Ha Ha
Goodness, me.
YOUR HIGHNESS.
HA HA HA
As you can see...
I WAS JUST PUNISHING THESE NAUGHTY GIRLS FOR FAILING TO RETRIEVE PRINCE KAITO.
I'm not as forgiving as his highness.
LADY VIITA, PLEASE UNDERSTAND! WE WERE JUST, UH...
That's my cue to scram!
Wait, wait!
THOSE THREE GUYS ARE TRICKING PRINCE KAITO!
I shall slice open my own belly.
SILENCE!
KA-BLAM
EEEEK!

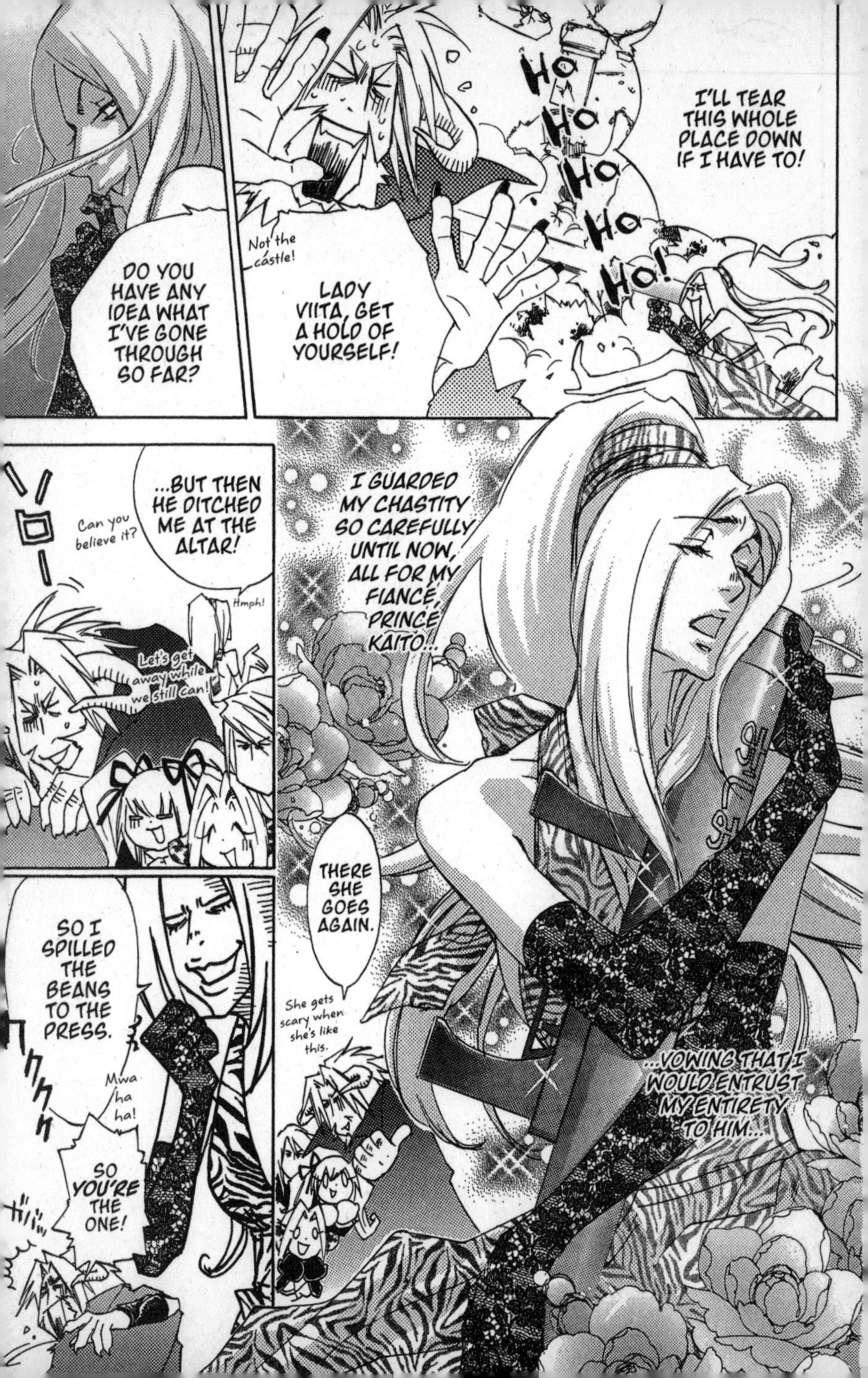
I'LL TEAR THIS WHOLE PLACE DOWN IF I HAVE TO!
HO HO HO HO HO!
Not the castle!
LADY VIITA, GET A HOLD OF YOURSELF!
DO YOU HAVE ANY IDEA WHAT I'VE GONE THROUGH SO FAR?
I GUARDED MY CHASTITY SO CAREFULLY UNTIL NOW, ALL FOR MY FIANCÉ, PRINCE KAITO...
...VOWING THAT I WOULD ENTRUST MY ENTIRETY TO HIM...
THERE SHE GOES AGAIN.
She gets scary when she's like this.
...BUT THEN HE DITCHED ME AT THE ALTAR!
Can you believe it?
Hmph!
Let's get away while we still can!
SO I SPILLED THE BEANS TO THE PRESS.
Mwa ha ha!
SO YOU'RE THE ONE!

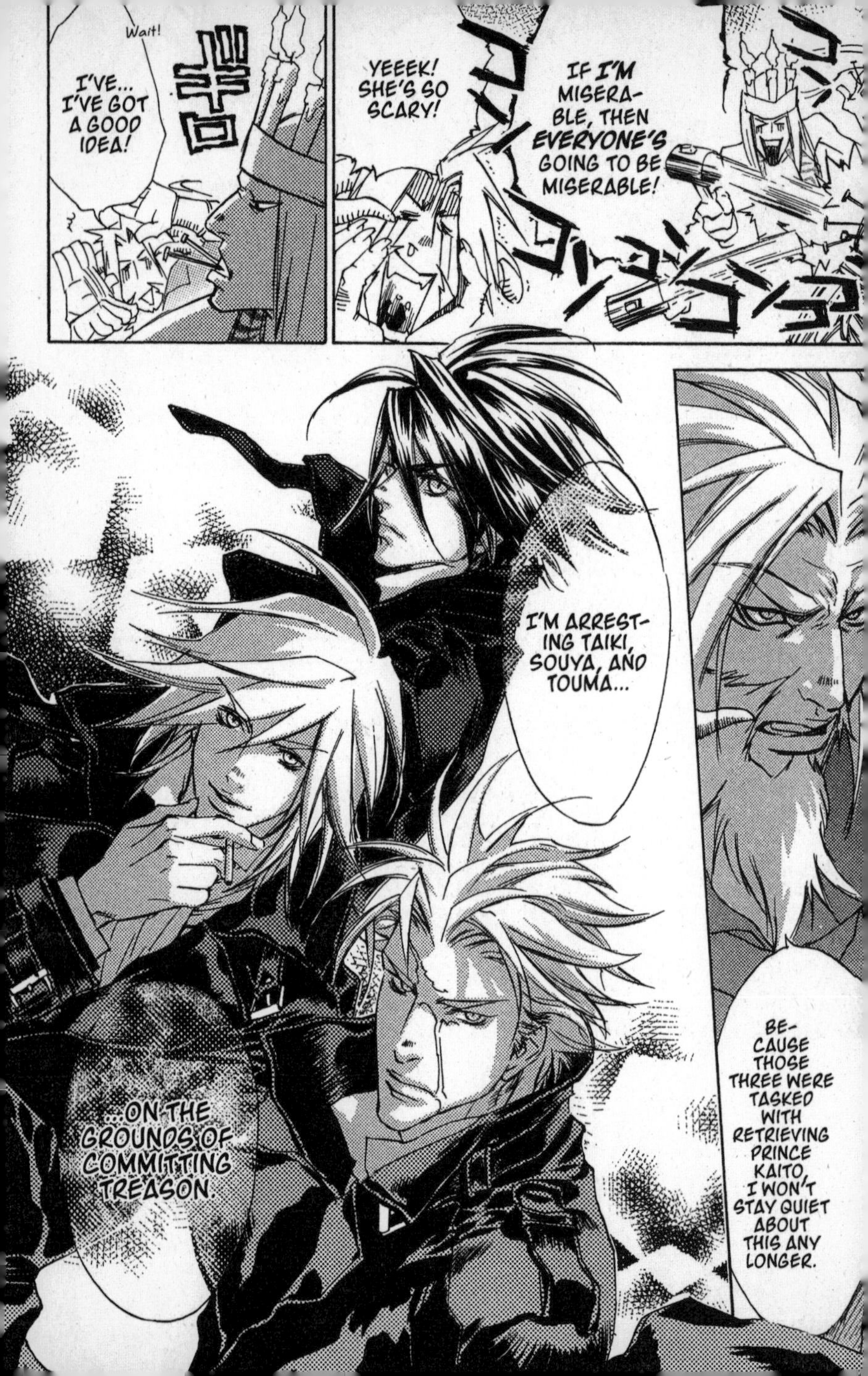
IF I'M MISERABLE, THEN EVERYONE'S GOING TO BE MISERABLE!
YEEEK! SHE'S SO SCARY!
I'VE... I'VE GOT A GOOD IDEA!
Wait!
BECAUSE THOSE THREE WERE TASKED WITH RETRIEVING PRINCE KAITO, I WON'T STAY QUIET ABOUT THIS ANY LONGER.
I'M ARRESTING TAIKI, SOUYA, AND TOUMA...
...ON THE GROUNDS OF COMMITTING TREASON.

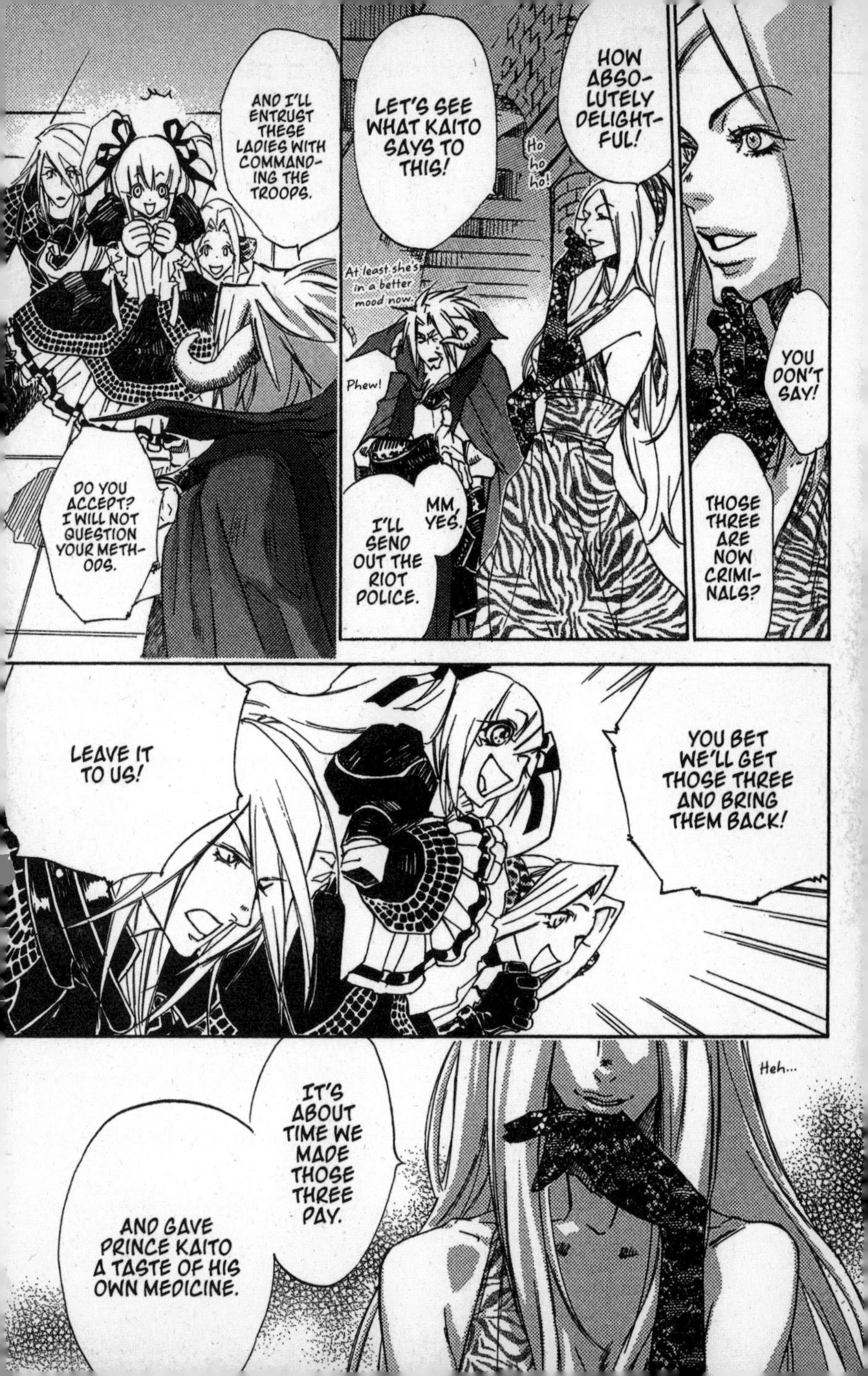
YOU DON'T SAY!
THOSE THREE ARE NOW CRIMINALS?
HOW ABSOLUTELY DELIGHTFUL!
Ho ho ho!
LET'S SEE WHAT KAITO SAYS TO THIS!
At least she's in a better mood now.
Phew!
MM, YES.
I'LL SEND OUT THE RIOT POLICE.
AND I'LL ENTRUST THESE LADIES WITH COMMANDING THE TROOPS.
DO YOU ACCEPT? I WILL NOT QUESTION YOUR METHODS.
YOU BET WE'LL GET THOSE THREE AND BRING THEM BACK!
LEAVE IT TO US!
Heh...
IT'S ABOUT TIME WE MADE THOSE THREE PAY.
AND GAVE PRINCE KAITO A TASTE OF HIS OWN MEDICINE.

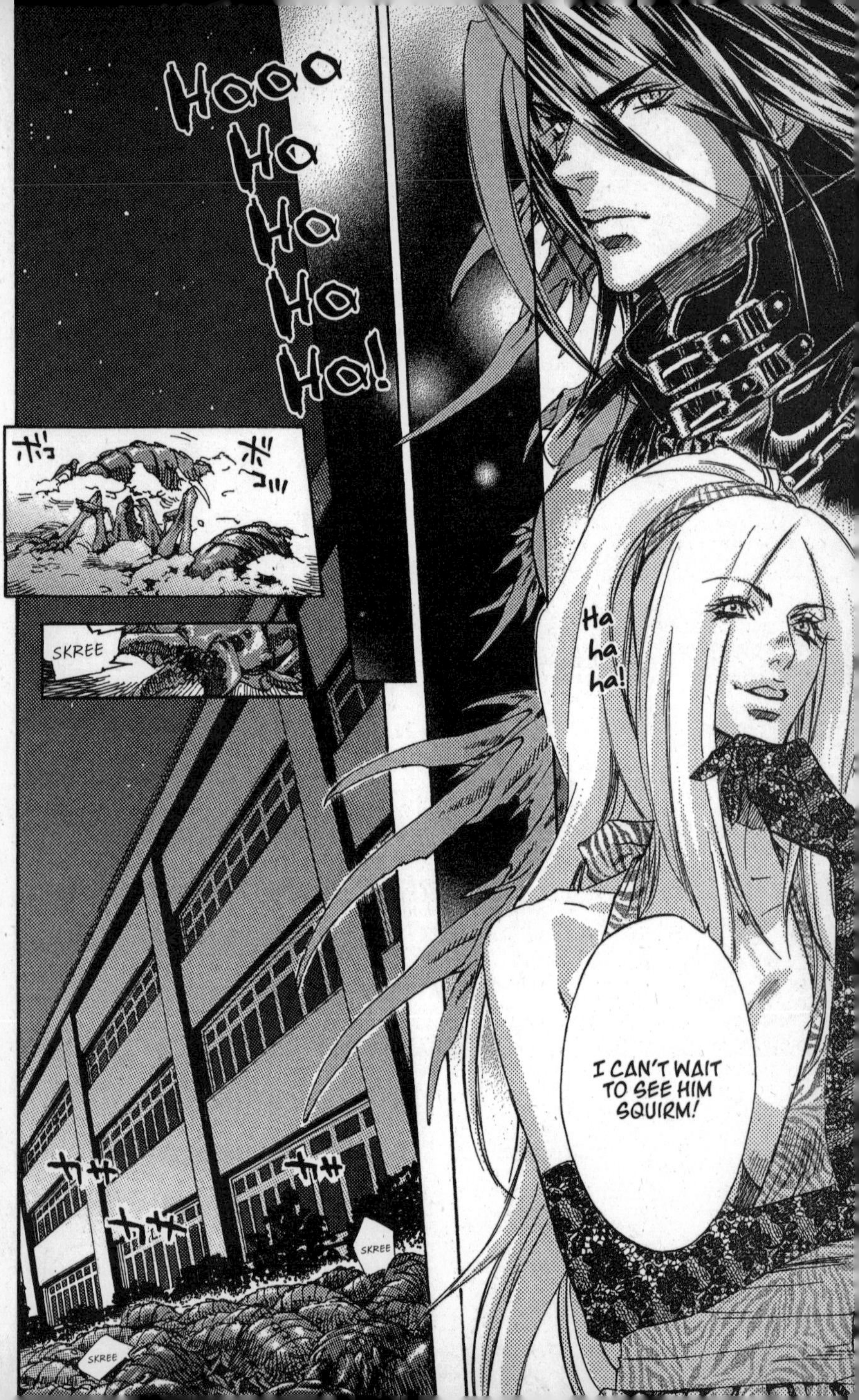
Ha ha ha!
I CAN'T WAIT TO SEE HIM SQUIRM!
Haaa Ha Ha Ha Ha!
ボコ
ボコッ
SKREE
カサ
カサ
カサ
SKREE
SKREE

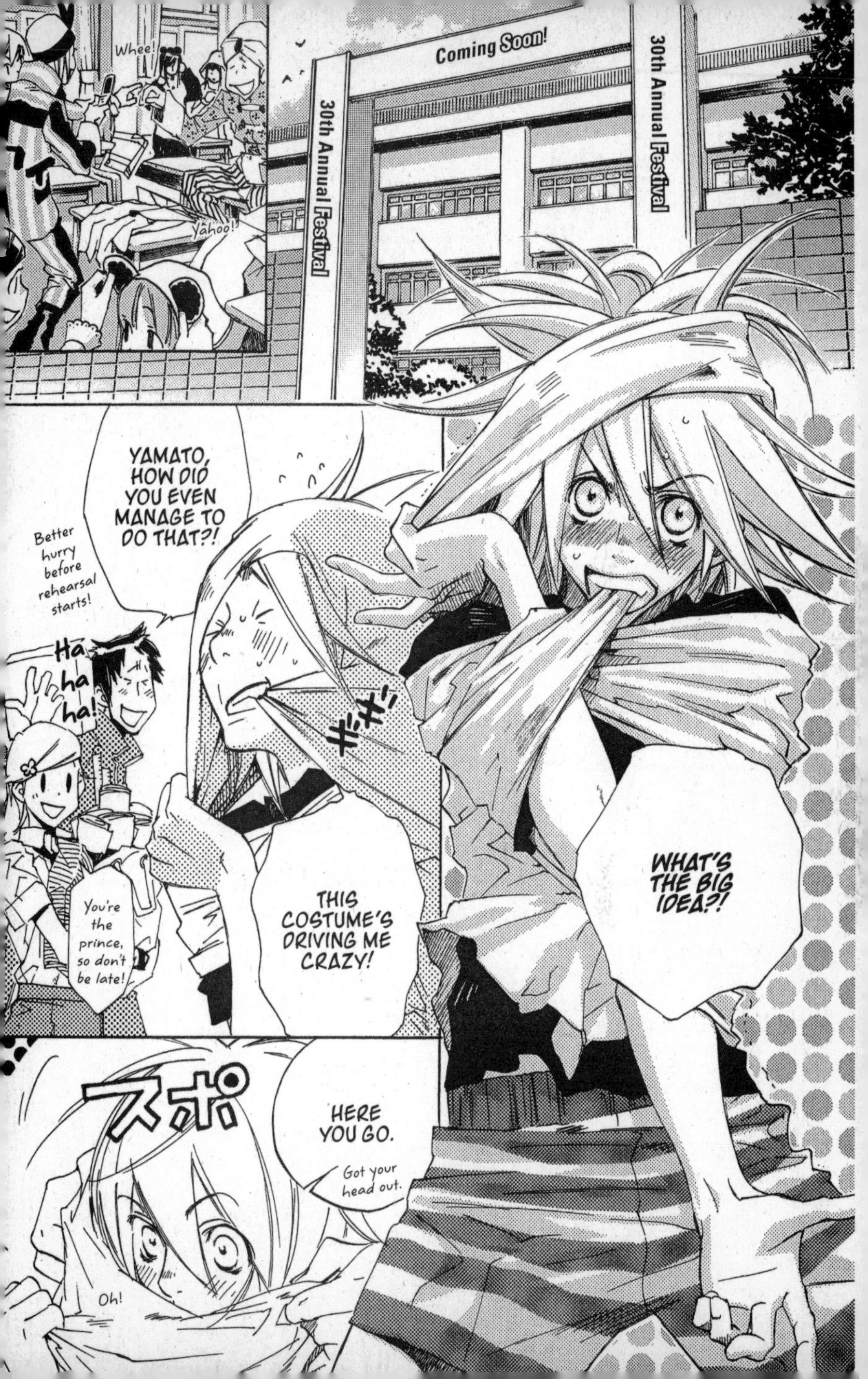
Coming Soon!
30th Annual Festival
30th Annual Festival
Whee!
Yahoo!
WHAT'S THE BIG IDEA?!
YAMATO, HOW DID YOU EVEN MANAGE TO DO THAT?!
Better hurry before rehearsal starts!
Ha ha ha!
ギギ
THIS COSTUME'S DRIVING ME CRAZY!
You're the prince, so don't be late!
HERE YOU GO.
Got your head out.
スポ
Oh!

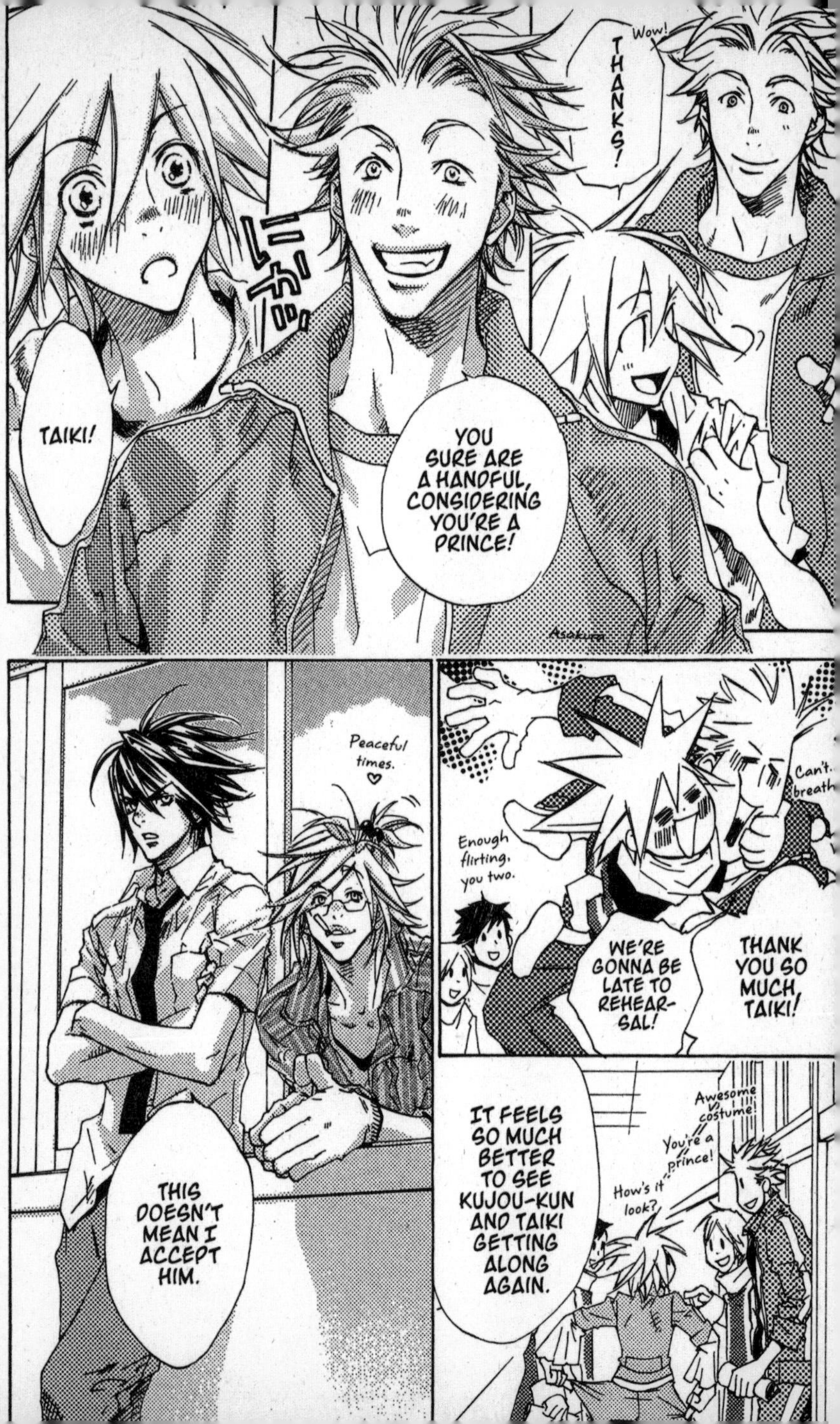
Wow!
THANKS!
にかっ
YOU SURE ARE A HANDFUL, CONSIDERING YOU'RE A PRINCE!
TAIKI!
Can't... breath
THANK YOU SO MUCH, TAIKI!
WE'RE GONNA BE LATE TO REHEAR-SAL!
Enough flirting, you two.
Awesome costume!
You're a prince!
How's it look?
IT FEELS SO MUCH BETTER TO SEE KUJOU-KUN AND TAIKI GETTING ALONG AGAIN.
Peaceful times. ♡
THIS DOESN'T MEAN I ACCEPT HIM.

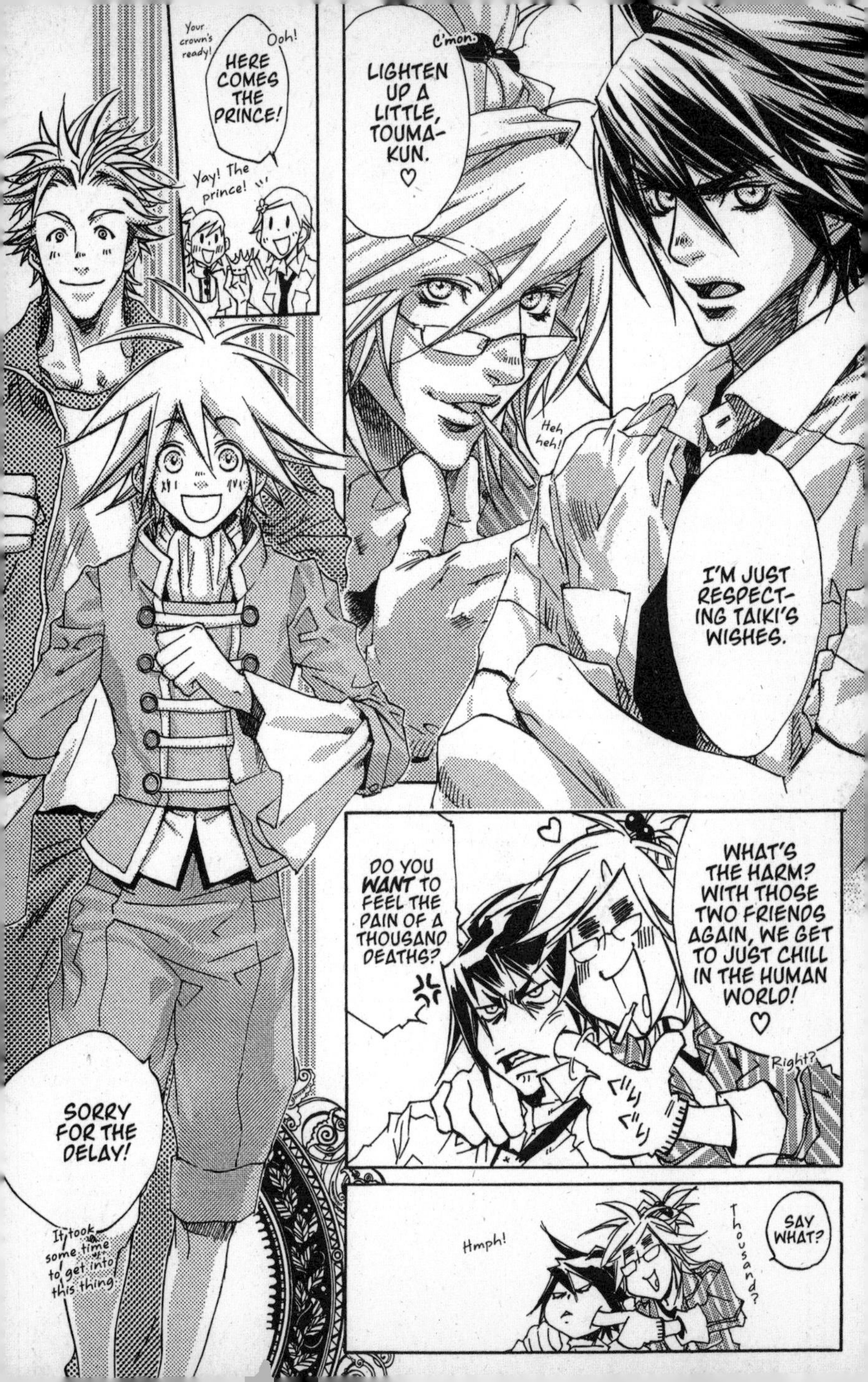
C'mon.
LIGHTEN UP A LITTLE, TOUMA-KUN. ♡
Heh heh!
I'M JUST RESPECTING TAIKI'S WISHES.
WHAT'S THE HARM? WITH THOSE TWO FRIENDS AGAIN, WE GET TO JUST CHILL IN THE HUMAN WORLD! ♡
Right?
DO YOU **WANT** TO FEEL THE PAIN OF A THOUSAND DEATHS?
SAY WHAT?
Thousand?
Hmph!
Ooh!
HERE COMES THE PRINCE!
Your crown's ready!
Yay! The prince!
SORRY FOR THE DELAY!
It took some time to get into this thing.

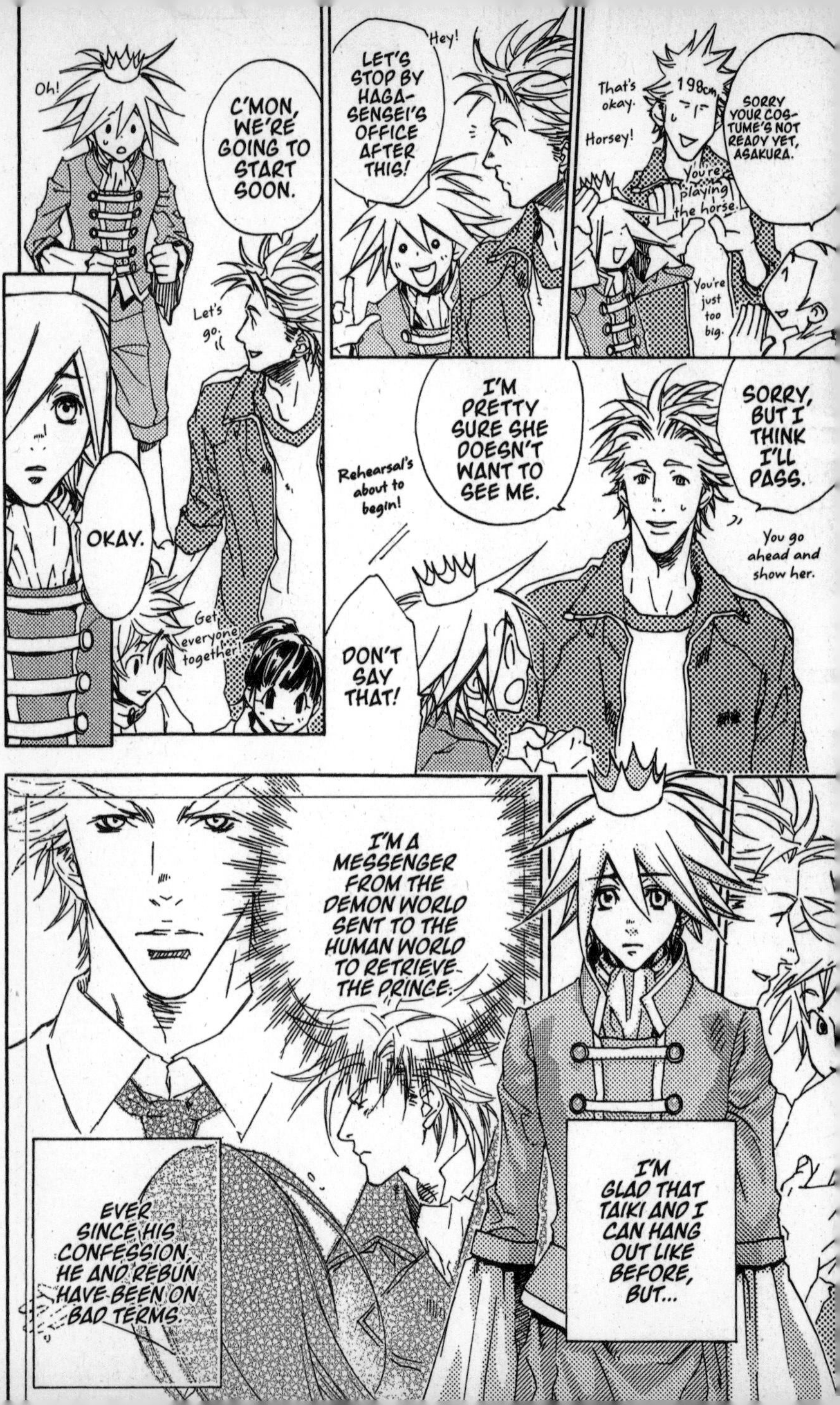

SORRY YOUR COSTUME'S NOT READY YET, ASAKURA.
198cm
That's okay.
Horsey!
You're playing the horse.
You're just too big.
Hey!
LET'S STOP BY HAGA-SENSEI'S OFFICE AFTER THIS!
SORRY, BUT I THINK I'LL PASS.
You go ahead and show her.
I'M PRETTY SURE SHE DOESN'T WANT TO SEE ME.
Rehearsal's about to begin!
DON'T SAY THAT!
C'MON, WE'RE GOING TO START SOON.
Oh!
Let's go.
OKAY.
Get everyone together!
I'M GLAD THAT TAIKI AND I CAN HANG OUT LIKE BEFORE, BUT...
I'M A MESSENGER FROM THE DEMON WORLD SENT TO THE HUMAN WORLD TO RETRIEVE THE PRINCE.
EVER SINCE HIS CONFESSION, HE AND REBUN HAVE BEEN ON BAD TERMS.

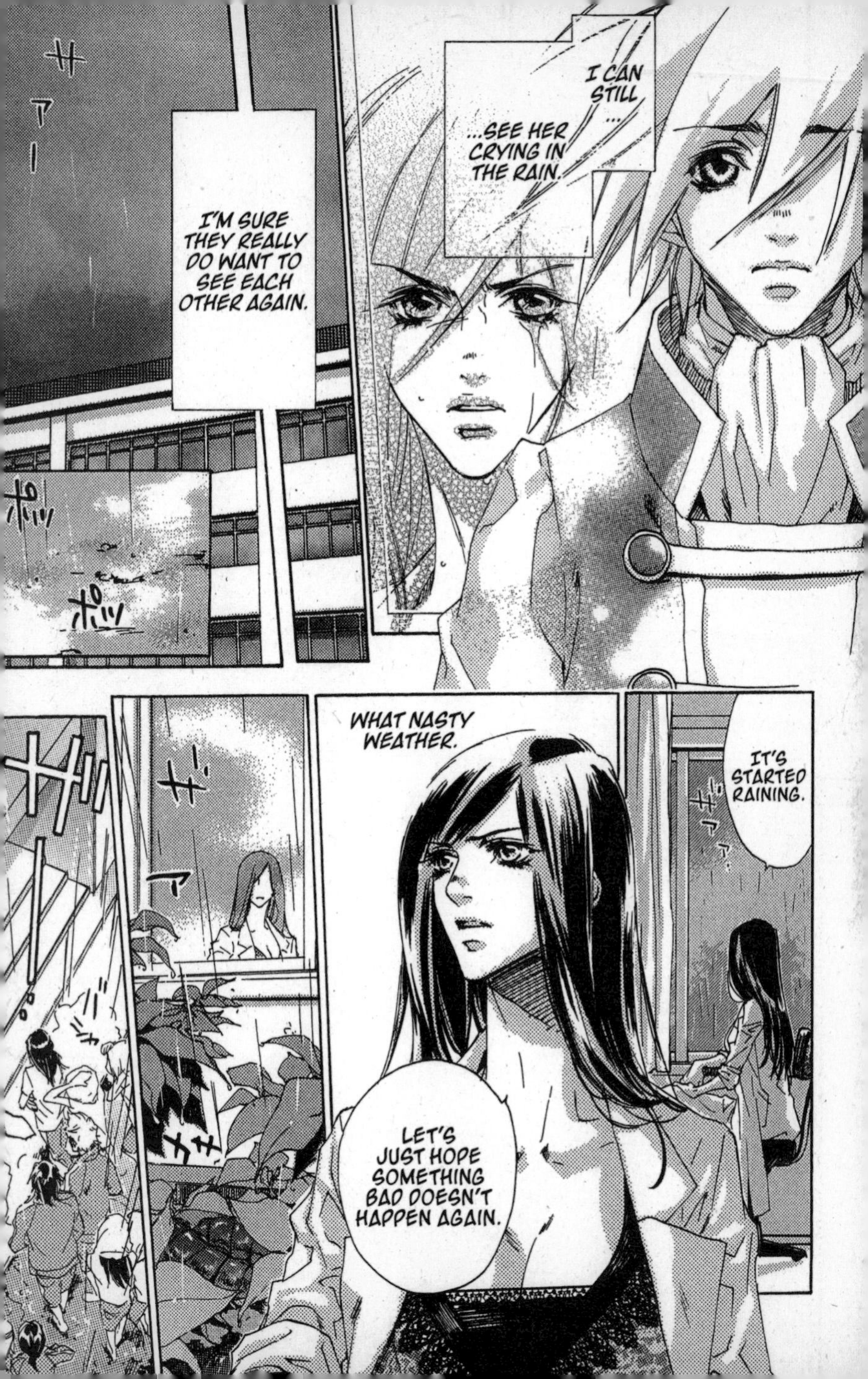
I CAN STILL ...
...SEE HER CRYING IN THE RAIN.
I'M SURE THEY REALLY DO WANT TO SEE EACH OTHER AGAIN.
IT'S STARTED RAINING.
WHAT NASTY WEATHER.
LET'S JUST HOPE SOMETHING BAD DOESN'T HAPPEN AGAIN.

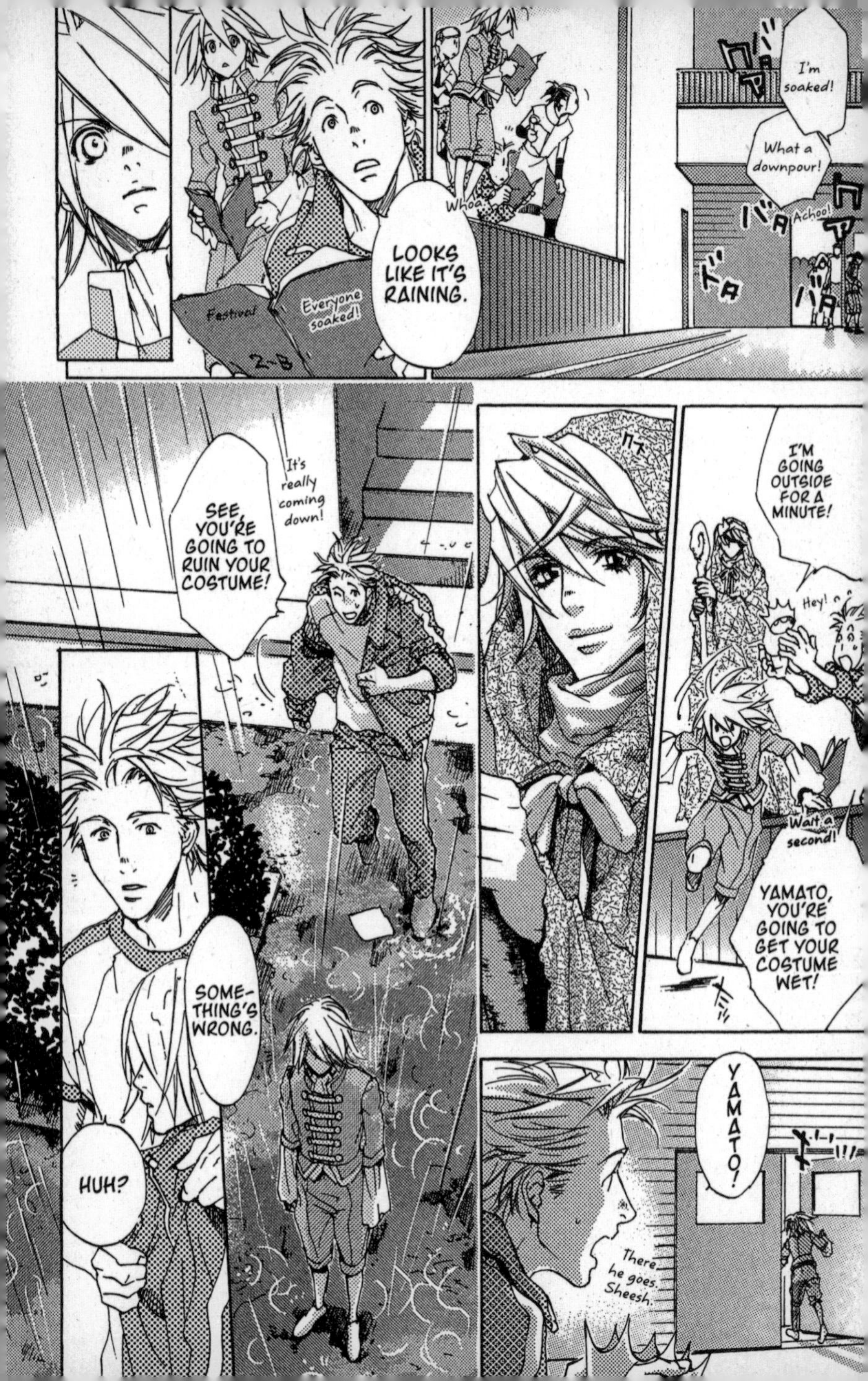
I'm soaked!
What a downpour!
Achoo!
Whoa.
LOOKS LIKE IT'S RAINING.
Everyone soaked!
Festival
2-B
I'M GOING OUTSIDE FOR A MINUTE!
Hey!
Wait a second!
YAMATO, YOU'RE GOING TO GET YOUR COSTUME WET!
YAMATO!
There he goes. Sheesh.
It's really coming down!
SEE, YOU'RE GOING TO RUIN YOUR COSTUME!
SOME-THING'S WRONG.
HUH?

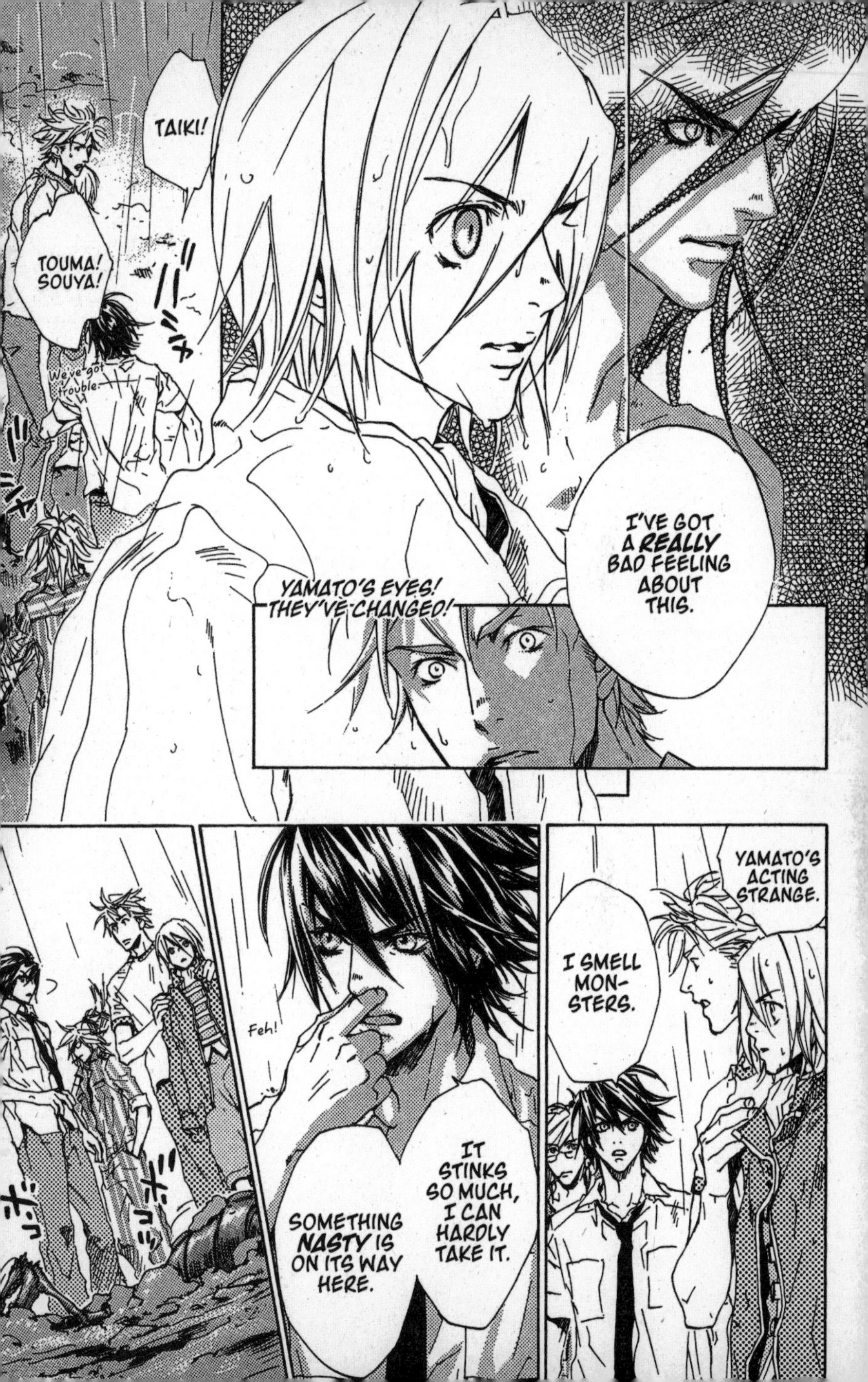
I'VE GOT A **REALLY** BAD FEELING ABOUT THIS.
YAMATO'S EYES! THEY'VE CHANGED!
TAIKI!
TOUMA! SOUYA!
We've got trouble.
YAMATO'S ACTING STRANGE.
I SMELL MON-STERS.
IT STINKS SO MUCH, I CAN HARDLY TAKE IT.
SOMETHING **NASTY** IS ON ITS WAY HERE.
Feh!

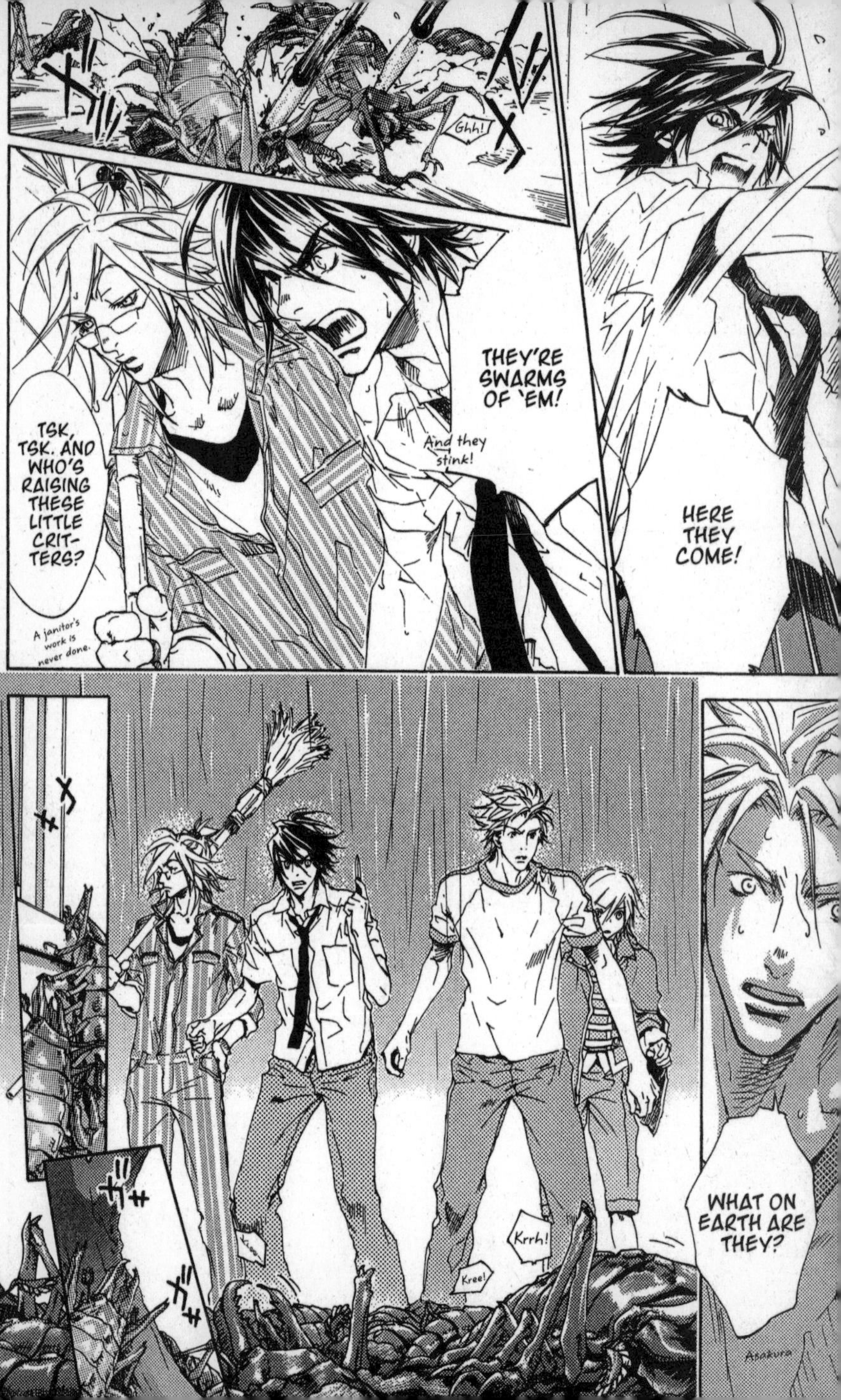
HERE THEY COME!
Ghh!
THEY'RE SWARMS OF 'EM!
And they stink!
TSK, TSK. AND WHO'S RAISING THESE LITTLE CRIT-TERS?
A janitor's work is never done.
WHAT ON EARTH ARE THEY?
Asakura
Krrh!
Kree!

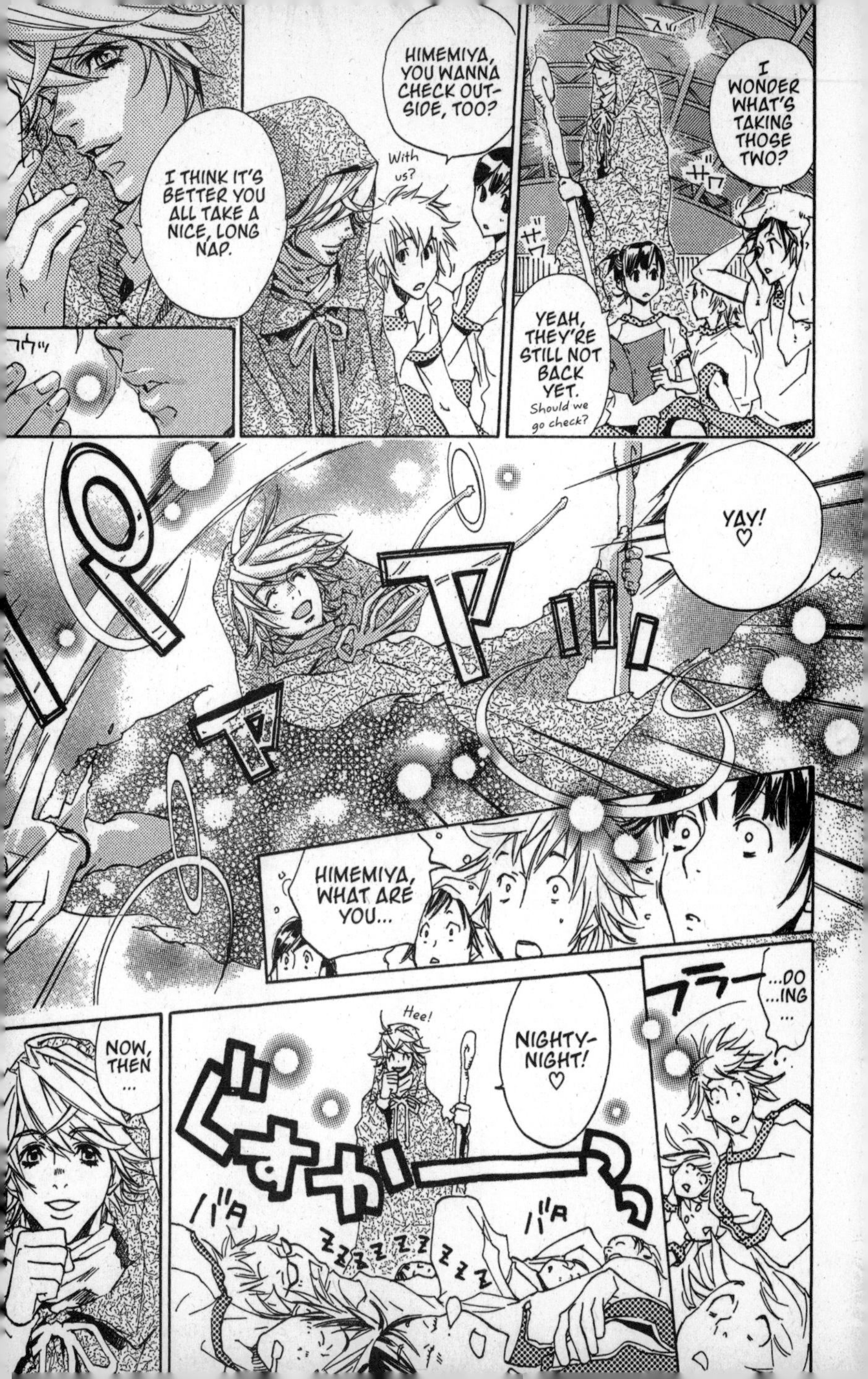
I WONDER WHAT'S TAKING THOSE TWO?
YEAH, THEY'RE STILL NOT BACK YET.
Should we go check?
HIMEMIYA, YOU WANNA CHECK OUT-SIDE, TOO?
With us?
I THINK IT'S BETTER YOU ALL TAKE A NICE, LONG NAP.
YAY! ♡
HIMEMIYA, WHAT ARE YOU...
...DOING ...ING ...
NIGHTY-NIGHT! ♡
Hee!
ZZZZZZZZZZ
NOW, THEN ...

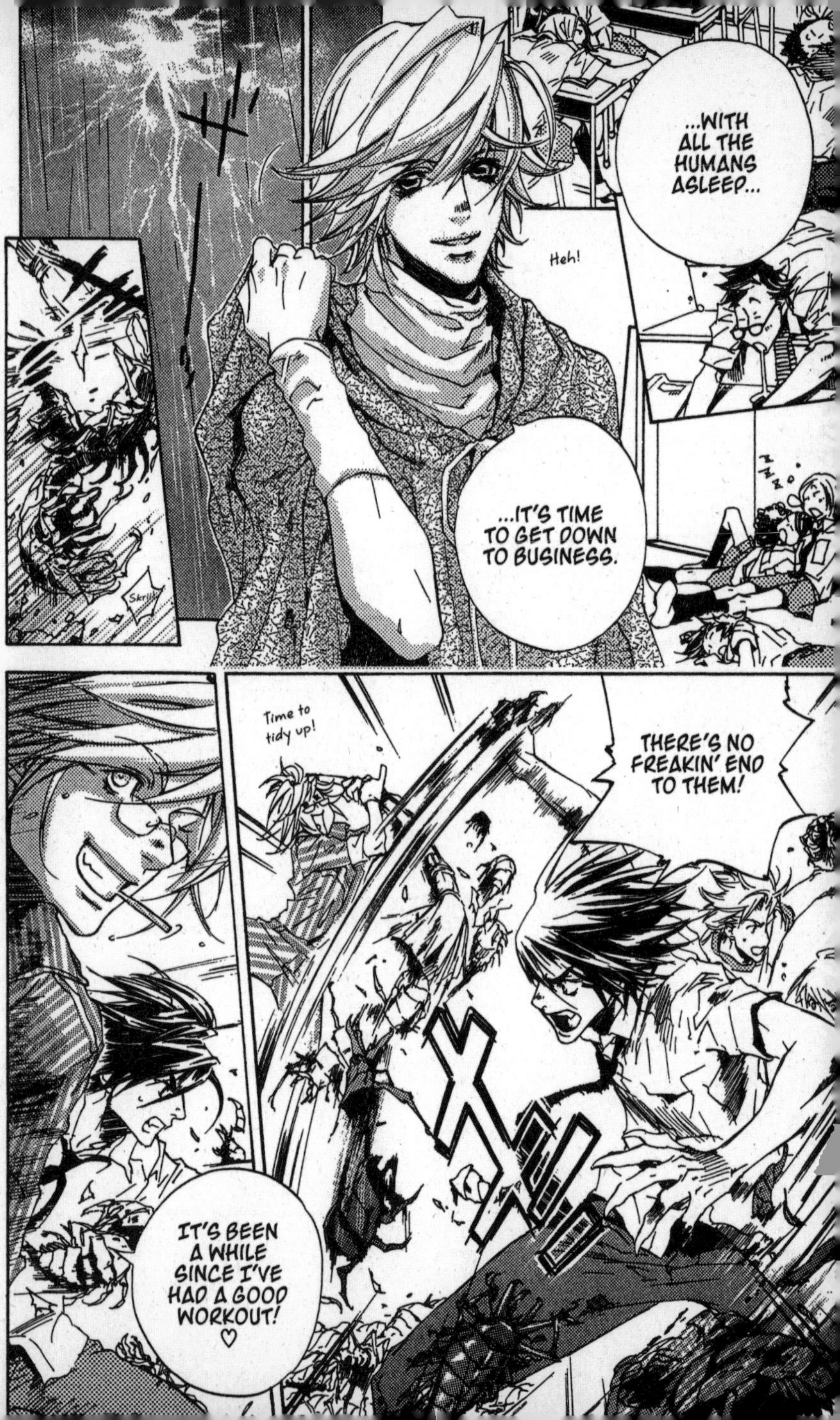
...WITH ALL THE HUMANS ASLEEP...
Heh!
...IT'S TIME TO GET DOWN TO BUSINESS.
THERE'S NO FREAKIN' END TO THEM!
Time to tidy up!
IT'S BEEN A WHILE SINCE I'VE HAD A GOOD WORKOUT! ♡

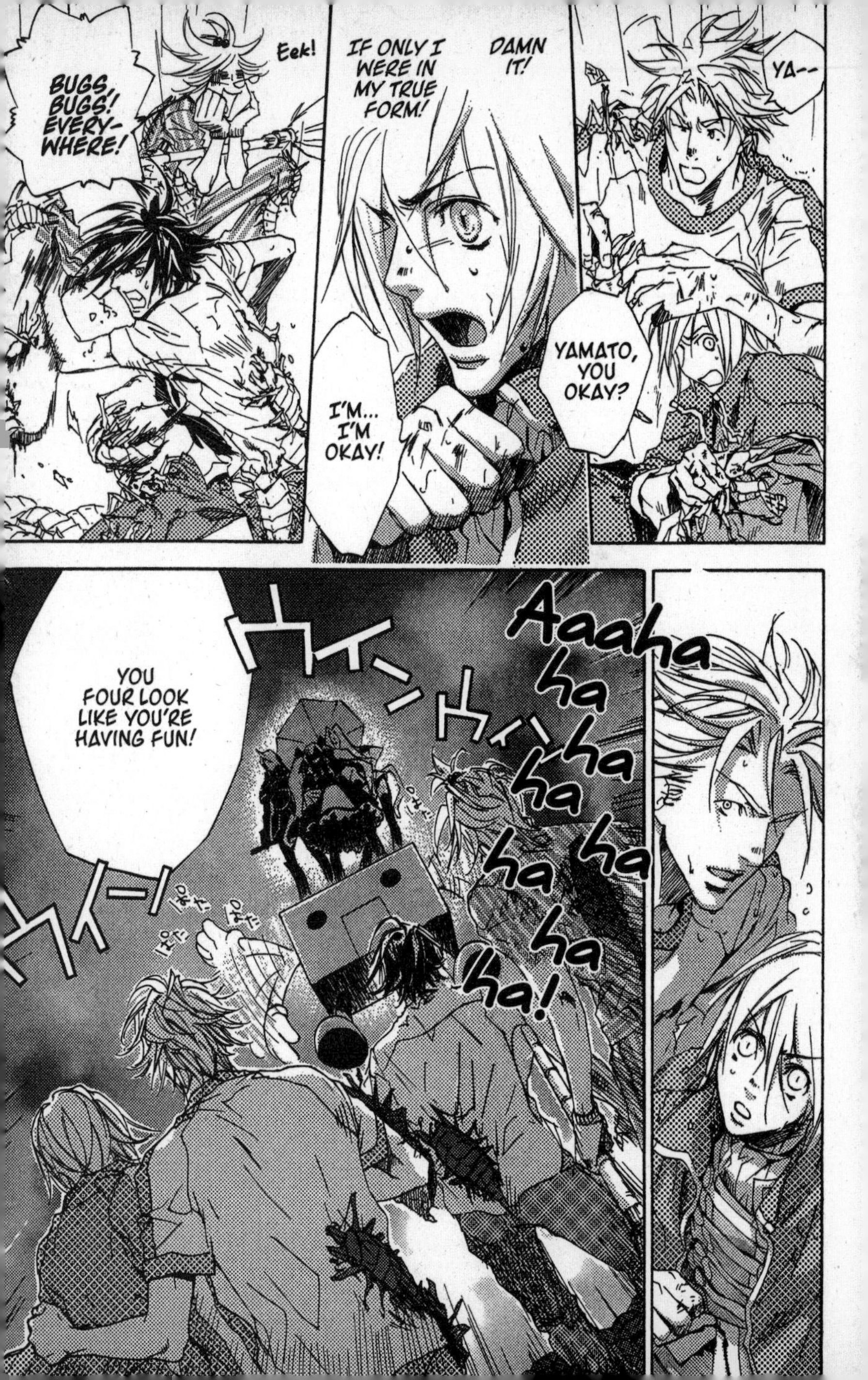
YA--
YAMATO, YOU OKAY?
DAMN IT!
IF ONLY I WERE IN MY TRUE FORM!
I'M... I'M OKAY!
Eek!
BUGS BUGS! EVERYWHERE!
Aaaha ha ha ha ha ha ha ha ha!
YOU FOUR LOOK LIKE YOU'RE HAVING FUN!

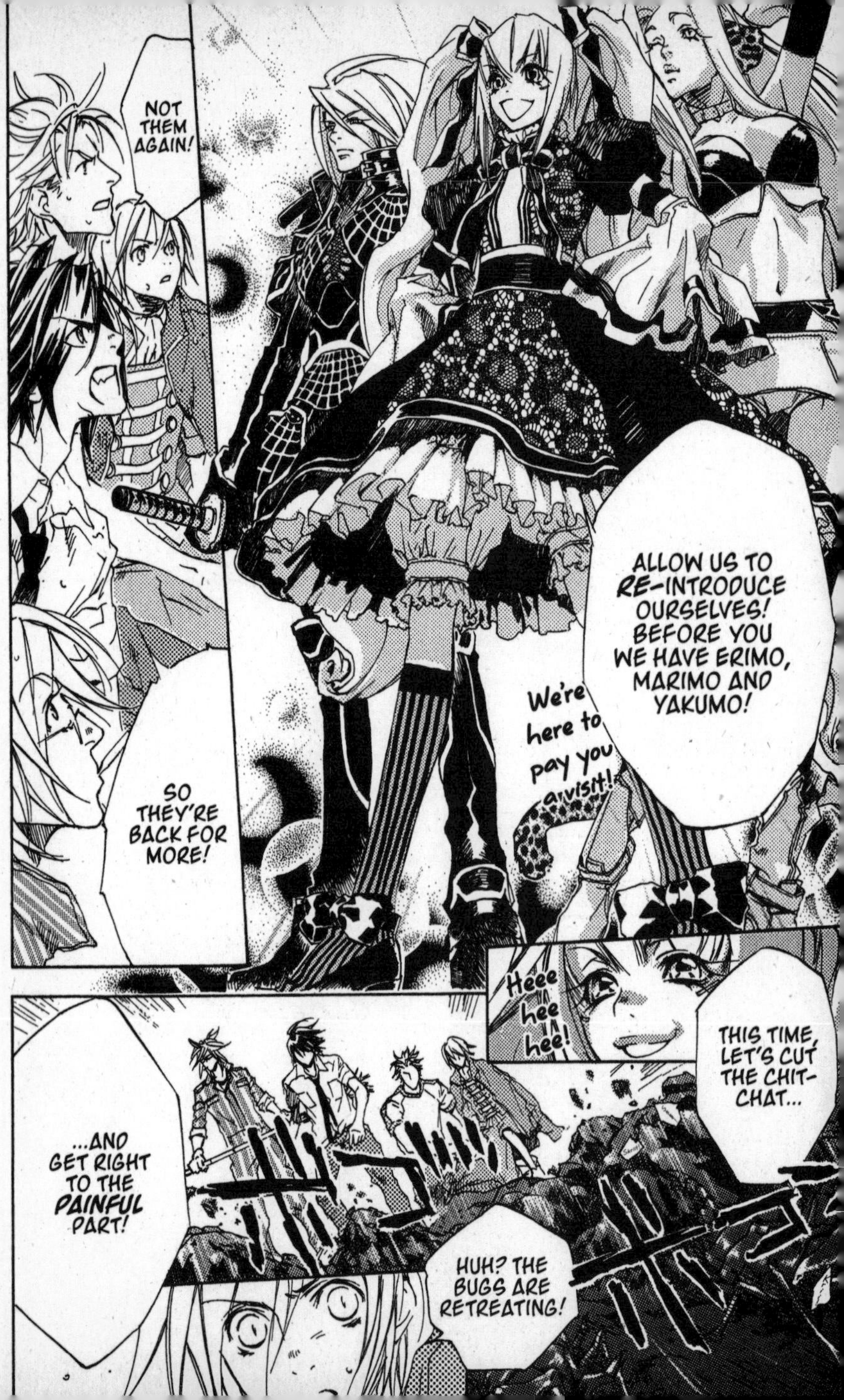
ALLOW US TO RE-INTRODUCE OURSELVES! BEFORE YOU WE HAVE ERIMO, MARIMO AND YAKUMO!
We're here to pay you a visit!
NOT THEM AGAIN!
SO THEY'RE BACK FOR MORE!
Heee hee hee!
THIS TIME, LET'S CUT THE CHIT-CHAT...
...AND GET RIGHT TO THE PAINFUL PART!
HUH? THE BUGS ARE RETREATING!

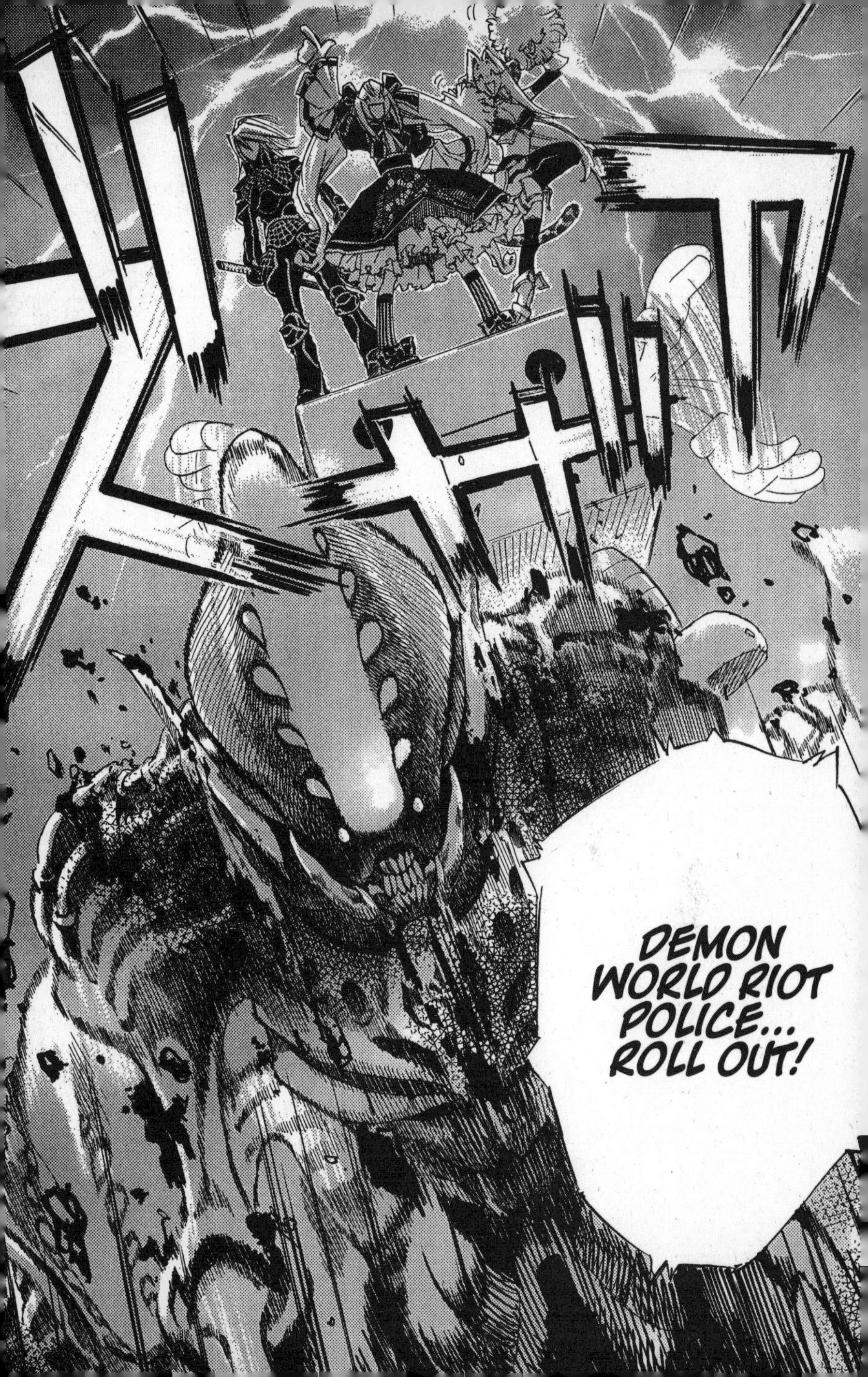
DEMON WORLD RIOT POLICE... ROLL OUT!

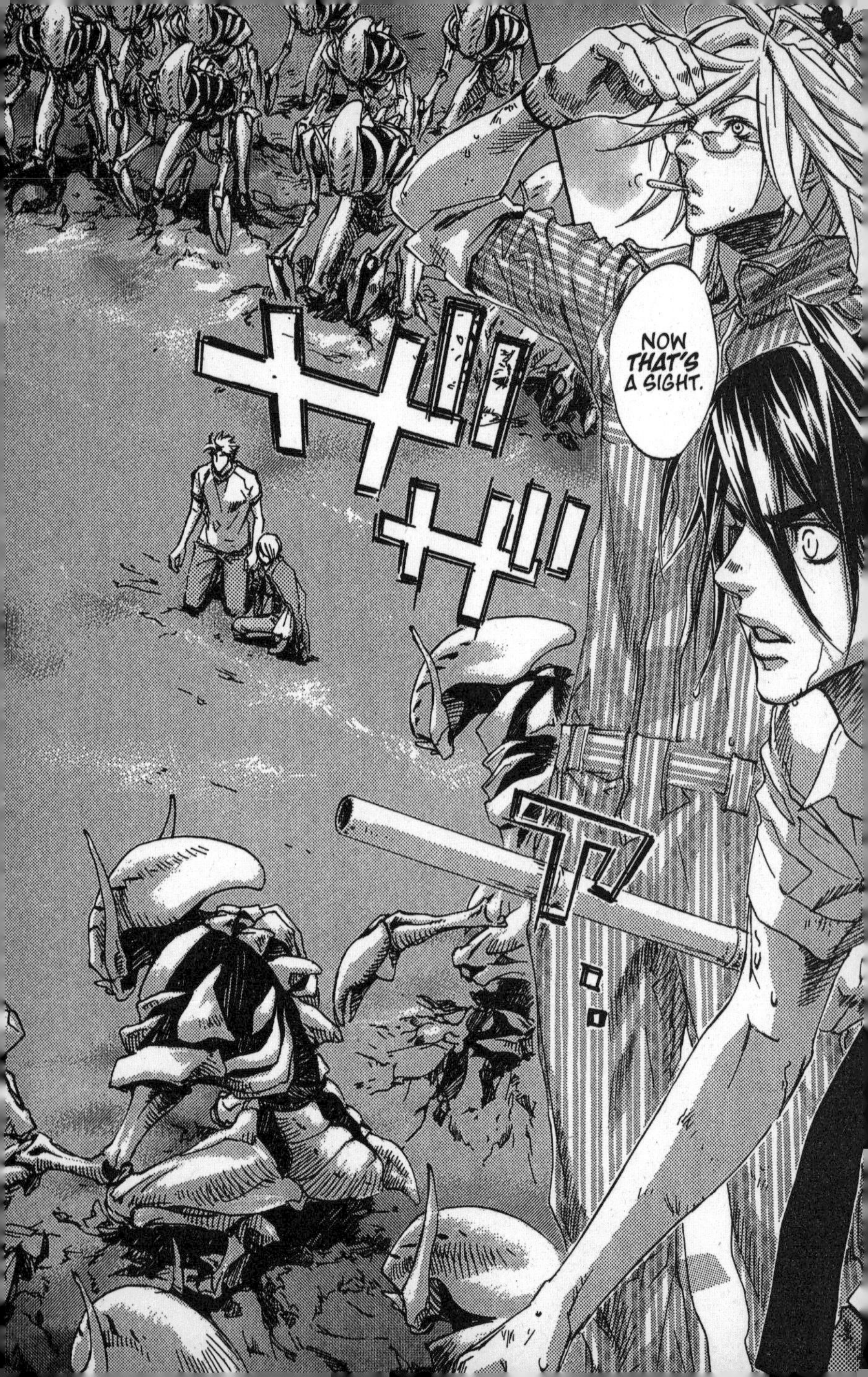
NOW THAT'S A SIGHT.

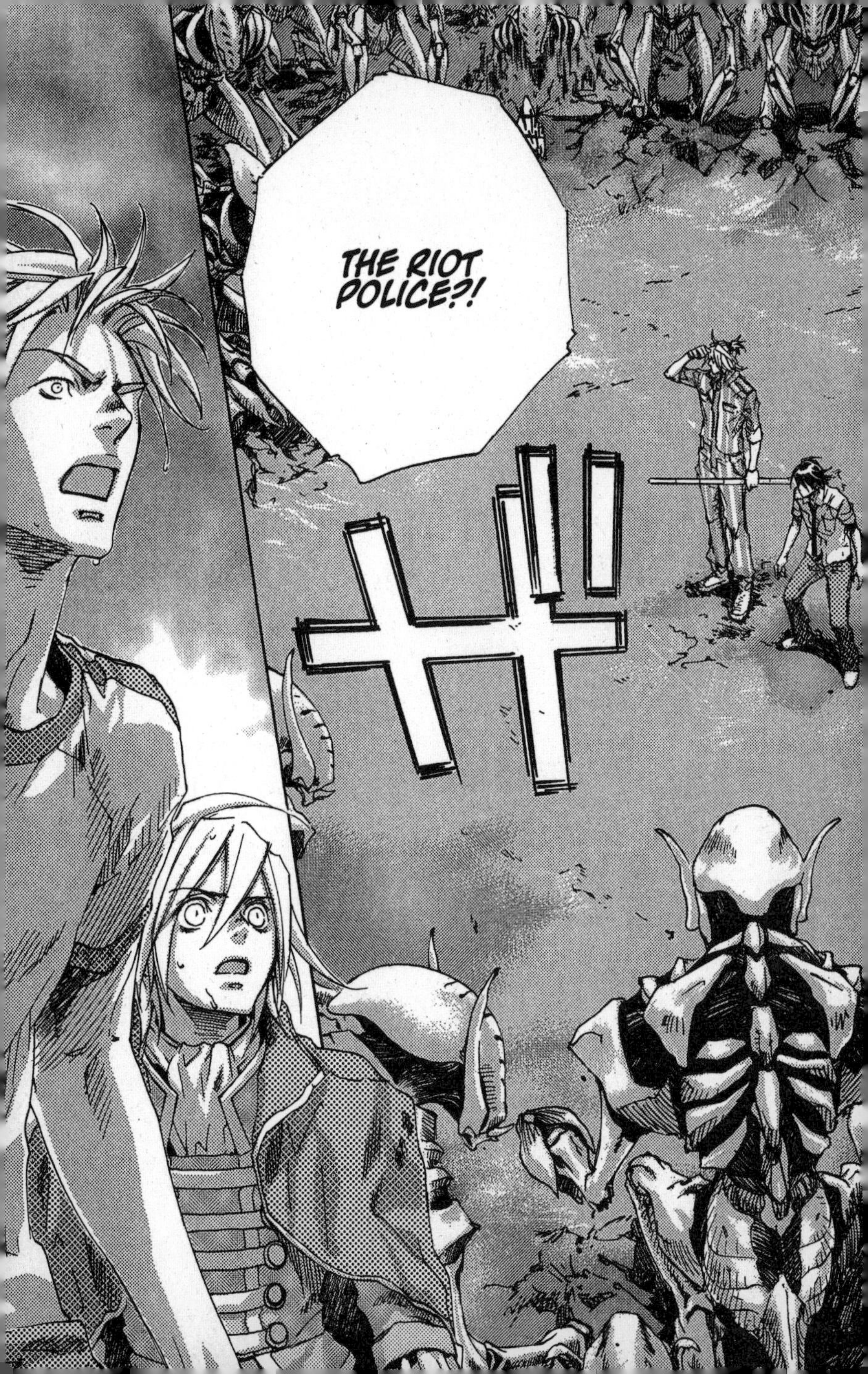
THE RIOT POLICE?!

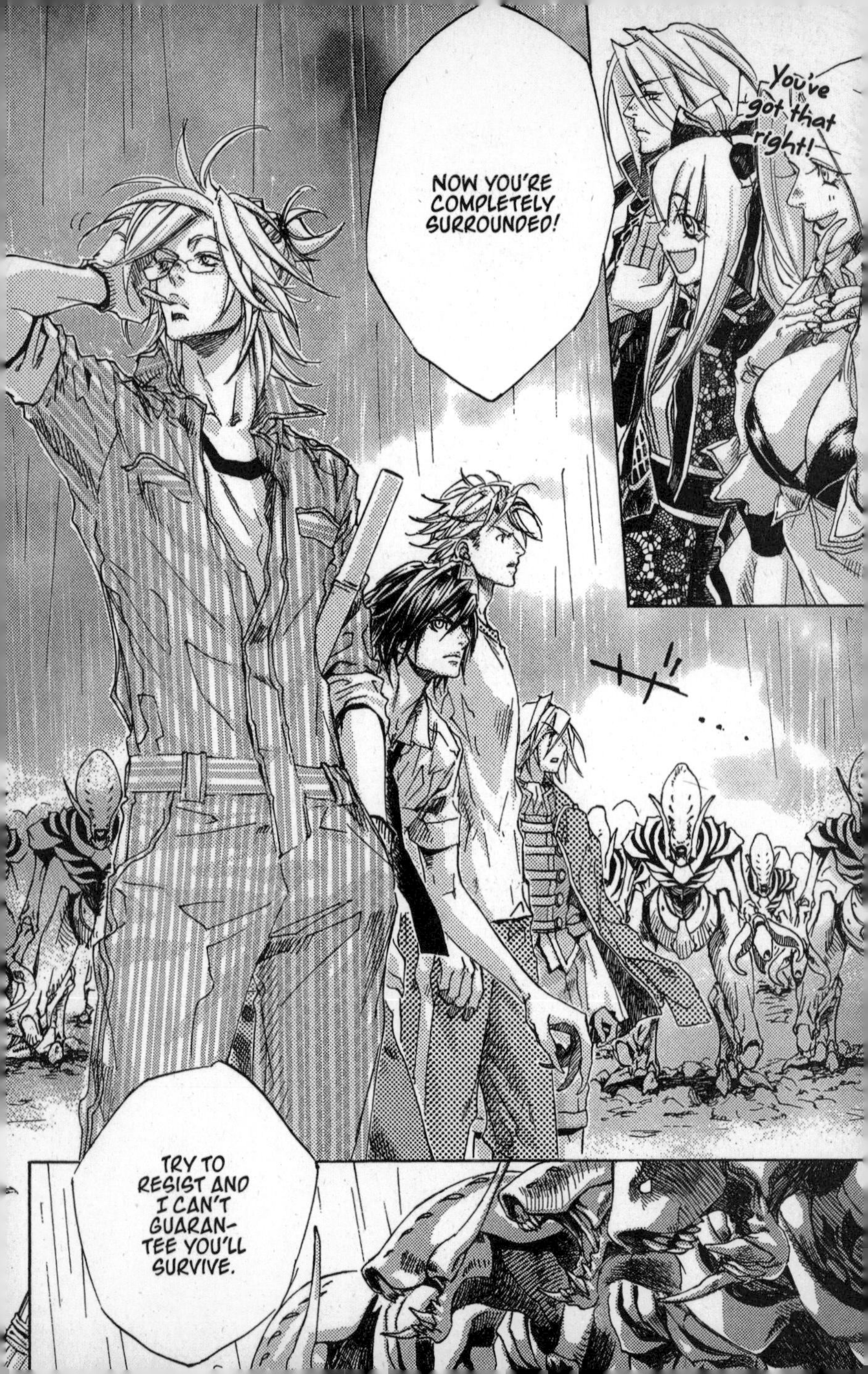
NOW YOU'RE COMPLETELY SURROUNDED!
You've got that right!
TRY TO RESIST AND I CAN'T GUARAN-TEE YOU'LL SURVIVE.

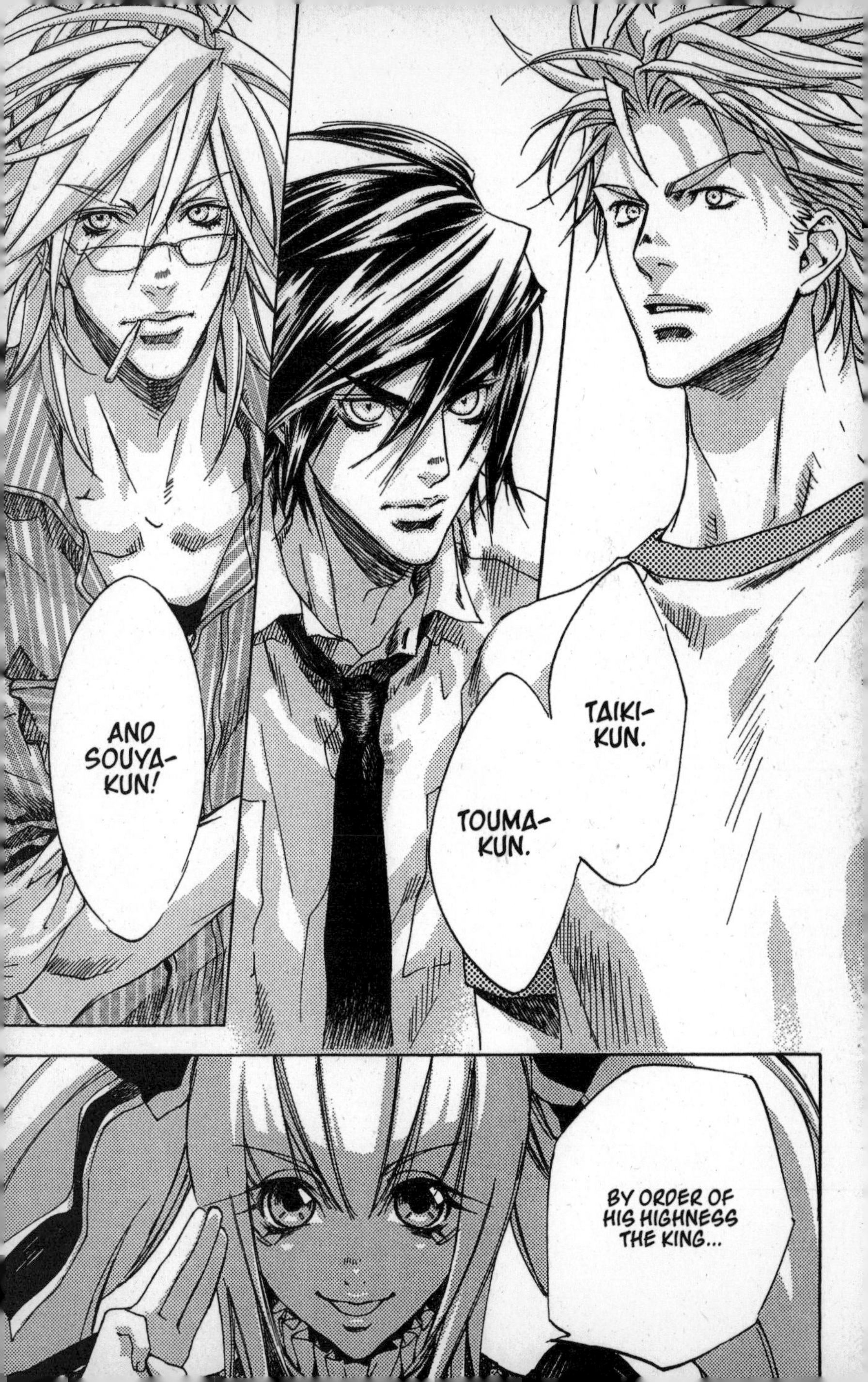
TAIKI-KUN.
TOUMA-KUN.
AND SOUYA-KUN!
BY ORDER OF HIS HIGHNESS THE KING...

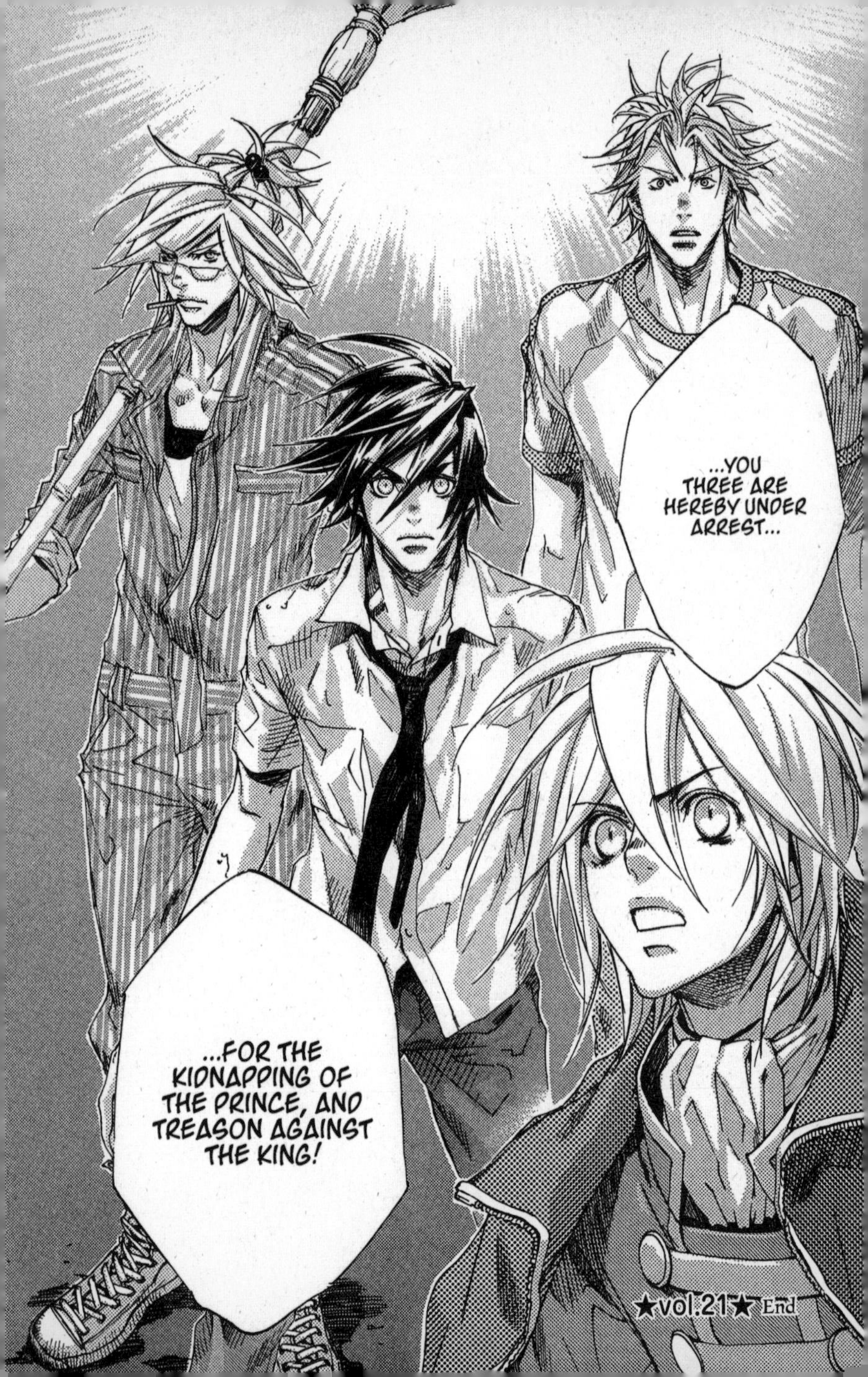
...YOU THREE ARE HEREBY UNDER ARREST...
...FOR THE KIDNAPPING OF THE PRINCE, AND TREASON AGAINST THE KING!
★vol.21★ End

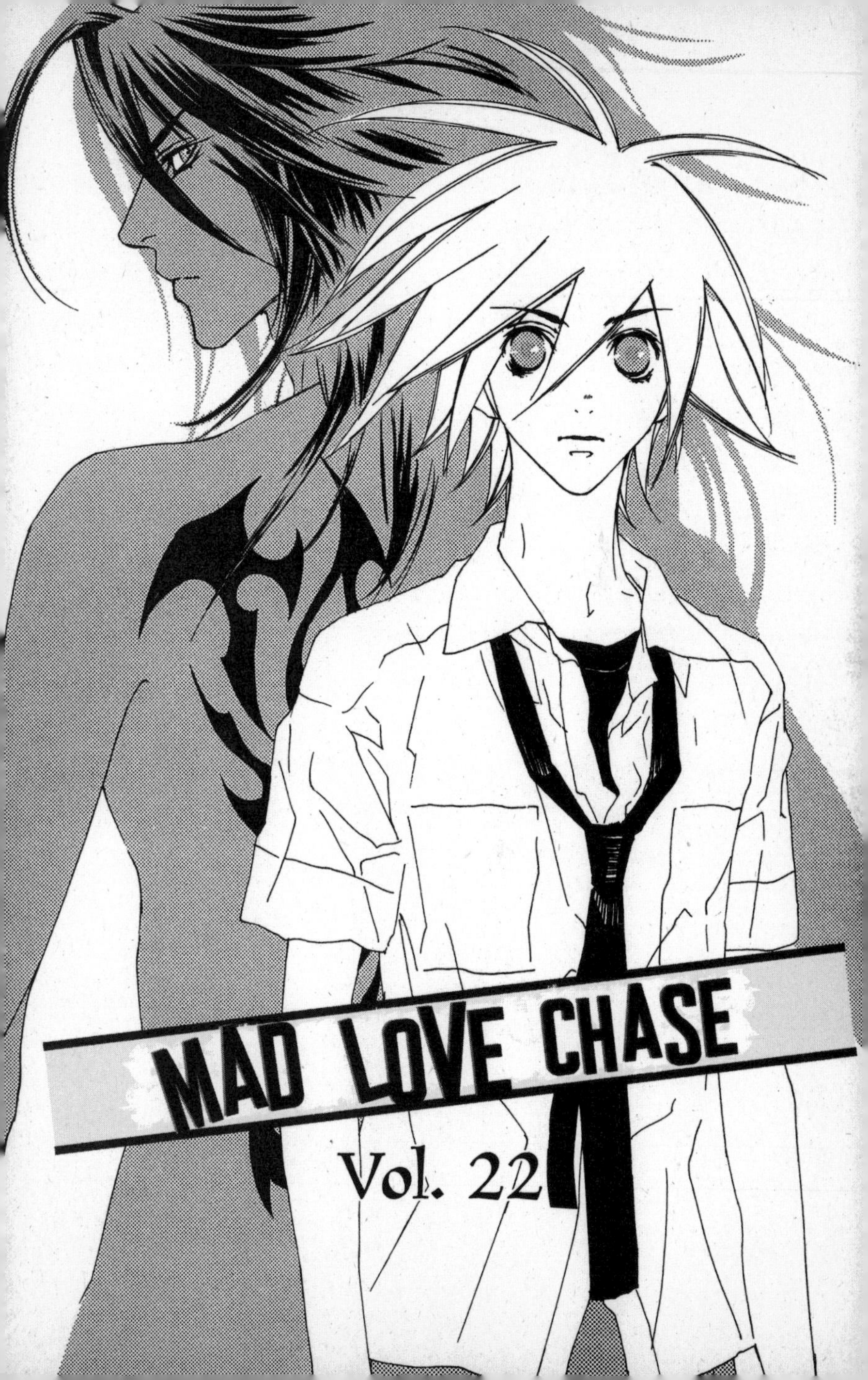
MAD LOVE CHASE
Vol. 22

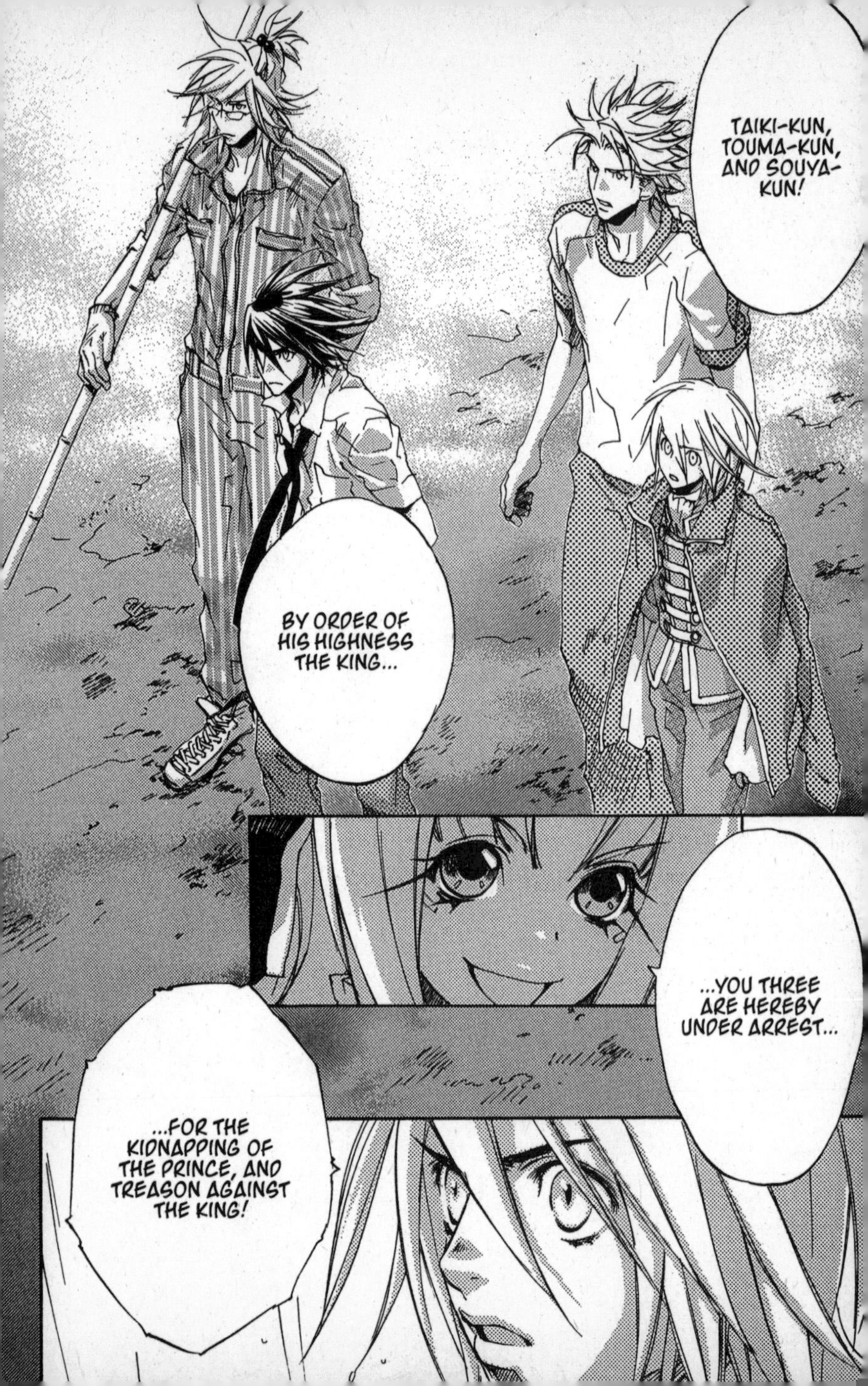
TAIKI-KUN, TOUMA-KUN, AND SOUYA-KUN!
BY ORDER OF HIS HIGHNESS THE KING...
...YOU THREE ARE HEREBY UNDER ARREST...
...FOR THE KIDNAPPING OF THE PRINCE, AND TREASON AGAINST THE KING!

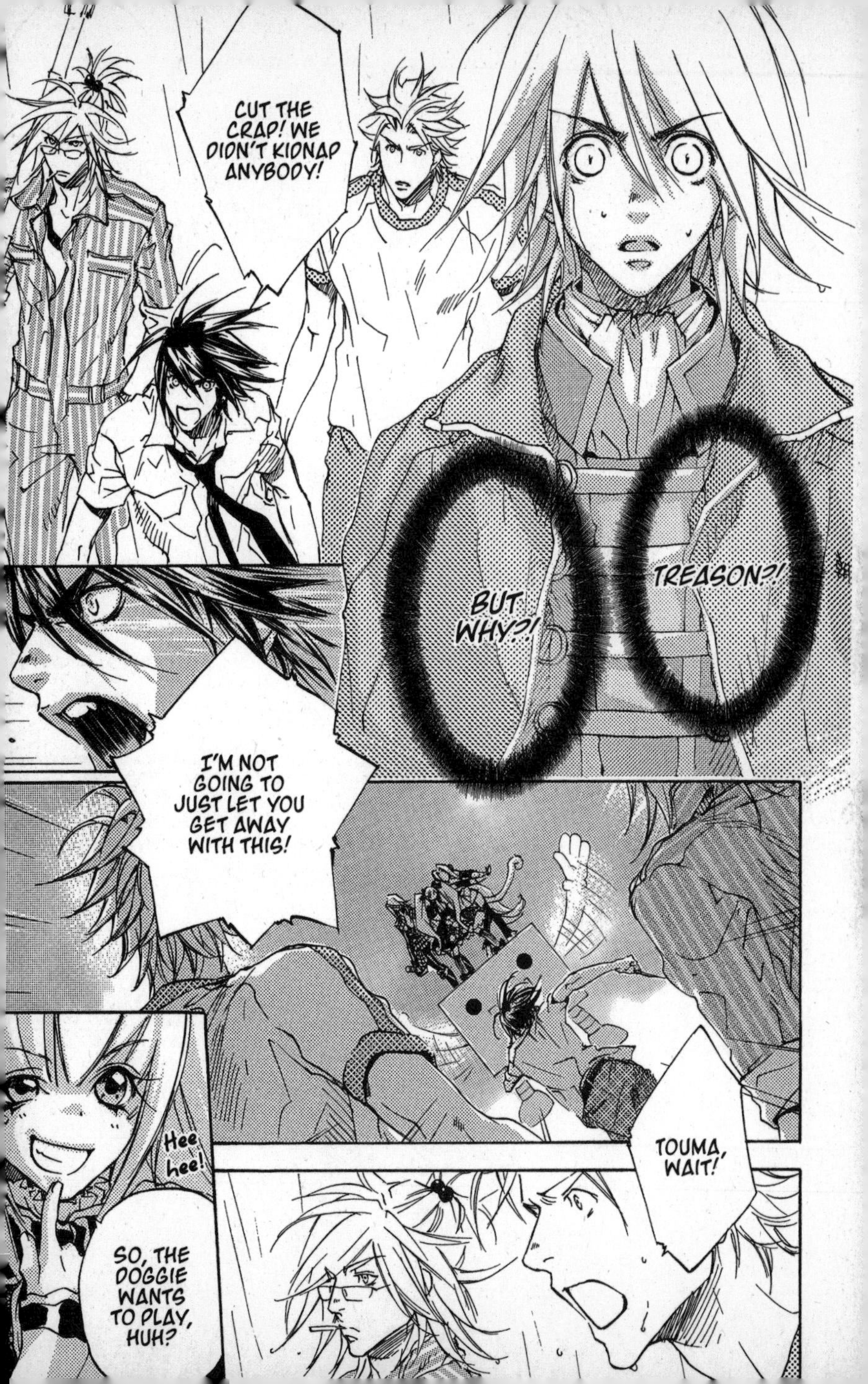
TREASON?!
BUT WHY?!
CUT THE CRAP! WE DIDN'T KIDNAP ANYBODY!
I'M NOT GOING TO JUST LET YOU GET AWAY WITH THIS!
TOUMA, WAIT!
Hee hee!
SO, THE DOGGIE WANTS TO PLAY, HUH?

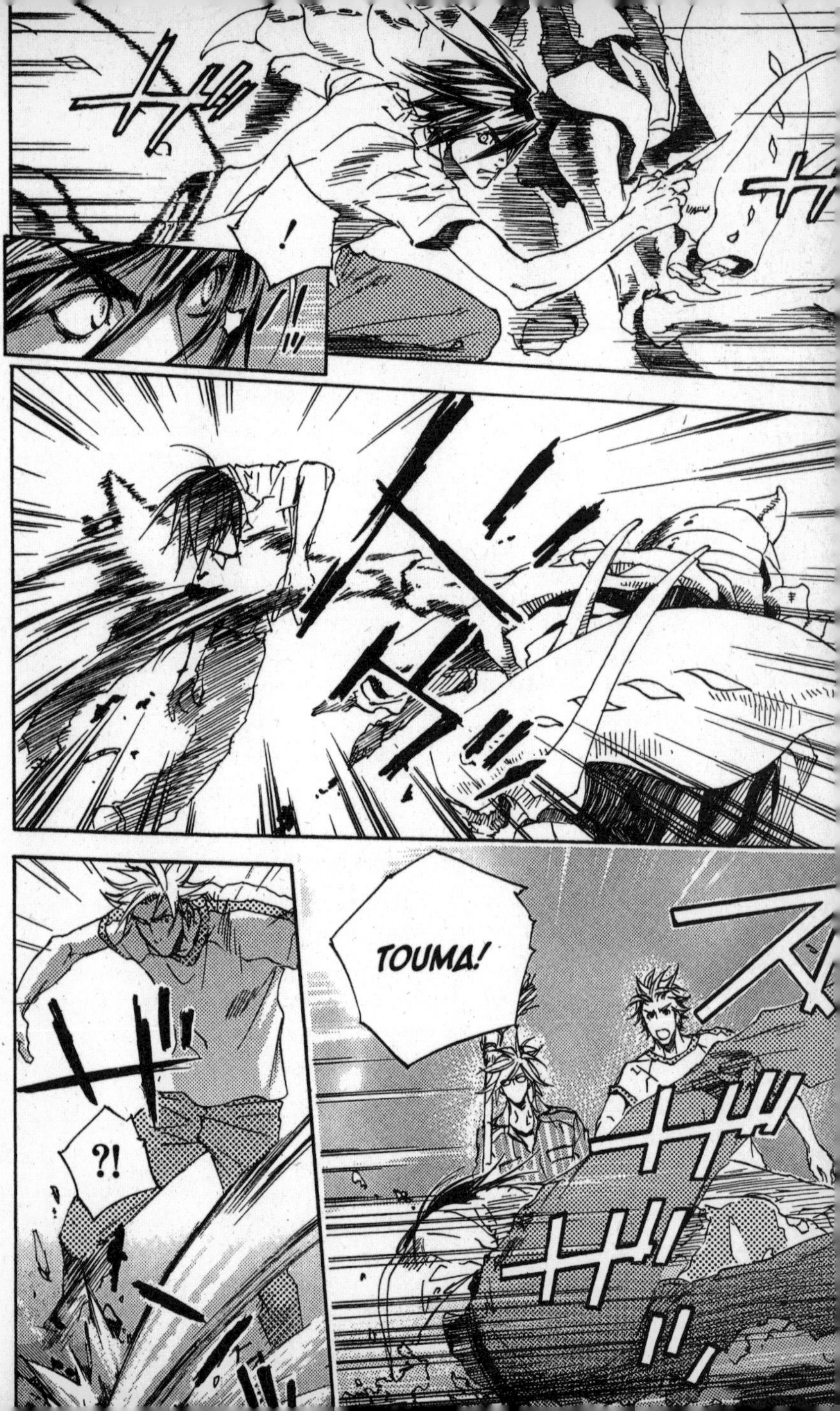
!
!!
TOUMA!
?!

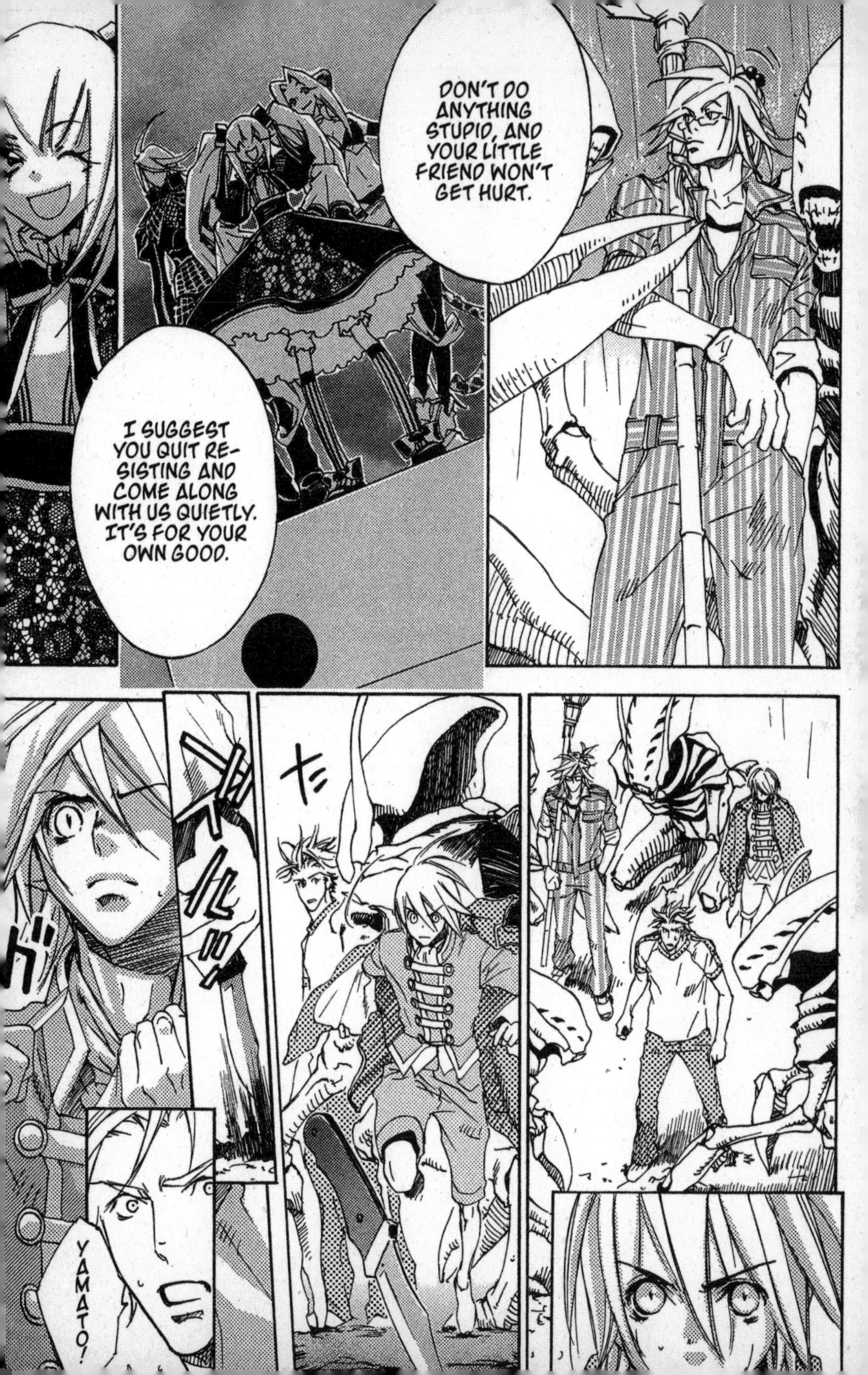
DON'T DO ANYTHING STUPID, AND YOUR LITTLE FRIEND WON'T GET HURT.
I SUGGEST YOU QUIT RE-SISTING AND COME ALONG WITH US QUIETLY. IT'S FOR YOUR OWN GOOD.
YAMATO!

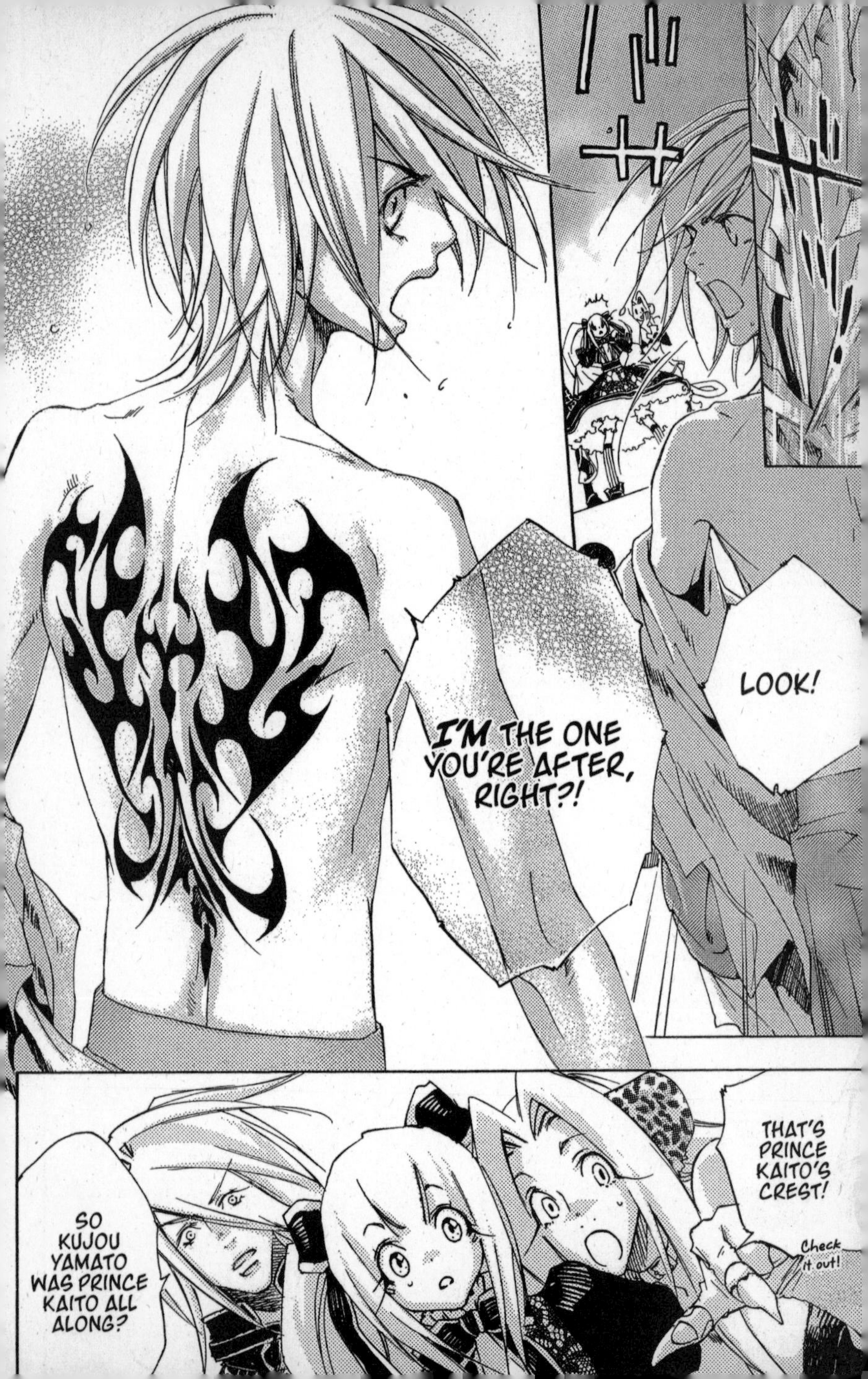
LOOK!
I'M THE ONE YOU'RE AFTER, RIGHT?!
THAT'S PRINCE KAITO'S CREST!
Check it out!
SO KUJOU YAMATO WAS PRINCE KAITO ALL ALONG?

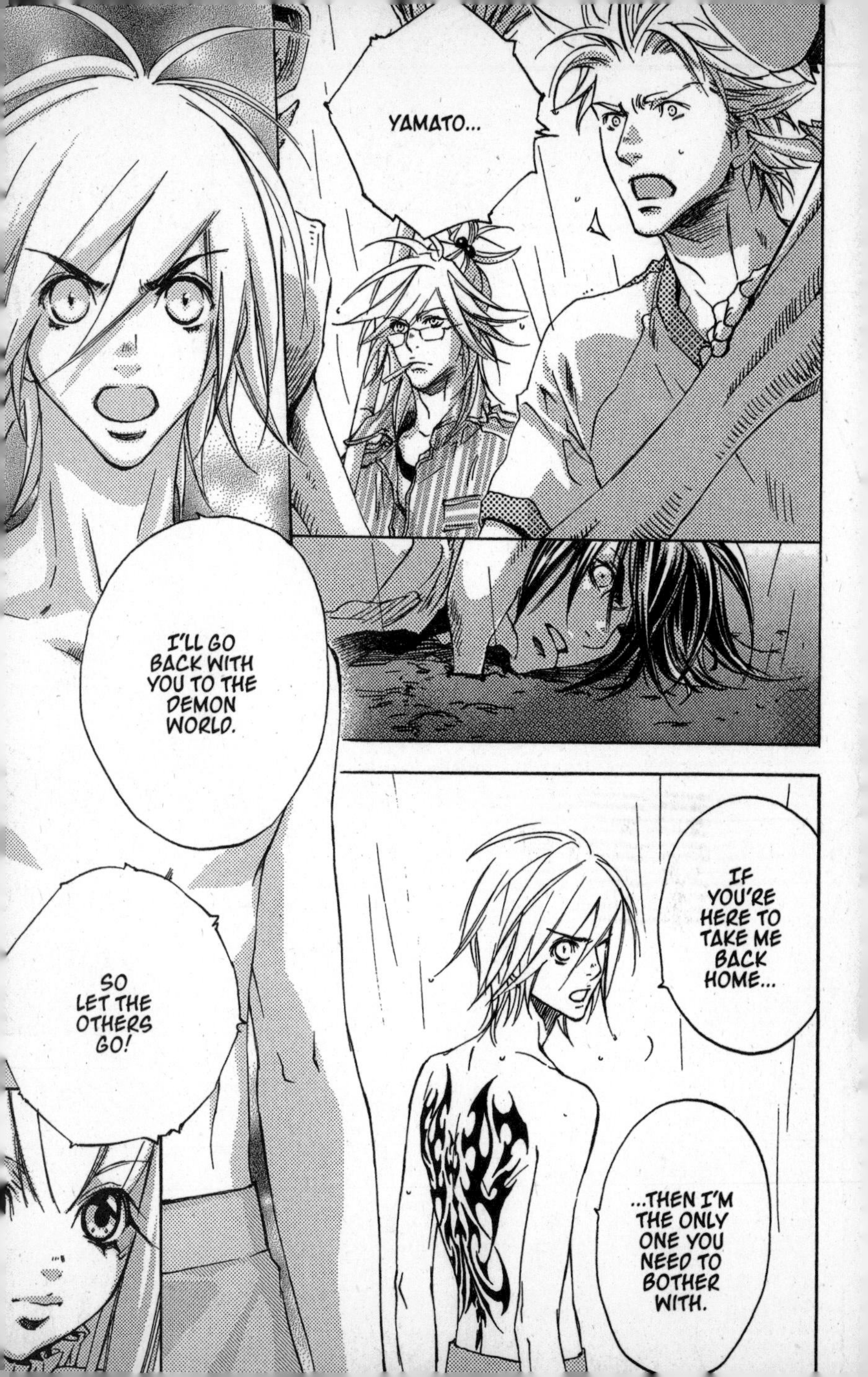
YAMATO...
I'LL GO BACK WITH YOU TO THE DEMON WORLD.
IF YOU'RE HERE TO TAKE ME BACK HOME...
...THEN I'M THE ONLY ONE YOU NEED TO BOTHER WITH.
SO LET THE OTHERS GO!

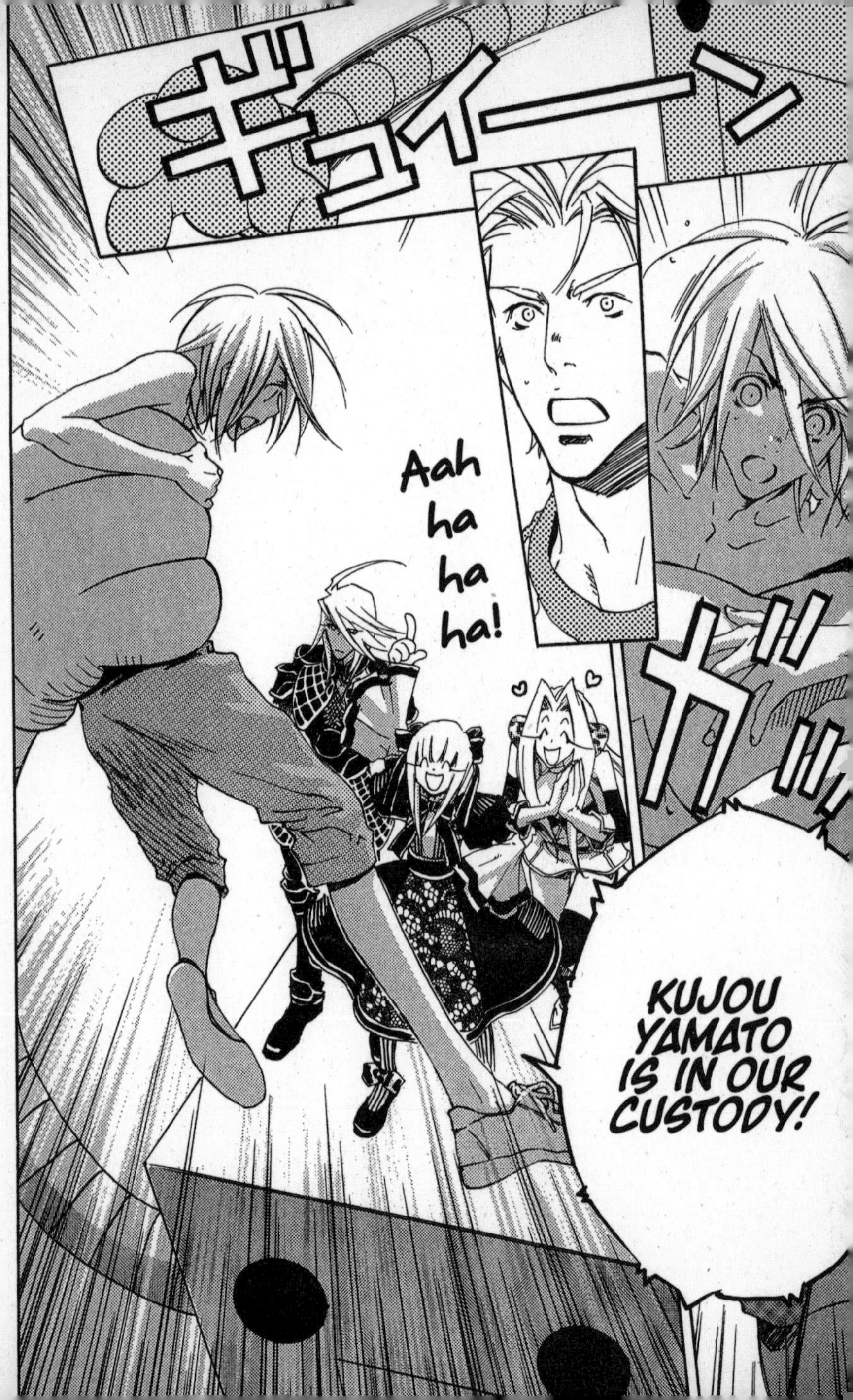
ギュイーーン
Aah ha ha ha!
ガッ
KUJOU YAMATO IS IN OUR CUSTODY!

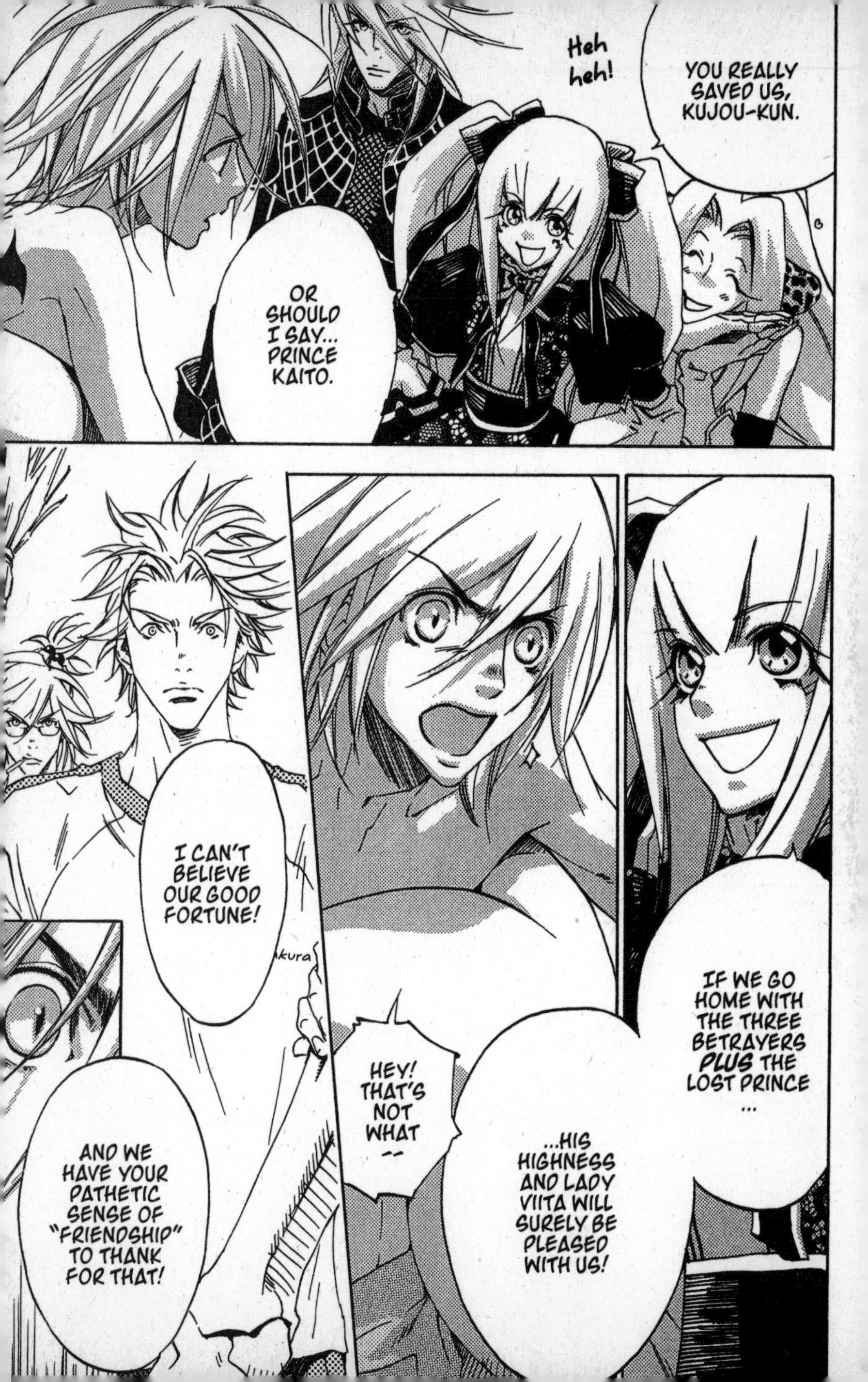
YOU REALLY SAVED US, KUJOU-KUN.
Heh heh!
OR SHOULD I SAY... PRINCE KAITO.
IF WE GO HOME WITH THE THREE BETRAYERS PLUS THE LOST PRINCE ...
...HIS HIGHNESS AND LADY VIITA WILL SURELY BE PLEASED WITH US!
HEY! THAT'S NOT WHAT --
I CAN'T BELIEVE OUR GOOD FORTUNE!
AND WE HAVE YOUR PATHETIC SENSE OF "FRIENDSHIP" TO THANK FOR THAT!

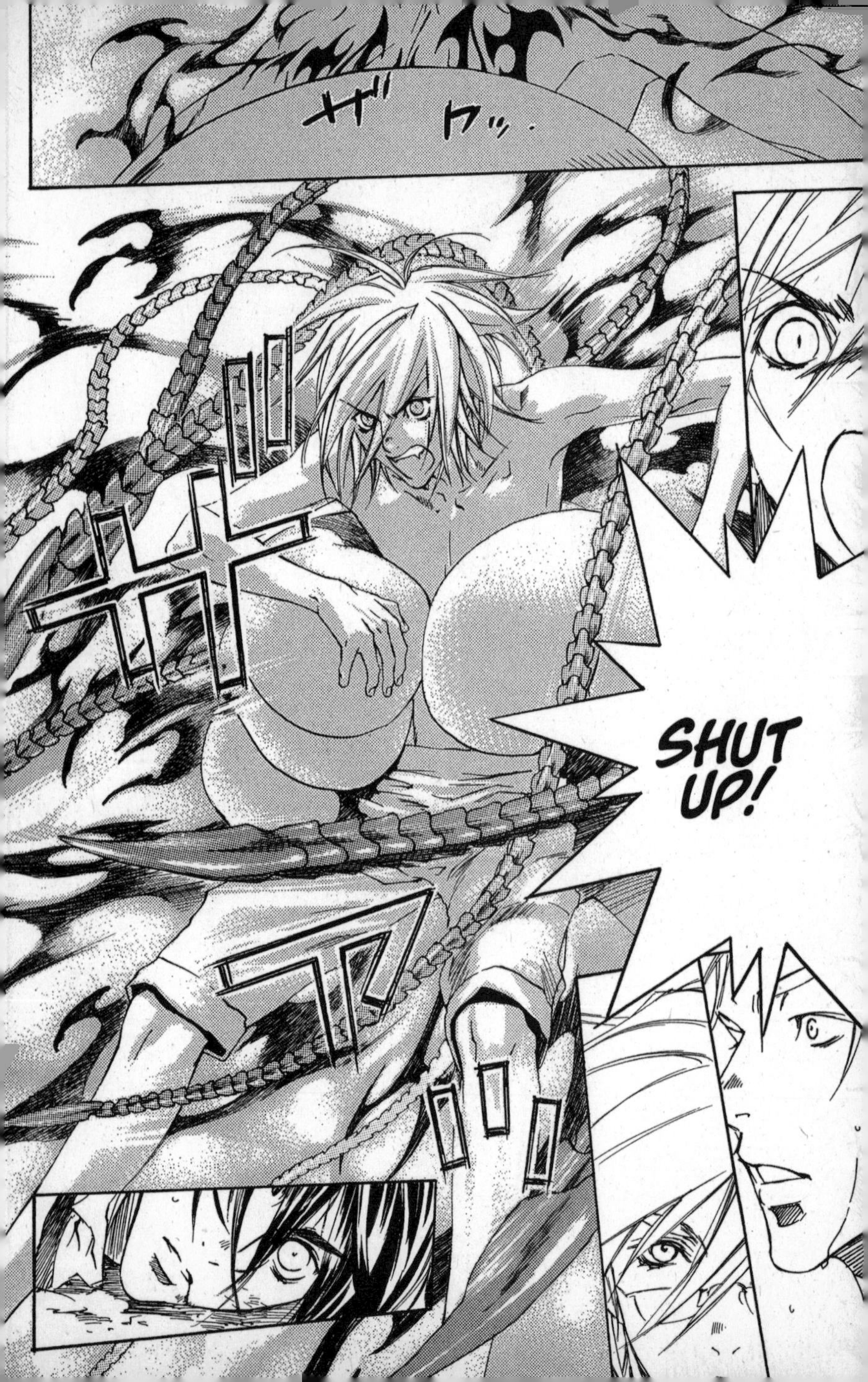
ザワッ
SHUT UP!

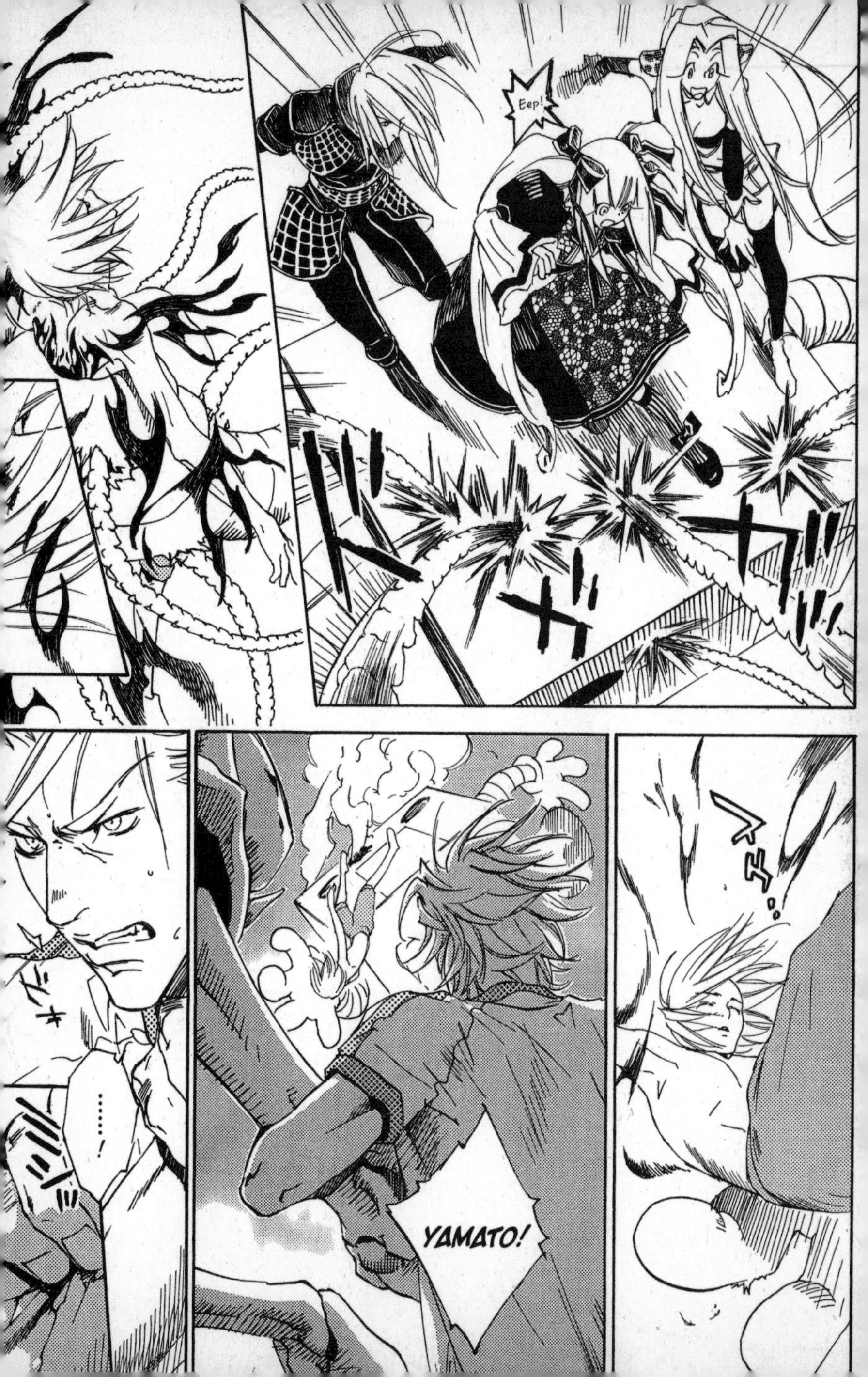
Eep!
YAMATO!
......!

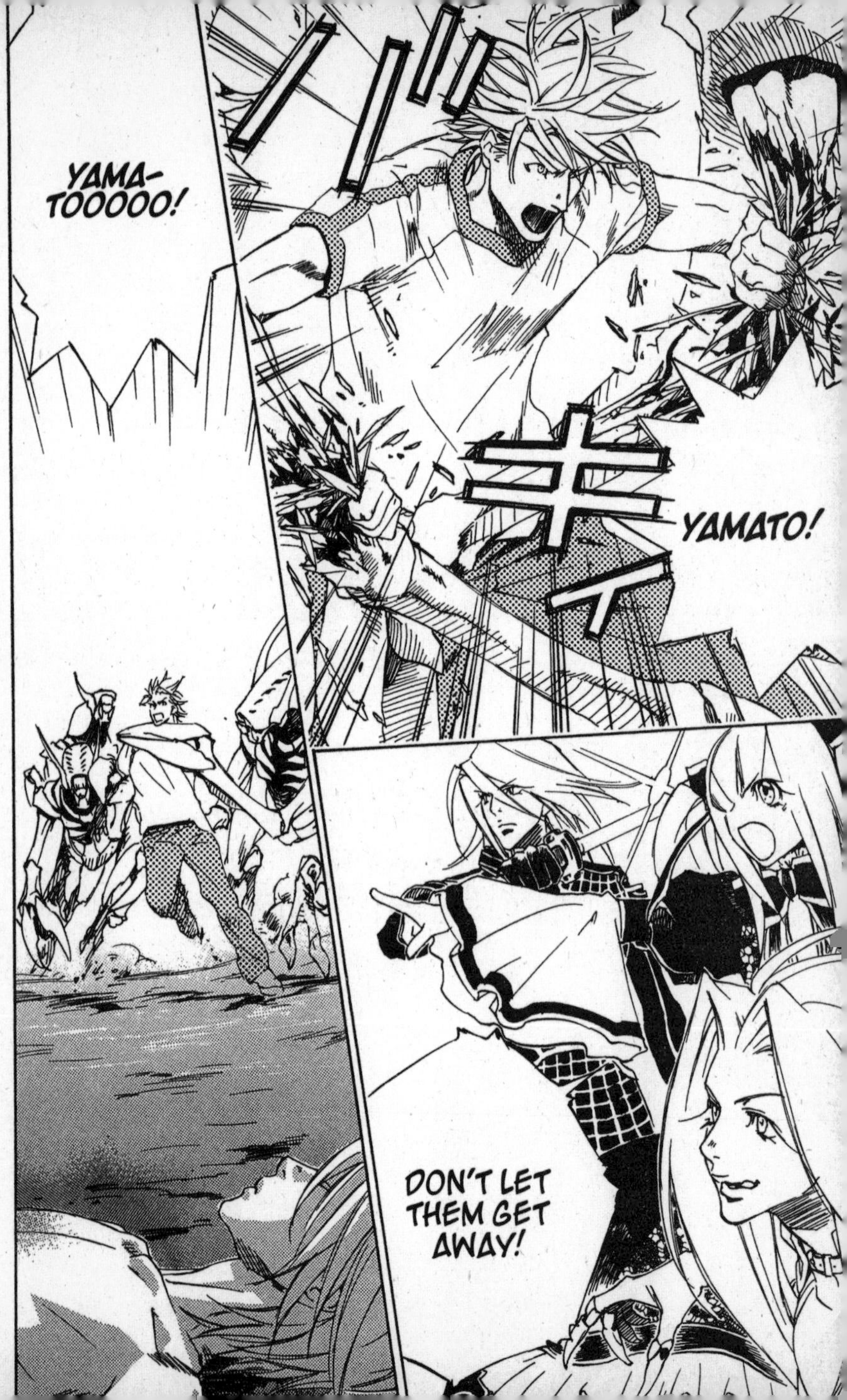
YAMATO!
DON'T LET THEM GET AWAY!
YAMA-TOOOOO!

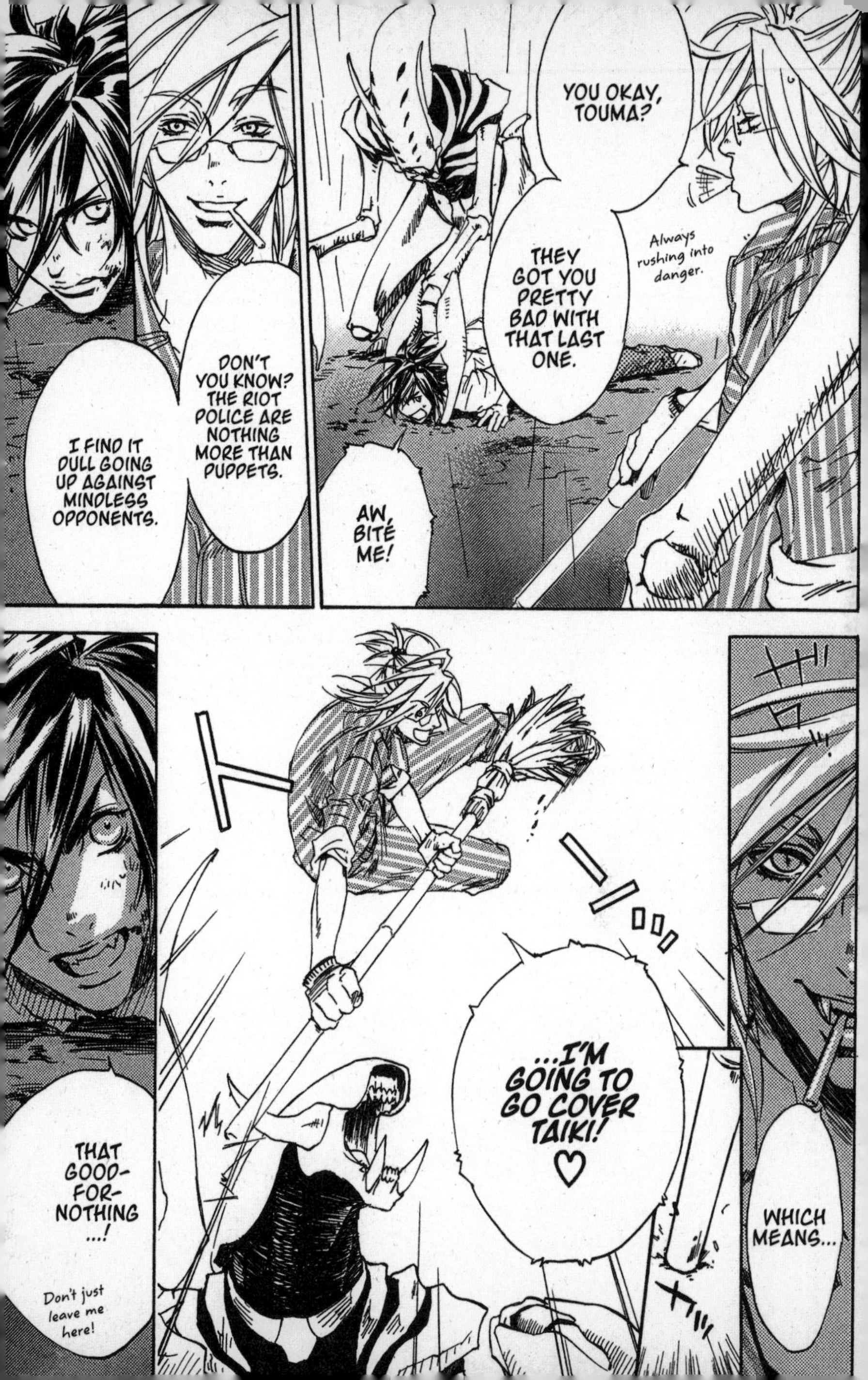
YOU OKAY, TOUMA?
Always rushing into danger.
THEY GOT YOU PRETTY BAD WITH THAT LAST ONE.
AW, BITE ME!
DON'T YOU KNOW? THE RIOT POLICE ARE NOTHING MORE THAN PUPPETS.
I FIND IT DULL GOING UP AGAINST MINDLESS OPPONENTS.
WHICH MEANS...
...I'M GOING TO GO COVER TAIKI! ♡
THAT GOOD-FOR-NOTHING...!
Don't just leave me here!

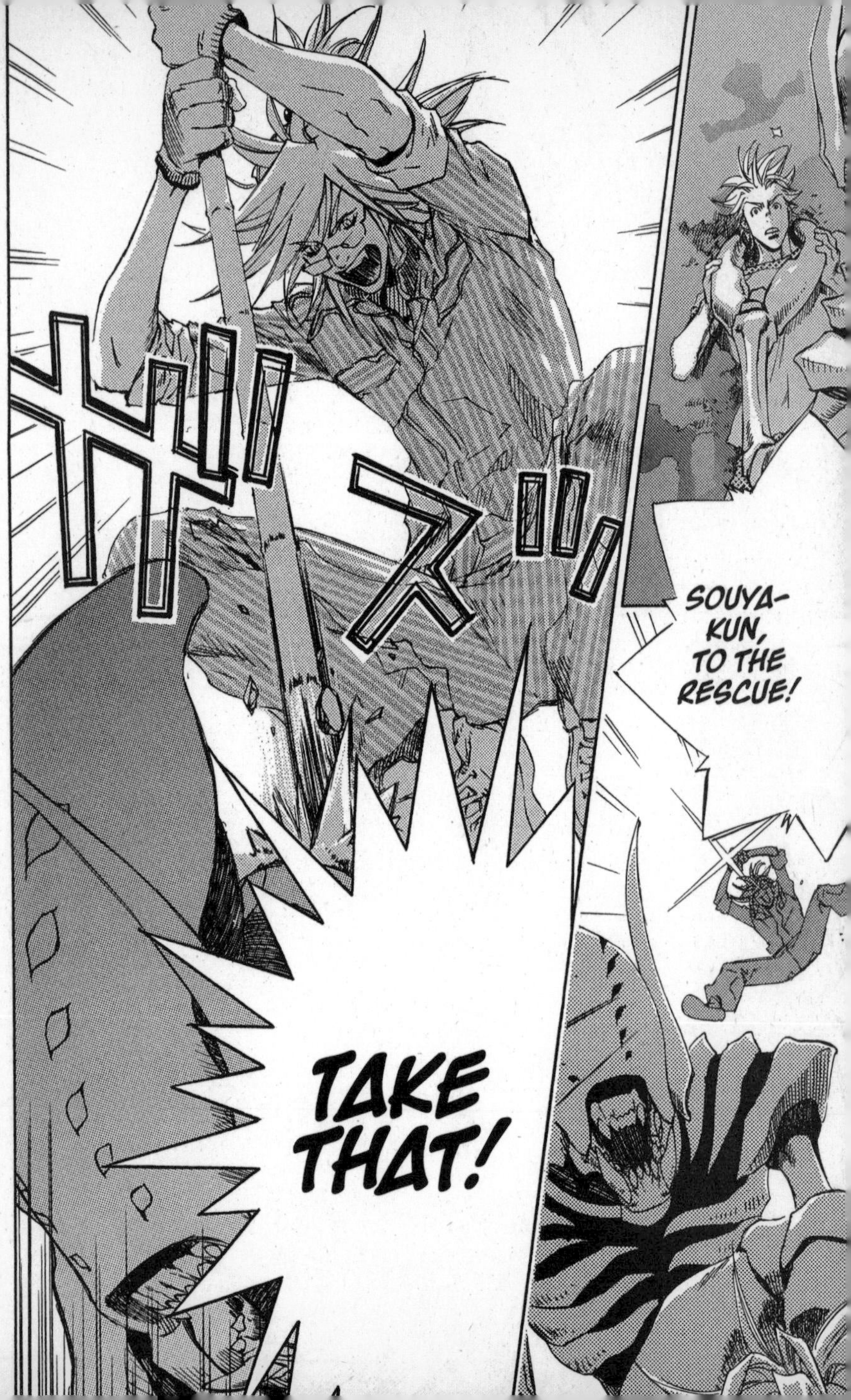
SOUYA-KUN, TO THE RESCUE!
TAKE THAT!

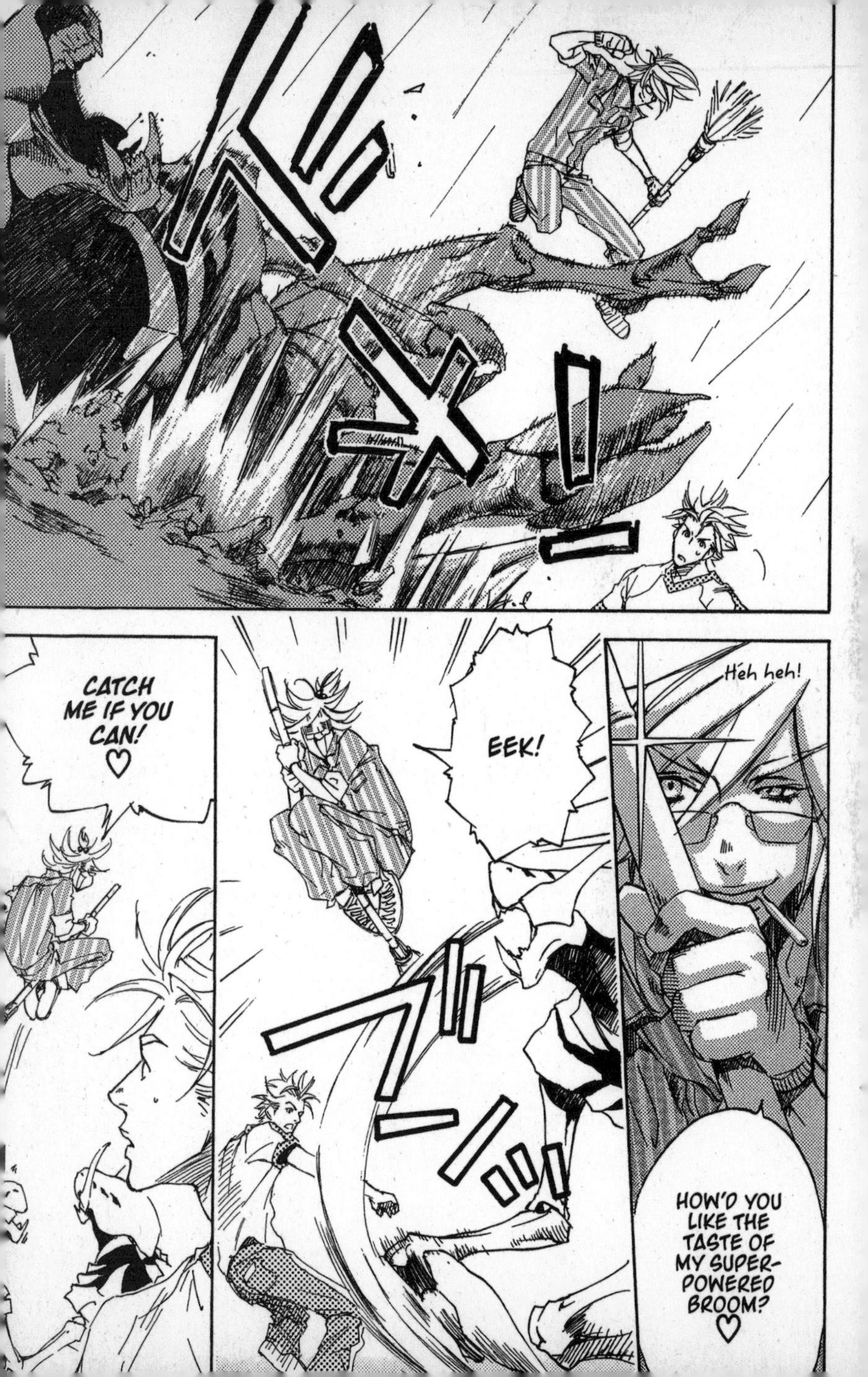
Heh heh!
HOW'D YOU LIKE THE TASTE OF MY SUPER-POWERED BROOM? ♡
EEK!
CATCH ME IF YOU CAN! ♡

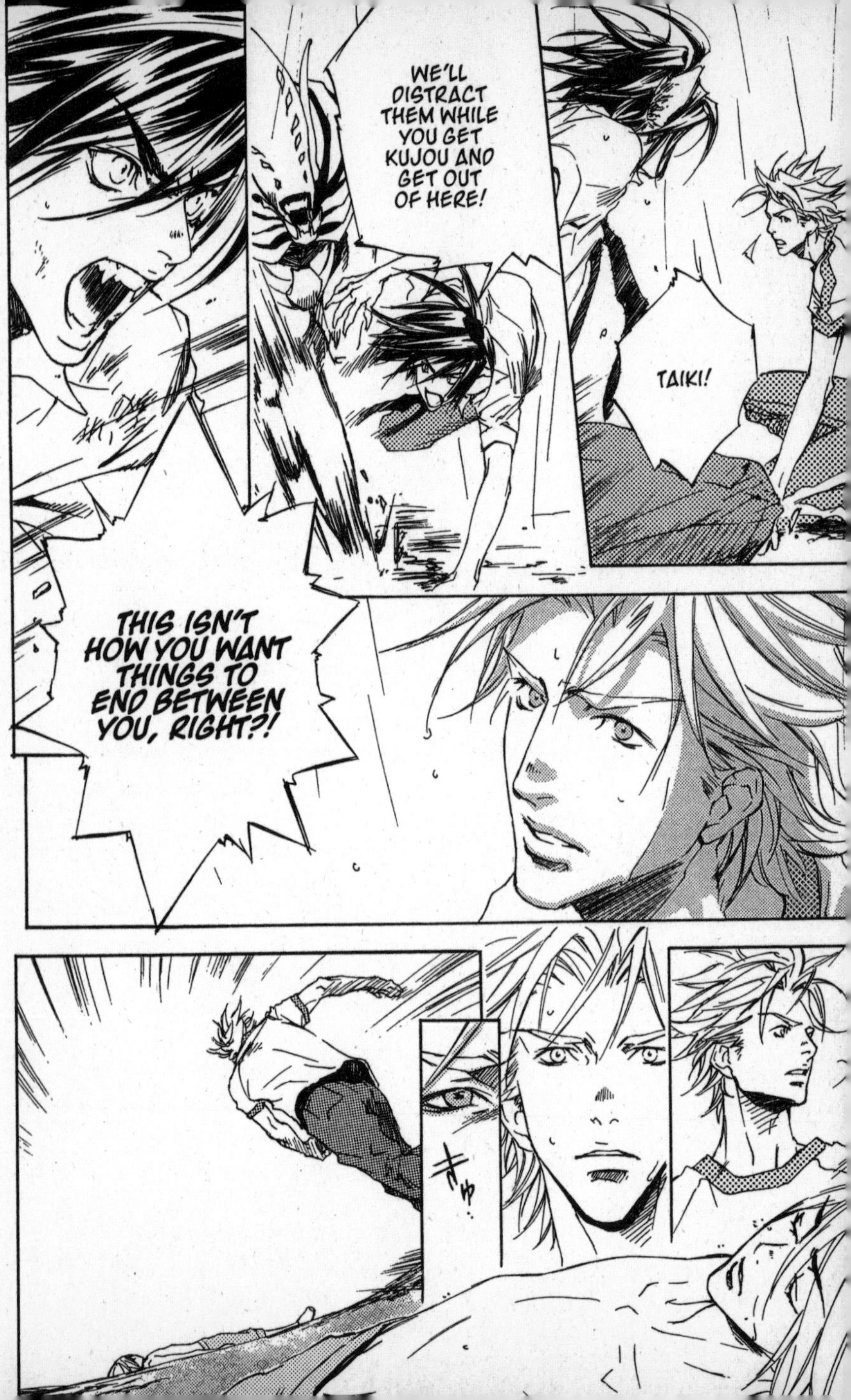
TAIKI!
WE'LL DISTRACT THEM WHILE YOU GET KUJOU AND GET OUT OF HERE!
THIS ISN'T HOW YOU WANT THINGS TO END BETWEEN YOU, RIGHT?!

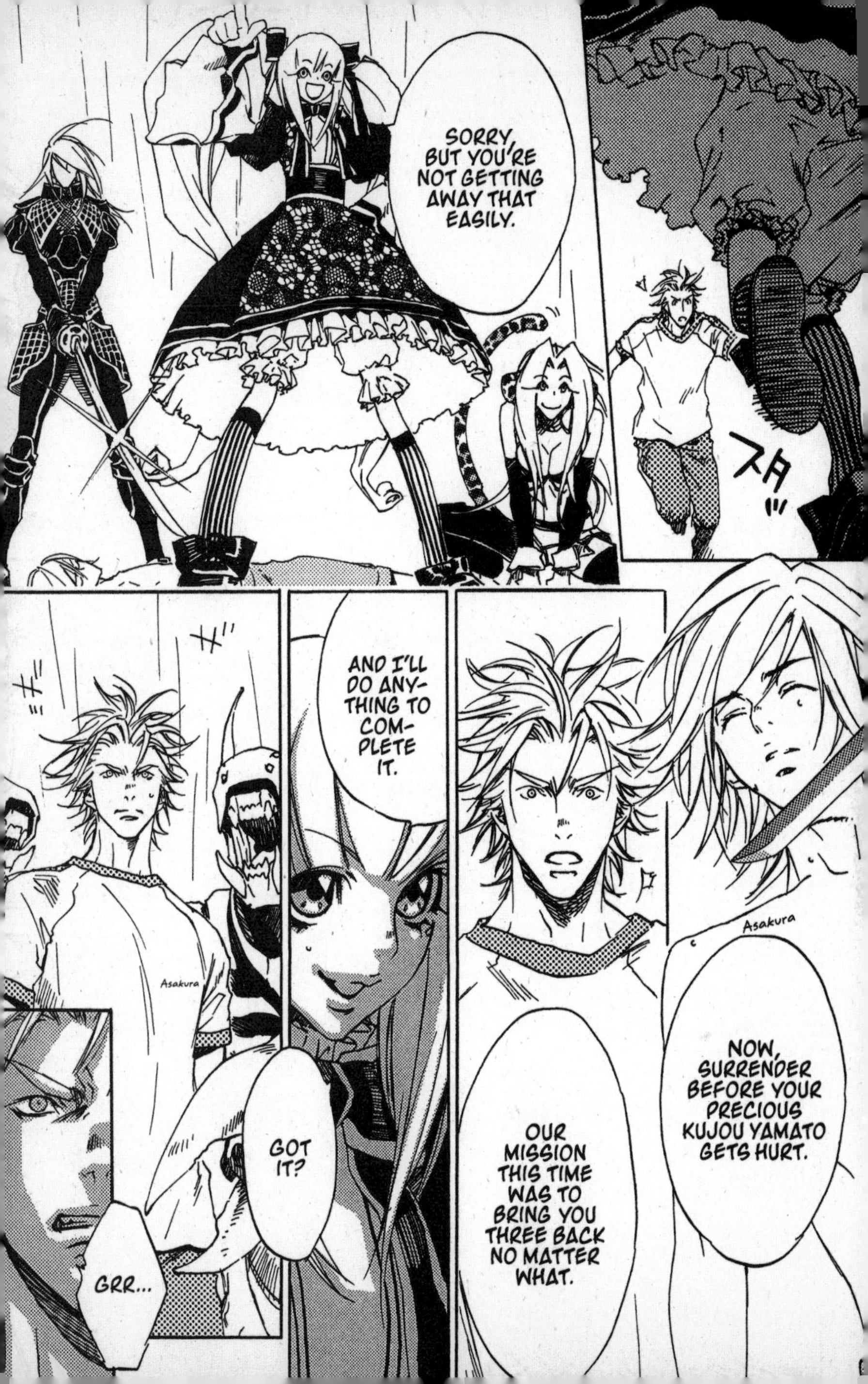
スタッ
SORRY, BUT YOU'RE NOT GETTING AWAY THAT EASILY.
NOW, SURRENDER BEFORE YOUR PRECIOUS KUJOU YAMATO GETS HURT.
OUR MISSION THIS TIME WAS TO BRING YOU THREE BACK NO MATTER WHAT.
Asakura
AND I'LL DO ANYTHING TO COMPLETE IT.
GOT IT?
Asakura
GRR...

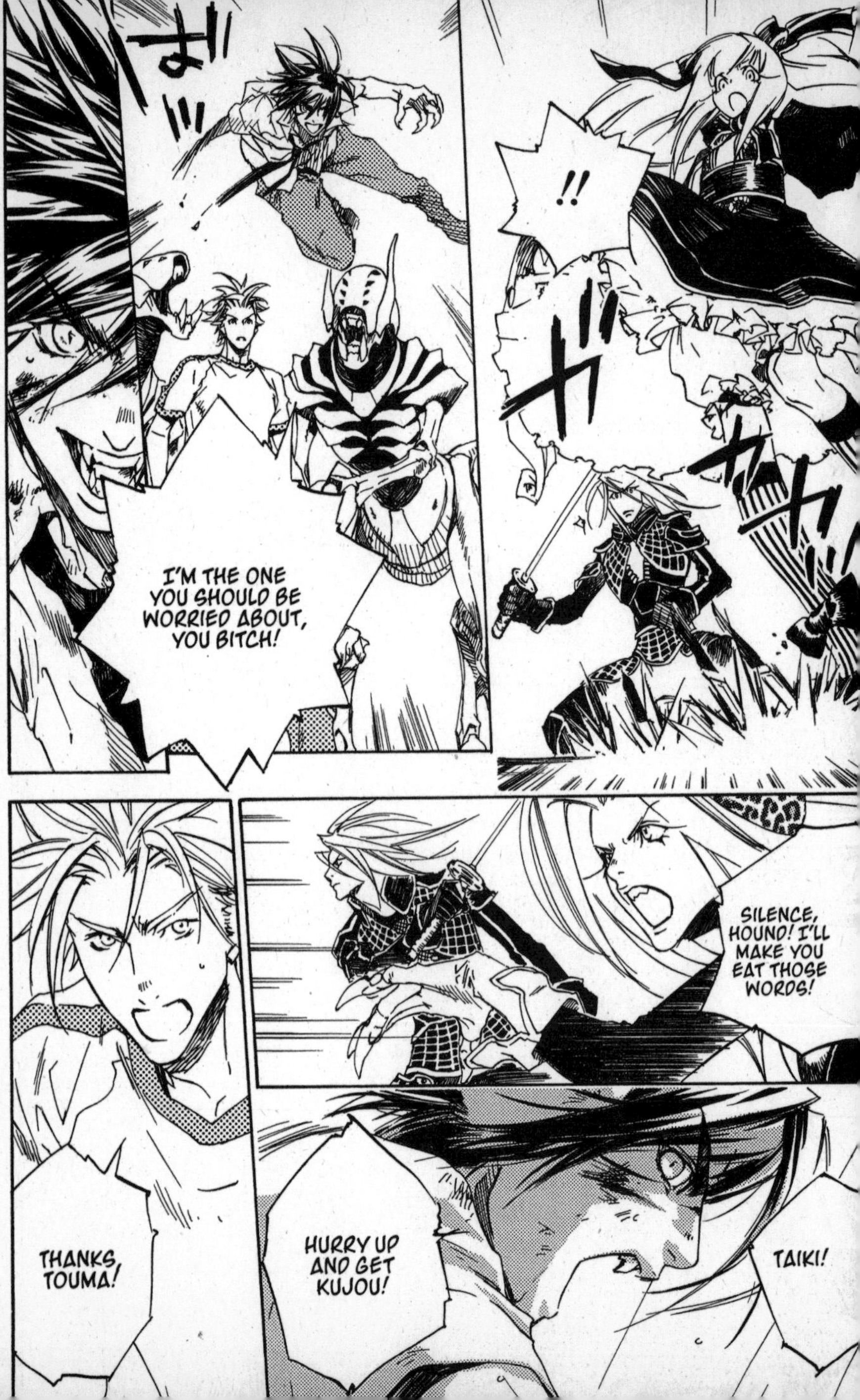
!!
I'M THE ONE YOU SHOULD BE WORRIED ABOUT, YOU BITCH!
SILENCE, HOUND! I'LL MAKE YOU EAT THOSE WORDS!
TAIKI!
HURRY UP AND GET KUJOU!
THANKS, TOUMA!

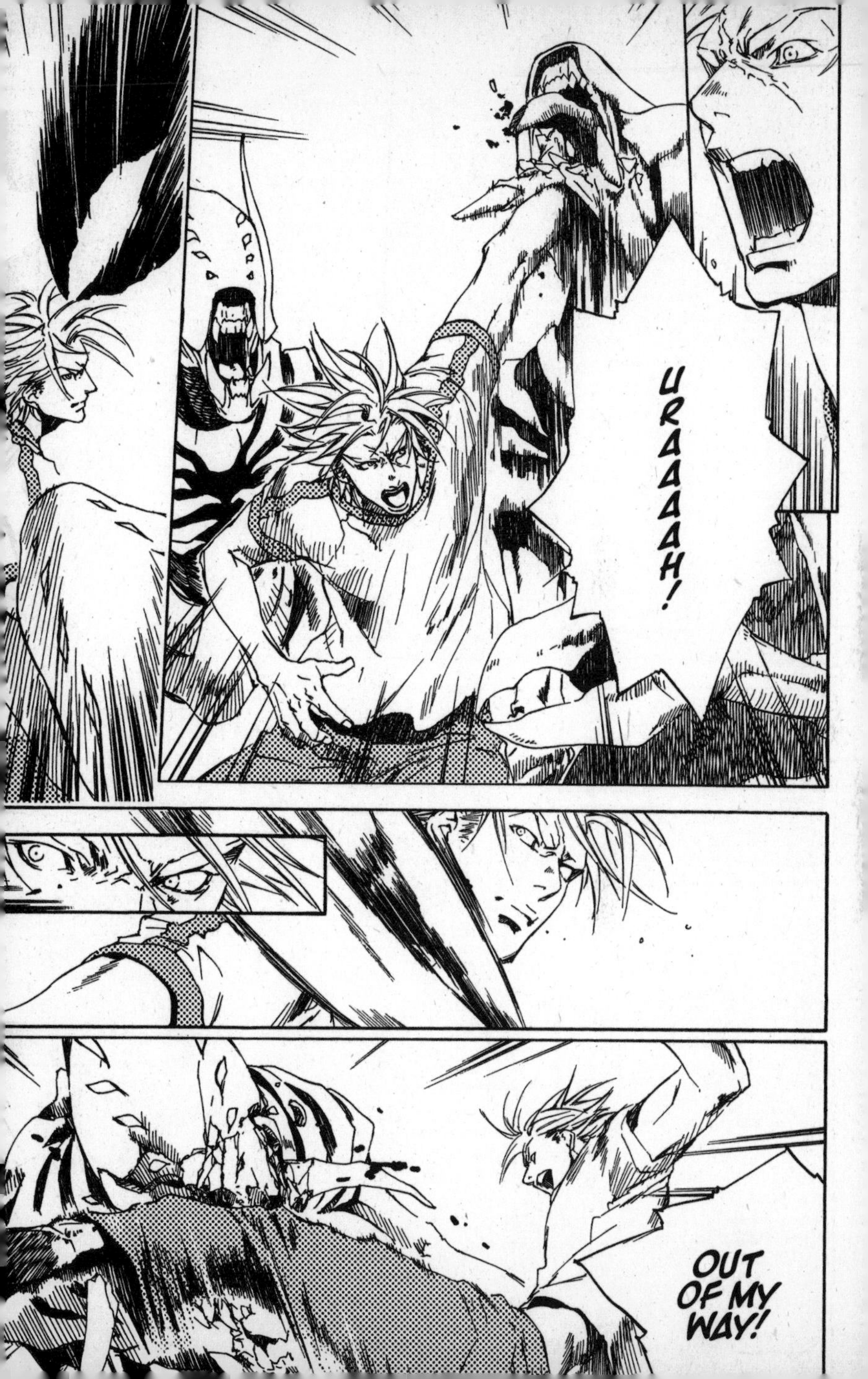
URAAAAAH!
OUT OF MY WAY!

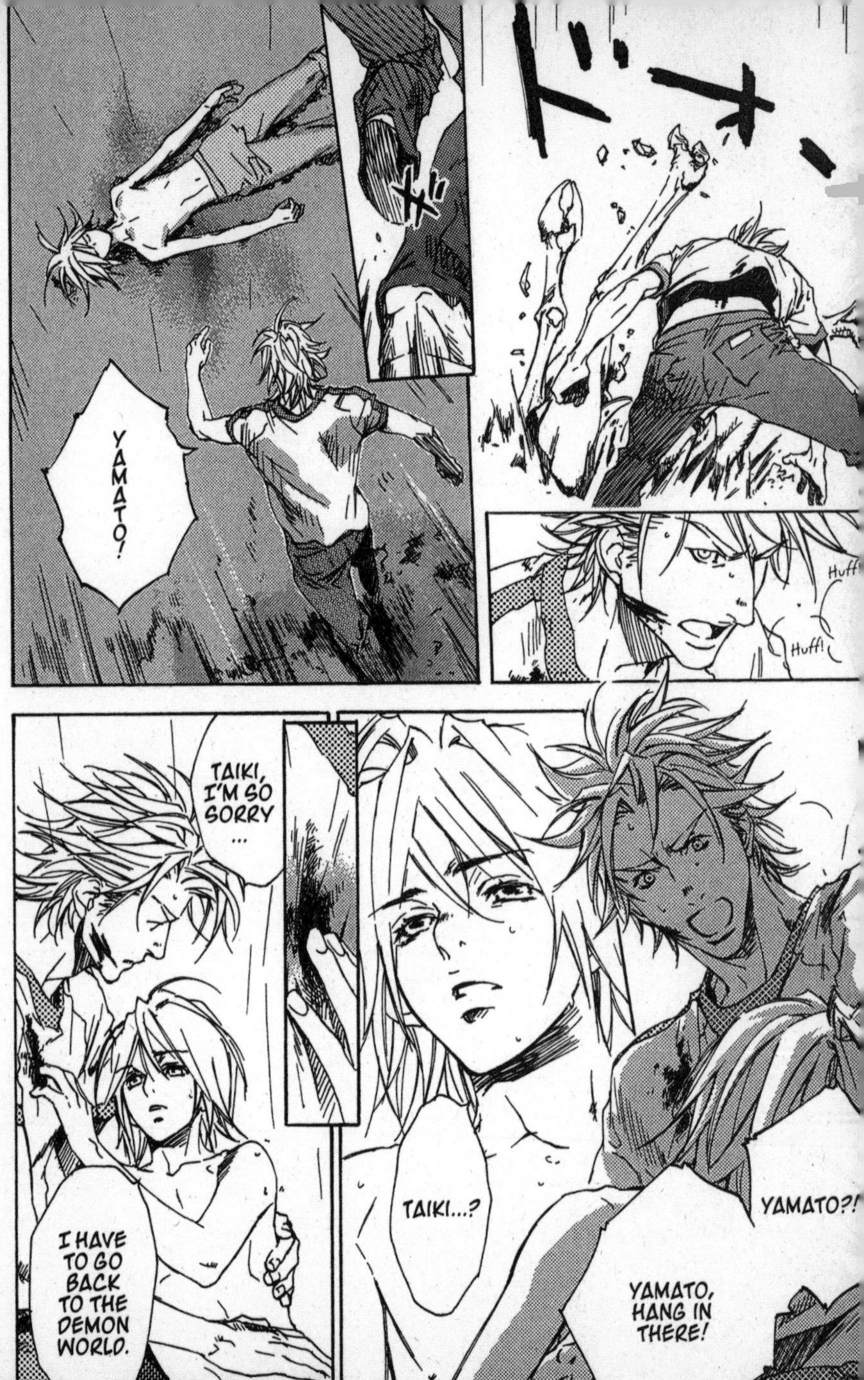
Huff!
Huff!
YAMATO!
YAMATO?!
YAMATO, HANG IN THERE!
TAIKI...?
TAIKI, I'M SO SORRY ...
I HAVE TO GO BACK TO THE DEMON WORLD.

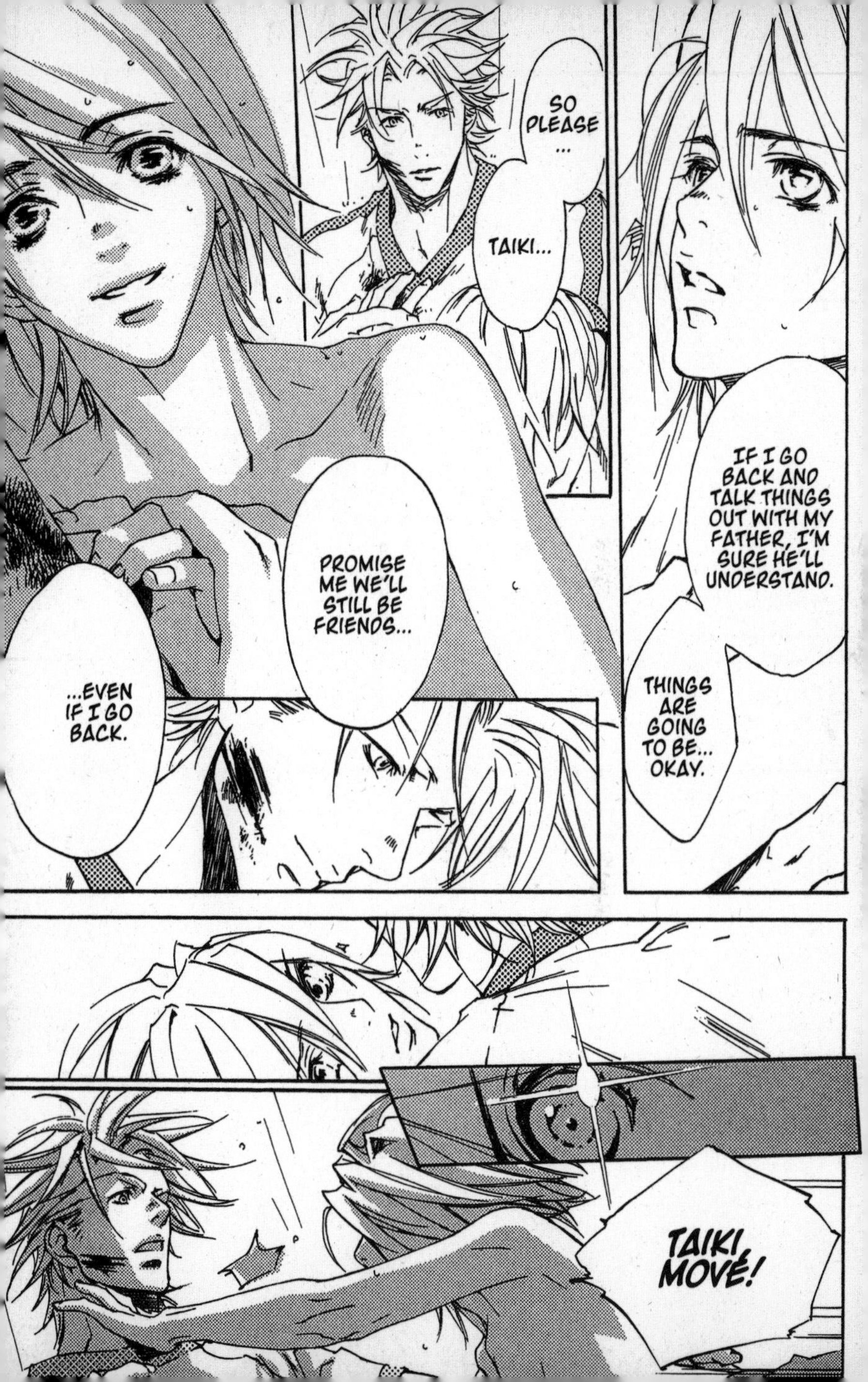
IF I GO BACK AND TALK THINGS OUT WITH MY FATHER, I'M SURE HE'LL UNDERSTAND.
THINGS ARE GOING TO BE... OKAY.
SO PLEASE ...
TAIKI...
PROMISE ME WE'LL STILL BE FRIENDS...
...EVEN IF I GO BACK.
TAIKI, MOVE!

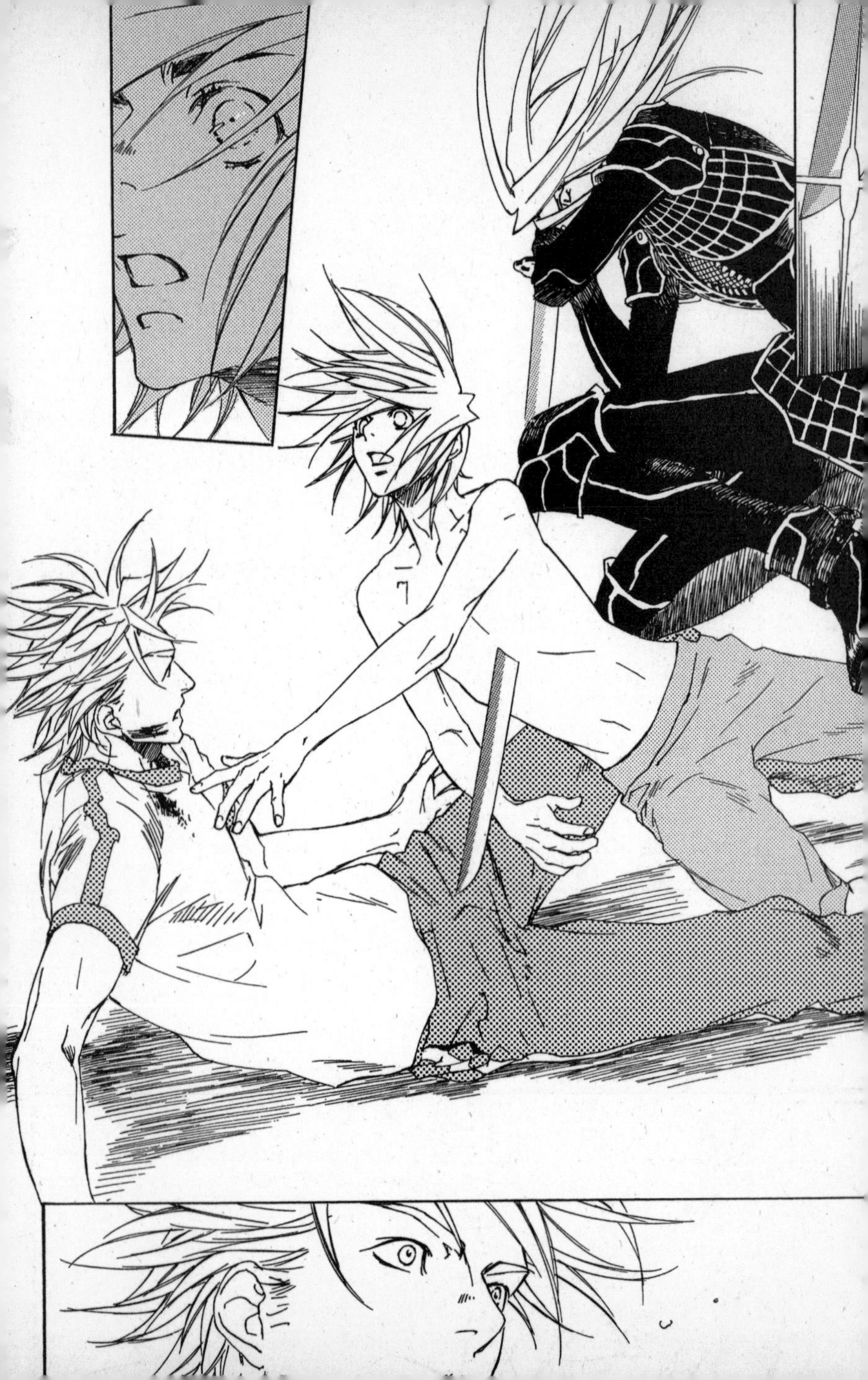

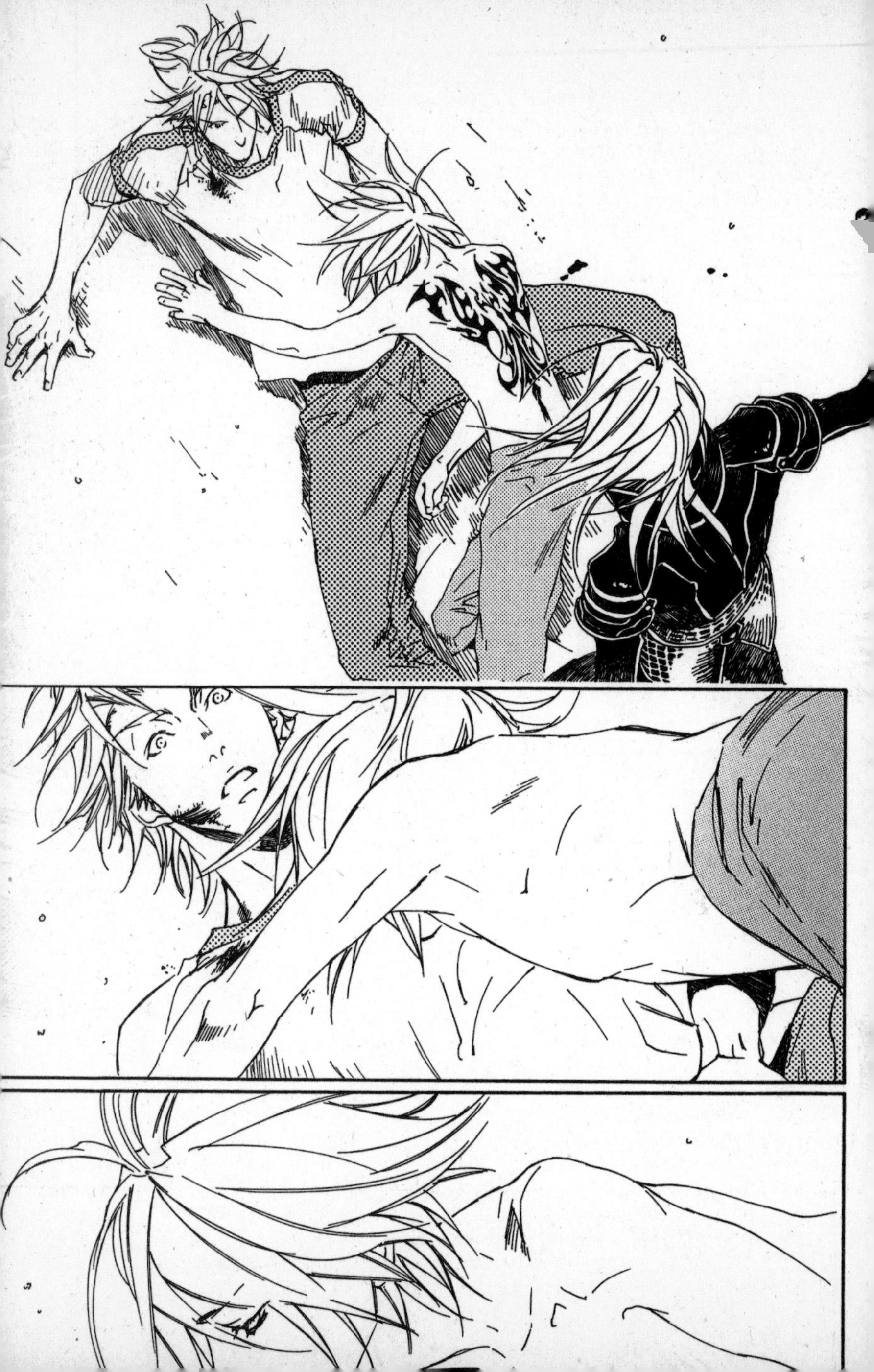

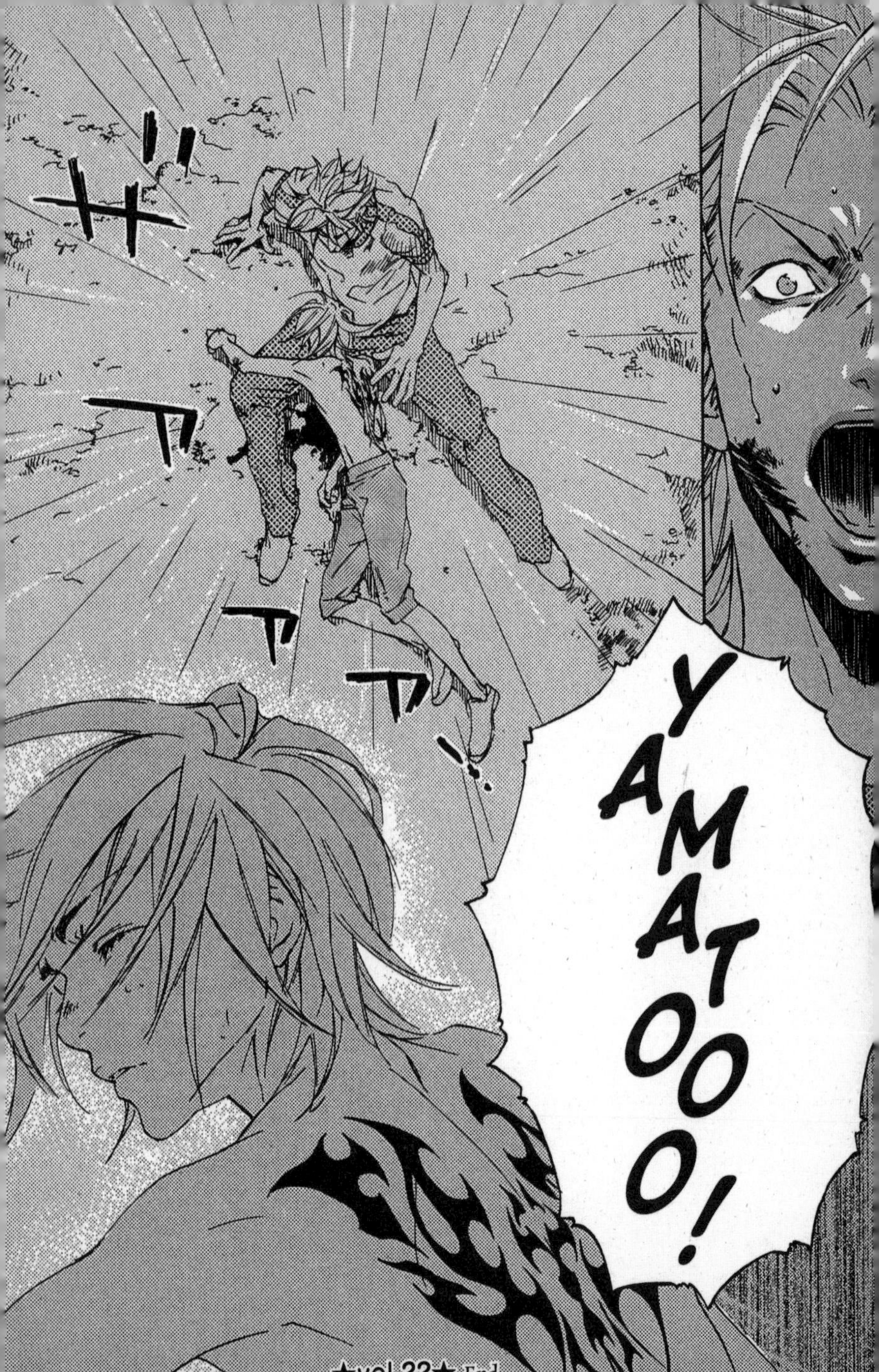
YAMATOOO!

★vol.22★ End

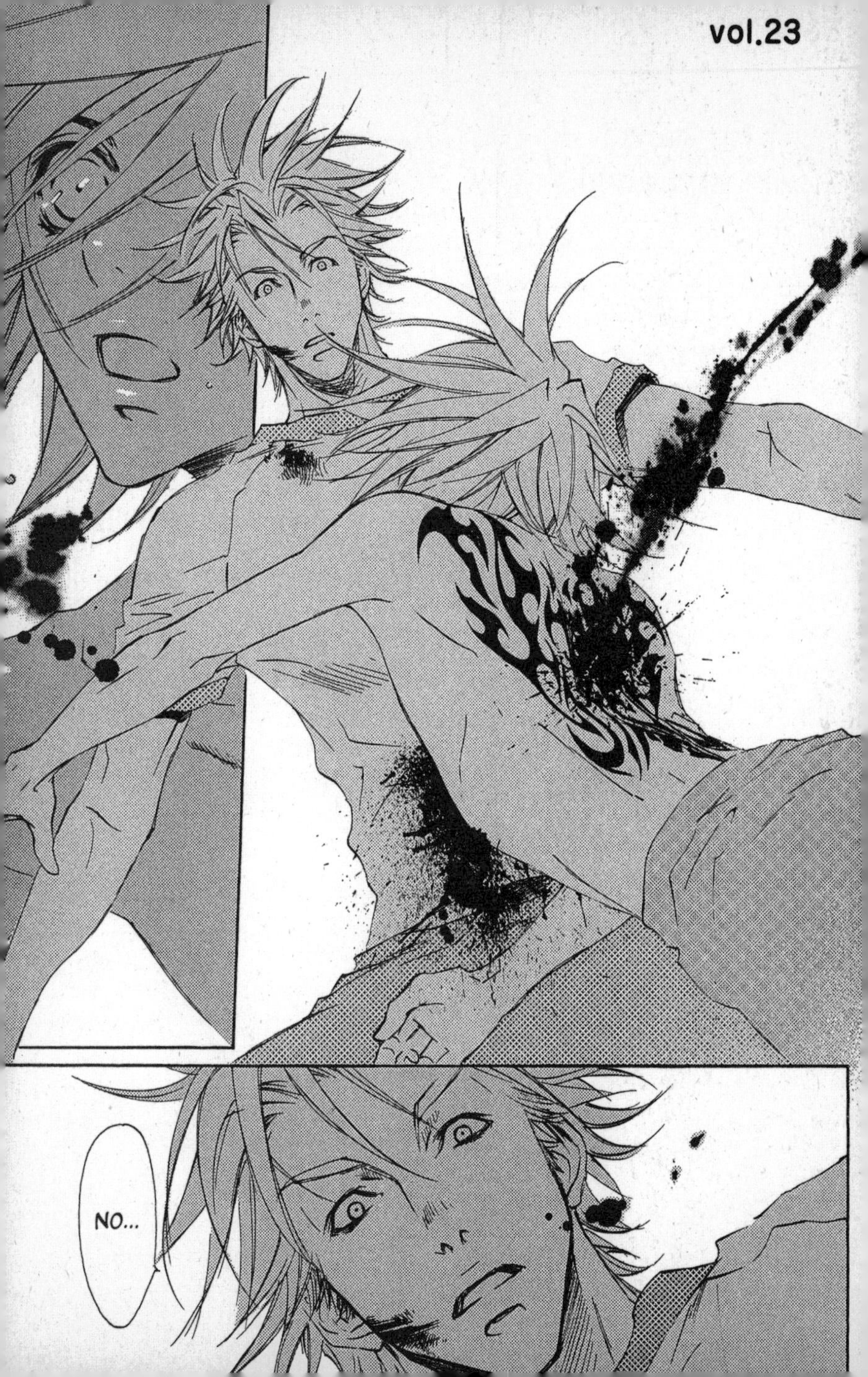
NO...

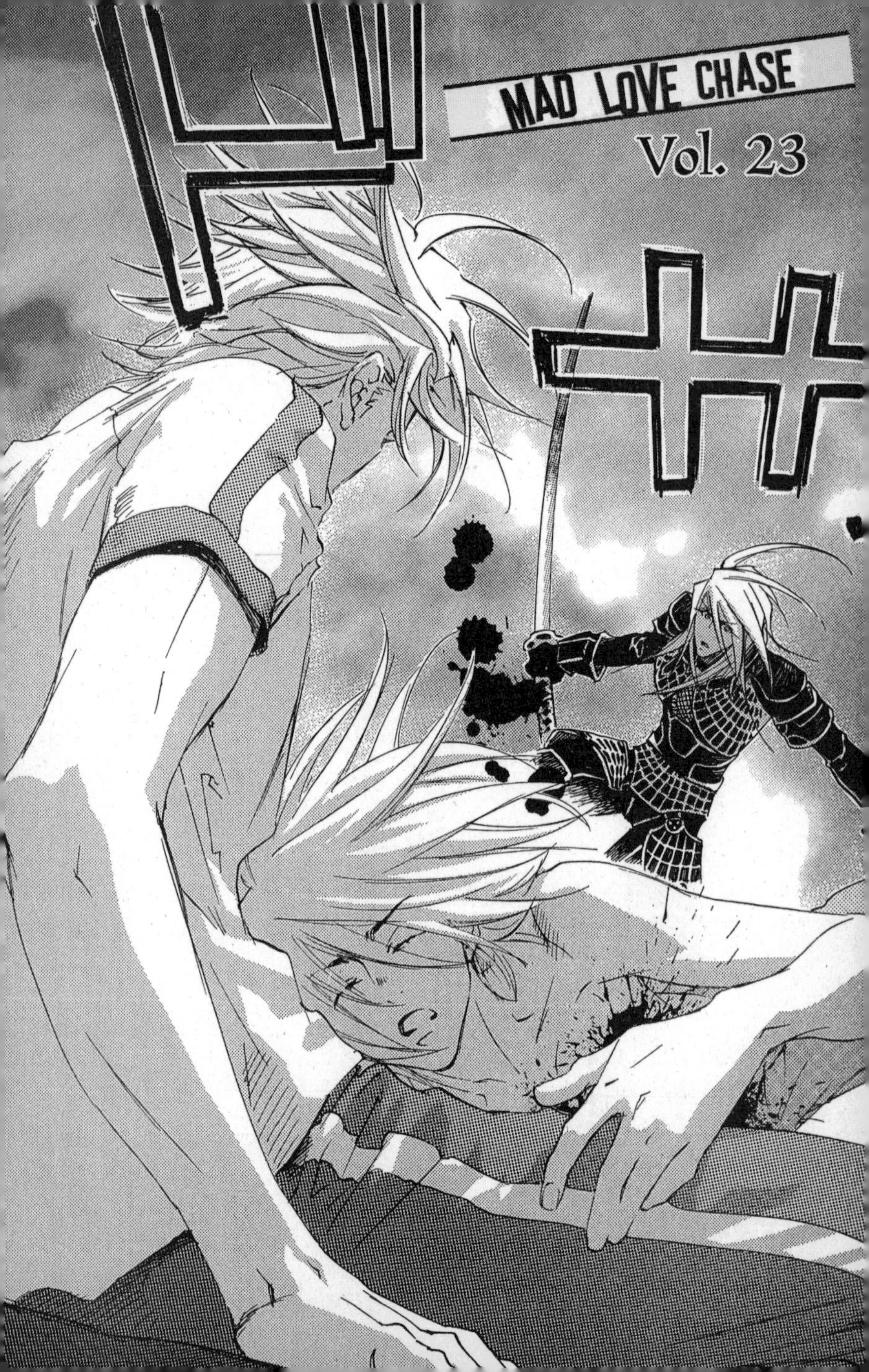
MAD LOVE CHASE
Vol. 23

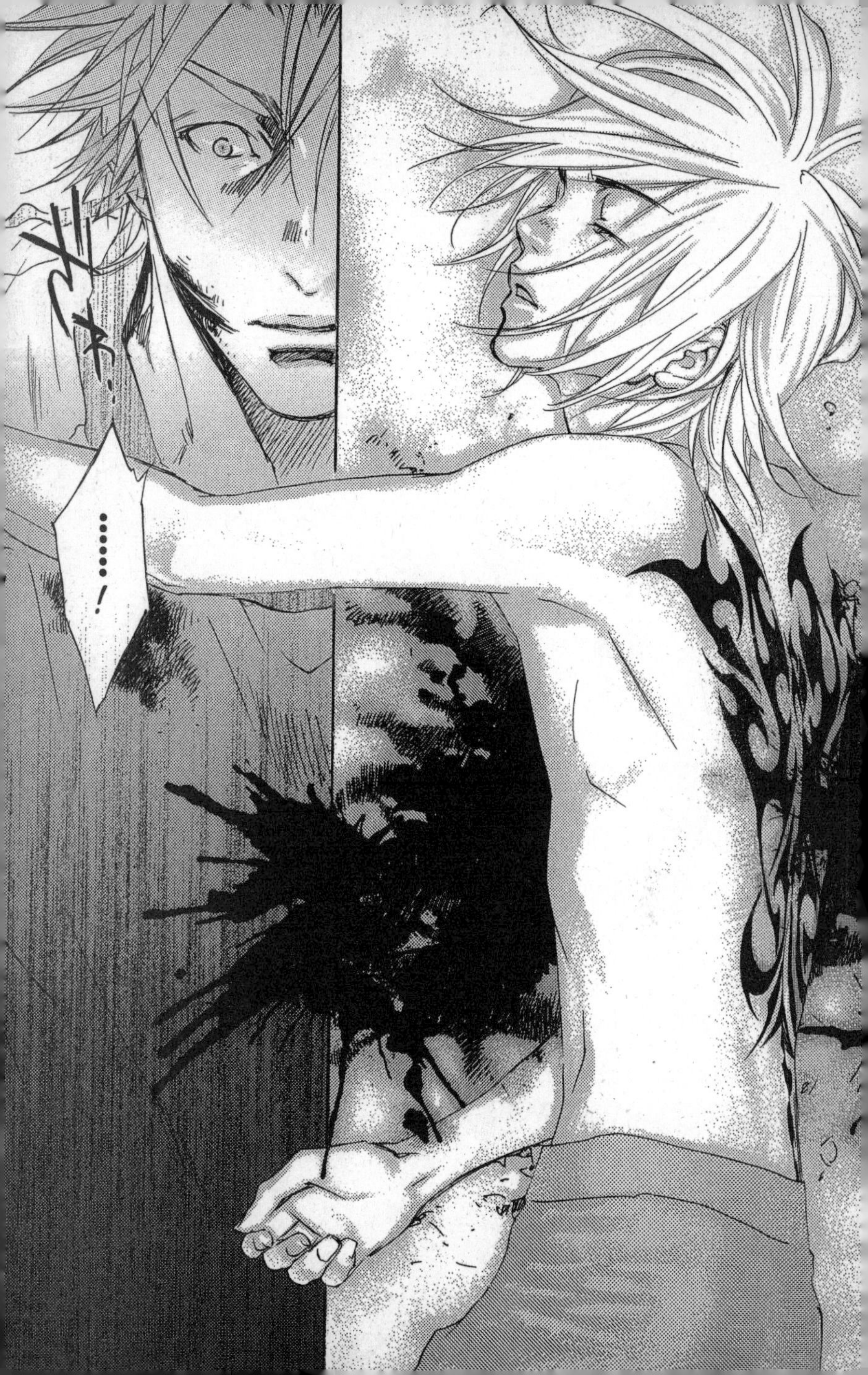
ズキ…
……!

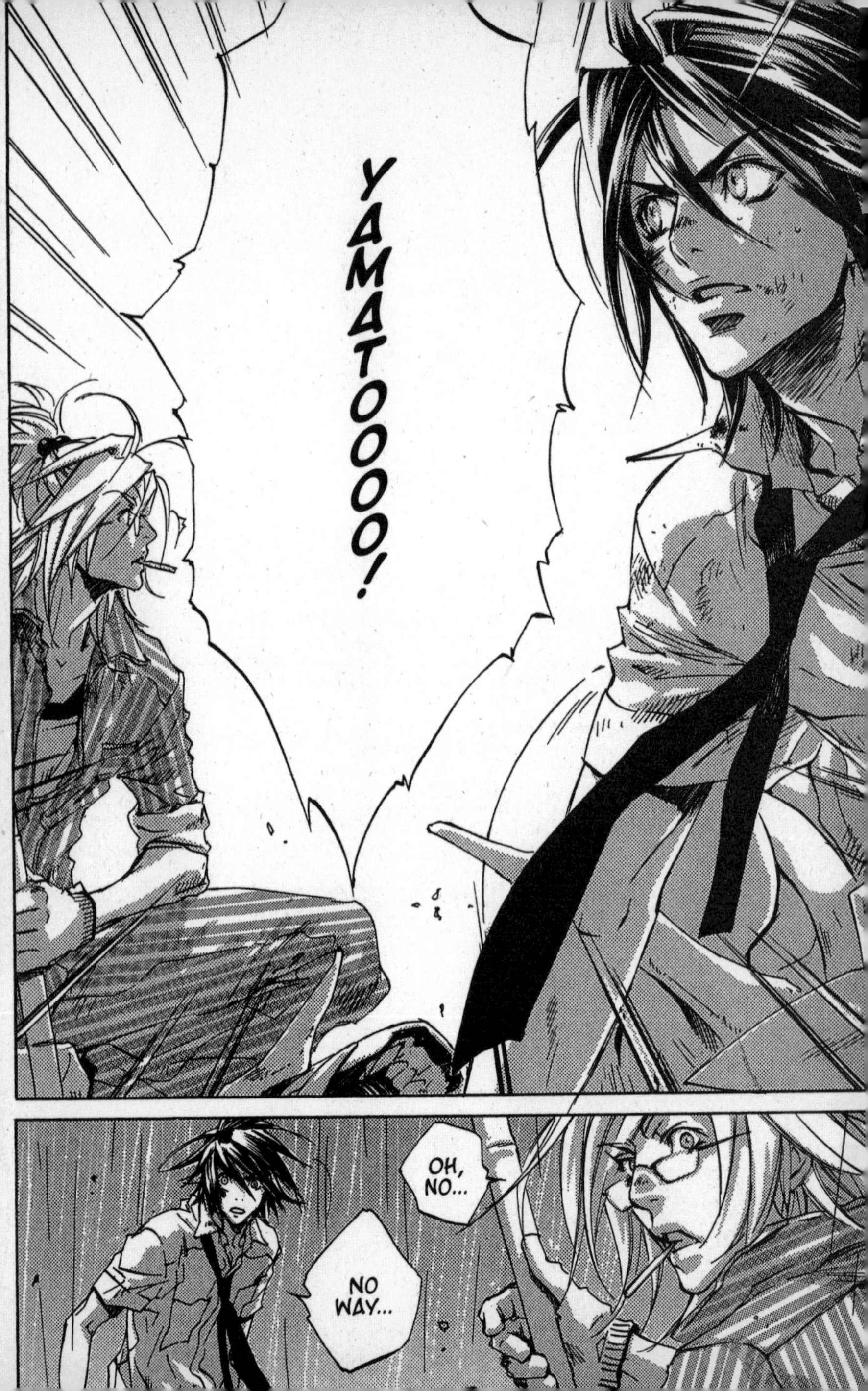
YAMATOOOOO!
OH, NO...
NO WAY...

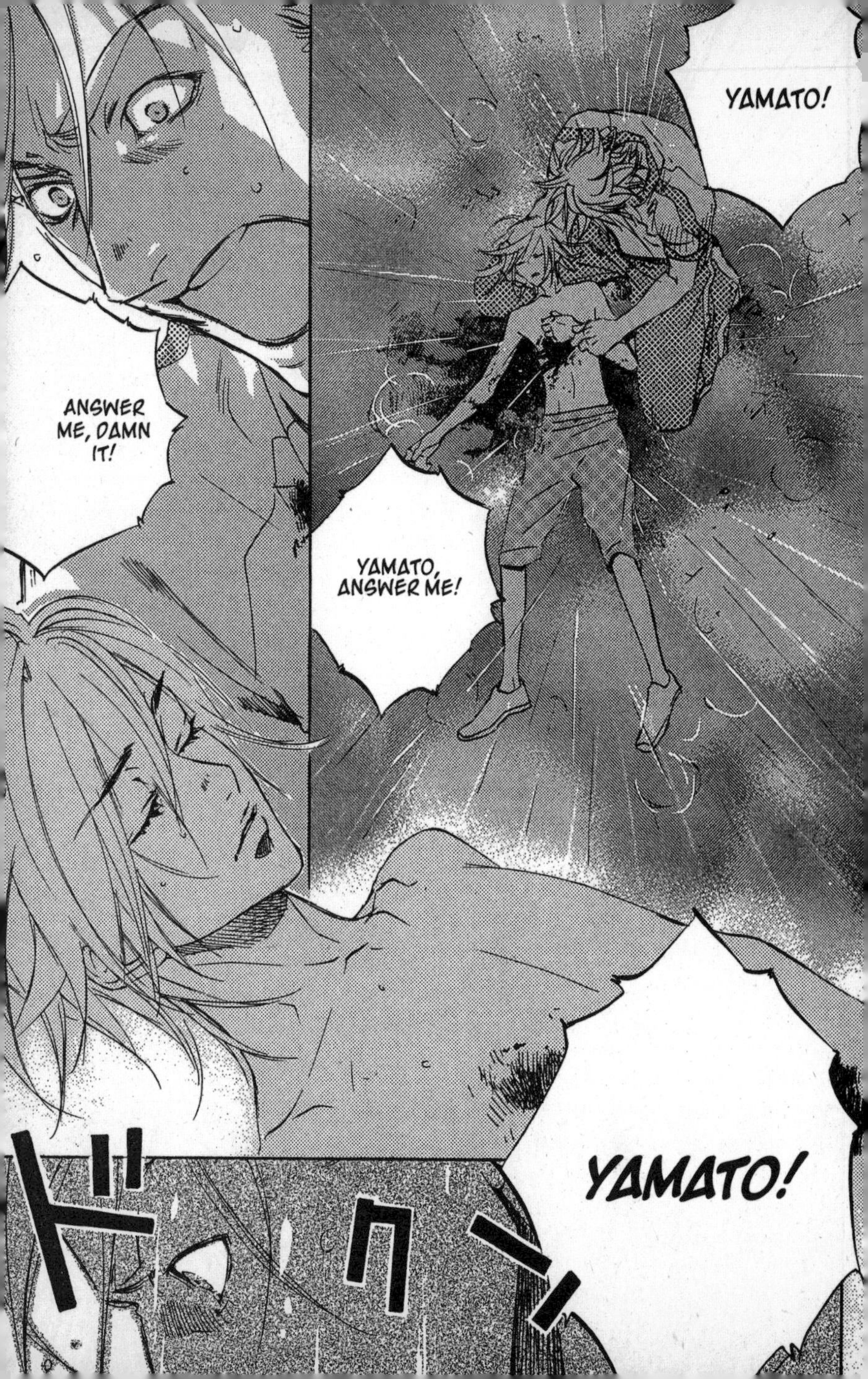
YAMATO!
YAMATO, ANSWER ME!
ANSWER ME, DAMN IT!
YAMATO!
ドクン

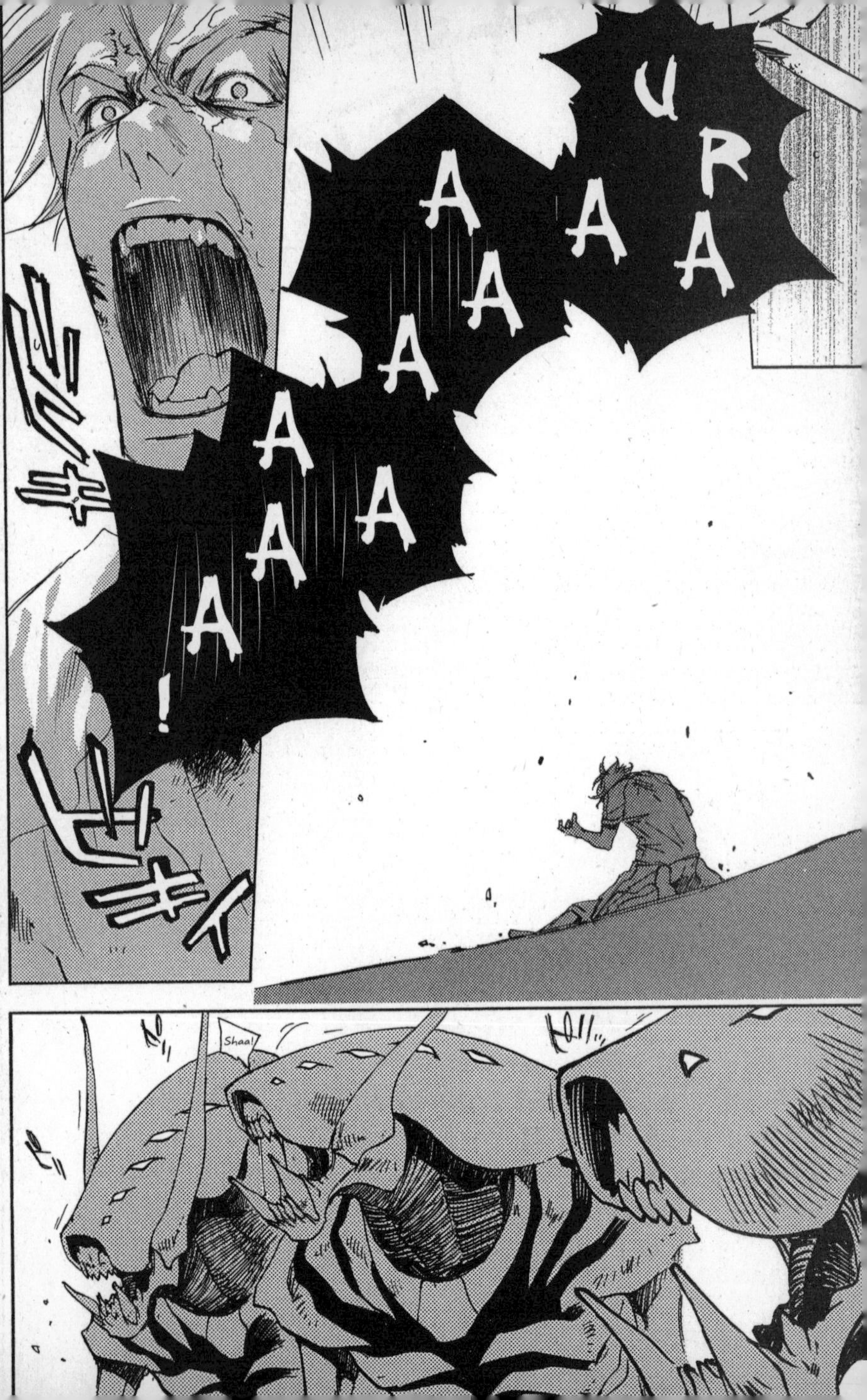
URAAAAAAAAA!
Shaa!

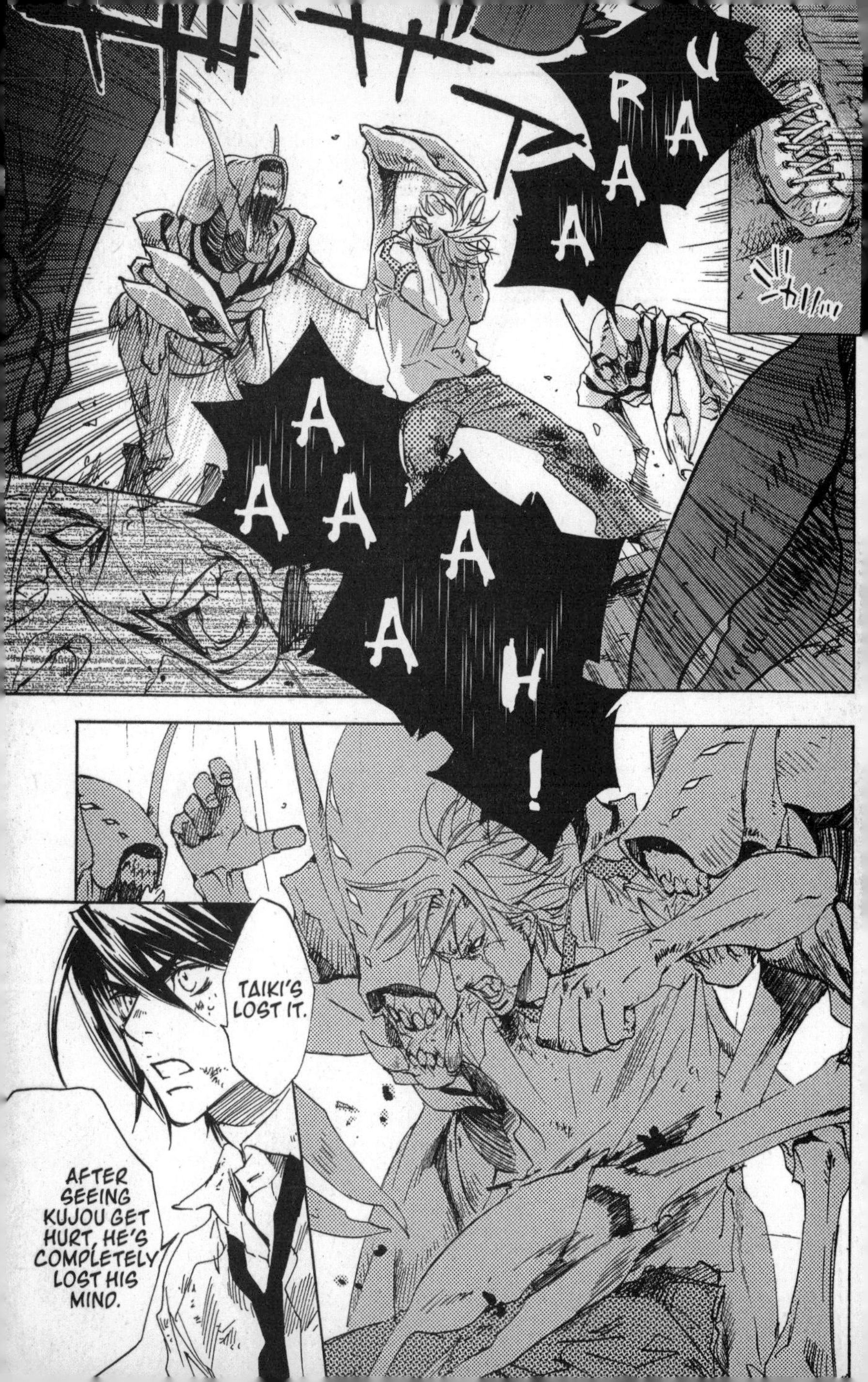
URAAAAAAAAH!
TAIKI'S LOST IT.
AFTER SEEING KUJOU GET HURT, HE'S COMPLETELY LOST HIS MIND.

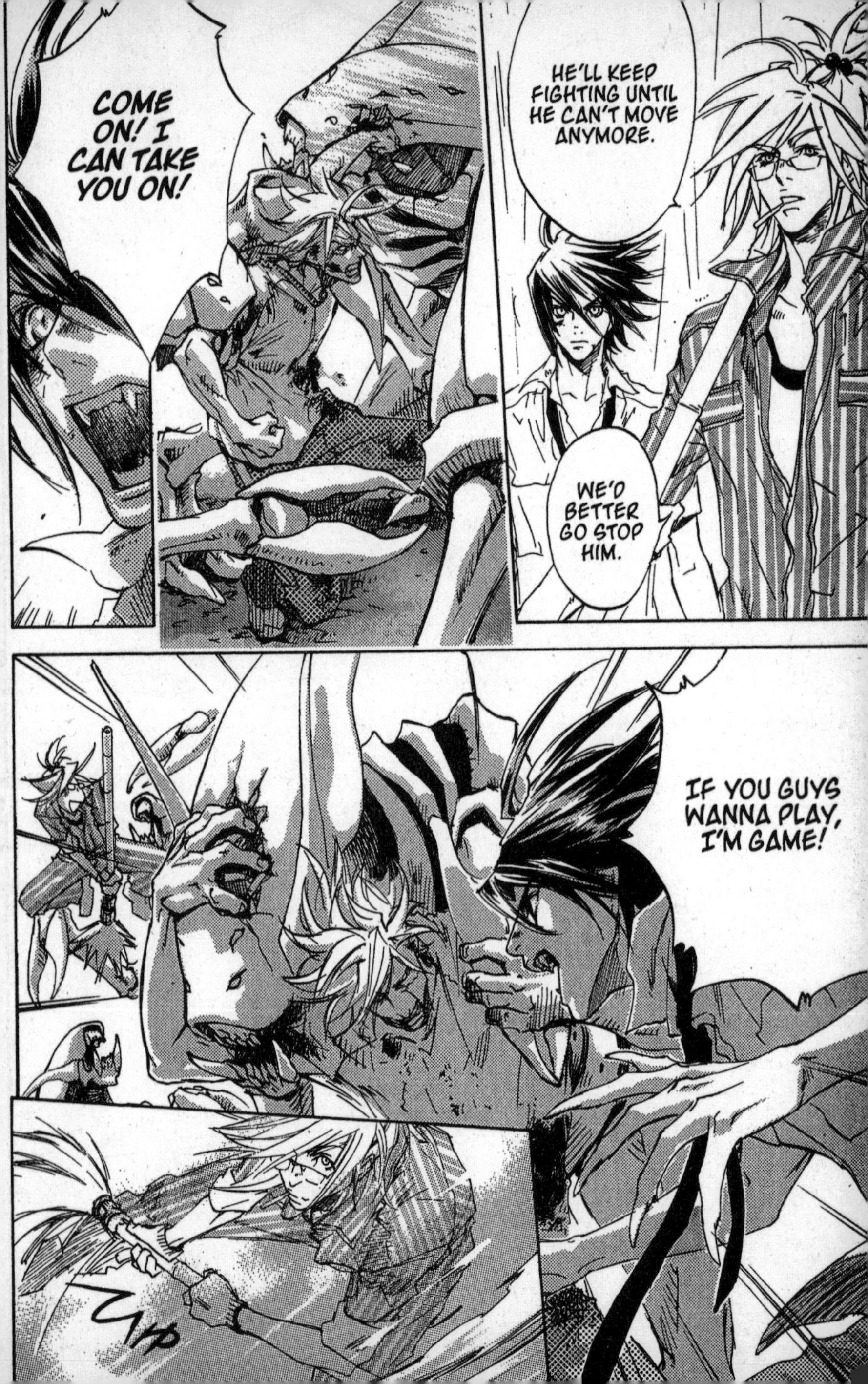
HE'LL KEEP FIGHTING UNTIL HE CAN'T MOVE ANYMORE.
WE'D BETTER GO STOP HIM.
COME ON! I CAN TAKE YOU ON!
IF YOU GUYS WANNA PLAY, I'M GAME!

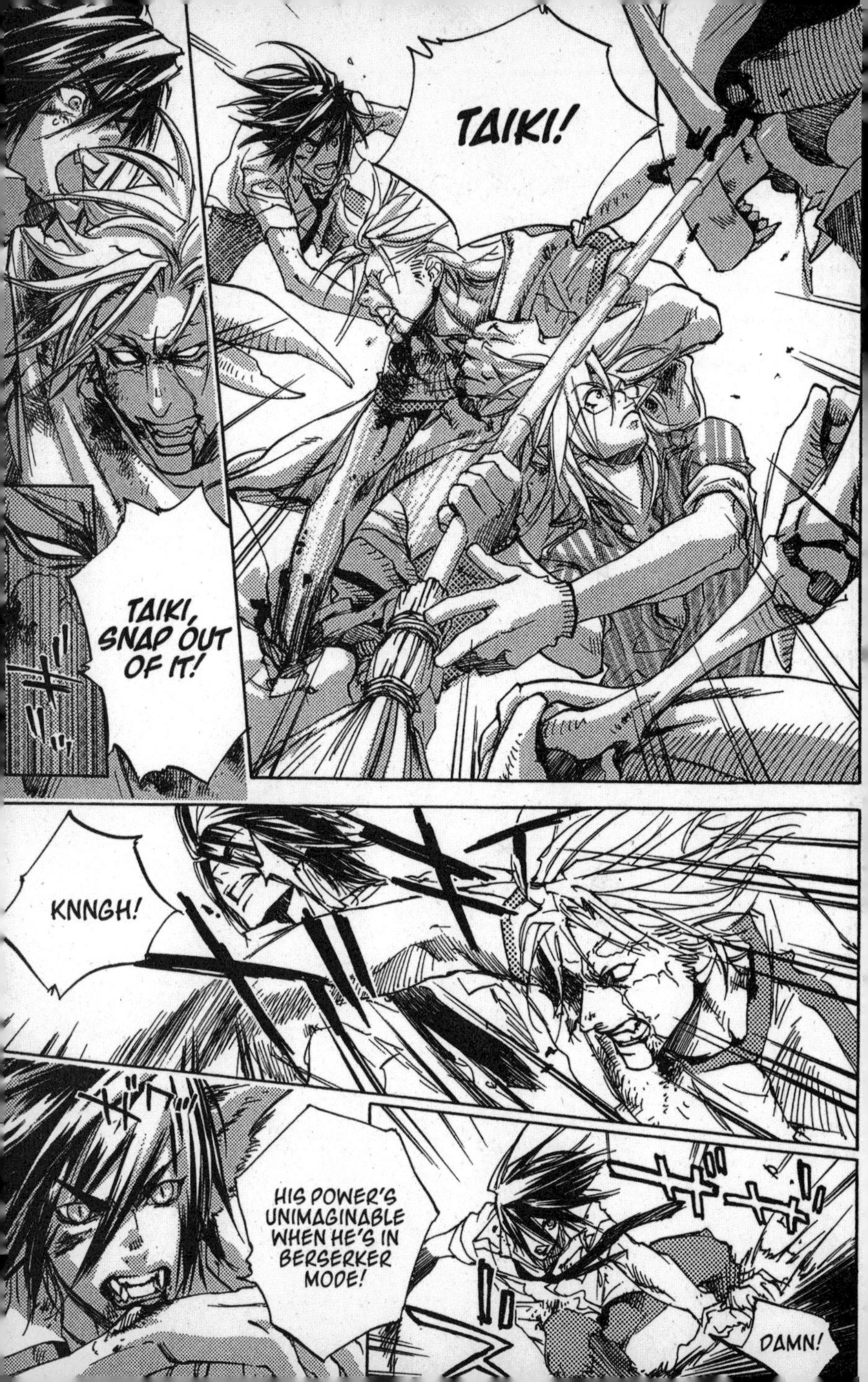
TAIKI!
TAIKI, SNAP OUT OF IT!
KNNGH!
HIS POWER'S UNIMAGINABLE WHEN HE'S IN BERSERKER MODE!
DAMN!

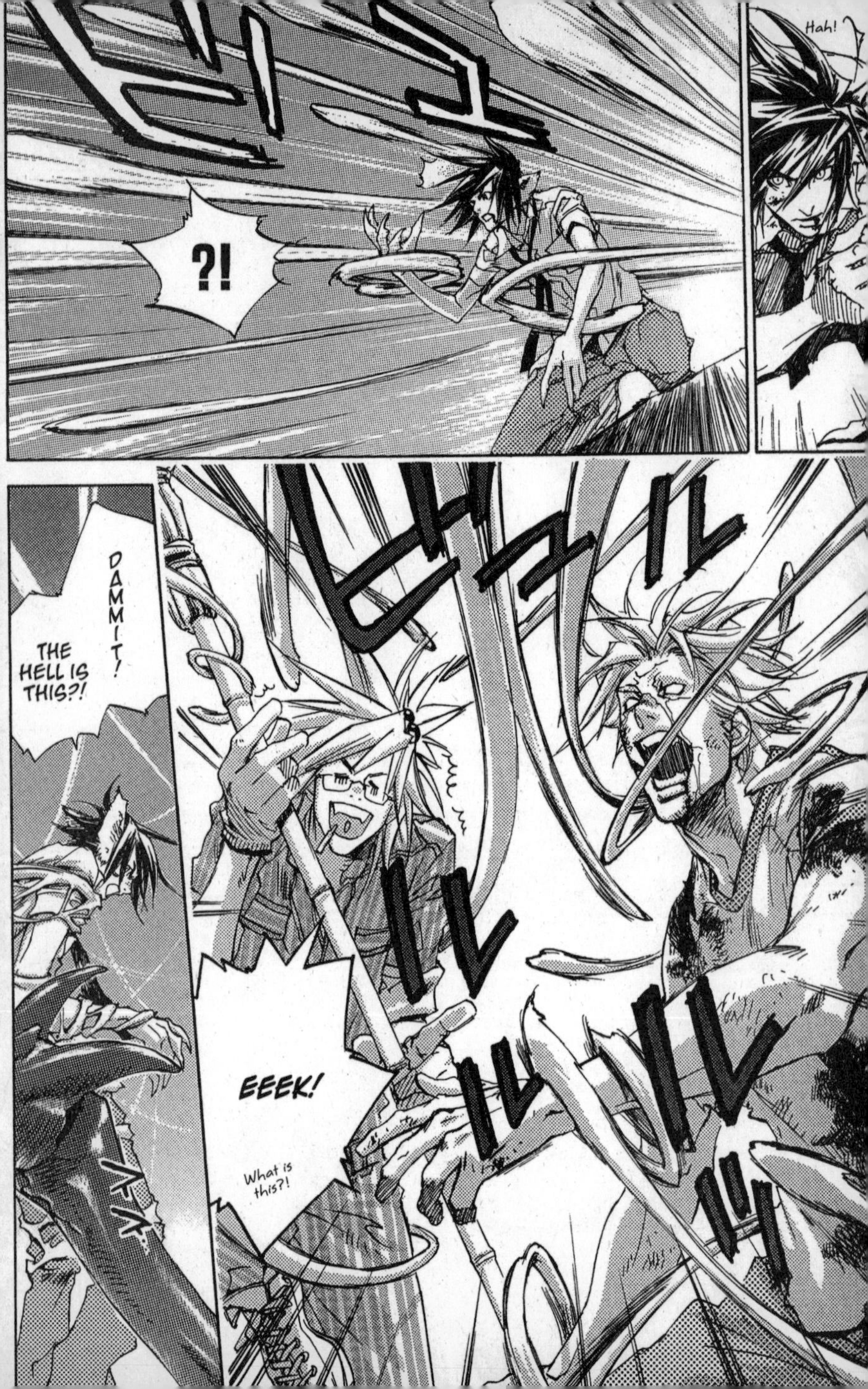
Hah!
?!
EEEK!
What is this?!
DAMMIT!
THE HELL IS THIS?!

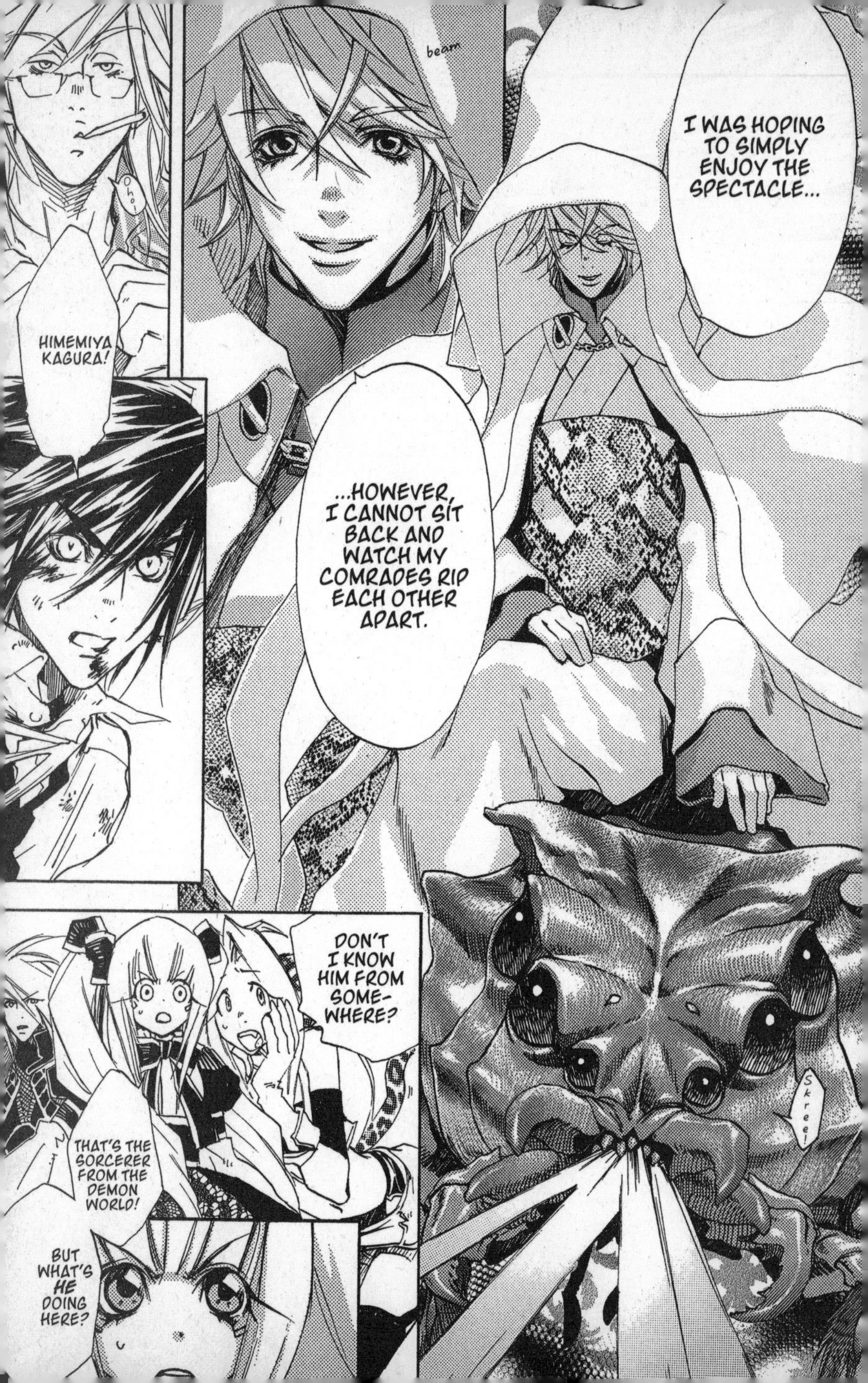

I WAS HOPING TO SIMPLY ENJOY THE SPECTACLE...
beam
...HOWEVER, I CANNOT SIT BACK AND WATCH MY COMRADES RIP EACH OTHER APART.
Oh...
HIMEMIYA KAGURA!
Skree!
DON'T I KNOW HIM FROM SOME-WHERE?
THAT'S THE SORCERER FROM THE DEMON WORLD!
BUT WHAT'S HE DOING HERE?

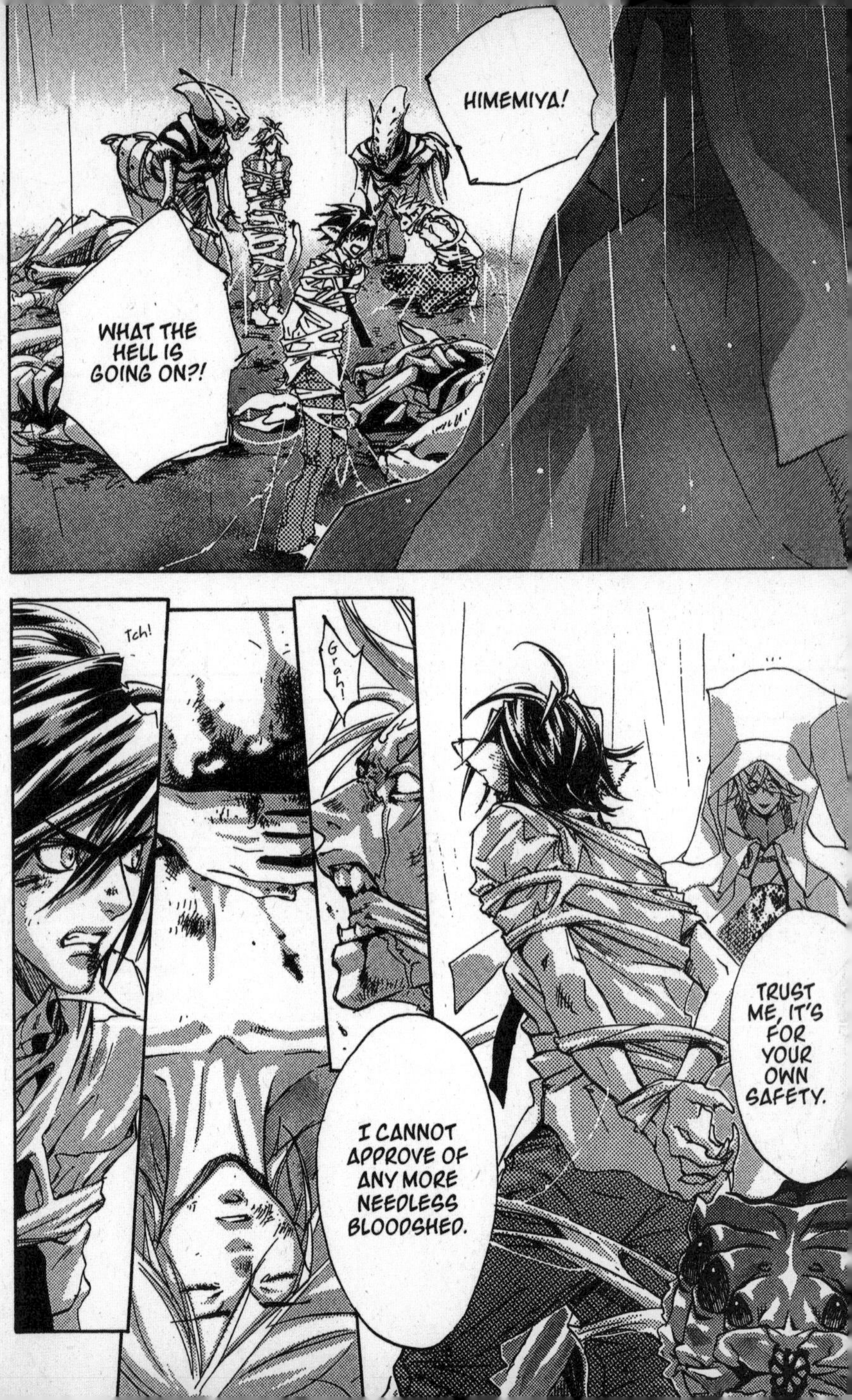
HIMEMIYA!
WHAT THE HELL IS GOING ON?!
...
TRUST ME, IT'S FOR YOUR OWN SAFETY.
I CANNOT APPROVE OF ANY MORE NEEDLESS BLOODSHED.
Grah!
...
Tch!

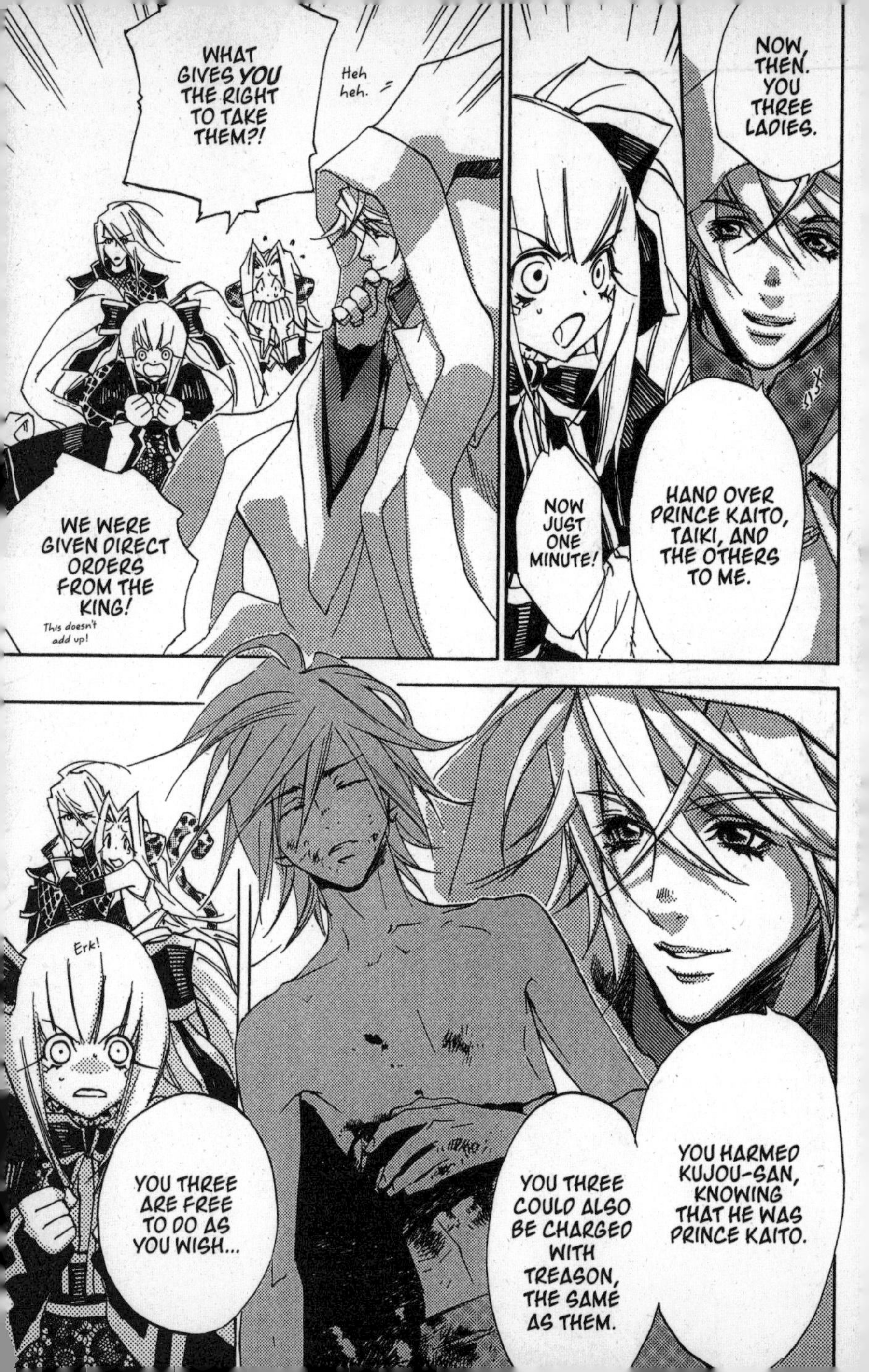
NOW, THEN. YOU THREE LADIES.
HAND OVER PRINCE KAITO, TAIKI, AND THE OTHERS TO ME.
NOW JUST ONE MINUTE!
Heh heh.
WHAT GIVES *YOU* THE RIGHT TO TAKE THEM?!
WE WERE GIVEN DIRECT ORDERS FROM THE KING!
This doesn't add up!
YOU HARMED KUJOU-SAN, KNOWING THAT HE WAS PRINCE KAITO.
YOU THREE COULD ALSO BE CHARGED WITH TREASON, THE SAME AS THEM.
Erk!
YOU THREE ARE FREE TO DO AS YOU WISH...

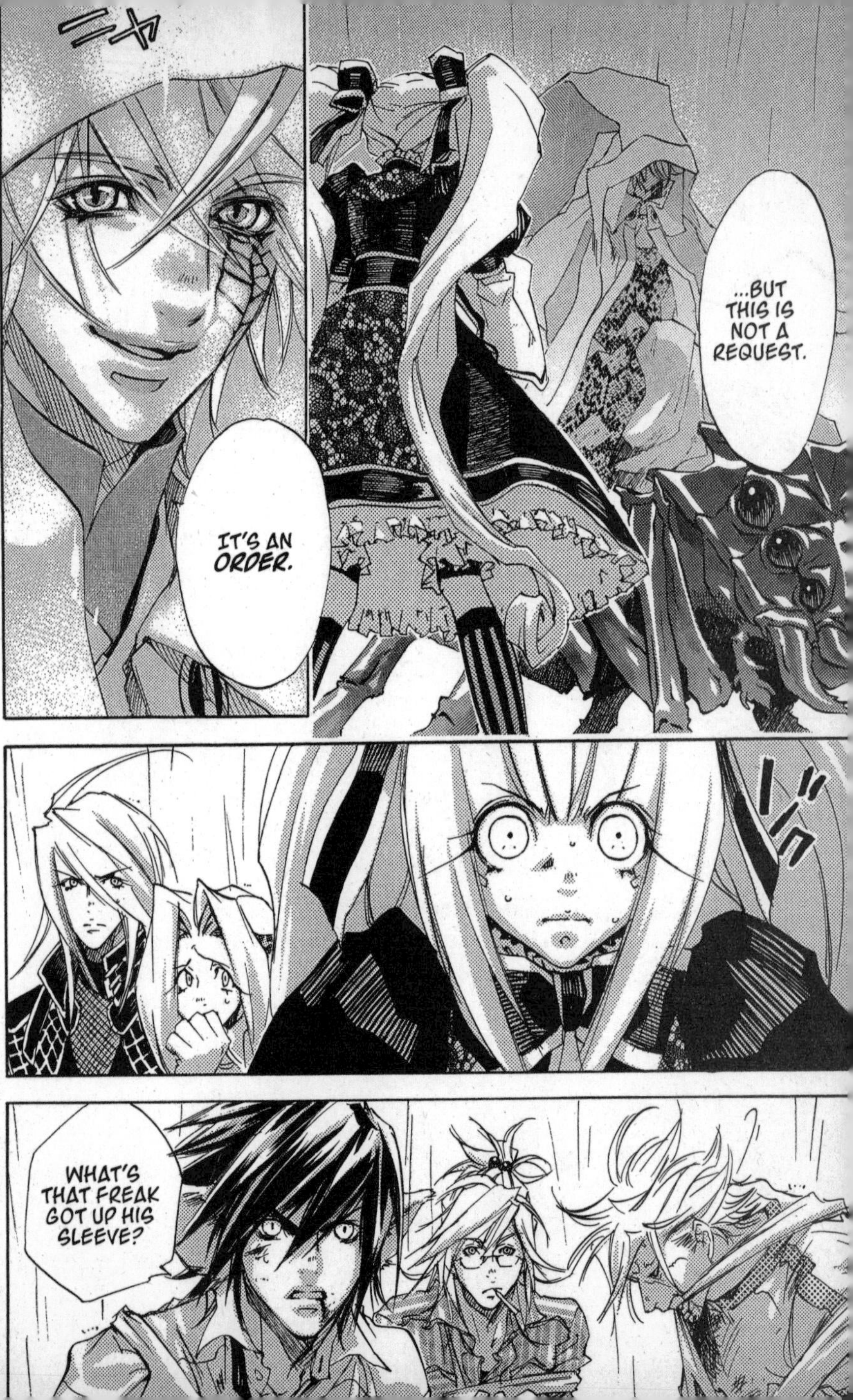
...BUT THIS IS NOT A REQUEST.
IT'S AN ORDER.
ニヤ
...
WHAT'S THAT FREAK GOT UP HIS SLEEVE?
...

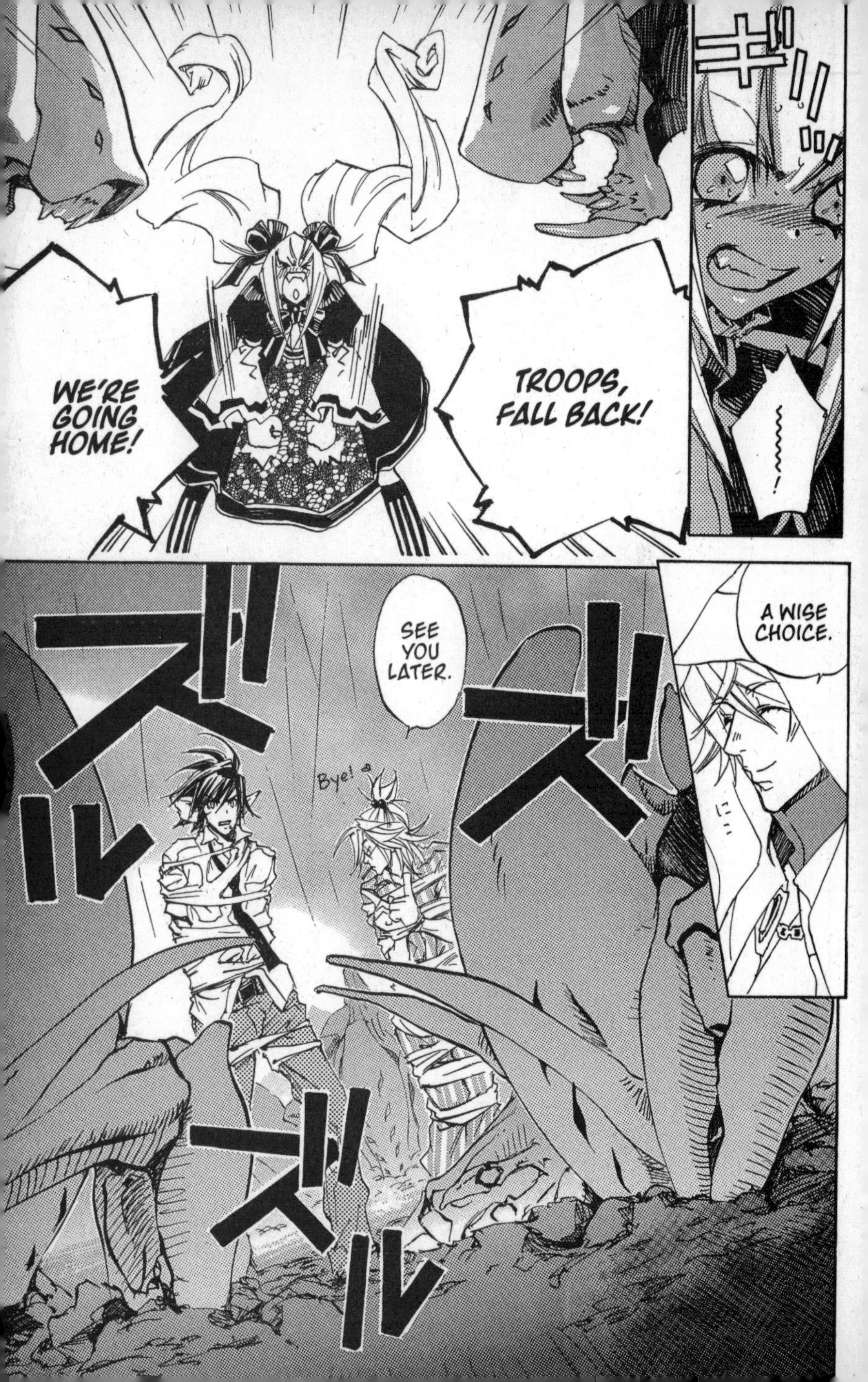
TROOPS, FALL BACK!
WE'RE GOING HOME!
A WISE CHOICE.
SEE YOU LATER.
Bye!

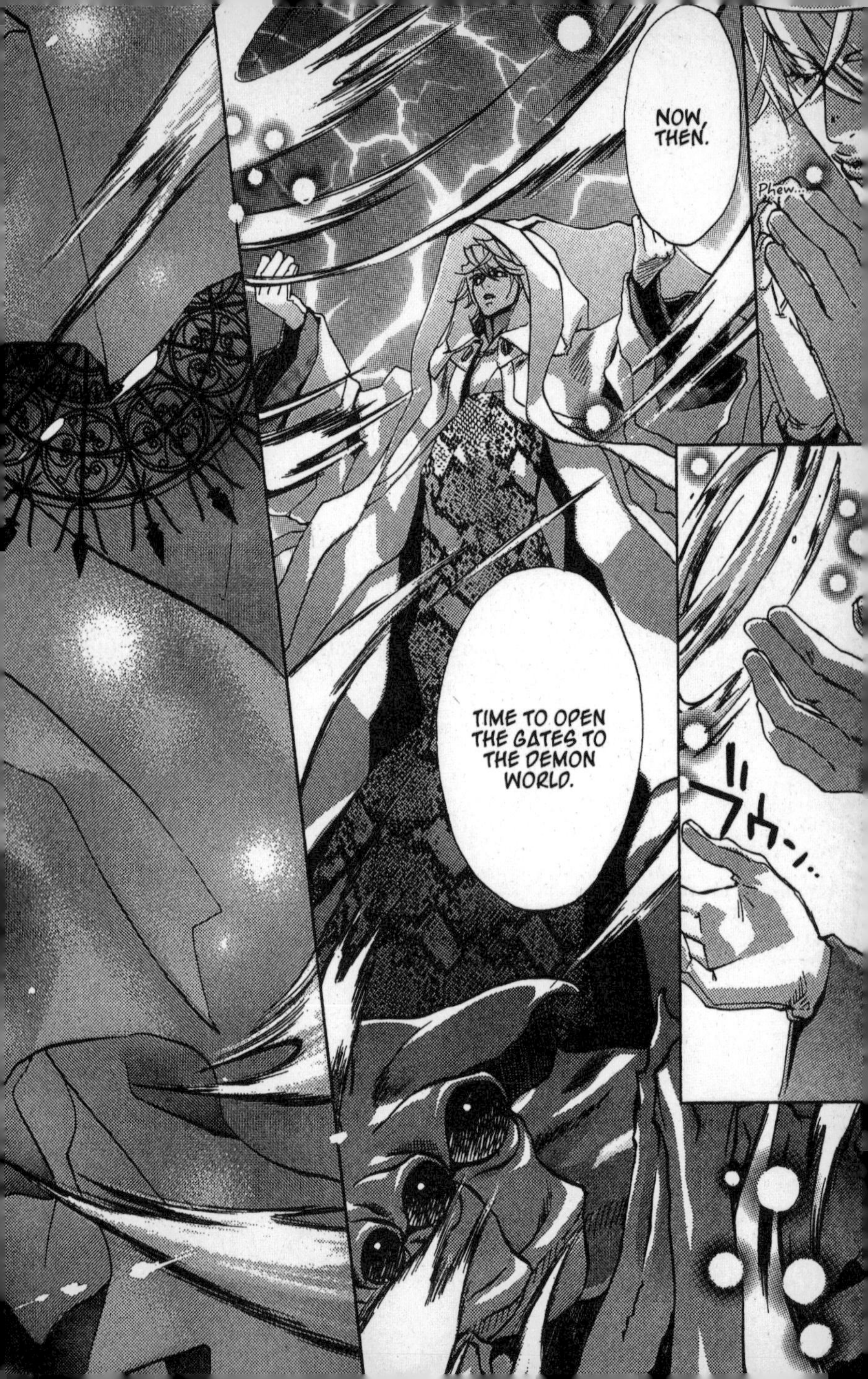
Phew...
ヴゥーン…
NOW, THEN.
TIME TO OPEN THE GATES TO THE DEMON WORLD.

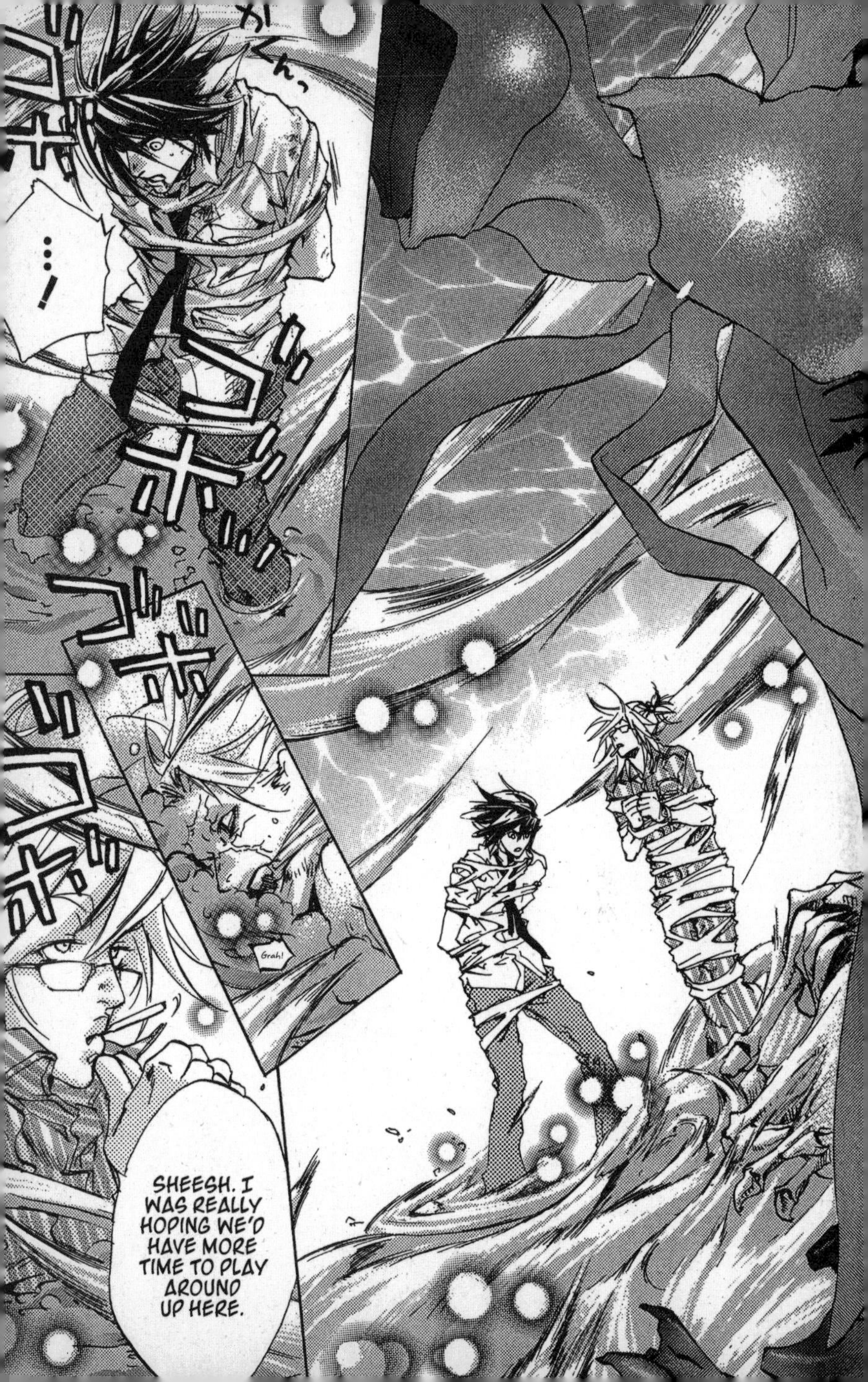
がくん
...!
Grah!
SHEESH. I WAS REALLY HOPING WE'D HAVE MORE TIME TO PLAY AROUND UP HERE.

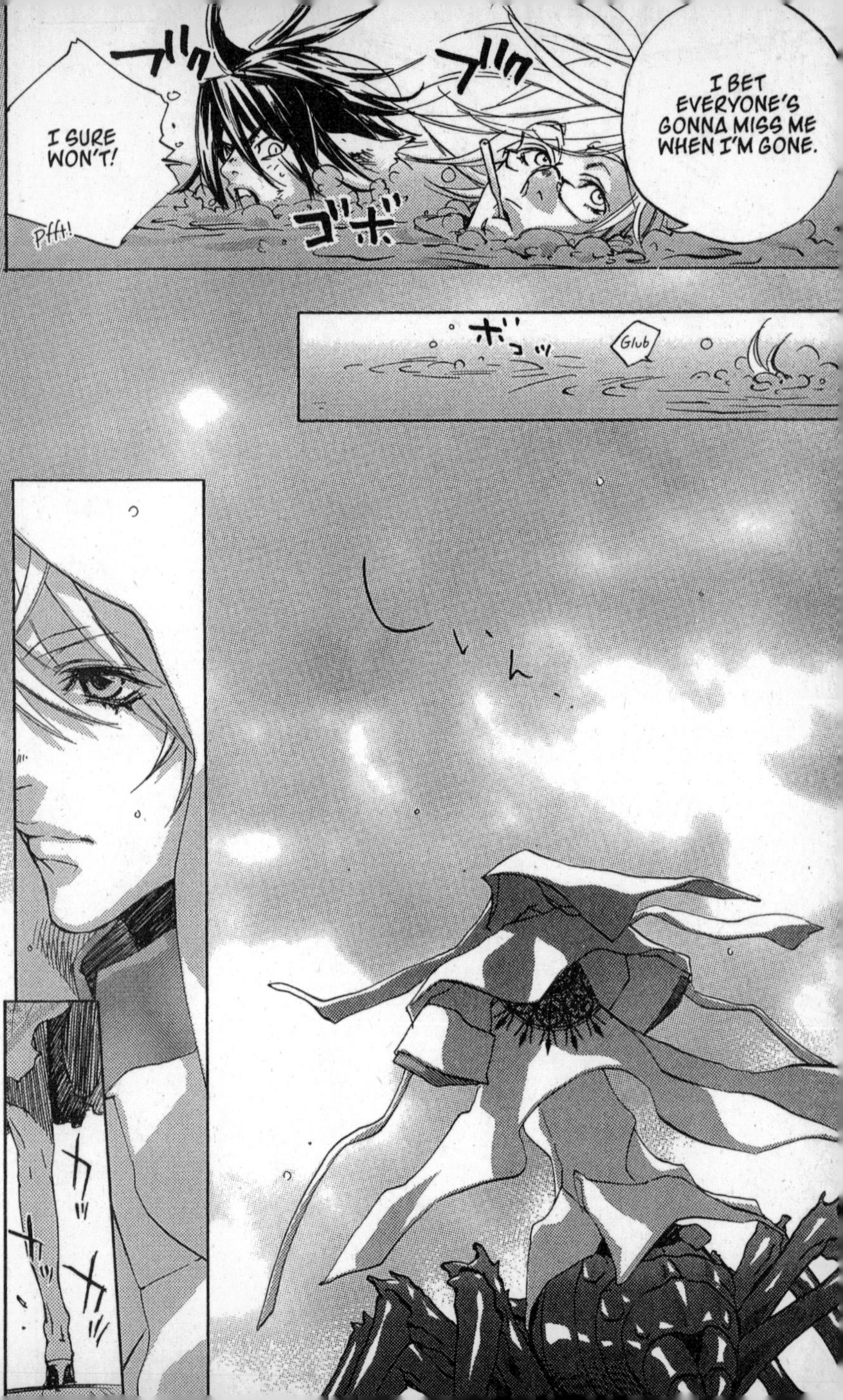
I BET EVERYONE'S GONNA MISS ME WHEN I'M GONE.
ブク
ブク
I SURE WON'T!
ゴボ
Pfft!
ボコッ
Glub
しぃん…
カツ
カツ

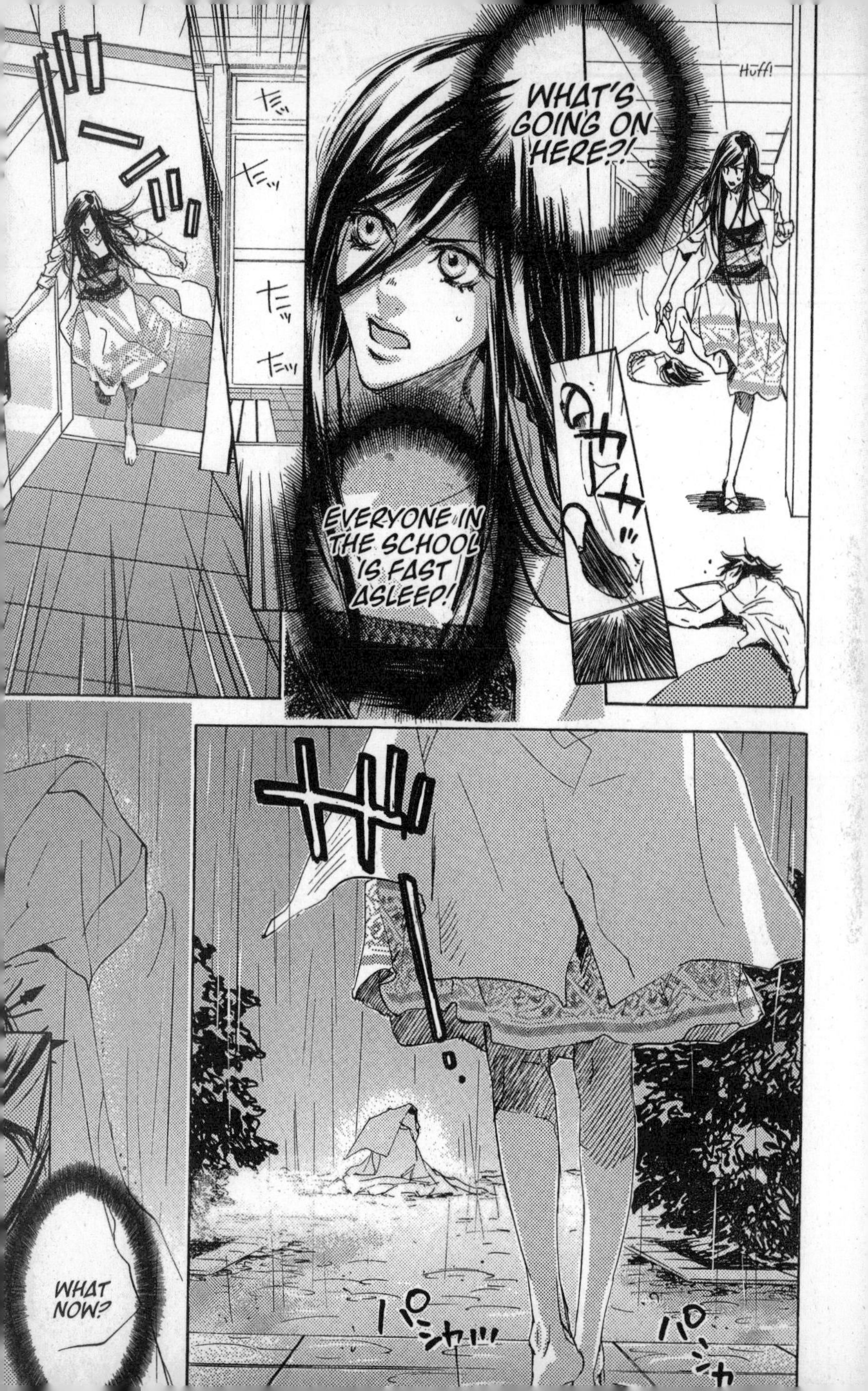
Huff!
WHAT'S GOING ON HERE?!
EVERYONE IN THE SCHOOL IS FAST ASLEEP!
WHAT NOW?

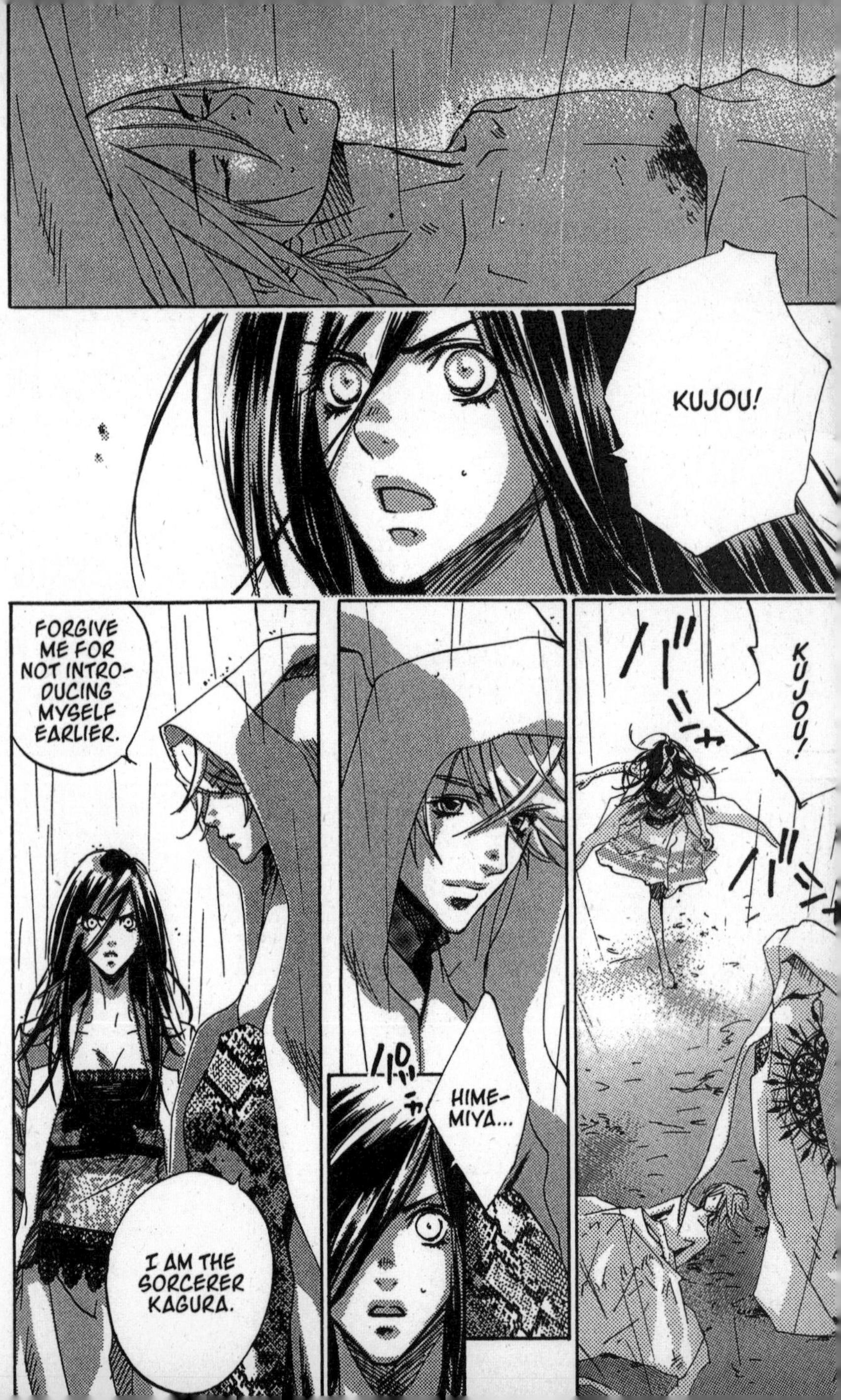
KUJOU!
KUJOU!
HIME-MIYA...
FORGIVE ME FOR NOT INTRO-DUCING MYSELF EARLIER.
I AM THE SORCERER KAGURA.

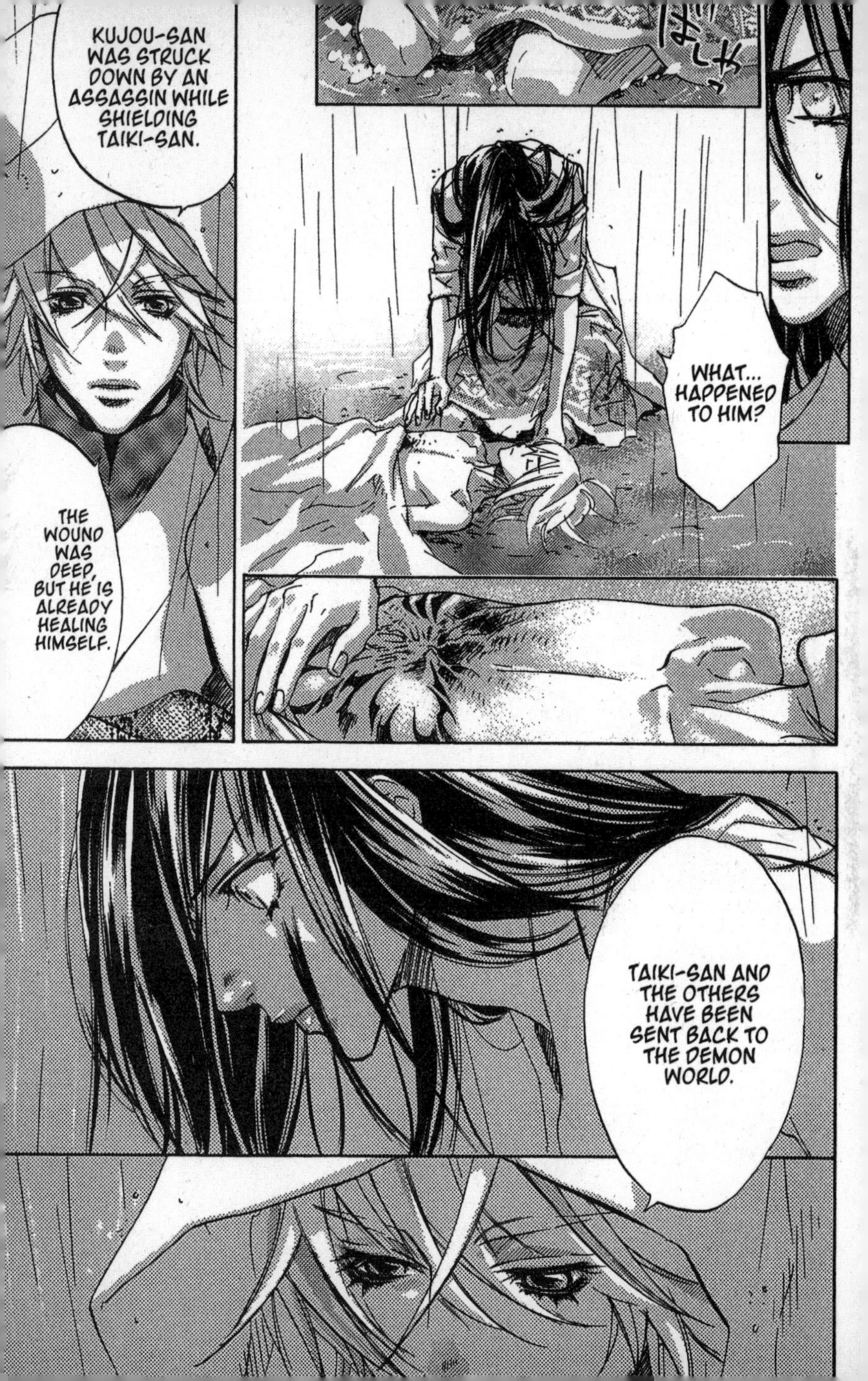
ばしゃっ
WHAT... HAPPENED TO HIM?
KUJOU-SAN WAS STRUCK DOWN BY AN ASSASSIN WHILE SHIELDING TAIKI-SAN.
THE WOUND WAS DEEP, BUT HE IS ALREADY HEALING HIMSELF.
TAIKI-SAN AND THE OTHERS HAVE BEEN SENT BACK TO THE DEMON WORLD.

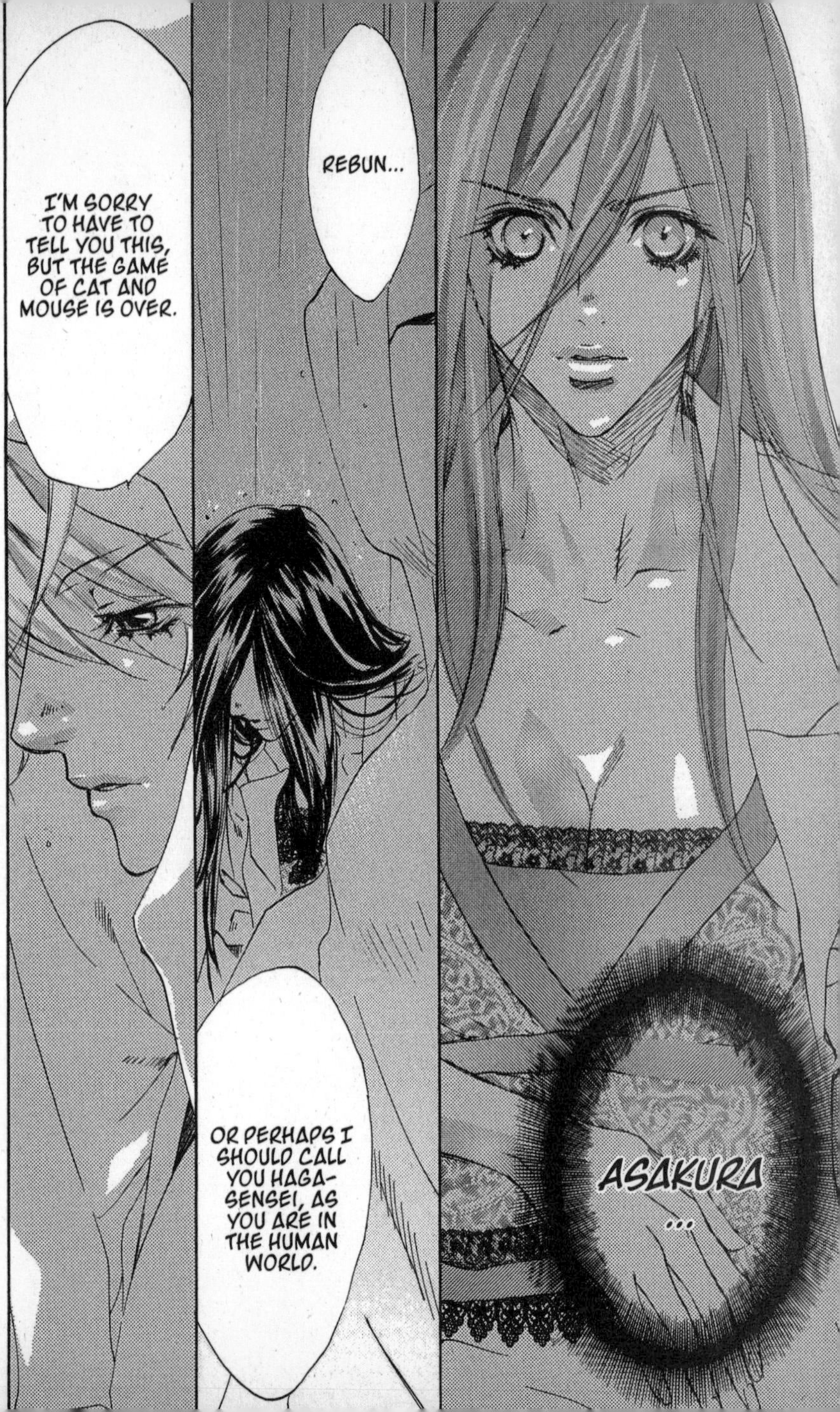
ASAKURA ...
REBUN...
OR PERHAPS I SHOULD CALL YOU HAGA-SENSEI, AS YOU ARE IN THE HUMAN WORLD.
I'M SORRY TO HAVE TO TELL YOU THIS, BUT THE GAME OF CAT AND MOUSE IS OVER.

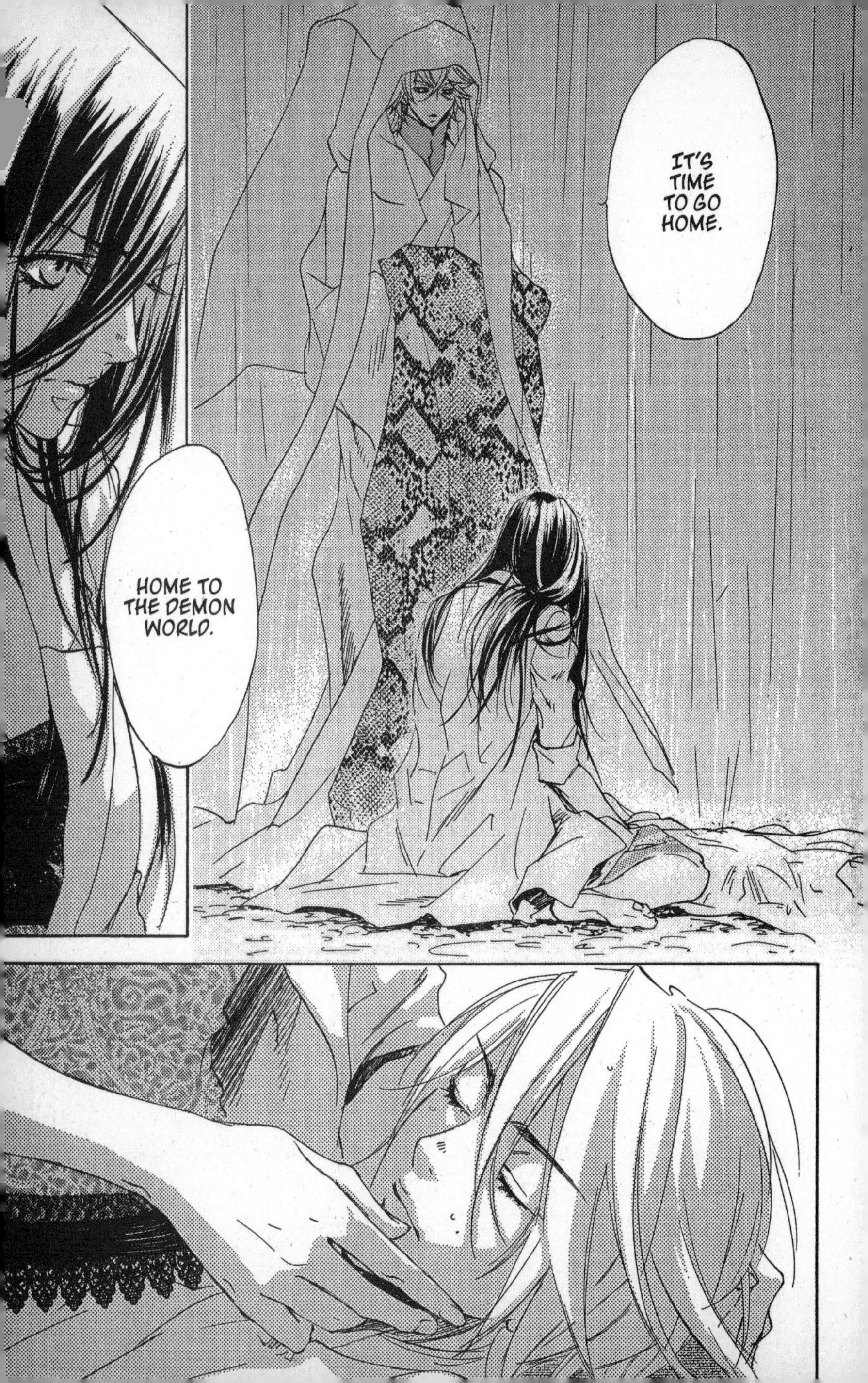
IT'S TIME TO GO HOME.
HOME TO THE DEMON WORLD.

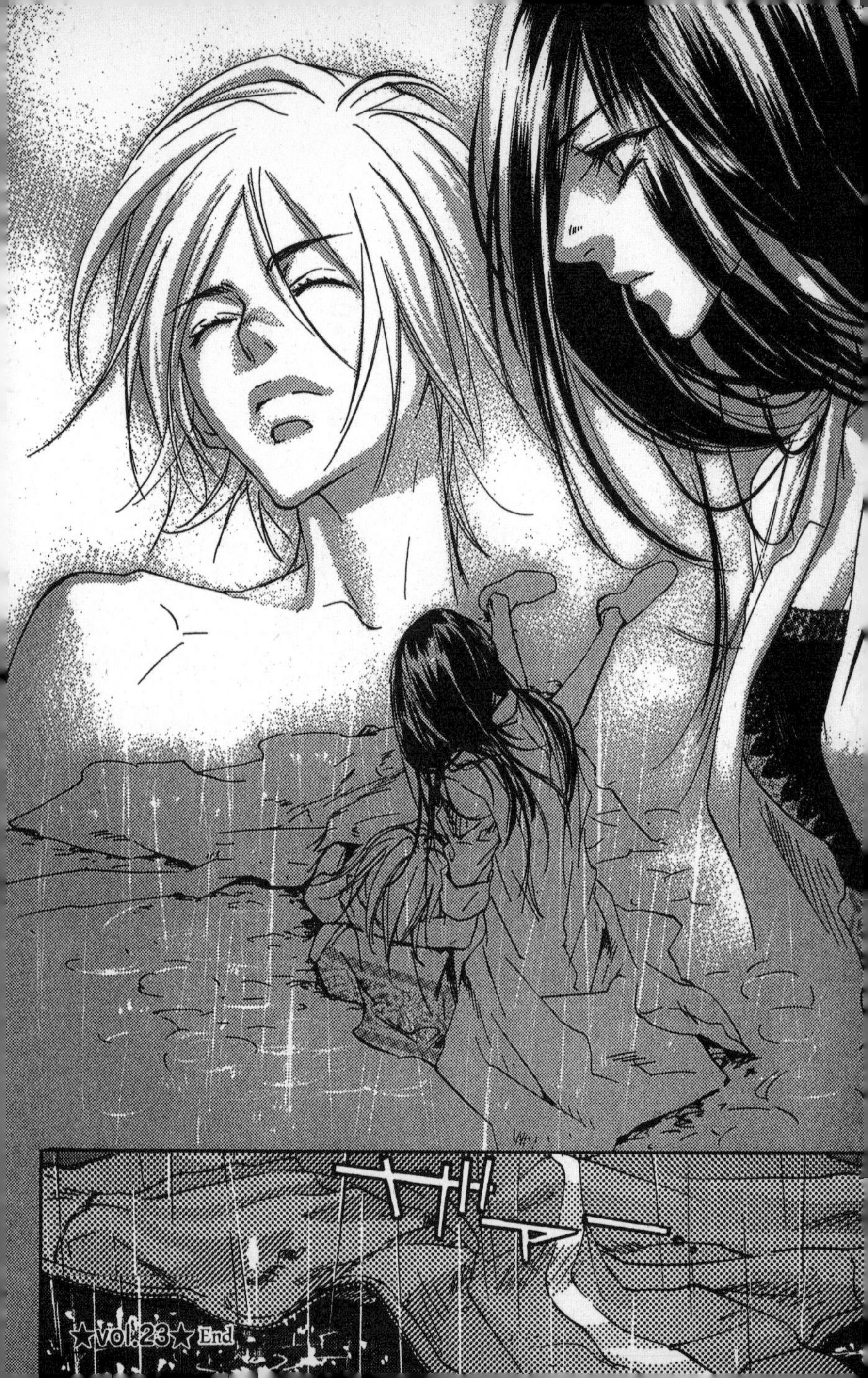
★Vol.23★ End

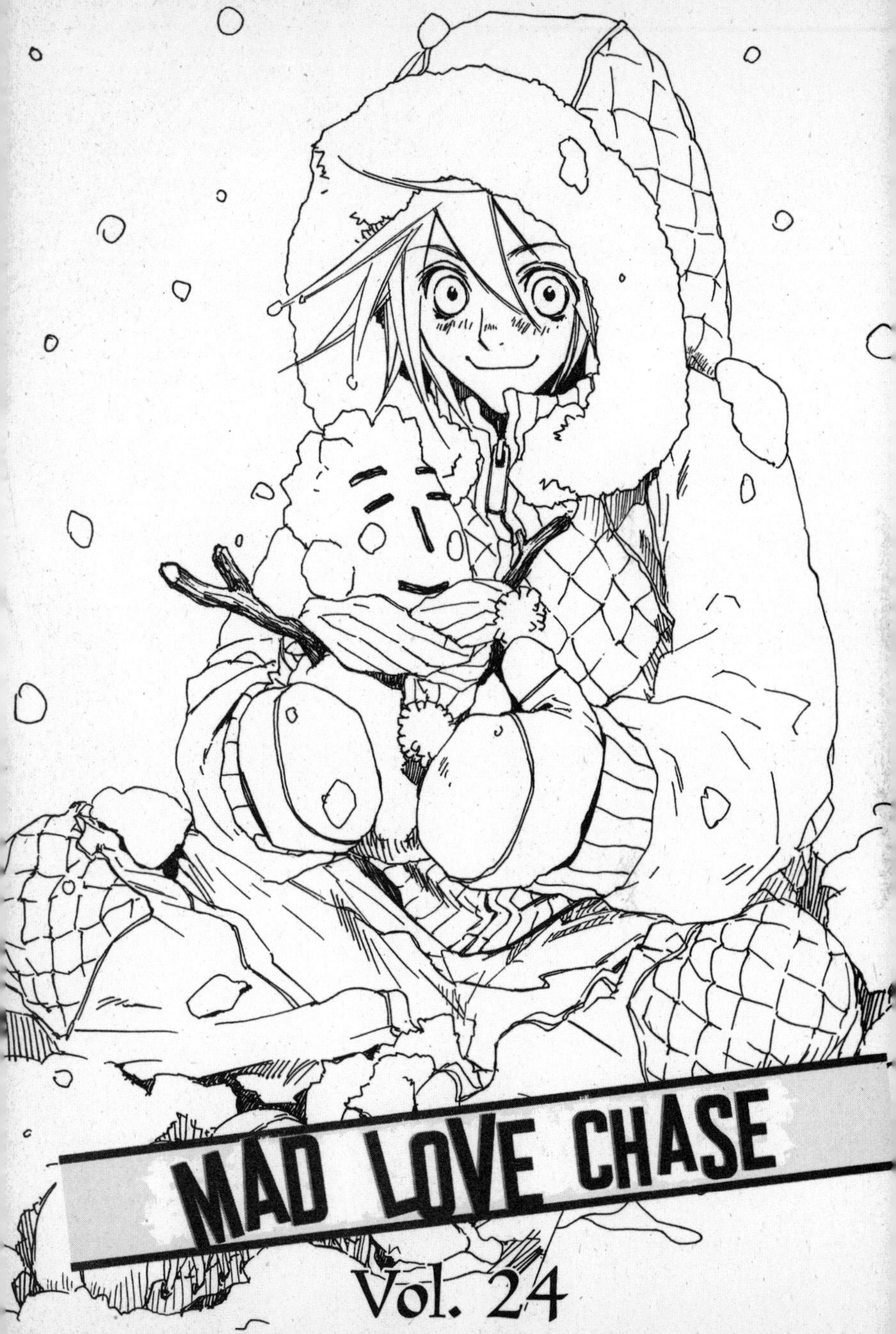
MAD LOVE CHASE
Vol. 24

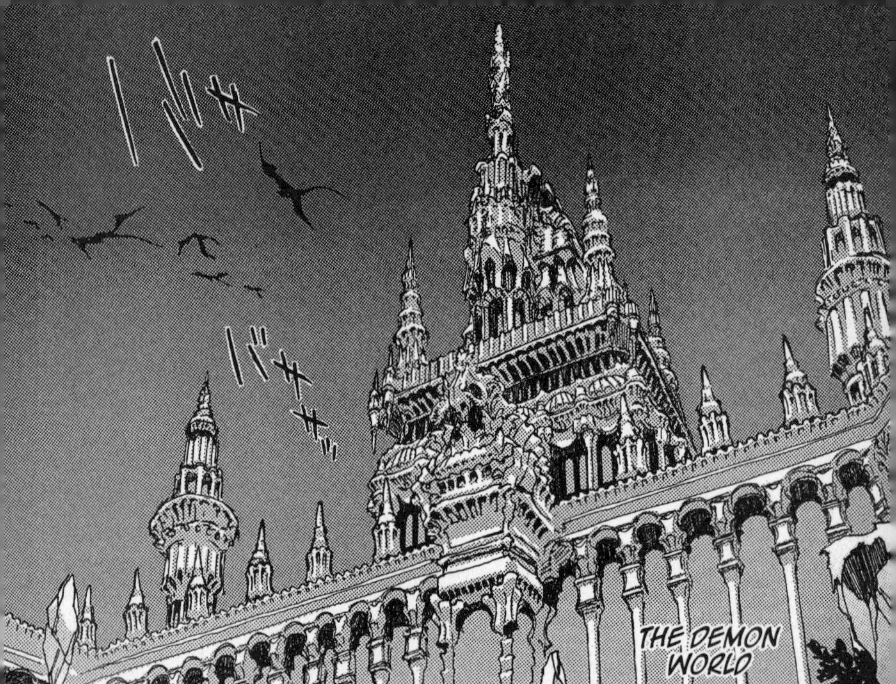
THE DEMON WORLD
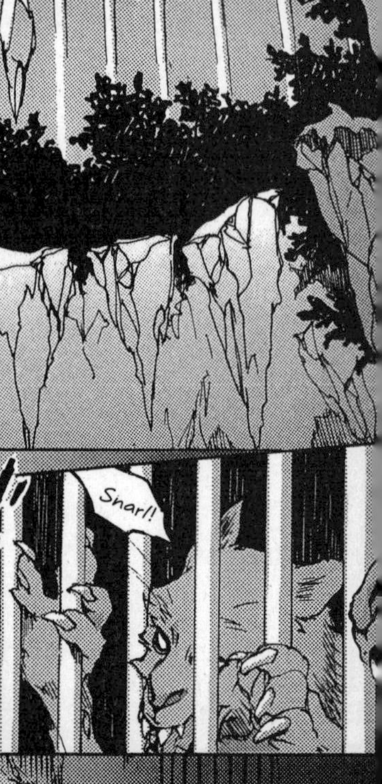
Snarl!!
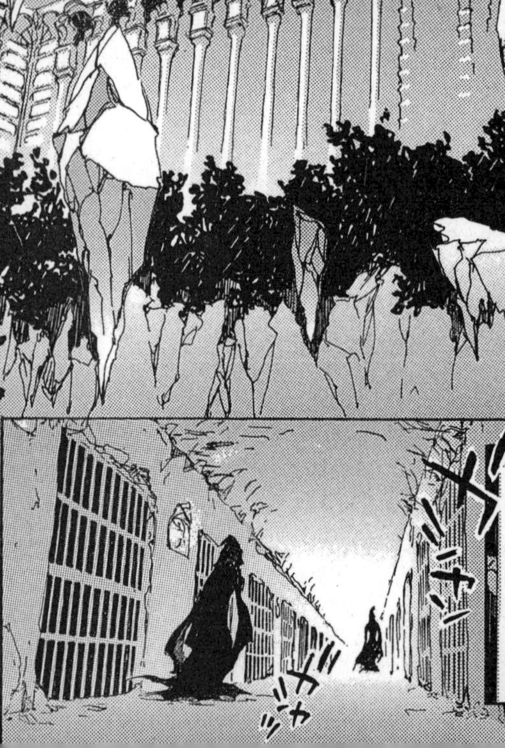

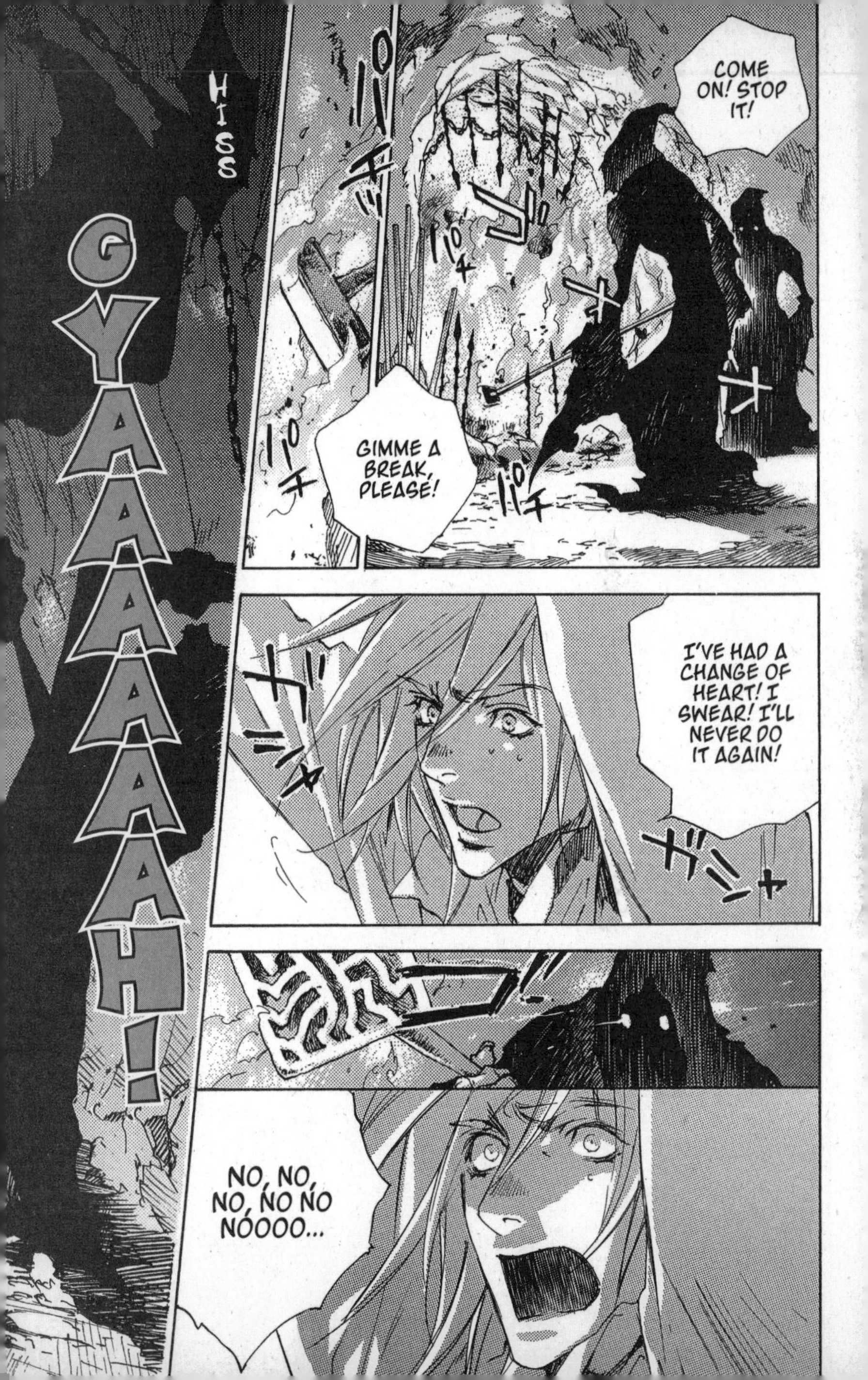
COME ON! STOP IT!
GIMME A BREAK, PLEASE!
I'VE HAD A CHANGE OF HEART! I SWEAR! I'LL NEVER DO IT AGAIN!
NO, NO, NO, NO NO NOOOO...
HISS
GYAAAAAAH!

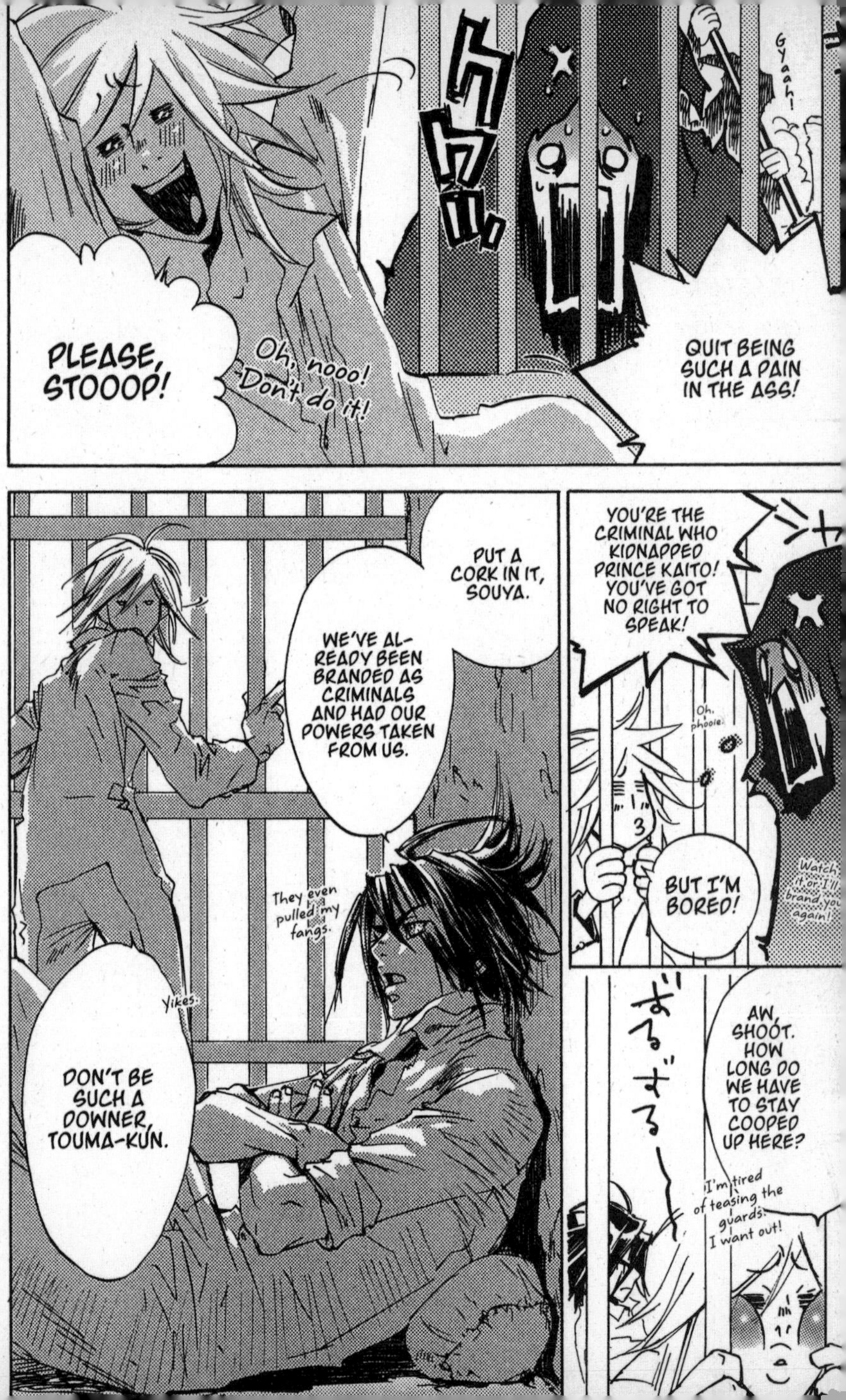
Gyaah!
QUIT BEING SUCH A PAIN IN THE ASS!
Oh, nooo! Don't do it!
PLEASE, STOOOP!
YOU'RE THE CRIMINAL WHO KIDNAPPED PRINCE KAITO! YOU'VE GOT NO RIGHT TO SPEAK!
Oh, phooie.
Watch it, or I'll brand you again!
BUT I'M BORED!
AW, SHOOT. HOW LONG DO WE HAVE TO STAY COOPED UP HERE?
ずるずる
I'm tired of teasing the guards. I want out!
PUT A CORK IN IT, SOUYA.
WE'VE ALREADY BEEN BRANDED AS CRIMINALS AND HAD OUR POWERS TAKEN FROM US.
They even pulled my fangs.
Yikes.
DON'T BE SUCH A DOWNER, TOUMA-KUN.

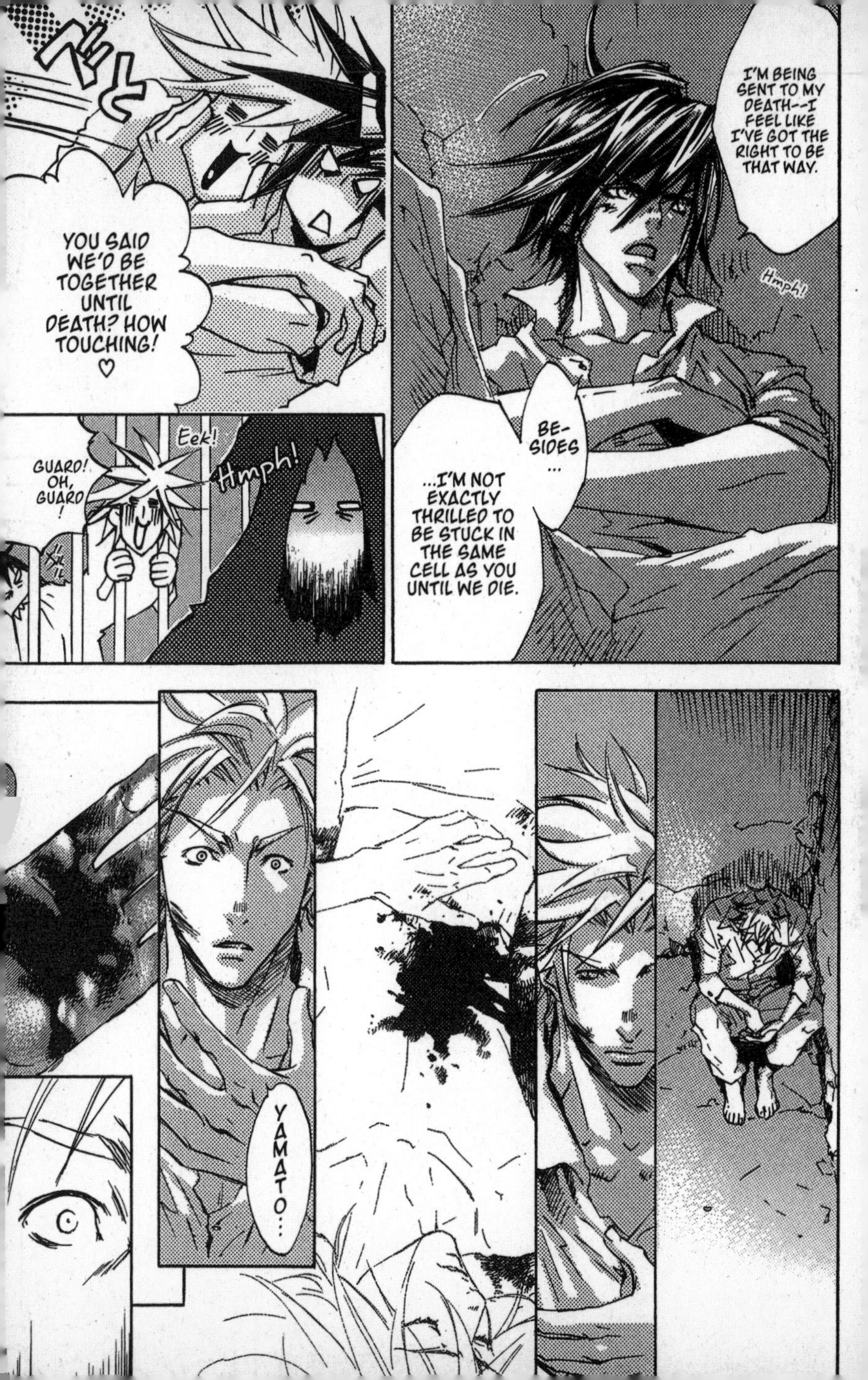
I'M BEING SENT TO MY DEATH--I FEEL LIKE I'VE GOT THE RIGHT TO BE THAT WAY.
Hmph!
BE-SIDES...
...I'M NOT EXACTLY THRILLED TO BE STUCK IN THE SAME CELL AS YOU UNTIL WE DIE.
YOU SAID WE'D BE TOGETHER UNTIL DEATH? HOW TOUCHING! ♡
Eek!
GUARD! OH, GUARD!
Hmph!
YAMATO...

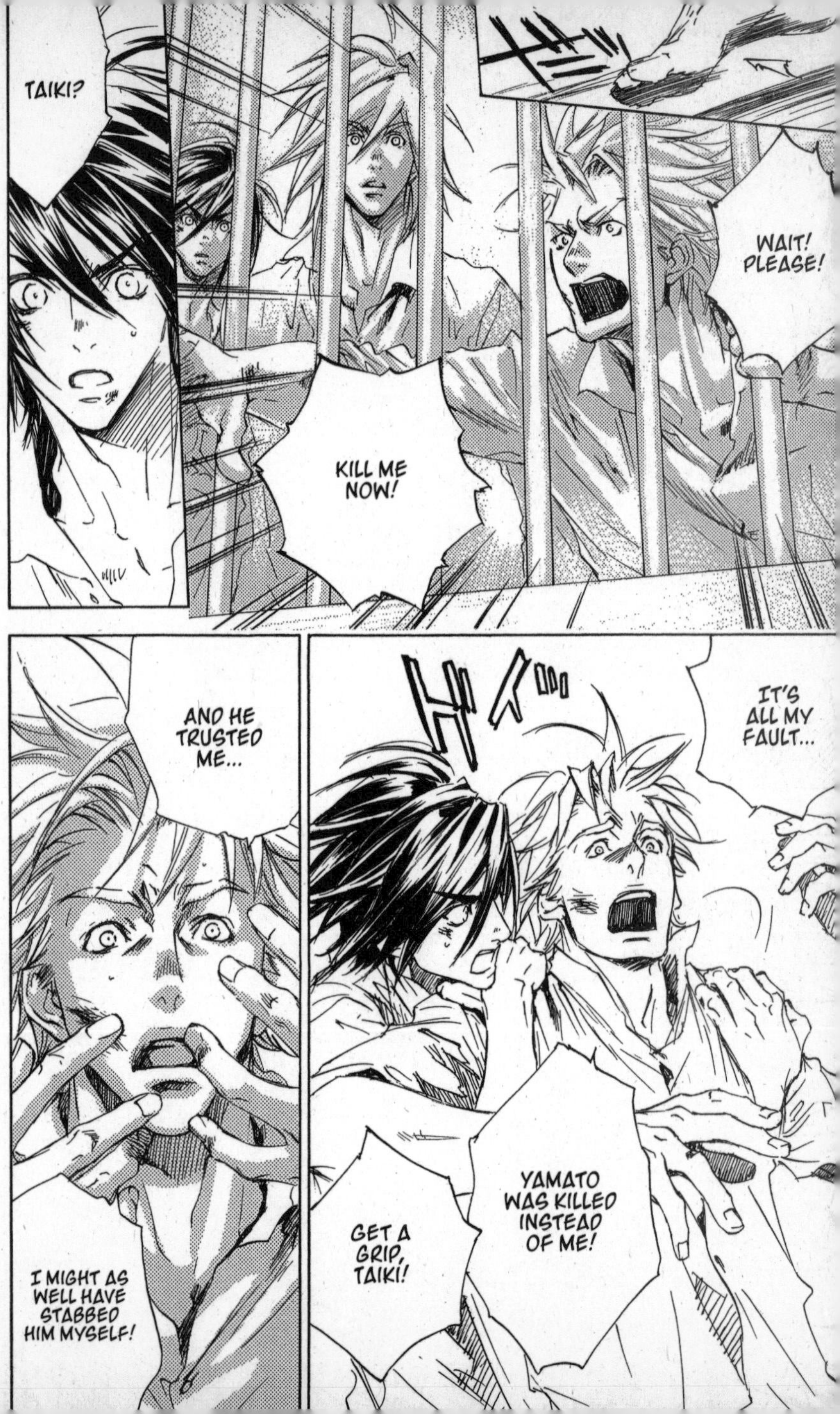
WAIT! PLEASE!
KILL ME NOW!
TAIKI?
IT'S ALL MY FAULT...
YAMATO WAS KILLED INSTEAD OF ME!
GET A GRIP, TAIKI!
AND HE TRUSTED ME...
I MIGHT AS WELL HAVE STABBED HIM MYSELF!

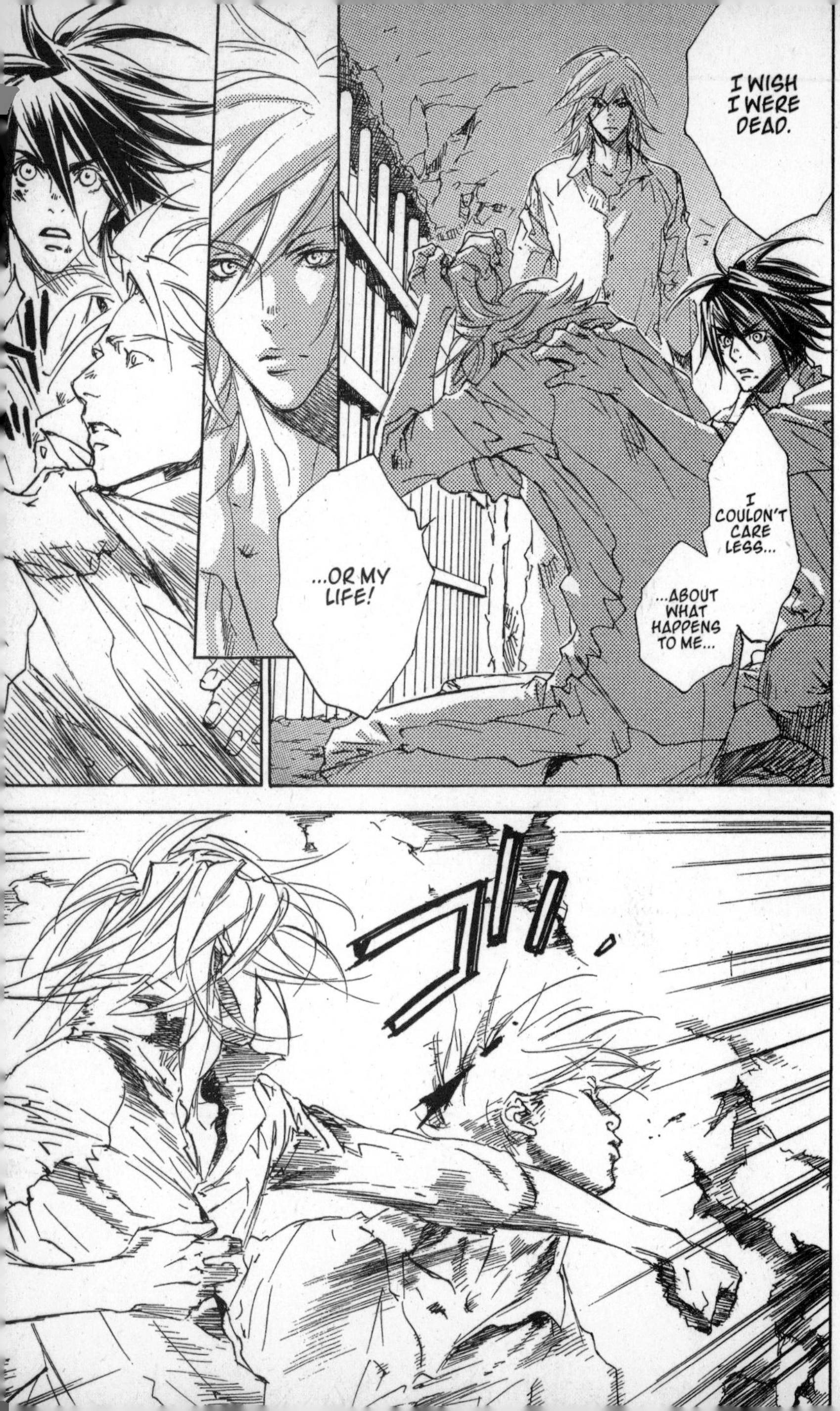
I WISH I WERE DEAD.
I COULDN'T CARE LESS...
...ABOUT WHAT HAPPENS TO ME...
...OR MY LIFE!

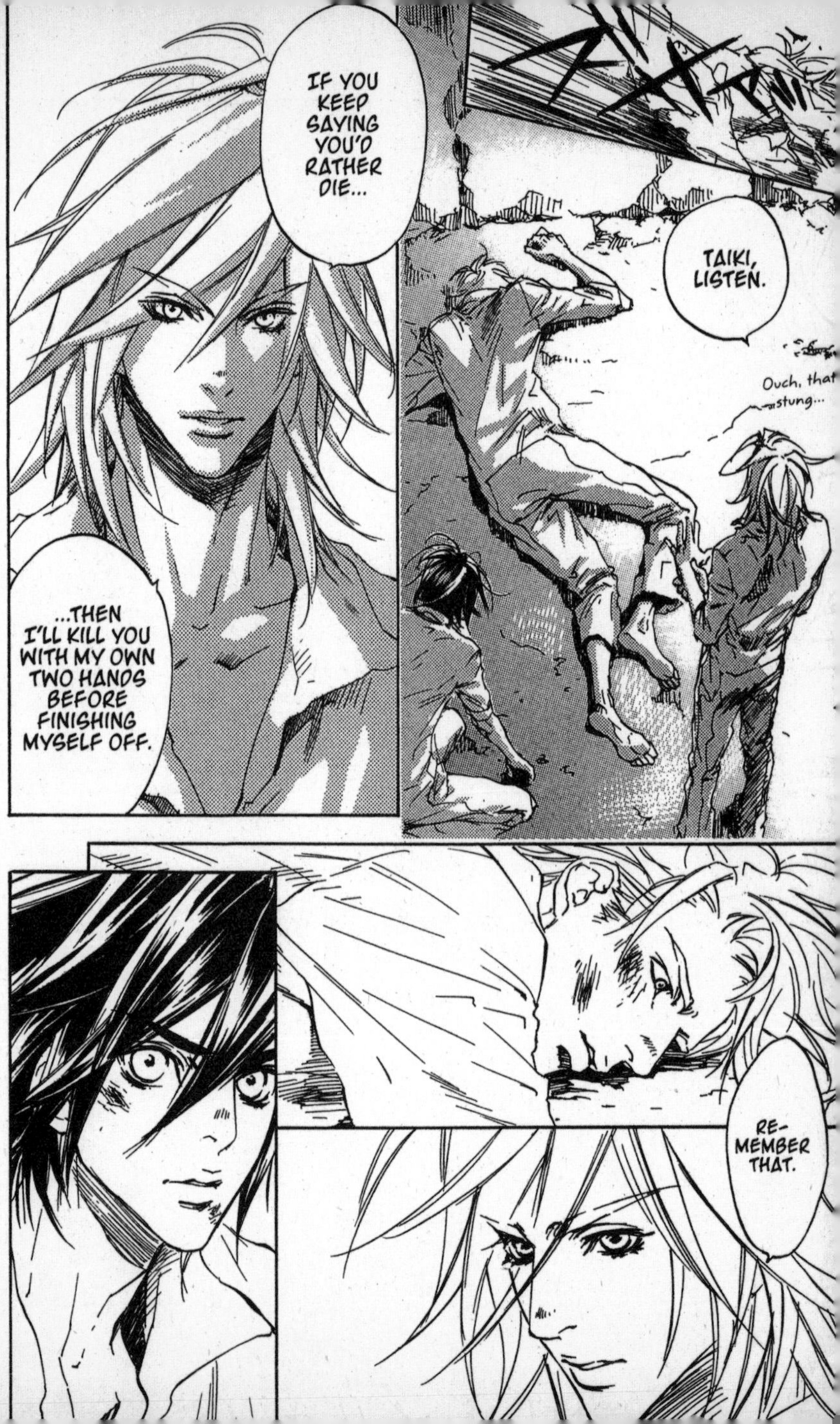
TAIKI, LISTEN.
Ouch, that stung...
IF YOU KEEP SAYING YOU'D RATHER DIE...
...THEN I'LL KILL YOU WITH MY OWN TWO HANDS BEFORE FINISHING MYSELF OFF.
RE-MEMBER THAT.

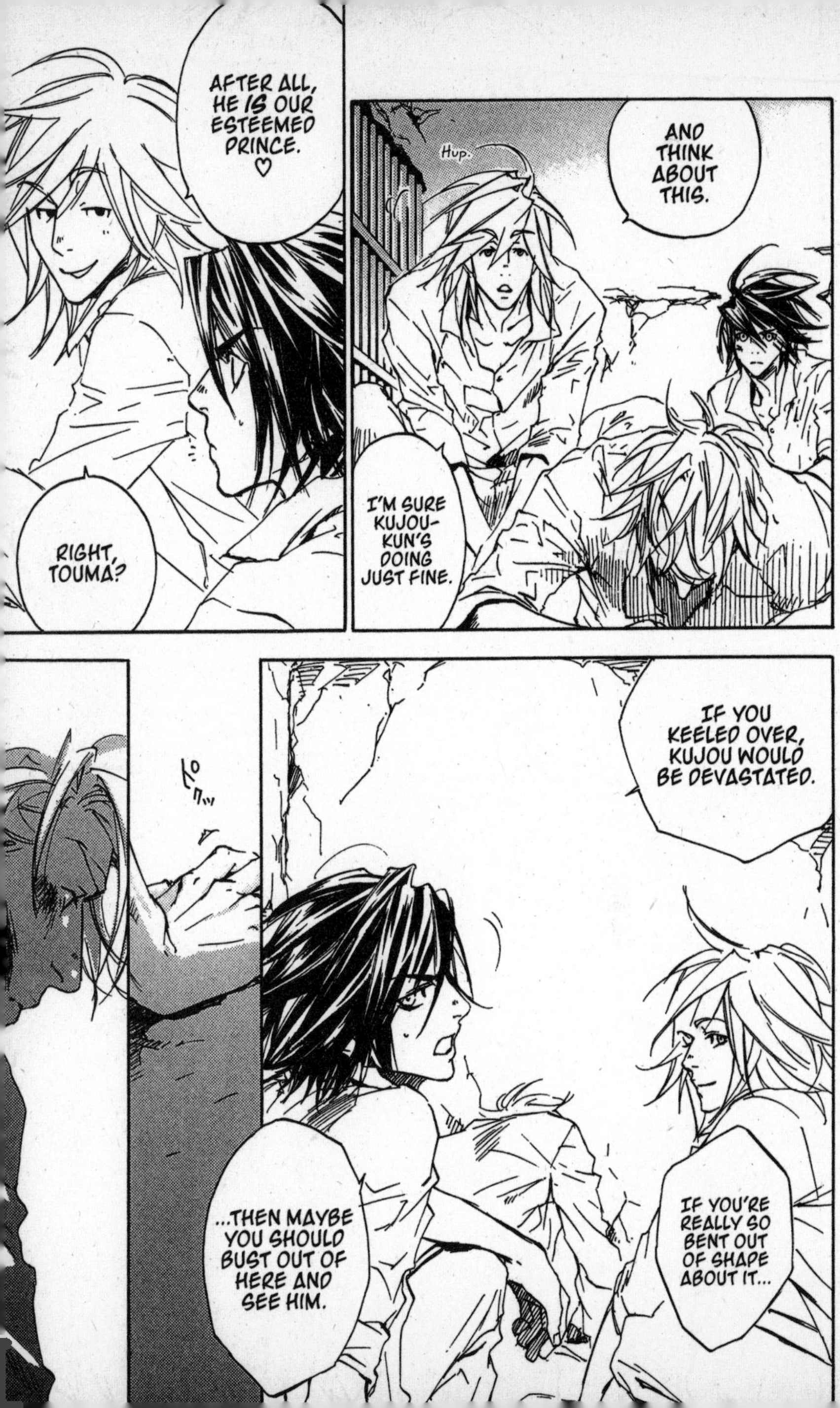
AND THINK ABOUT THIS.
Hup.
I'M SURE KUJOU-KUN'S DOING JUST FINE.
AFTER ALL, HE *IS* OUR ESTEEMED PRINCE. ♡
RIGHT, TOUMA?
IF YOU KEELED OVER, KUJOU WOULD BE DEVASTATED.
IF YOU'RE REALLY SO BENT OUT OF SHAPE ABOUT IT...
...THEN MAYBE YOU SHOULD BUST OUT OF HERE AND SEE HIM.

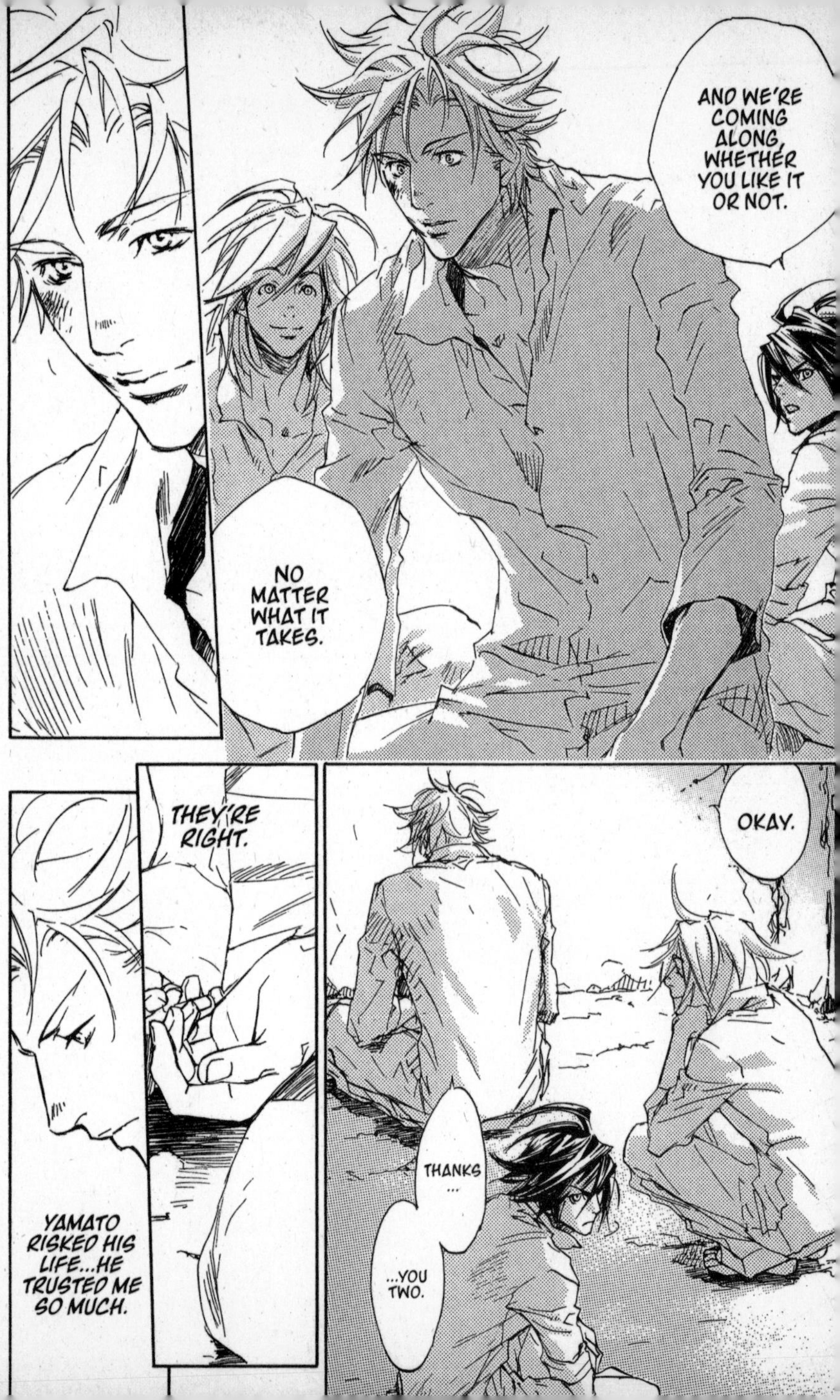
AND WE'RE COMING ALONG, WHETHER YOU LIKE IT OR NOT.
NO MATTER WHAT IT TAKES.
OKAY.
THANKS...
...YOU TWO.
THEY'RE RIGHT.
YAMATO RISKED HIS LIFE...HE TRUSTED ME SO MUCH.

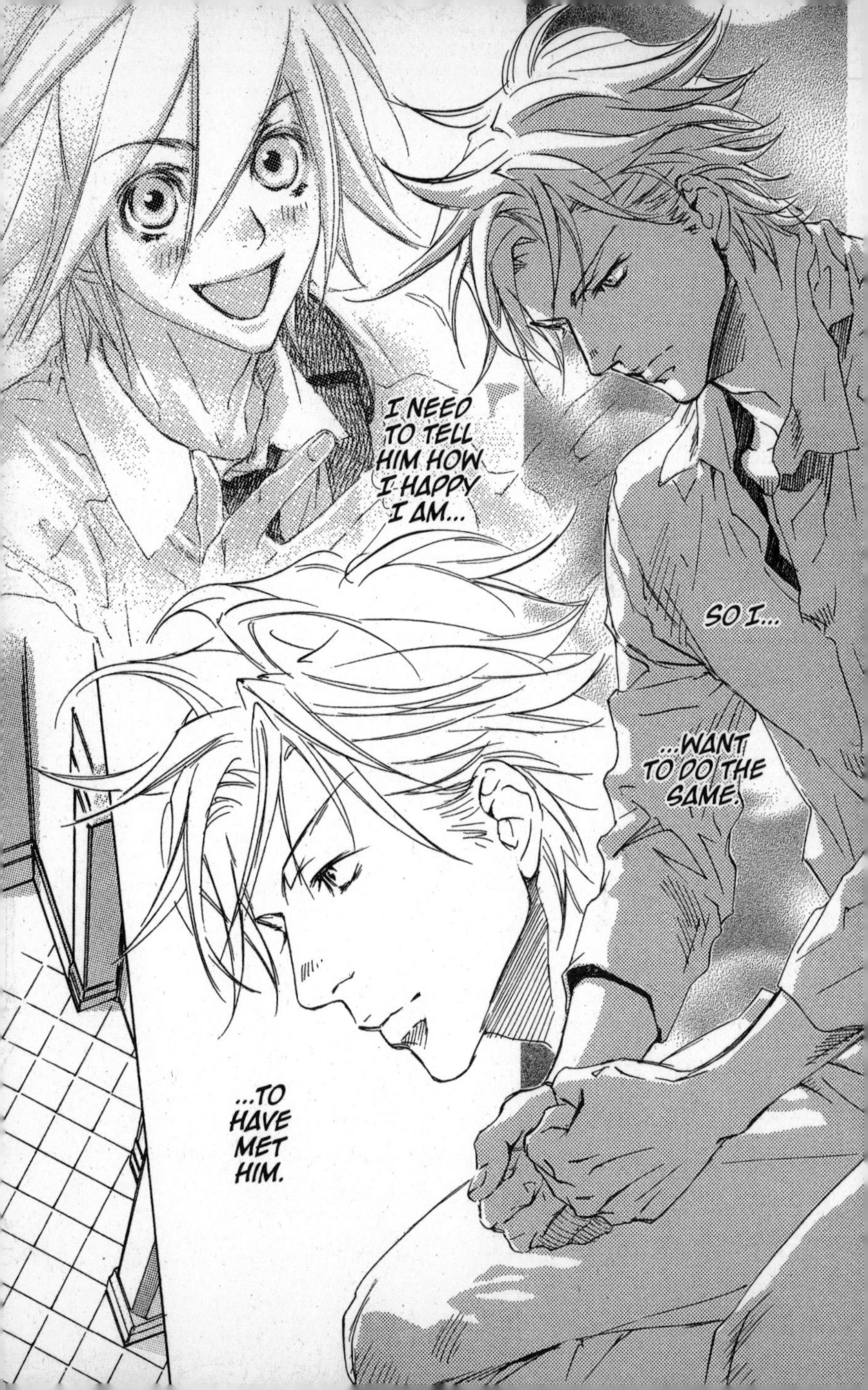
I NEED TO TELL HIM HOW I HAPPY I AM...
SO I...
...WANT TO DO THE SAME.
...TO HAVE MET HIM.

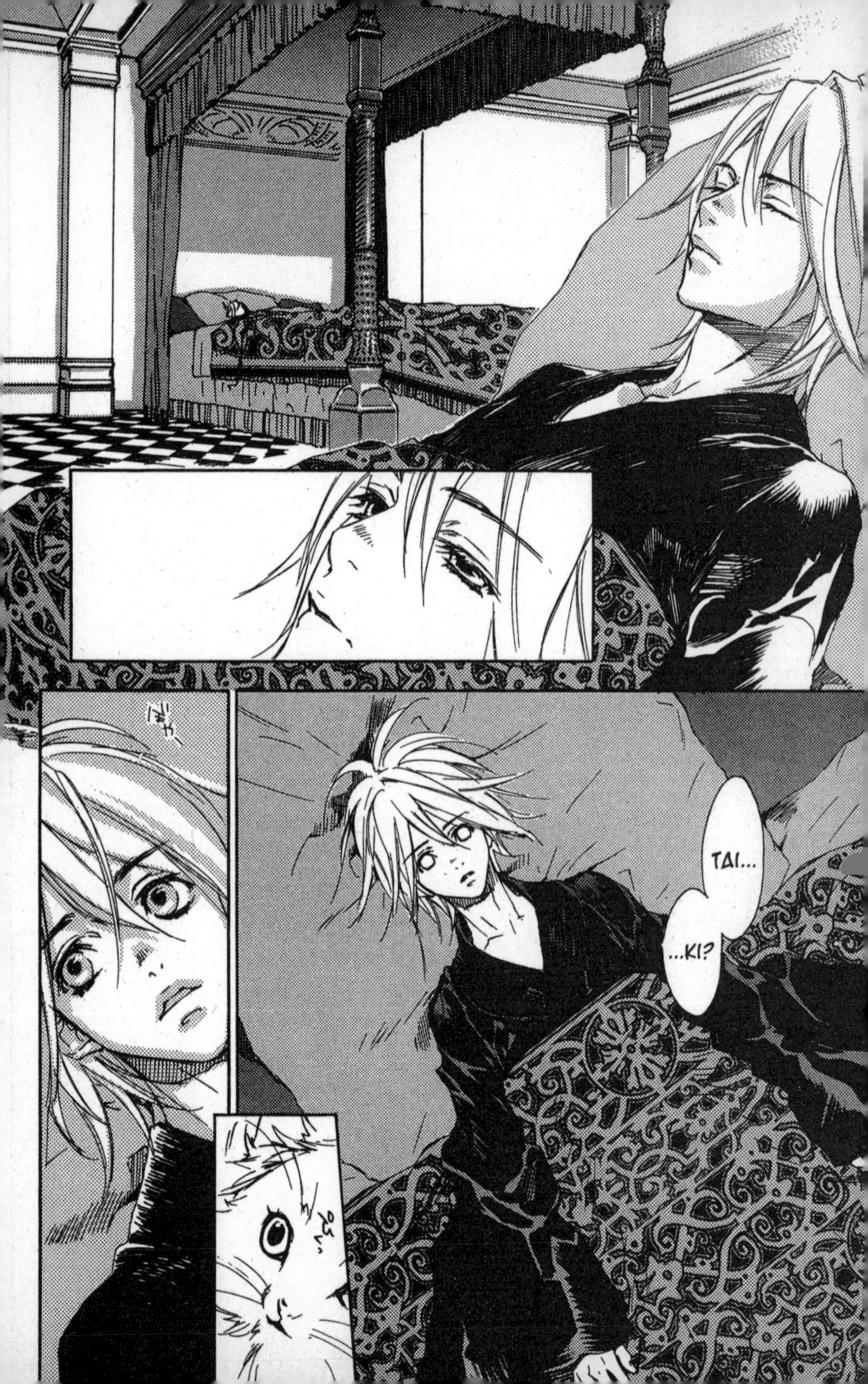
TAI...
...KI?

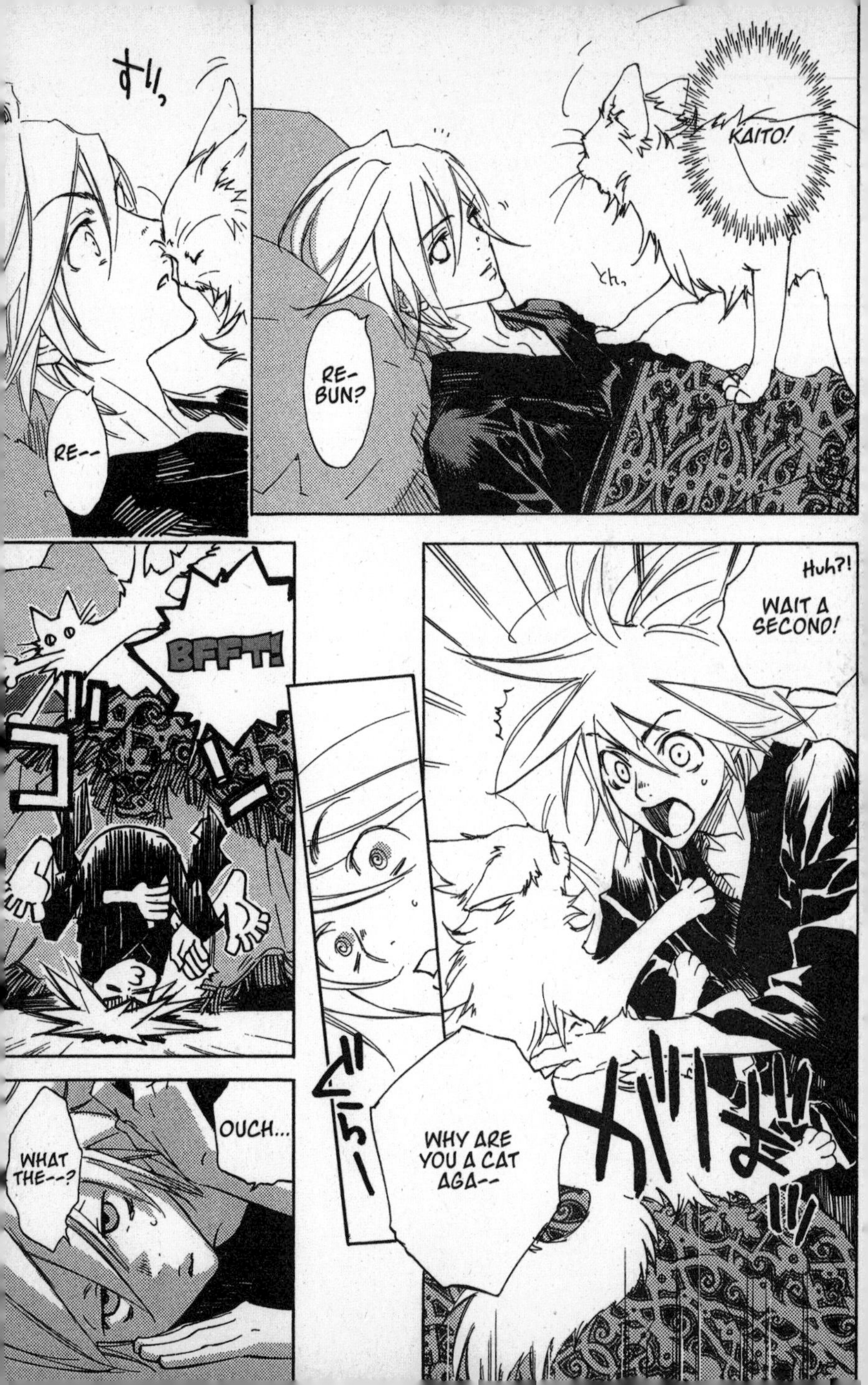
KAITO!
RE-BUN?
すりっ
RE--
Huh?!
WAIT A SECOND!
WHY ARE YOU A CAT AGA--
BFFT!
OUCH...
WHAT THE--?

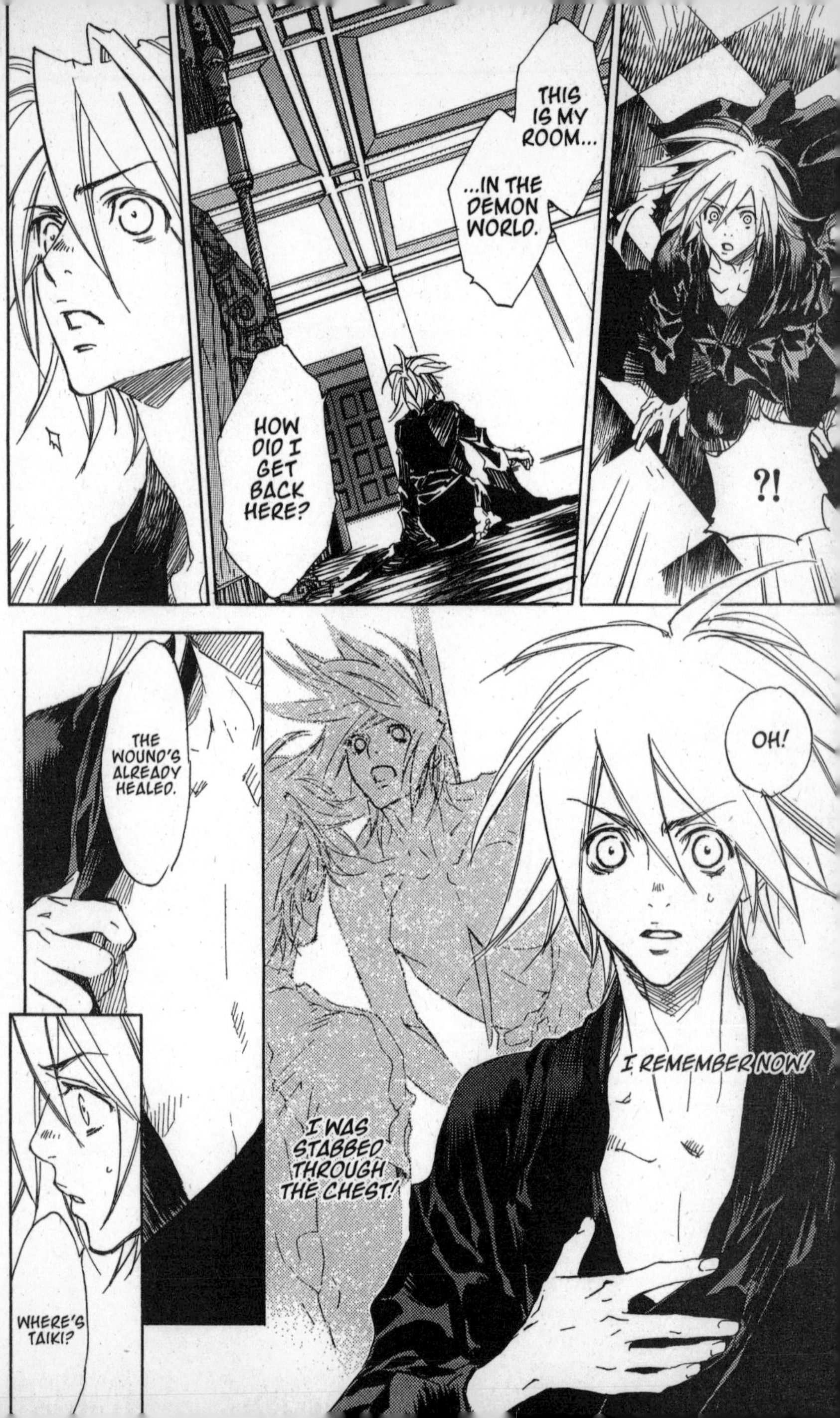
?!
THIS IS MY ROOM...
...IN THE DEMON WORLD.
HOW DID I GET BACK HERE?
OH!
I REMEMBER NOW!
I WAS STABBED THROUGH THE CHEST!
THE WOUND'S ALREADY HEALED.
WHERE'S TAIKI?

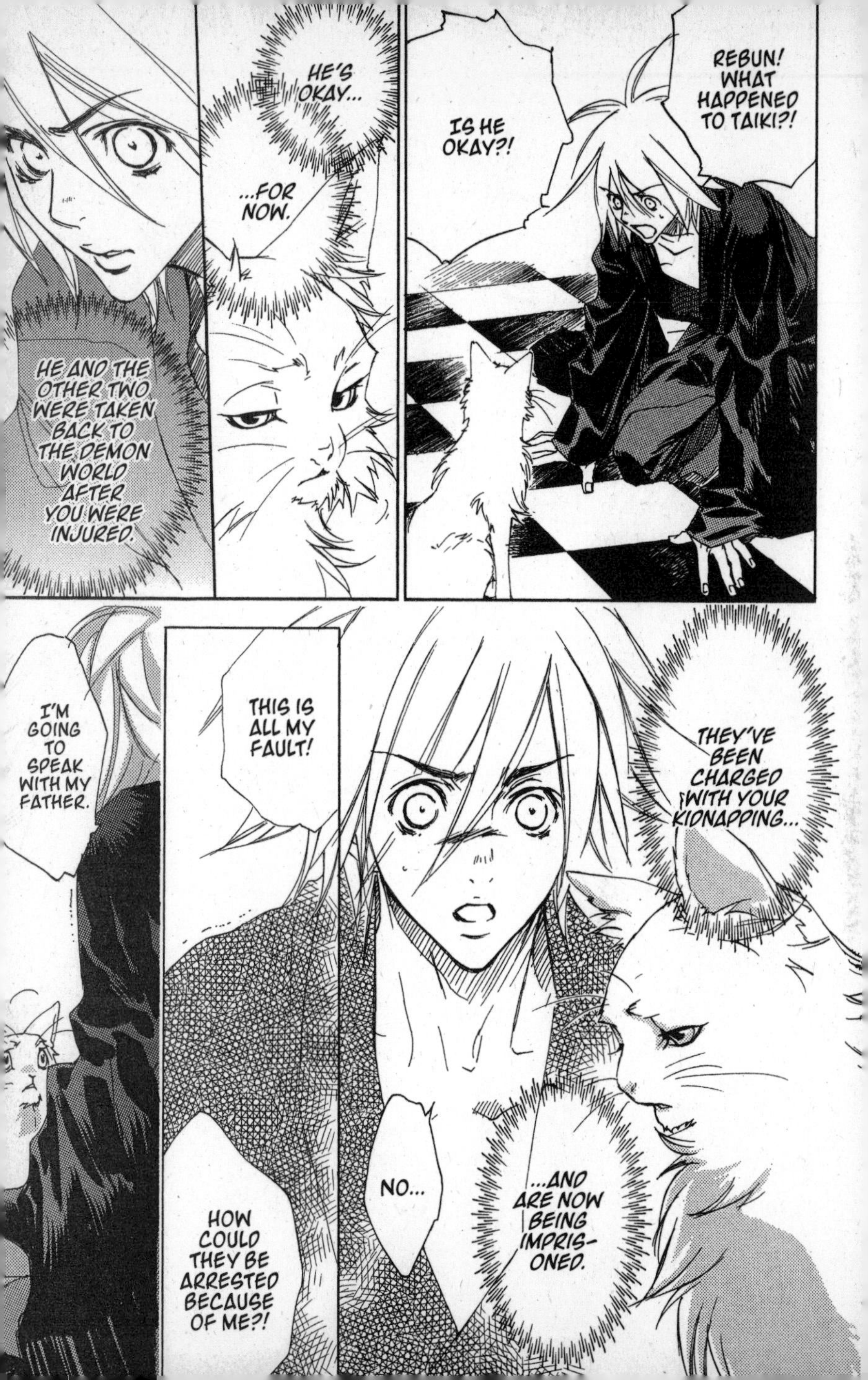
REBUN! WHAT HAPPENED TO TAIKI?!
IS HE OKAY?!
HE'S OKAY...
...FOR NOW.
HE AND THE OTHER TWO WERE TAKEN BACK TO THE DEMON WORLD AFTER YOU WERE INJURED.
THEY'VE BEEN CHARGED WITH YOUR KIDNAPPING...
...AND ARE NOW BEING IMPRISONED.
NO...
HOW COULD THEY BE ARRESTED BECAUSE OF ME?!
THIS IS ALL MY FAULT!
I'M GOING TO SPEAK WITH MY FATHER.

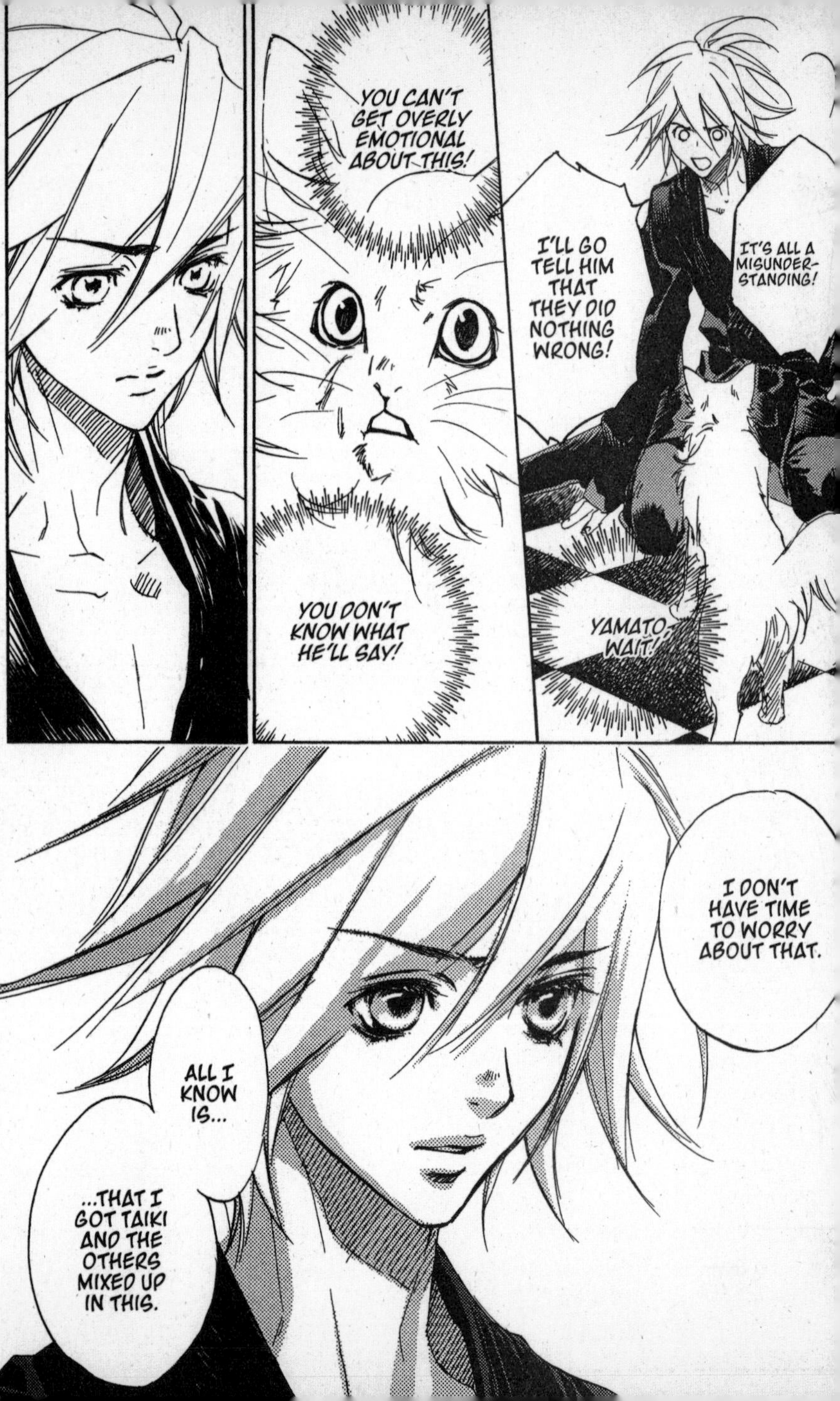
IT'S ALL A MISUNDERSTANDING!
I'LL GO TELL HIM THAT THEY DID NOTHING WRONG!
YAMATO-WAIT!
YOU CAN'T GET OVERLY EMOTIONAL ABOUT THIS!
YOU DON'T KNOW WHAT HE'LL SAY!
I DON'T HAVE TIME TO WORRY ABOUT THAT.
ALL I KNOW IS...
...THAT I GOT TAIKI AND THE OTHERS MIXED UP IN THIS.

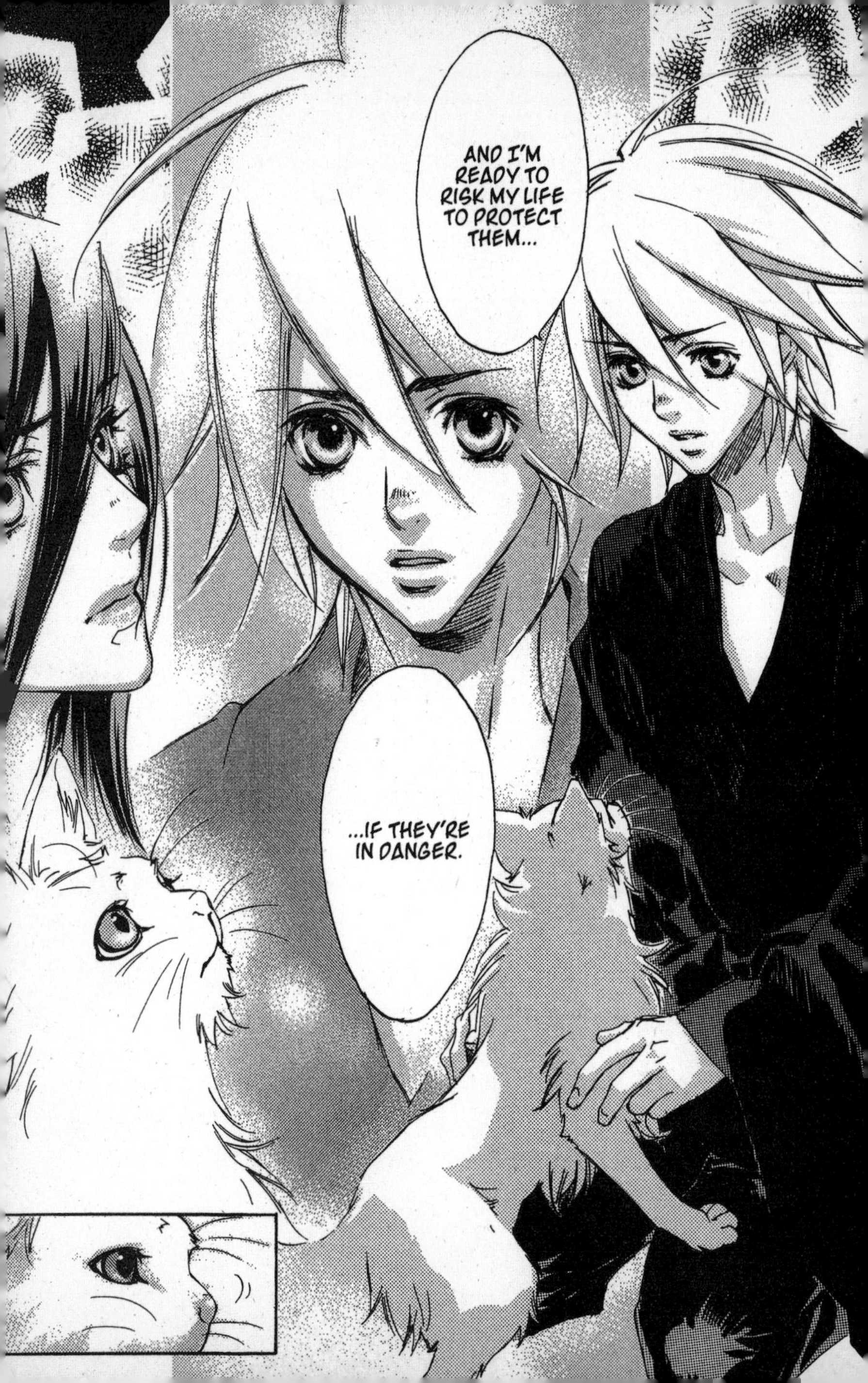
AND I'M READY TO RISK MY LIFE TO PROTECT THEM...
...IF THEY'RE IN DANGER.

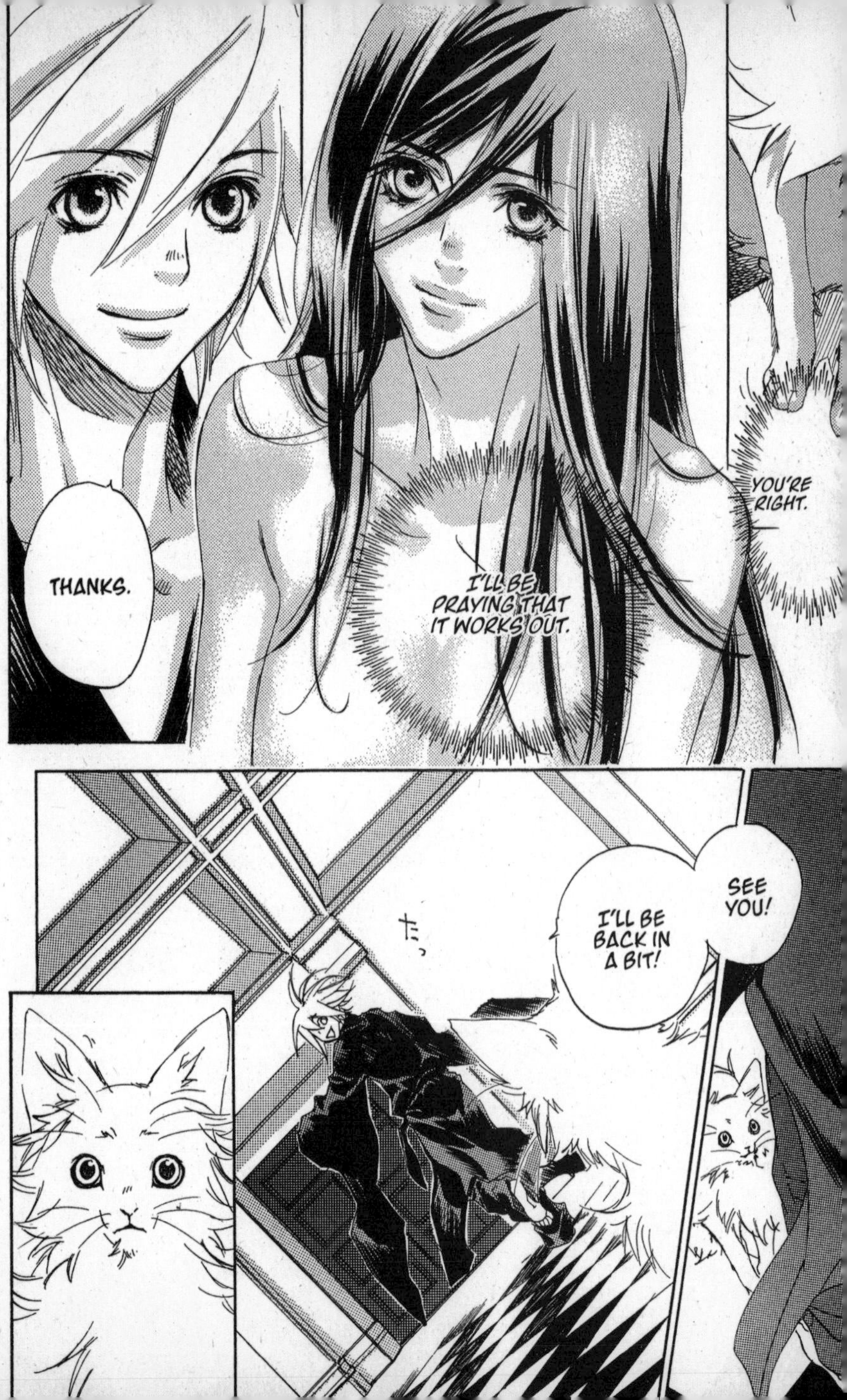
YOU'RE RIGHT.
I'LL BE PRAYING THAT IT WORKS OUT.
THANKS.
SEE YOU!
I'LL BE BACK IN A BIT!
たっ

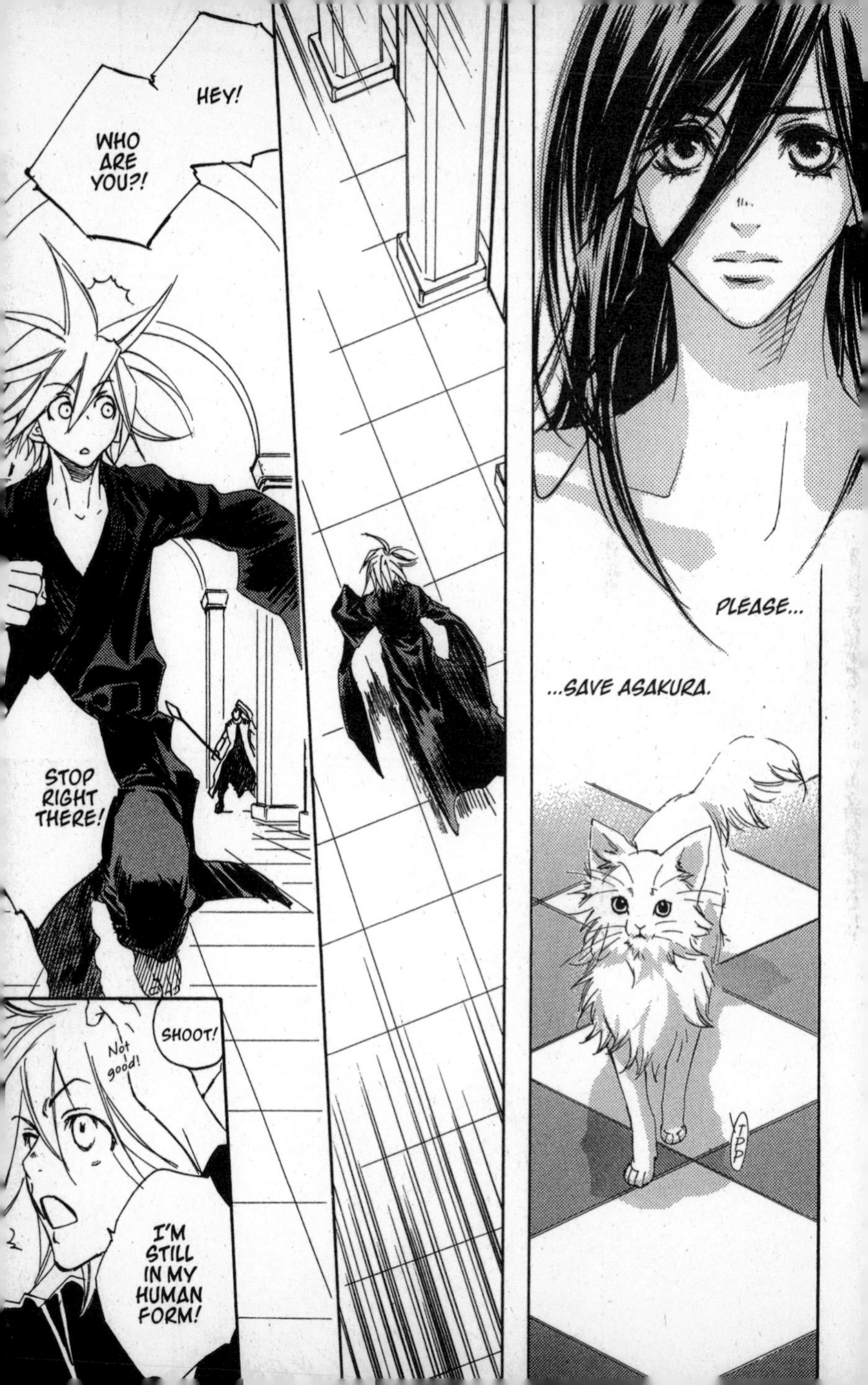
PLEASE...
...SAVE ASAKURA.
TPP
HEY!
WHO ARE YOU?!
STOP RIGHT THERE!
SHOOT!
Not good!
I'M STILL IN MY HUMAN FORM!

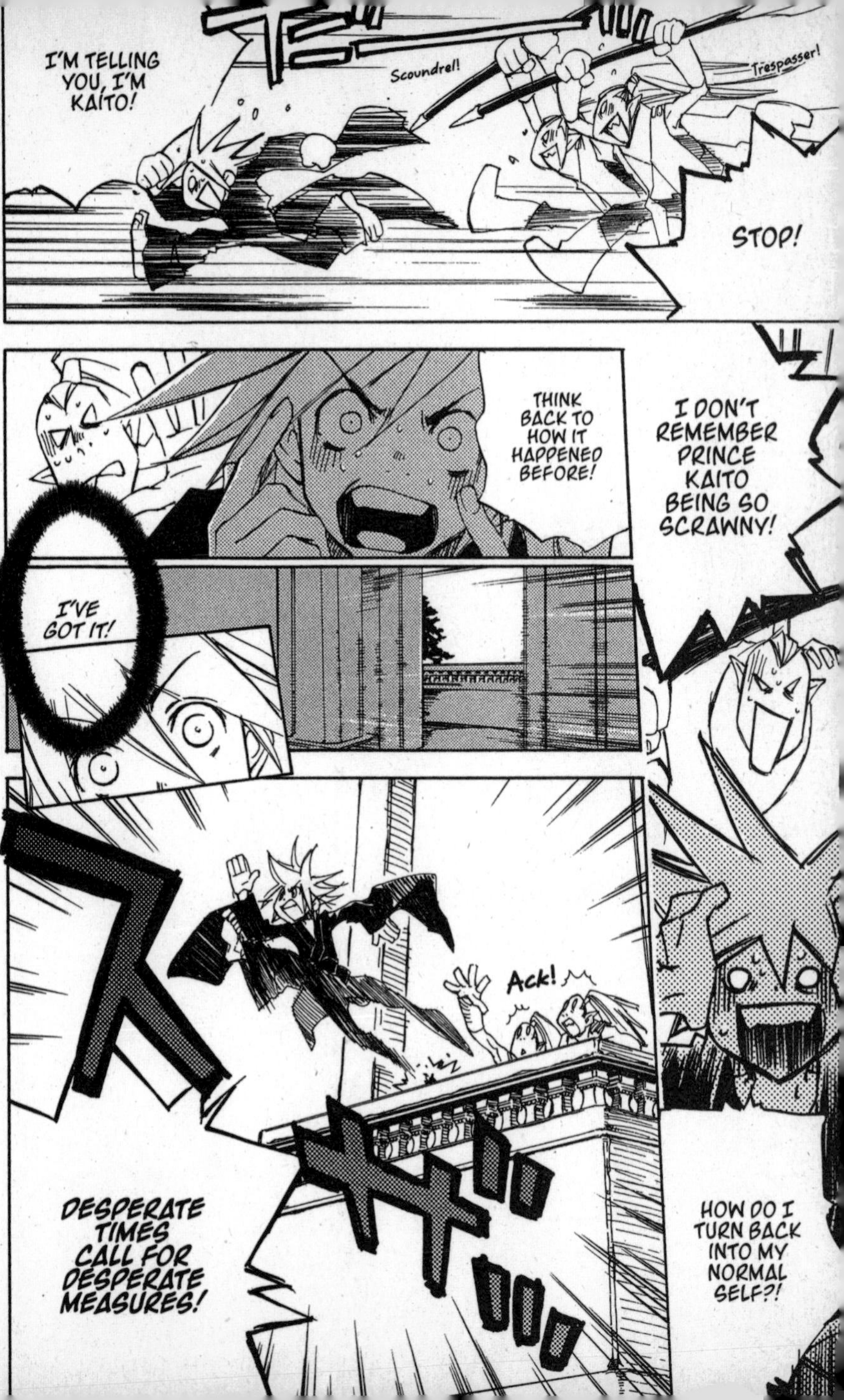
Trespasser!
Scoundrel!
STOP!
I'M TELLING YOU, I'M KAITO!
I DON'T REMEMBER PRINCE KAITO BEING SO SCRAWNY!
HOW DO I TURN BACK INTO MY NORMAL SELF?!
THINK BACK TO HOW IT HAPPENED BEFORE!
I'VE GOT IT!
Ack!
DESPERATE TIMES CALL FOR DESPERATE MEASURES!

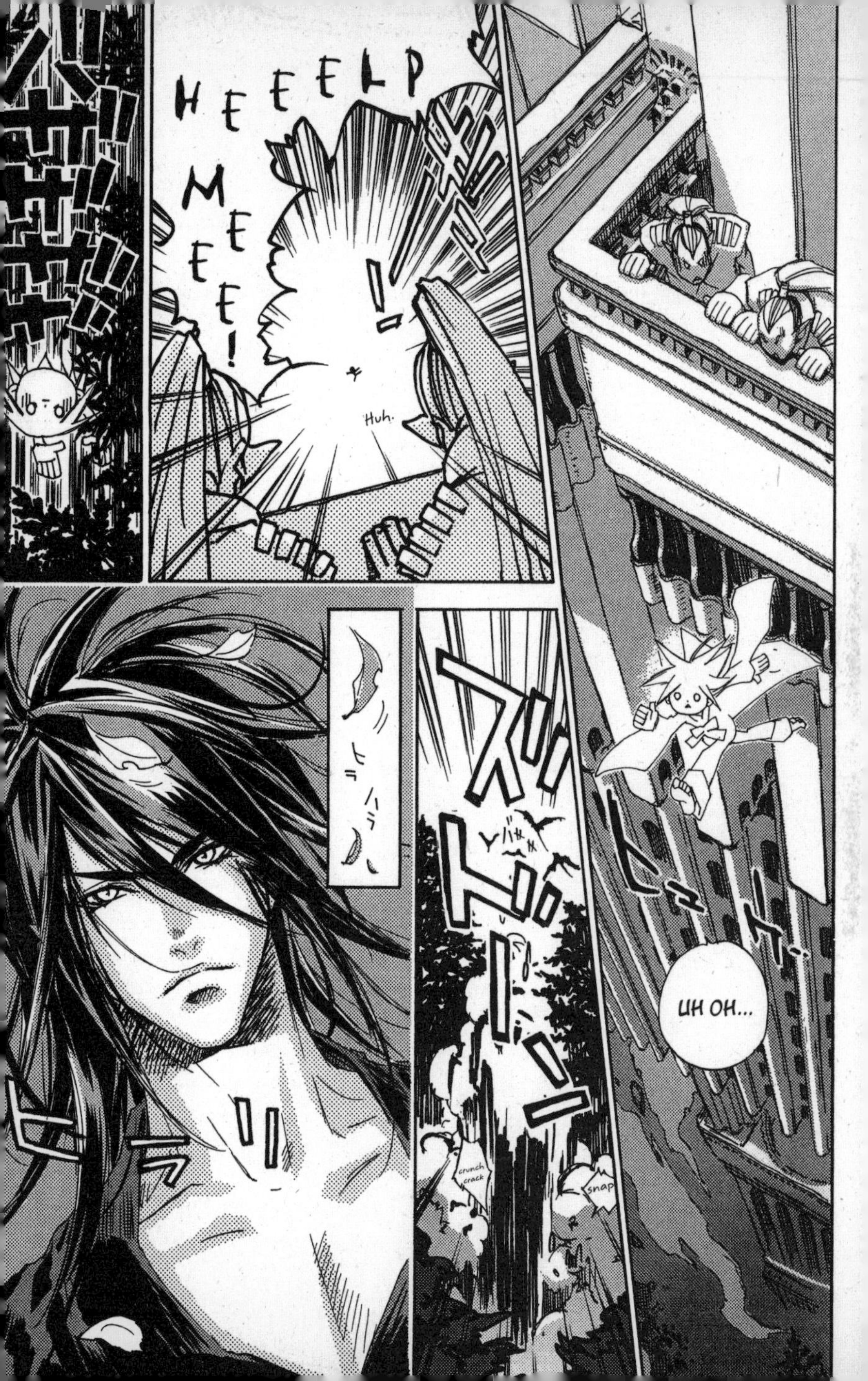
UH OH...
HEEELP MEEEE!
Huh.
crunch crack
snap

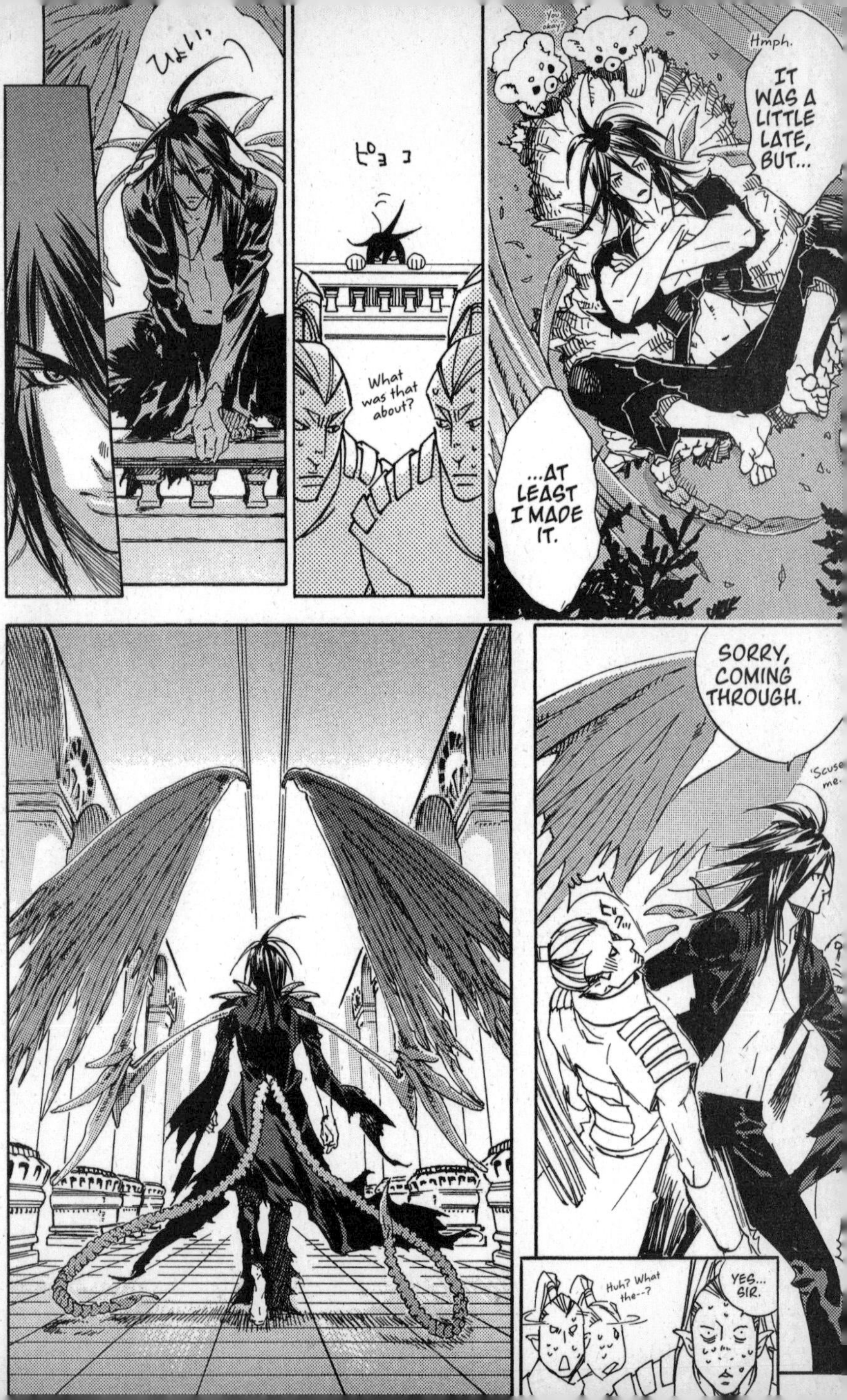
You okay?
Hmph.
IT WAS A LITTLE LATE, BUT...
...AT LEAST I MADE IT.
ピョコ
What was that about?
ひょい
SORRY, COMING THROUGH.
'Scuse me.
YES... SIR.
Huh? What the--?

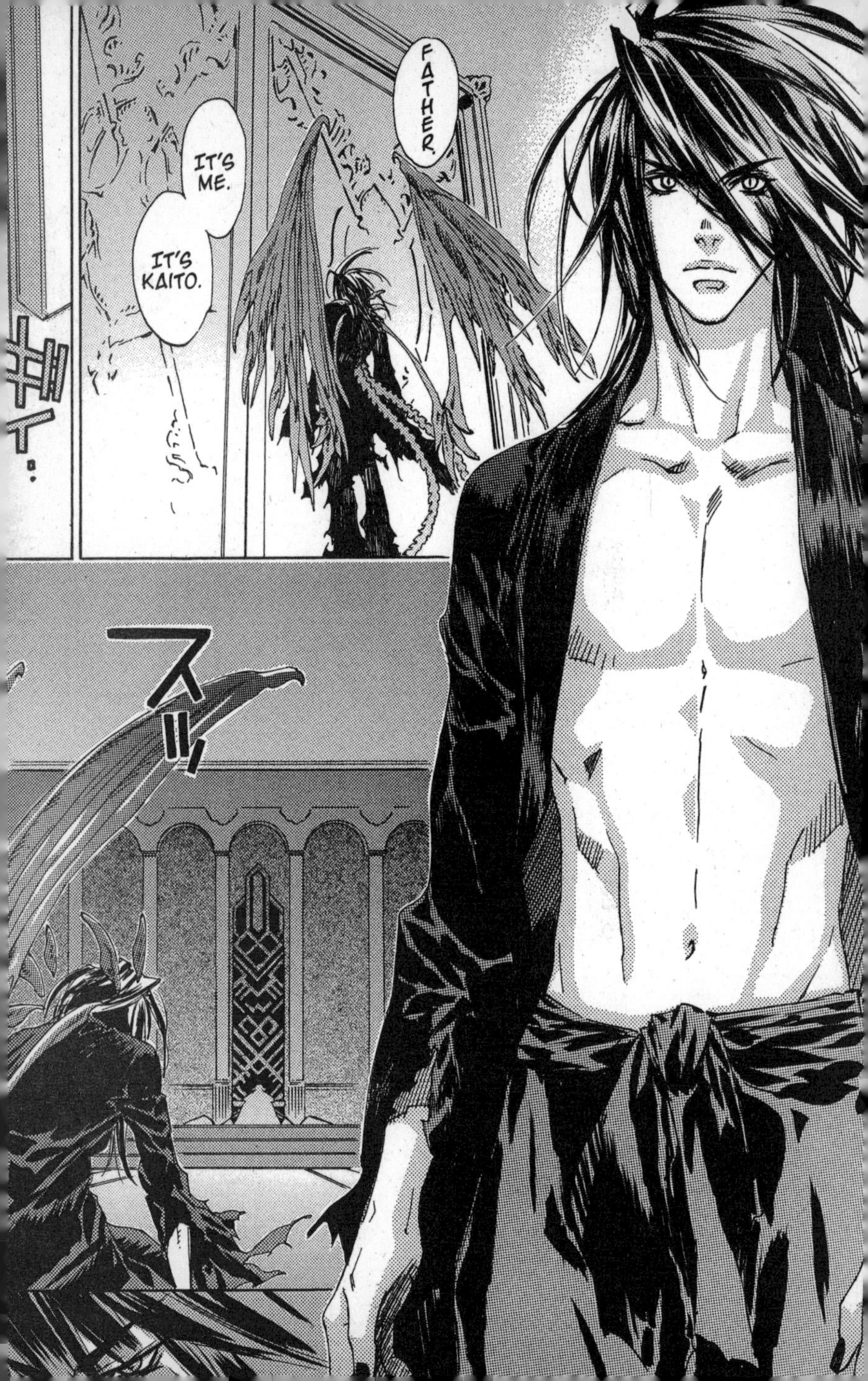
FATHER,
IT'S ME.
IT'S KAITO.
ギィ…
スッ

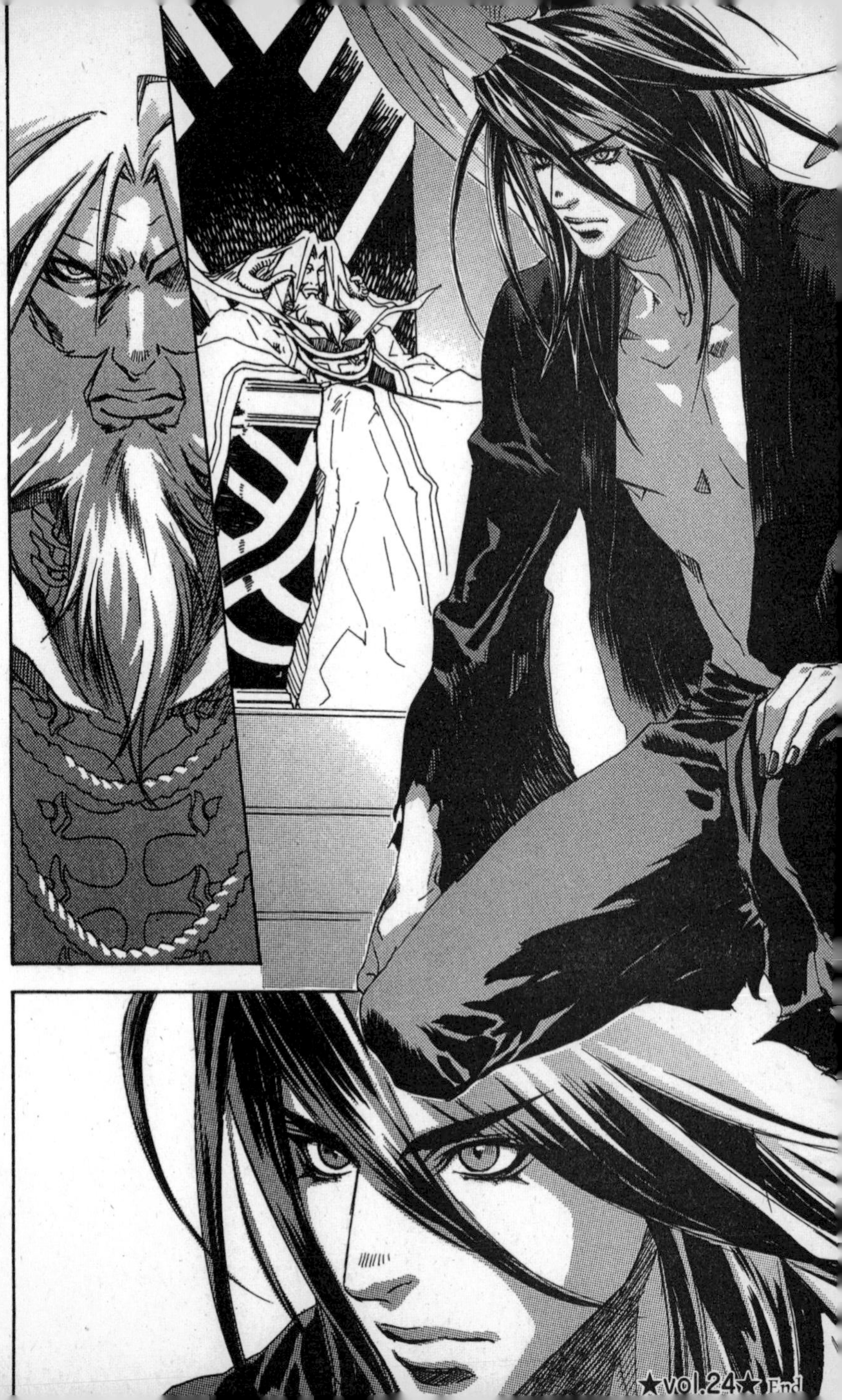
★vol.24★ End

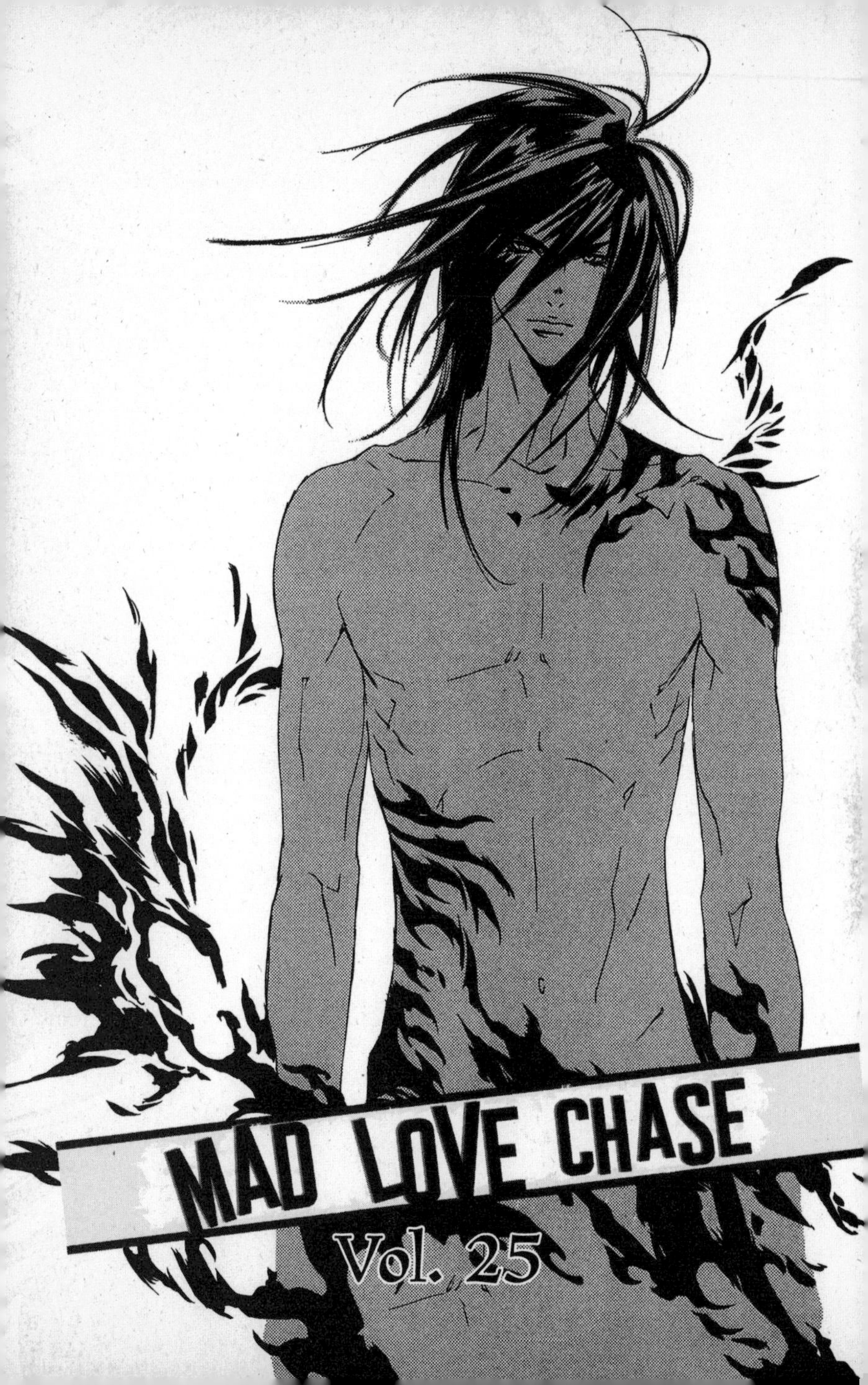
MAD LOVE CHASE
Vol. 25

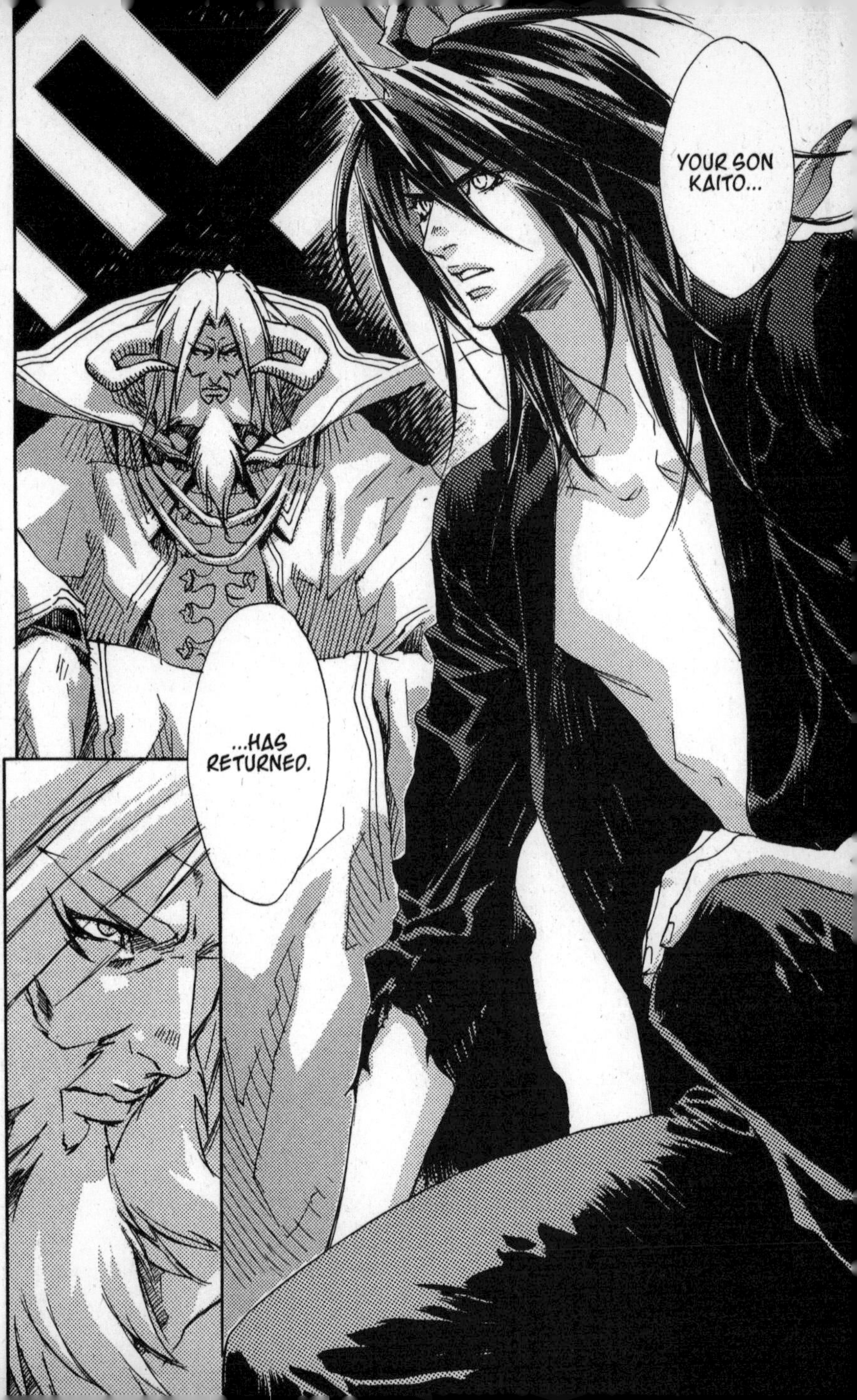
YOUR SON KAITO...
...HAS RETURNED.

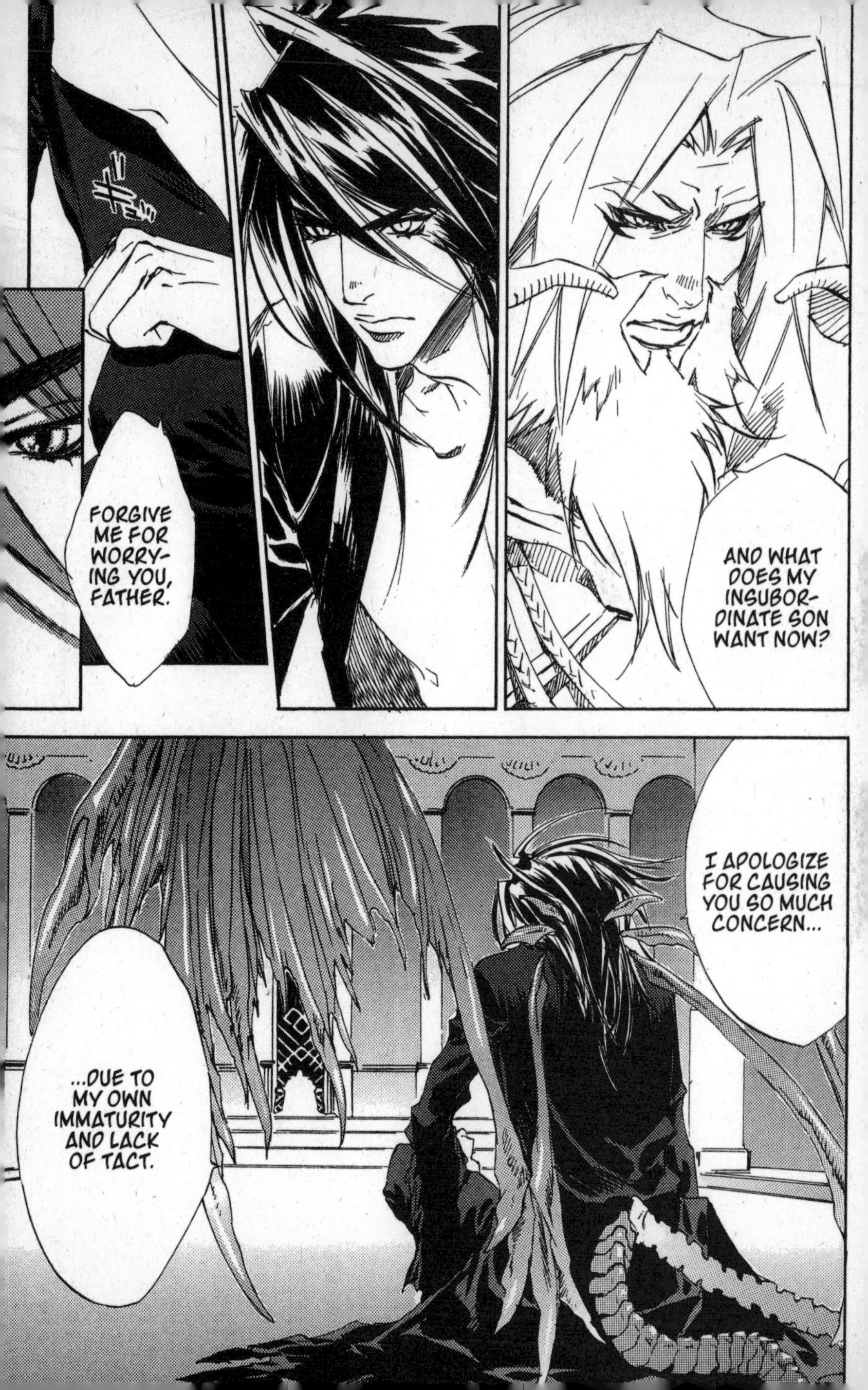
AND WHAT DOES MY INSUBOR-DINATE SON WANT NOW?
FORGIVE ME FOR WORRY-ING YOU, FATHER.
I APOLOGIZE FOR CAUSING YOU SO MUCH CONCERN...
...DUE TO MY OWN IMMATURITY AND LACK OF TACT.

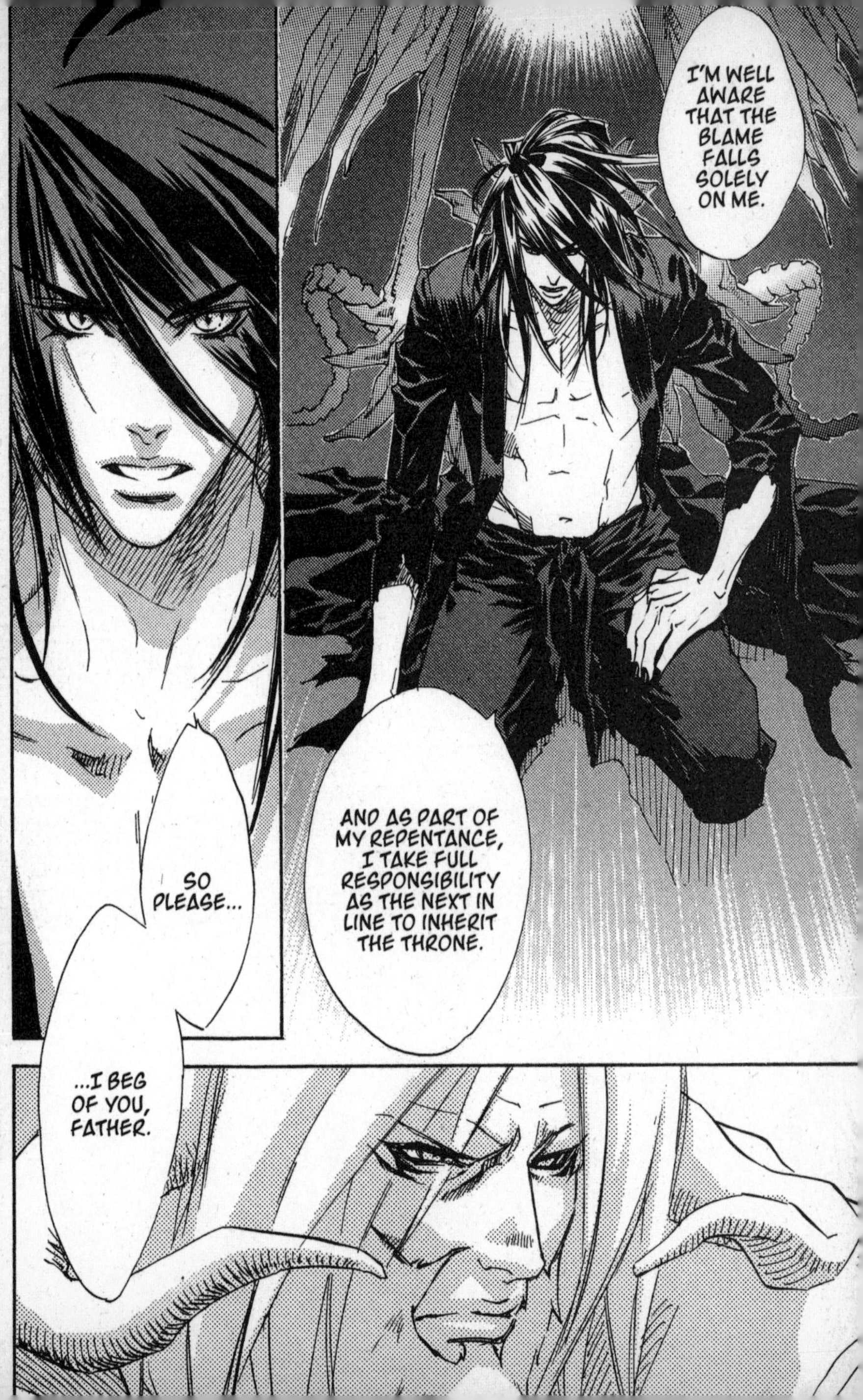
I'M WELL AWARE THAT THE BLAME FALLS SOLELY ON ME.
AND AS PART OF MY REPENTANCE, I TAKE FULL RESPONSIBILITY AS THE NEXT IN LINE TO INHERIT THE THRONE.
SO PLEASE...
...I BEG OF YOU, FATHER.

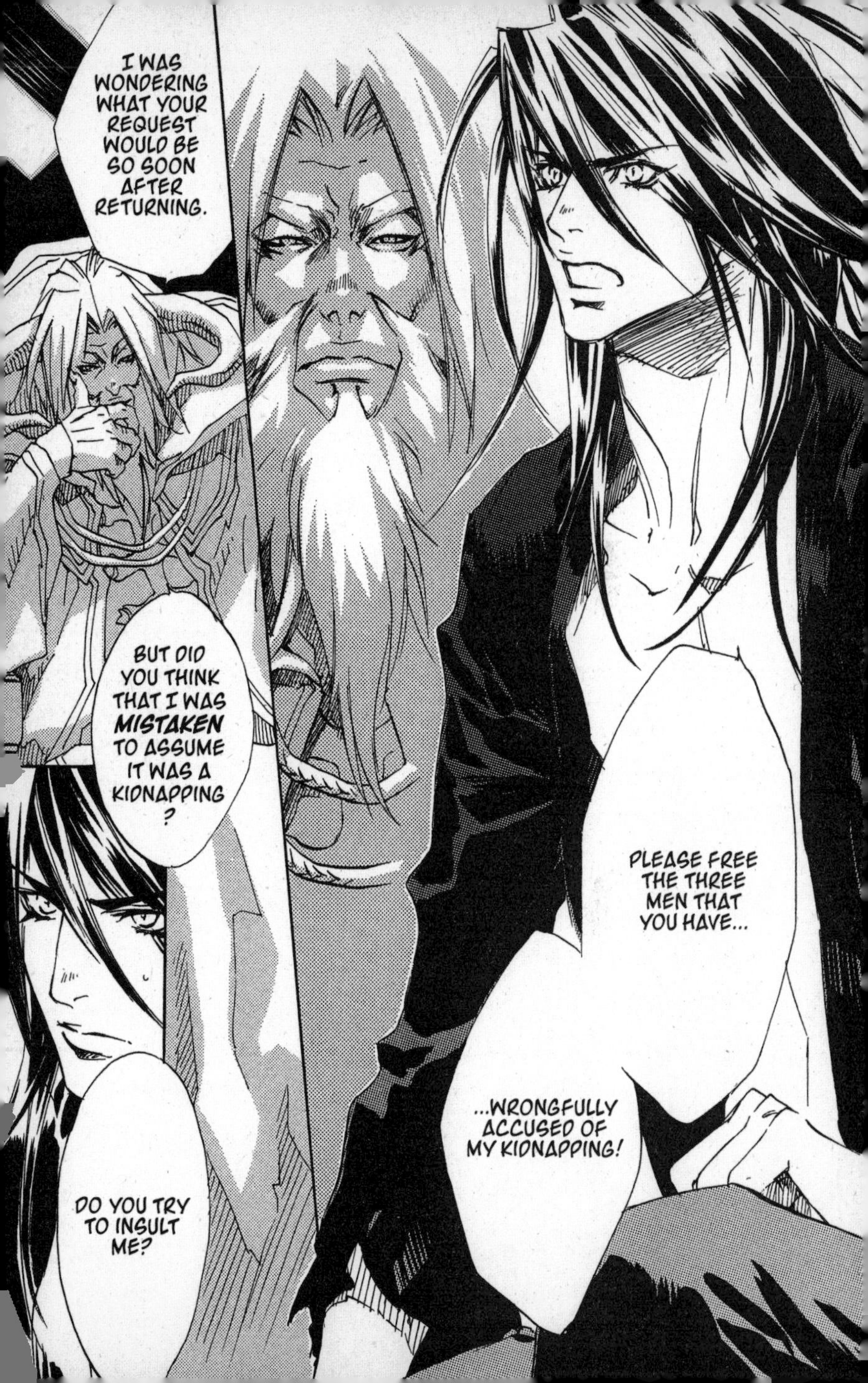
PLEASE FREE THE THREE MEN THAT YOU HAVE...
...WRONGFULLY ACCUSED OF MY KIDNAPPING!
I WAS WONDERING WHAT YOUR REQUEST WOULD BE SO SOON AFTER RETURNING.
BUT DID YOU THINK THAT I WAS **MISTAKEN** TO ASSUME IT WAS A KIDNAPPING?
DO YOU TRY TO INSULT ME?

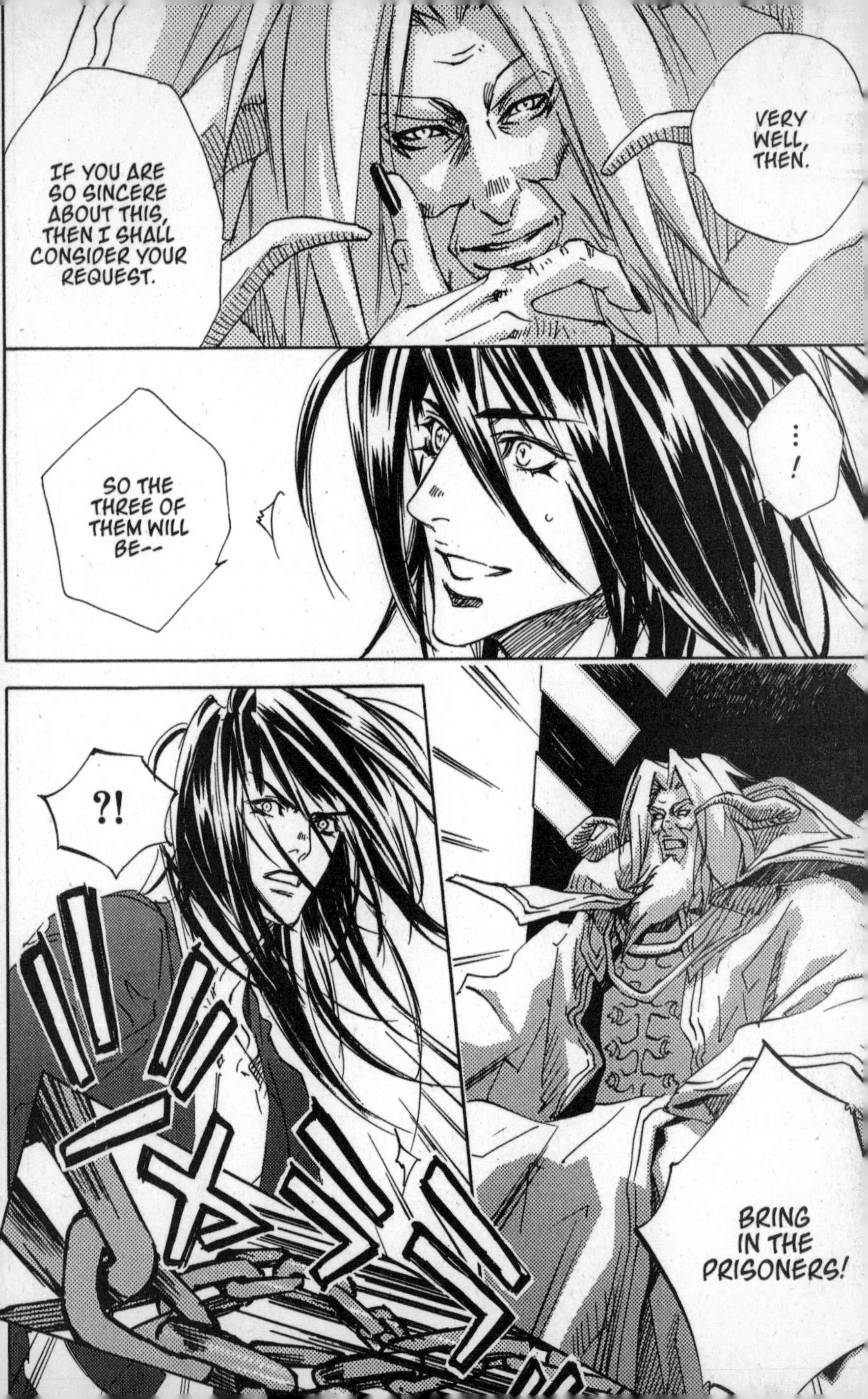
VERY WELL, THEN.
IF YOU ARE SO SINCERE ABOUT THIS, THEN I SHALL CONSIDER YOUR REQUEST.
...!
SO THE THREE OF THEM WILL BE--
BRING IN THE PRISONERS!
?!

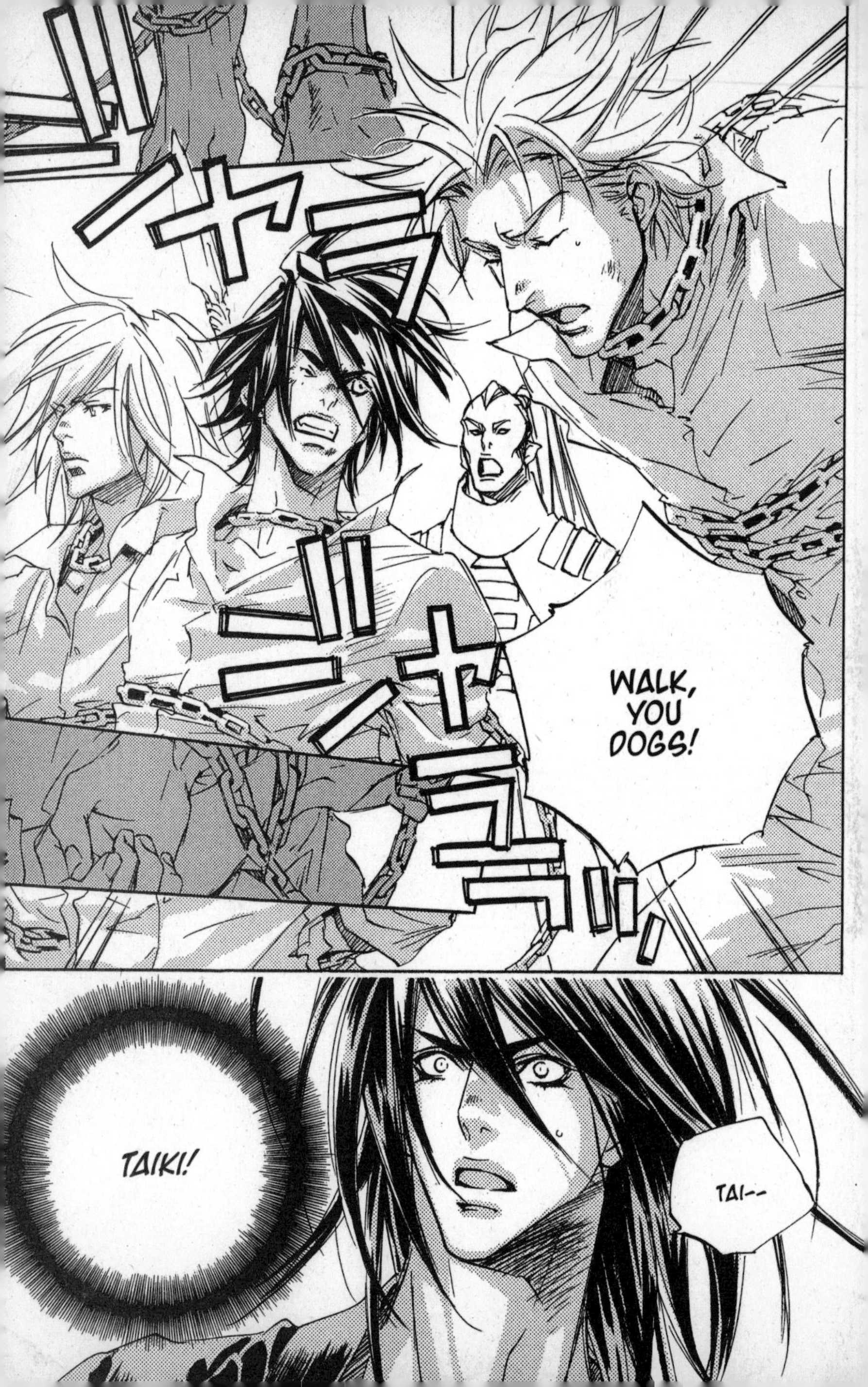
ジャラ
ジャララッ
WALK, YOU DOGS!
TAI--
TAIKI!

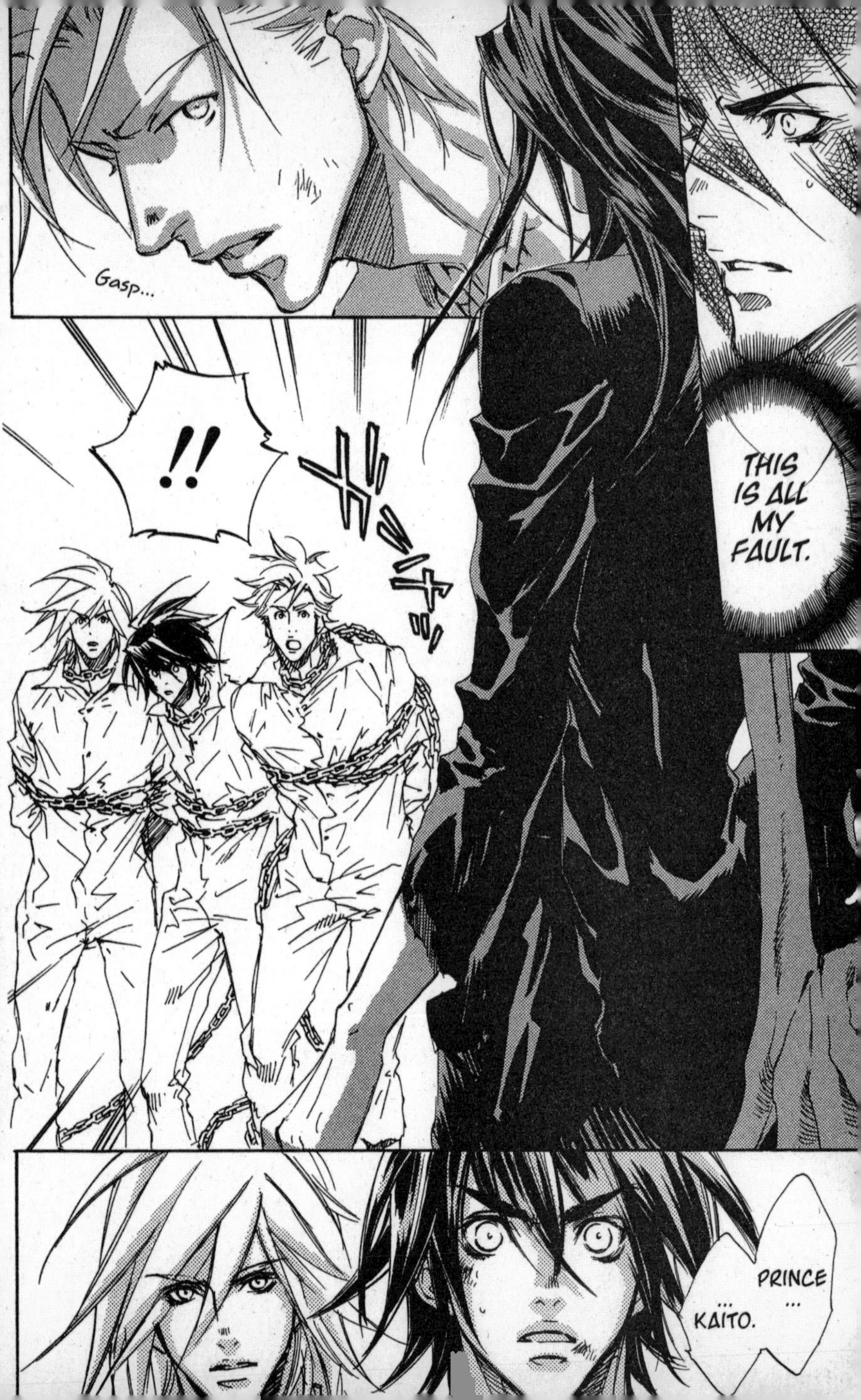
THIS IS ALL MY FAULT.
Gasp...
!!
PRINCE... ...KAITO.

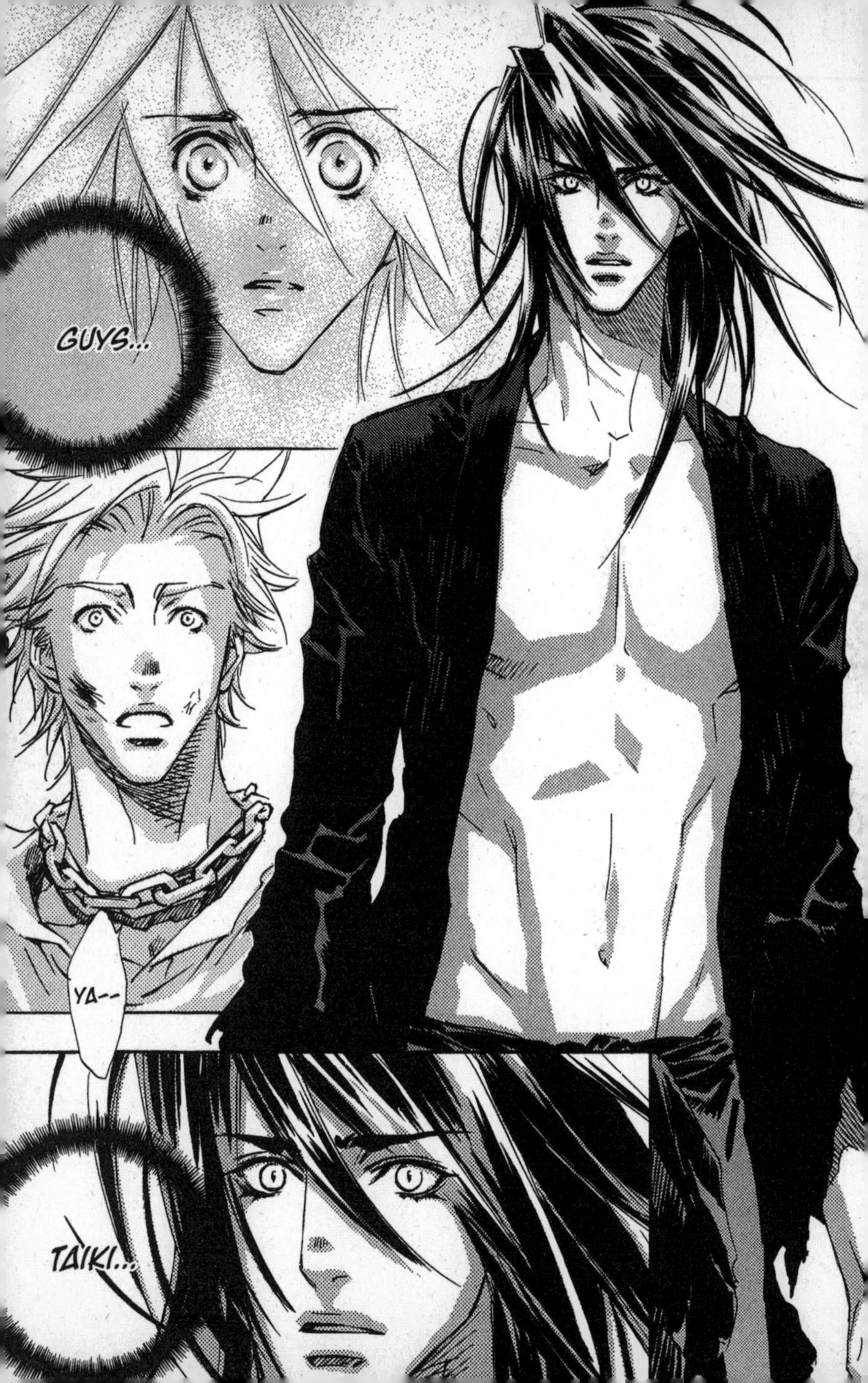
GUYS...
YA--
TAIKI...

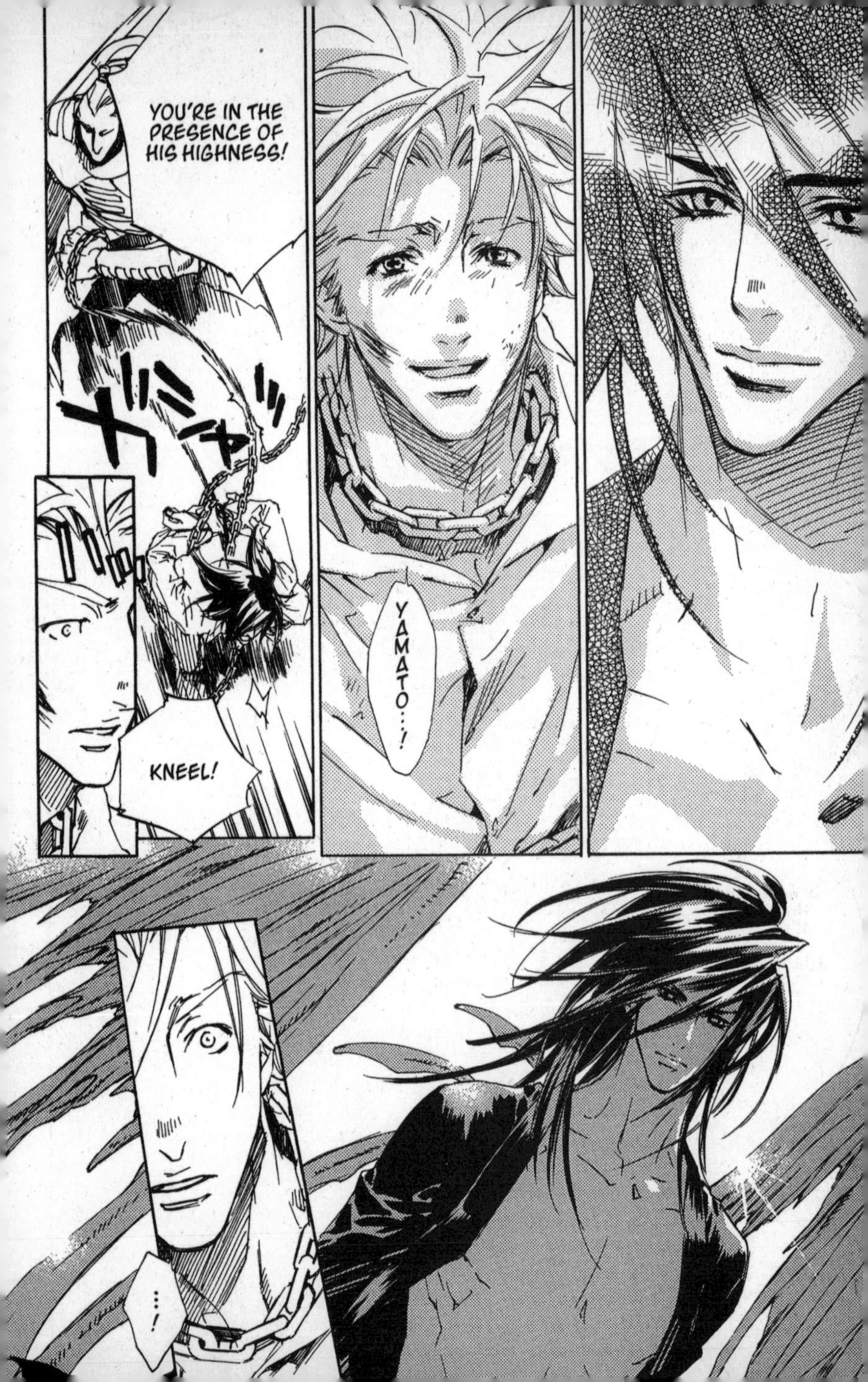
YAMATO...!
YOU'RE IN THE PRESENCE OF HIS HIGHNESS!
ガシャッ
KNEEL!
...!

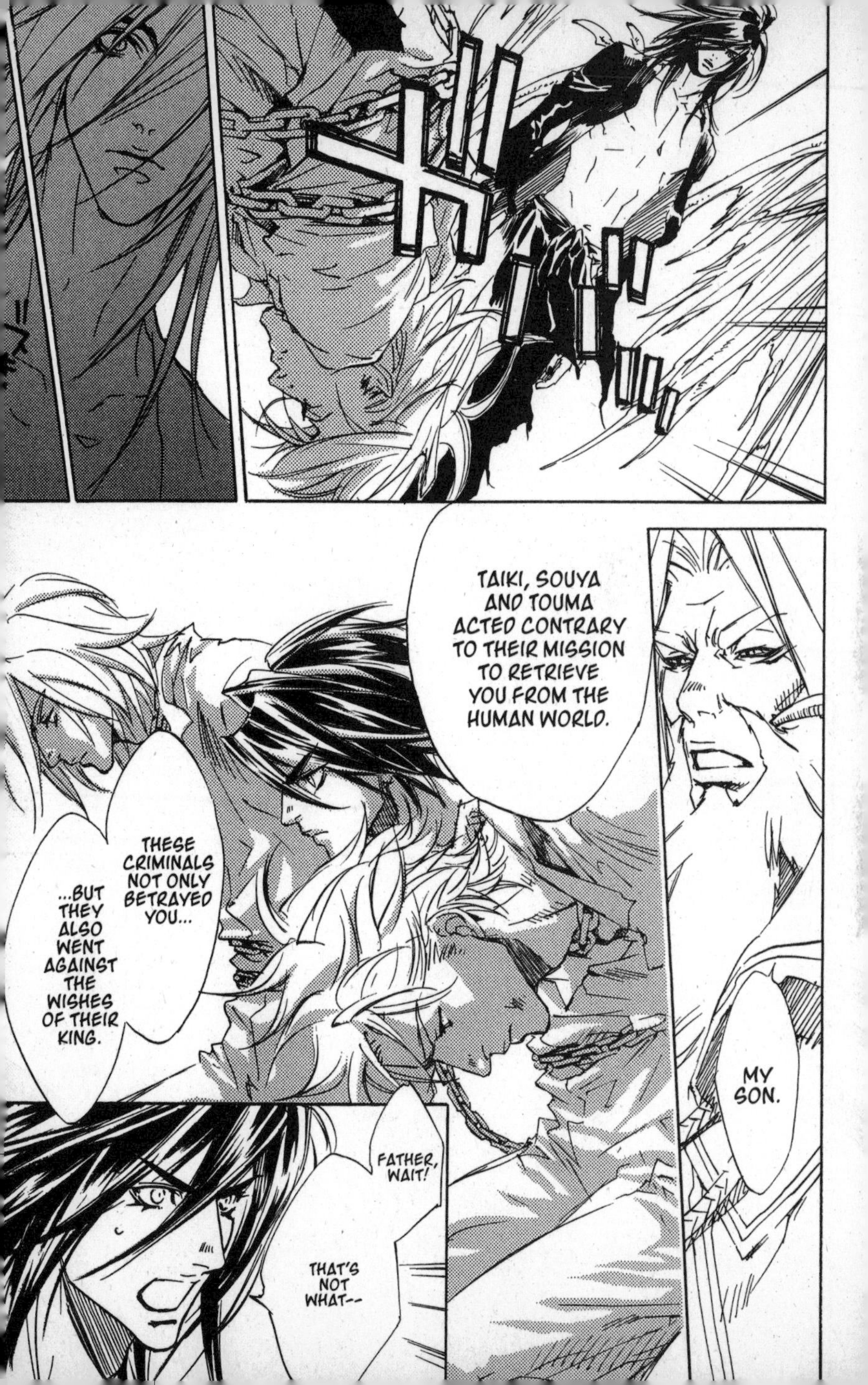
TAIKI, SOUYA AND TOUMA ACTED CONTRARY TO THEIR MISSION TO RETRIEVE YOU FROM THE HUMAN WORLD.
THESE CRIMINALS NOT ONLY BETRAYED YOU...
...BUT THEY ALSO WENT AGAINST THE WISHES OF THEIR KING.
MY SON.
FATHER, WAIT!
THAT'S NOT WHAT--

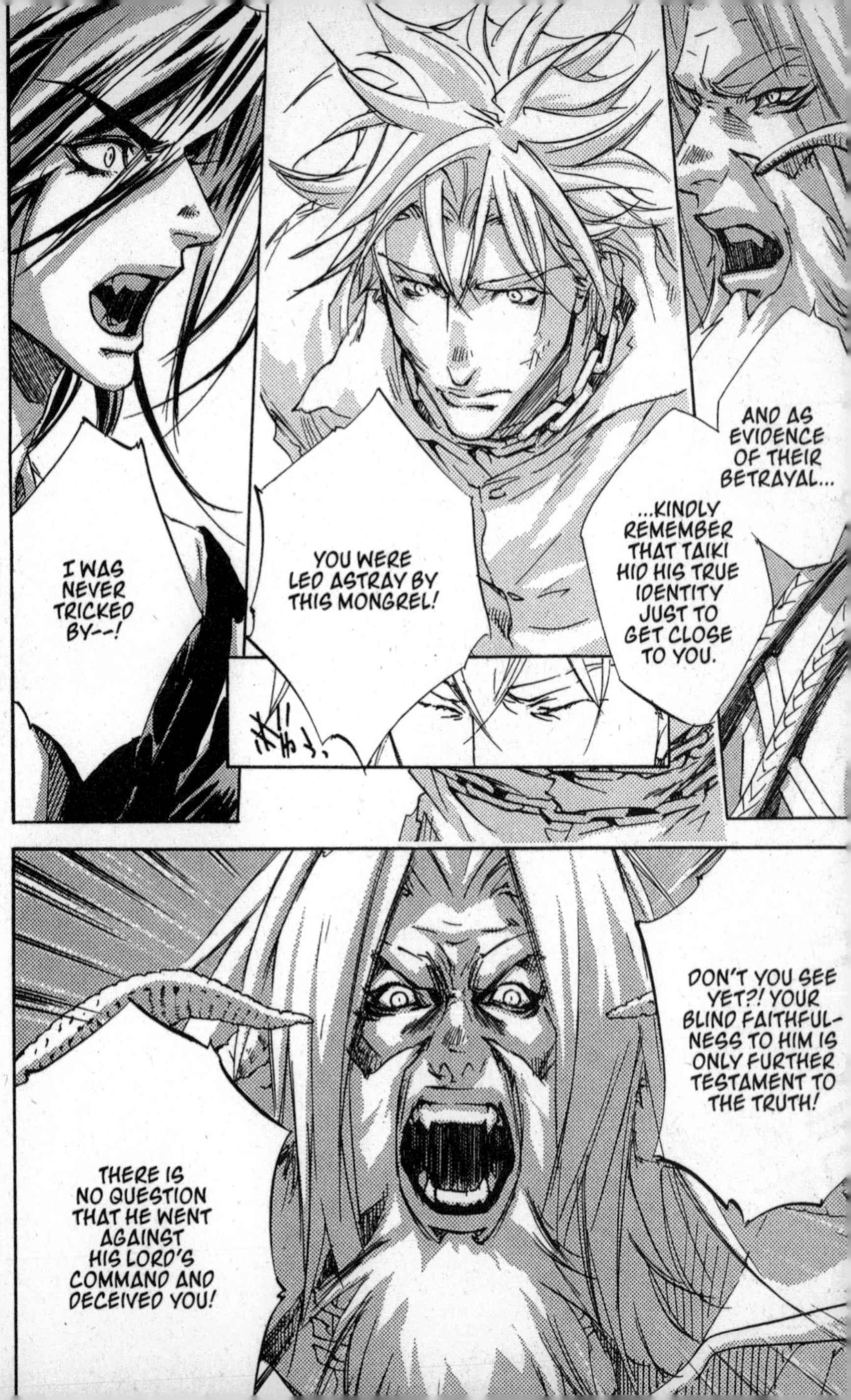
AND AS EVIDENCE OF THEIR BETRAYAL...
...KINDLY REMEMBER THAT TAIKI HID HIS TRUE IDENTITY JUST TO GET CLOSE TO YOU.
YOU WERE LED ASTRAY BY THIS MONGREL!
I WAS NEVER TRICKED BY--!
DON'T YOU SEE YET?! YOUR BLIND FAITHFUL-NESS TO HIM IS ONLY FURTHER TESTAMENT TO THE TRUTH!
THERE IS NO QUESTION THAT HE WENT AGAINST HIS LORD'S COMMAND AND DECEIVED YOU!

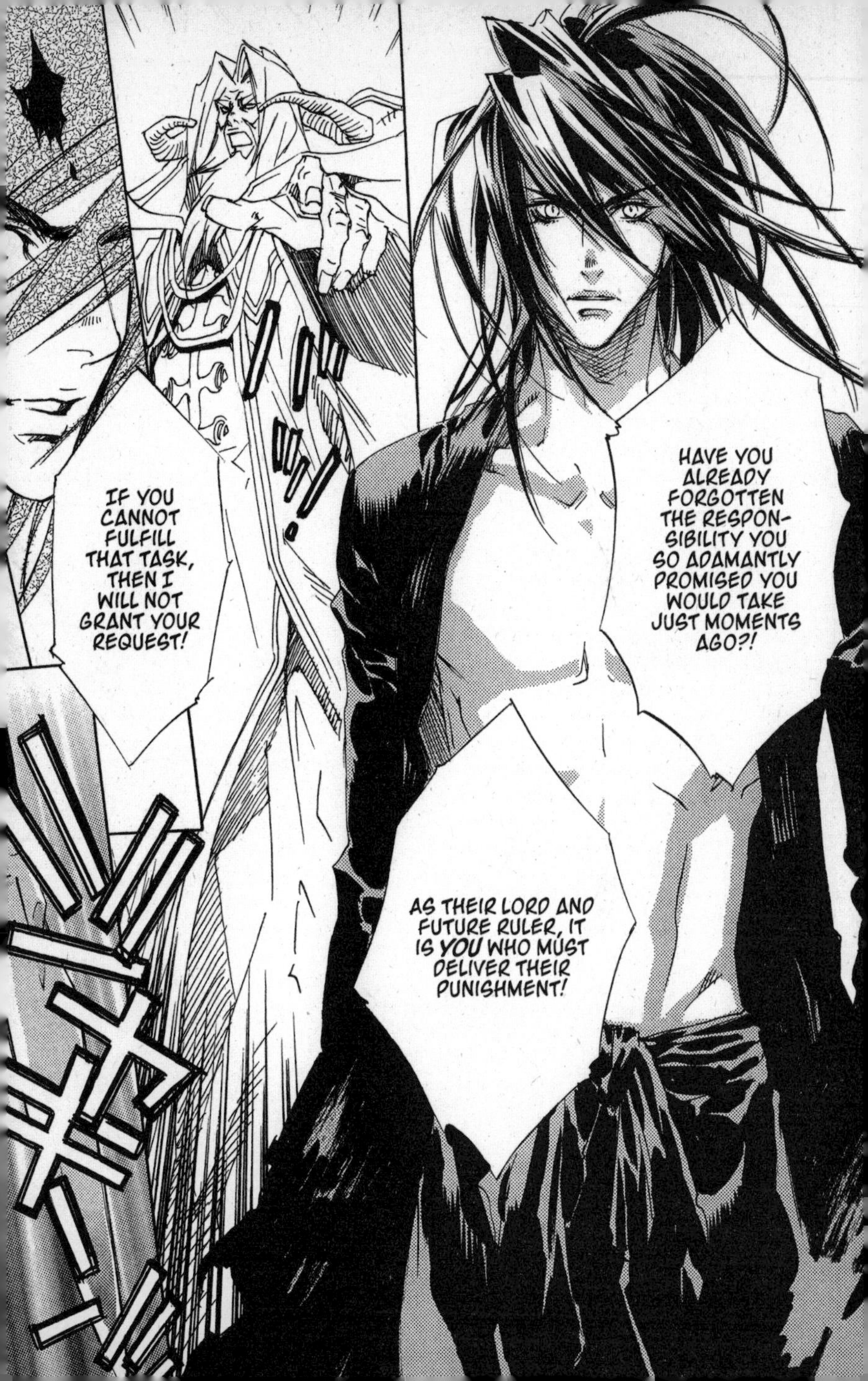
HAVE YOU ALREADY FORGOTTEN THE RESPON-SIBILITY YOU SO ADAMANTLY PROMISED YOU WOULD TAKE JUST MOMENTS AGO?!
AS THEIR LORD AND FUTURE RULER, IT IS *YOU* WHO MUST DELIVER THEIR PUNISHMENT!
IF YOU CANNOT FULFILL THAT TASK, THEN I WILL NOT GRANT YOUR REQUEST!

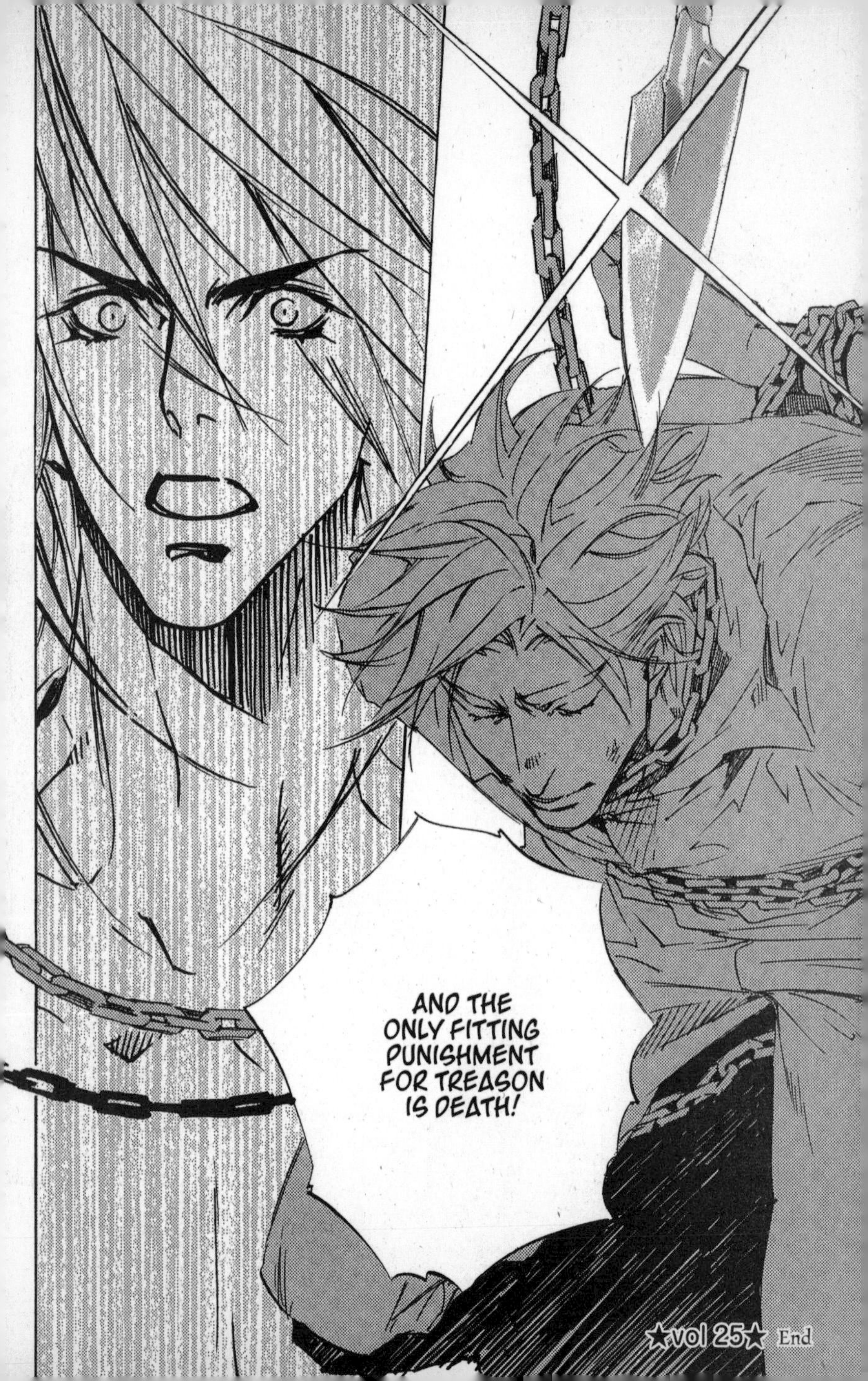
AND THE ONLY FITTING PUNISHMENT FOR TREASON IS DEATH!
★vol 25★ End

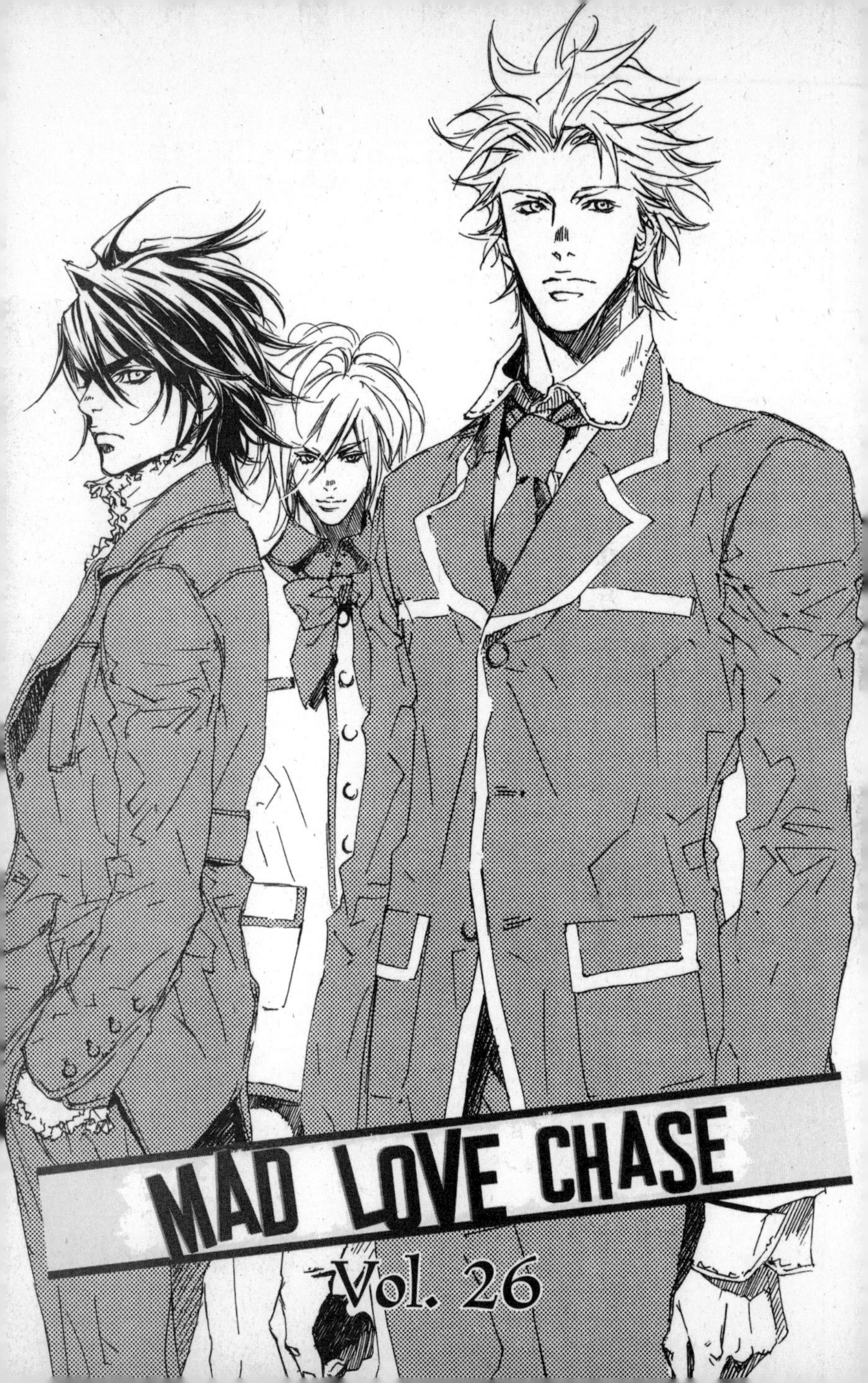
MAD LOVE CHASE
Vol. 26

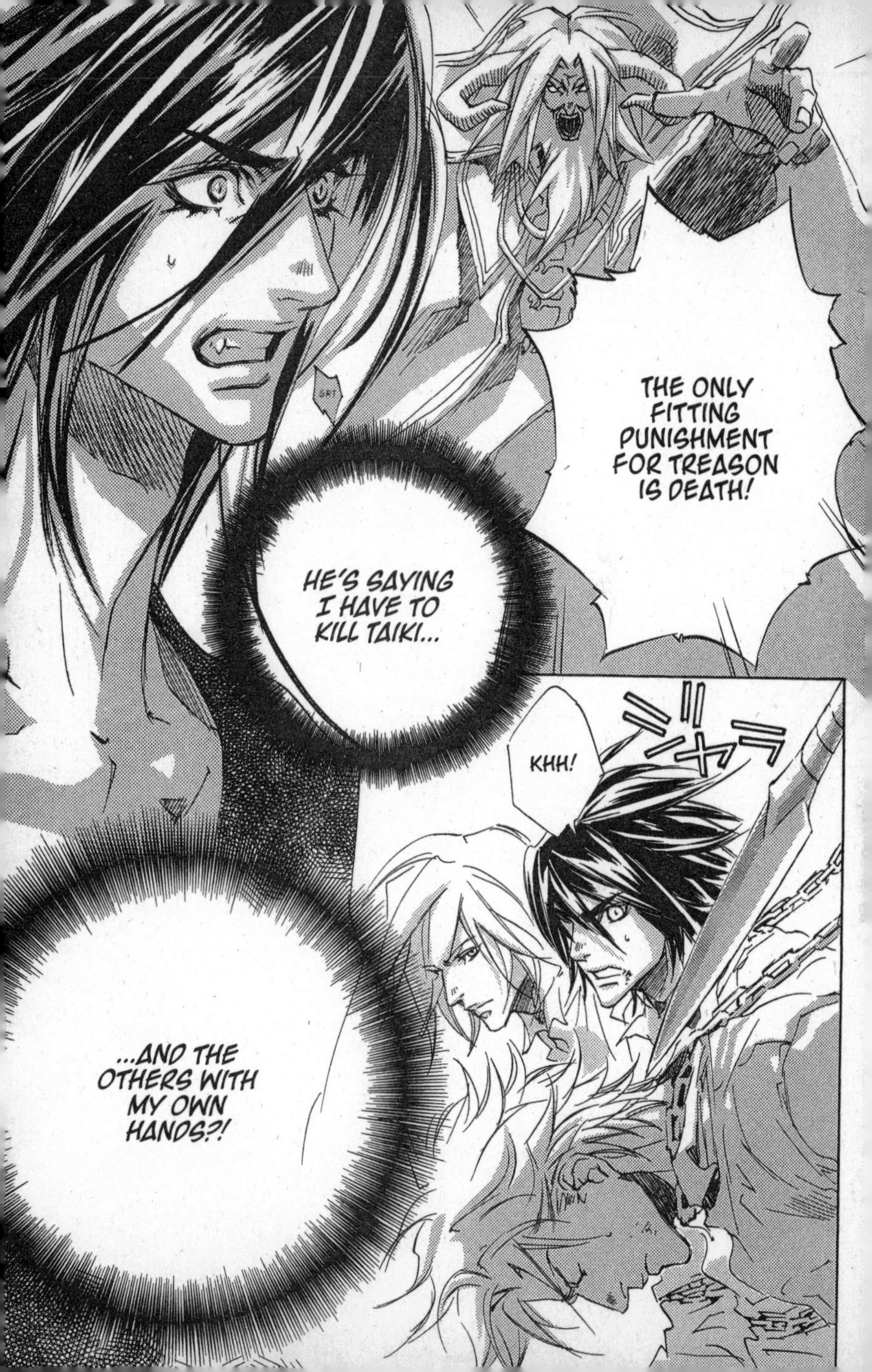
THE ONLY FITTING PUNISHMENT FOR TREASON IS DEATH!
GRT
HE'S SAYING I HAVE TO KILL TAIKI...
KHH!
...AND THE OTHERS WITH MY OWN HANDS?!

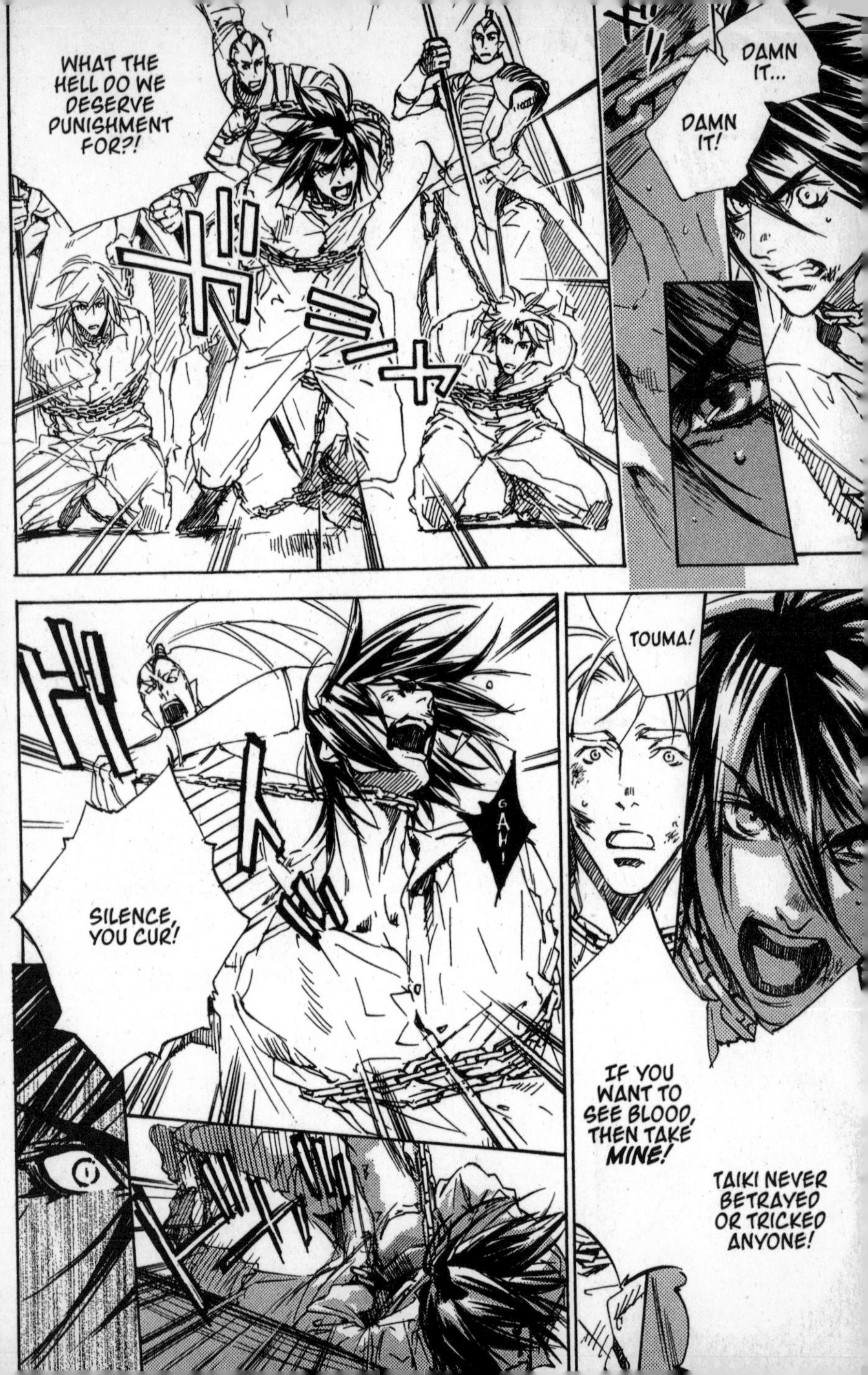
DAMN IT...
DAMN IT!
WHAT THE HELL DO WE DESERVE PUNISHMENT FOR?!
TOUMA!
IF YOU WANT TO SEE BLOOD, THEN TAKE MINE!
TAIKI NEVER BETRAYED OR TRICKED ANYONE!
SILENCE, YOU CUR!
GAH!

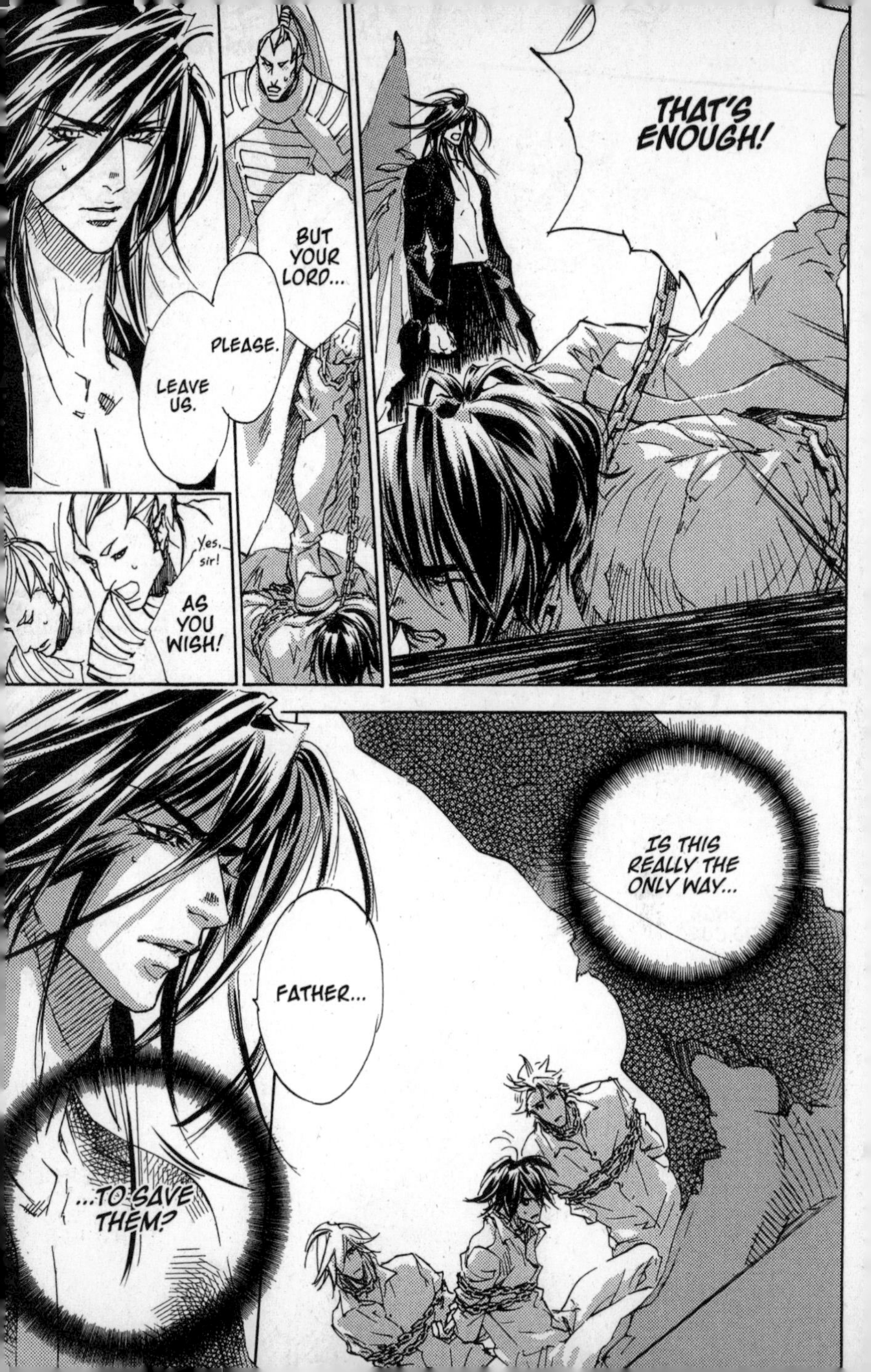

THAT'S ENOUGH!
BUT YOUR LORD...
PLEASE.
LEAVE US.
AS YOU WISH!
Yes, sir!
IS THIS REALLY THE ONLY WAY...
FATHER...
...TO SAVE THEM?

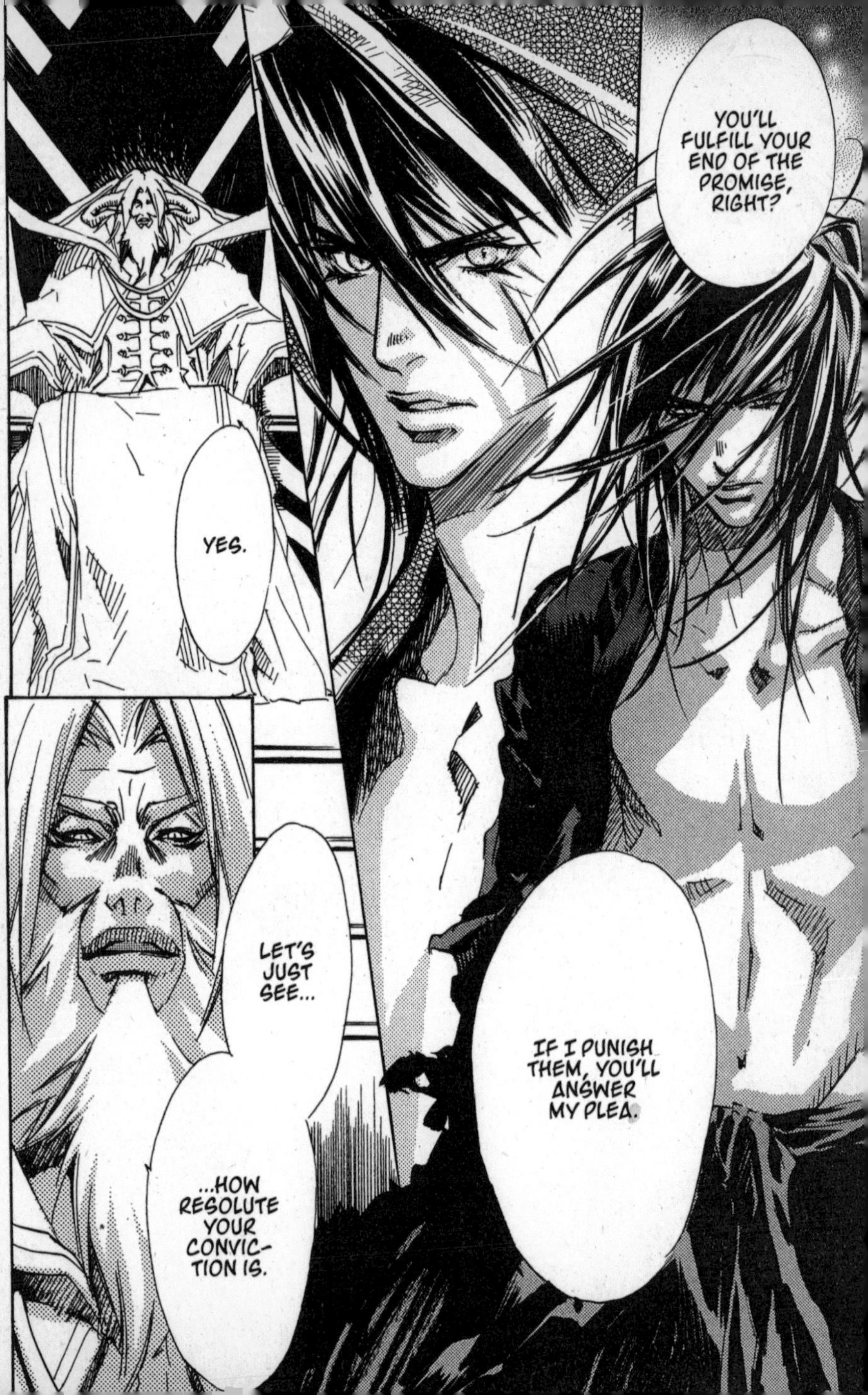
YOU'LL FULFILL YOUR END OF THE PROMISE, RIGHT?
IF I PUNISH THEM, YOU'LL ANSWER MY PLEA.
YES.
LET'S JUST SEE...
...HOW RESOLUTE YOUR CONVICTION IS.

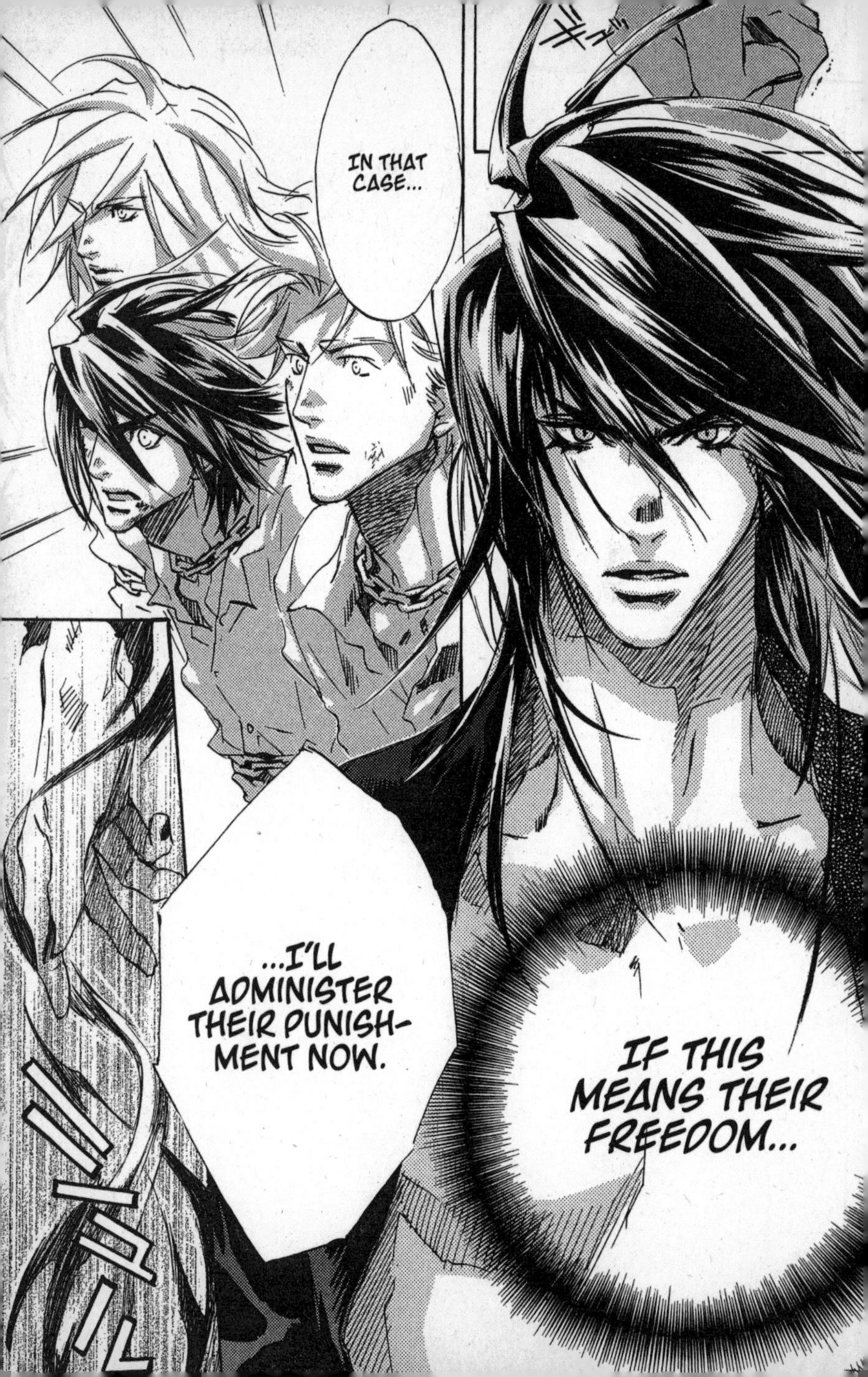
IN THAT CASE...
IF THIS MEANS THEIR FREEDOM...
...I'LL ADMINISTER THEIR PUNISHMENT NOW.

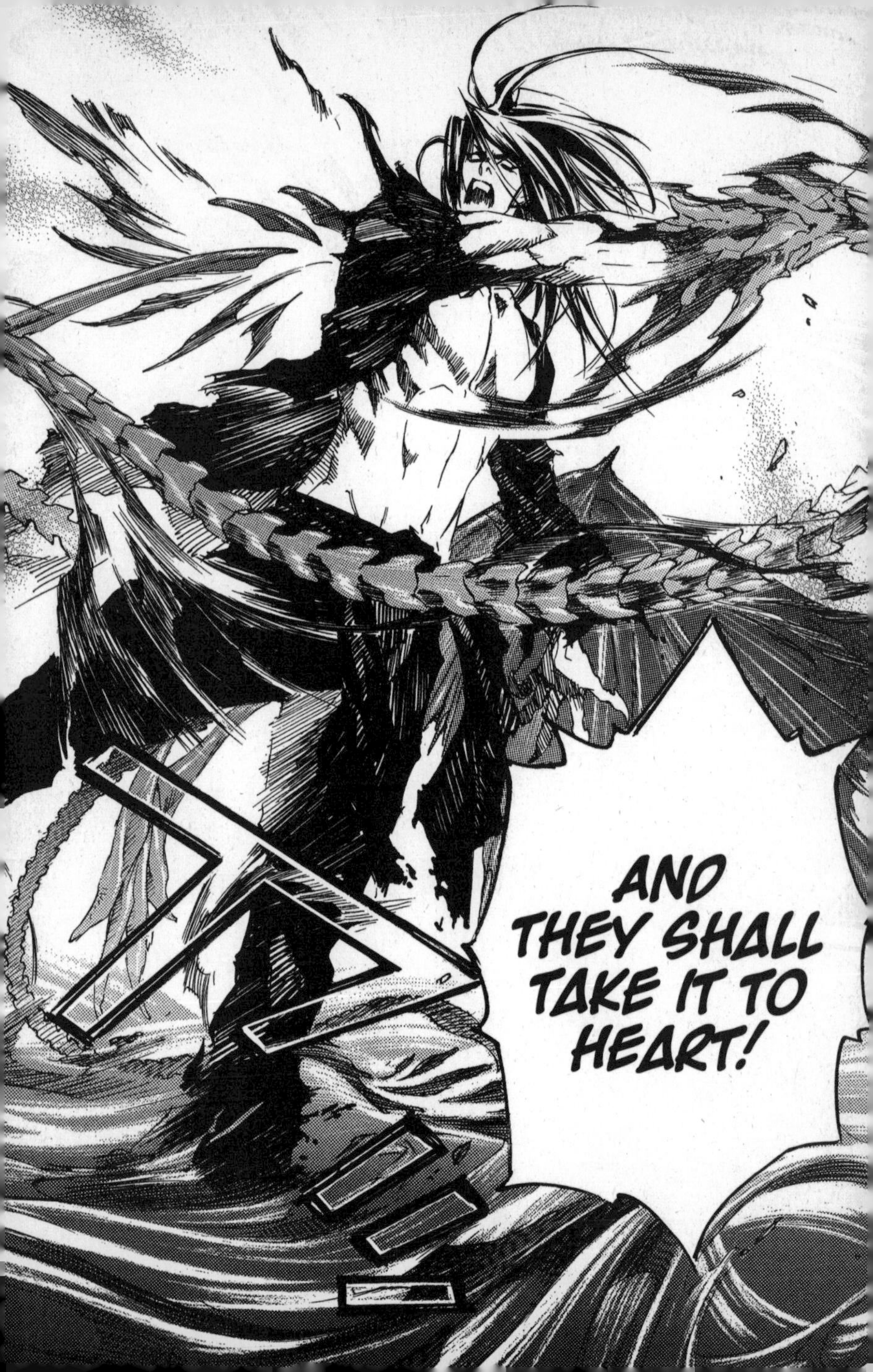
AND THEY SHALL TAKE IT TO HEART!

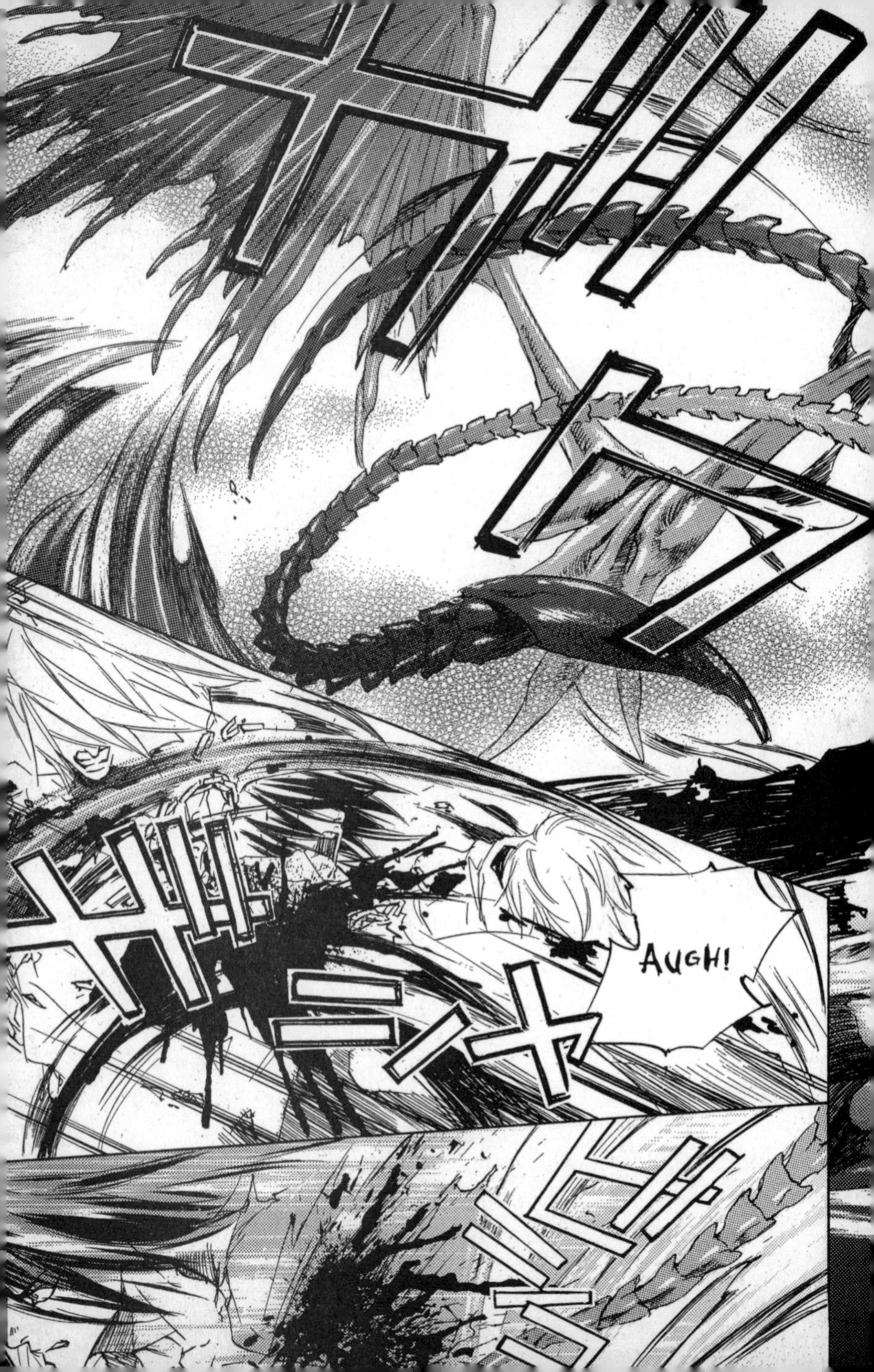
AUGH!

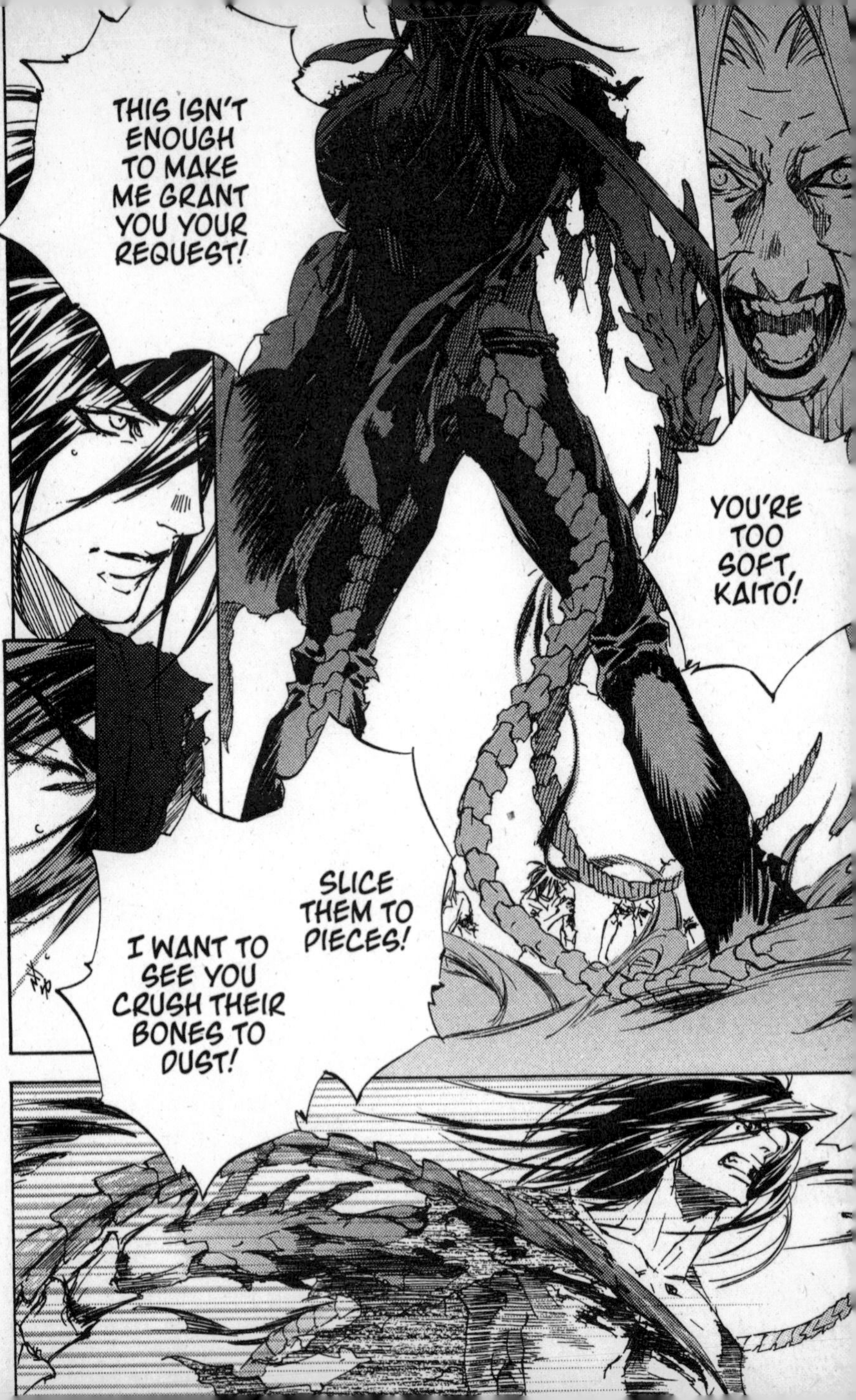
THIS ISN'T ENOUGH TO MAKE ME GRANT YOU YOUR REQUEST!
YOU'RE TOO SOFT, KAITO!
SLICE THEM TO PIECES!
I WANT TO SEE YOU CRUSH THEIR BONES TO DUST!

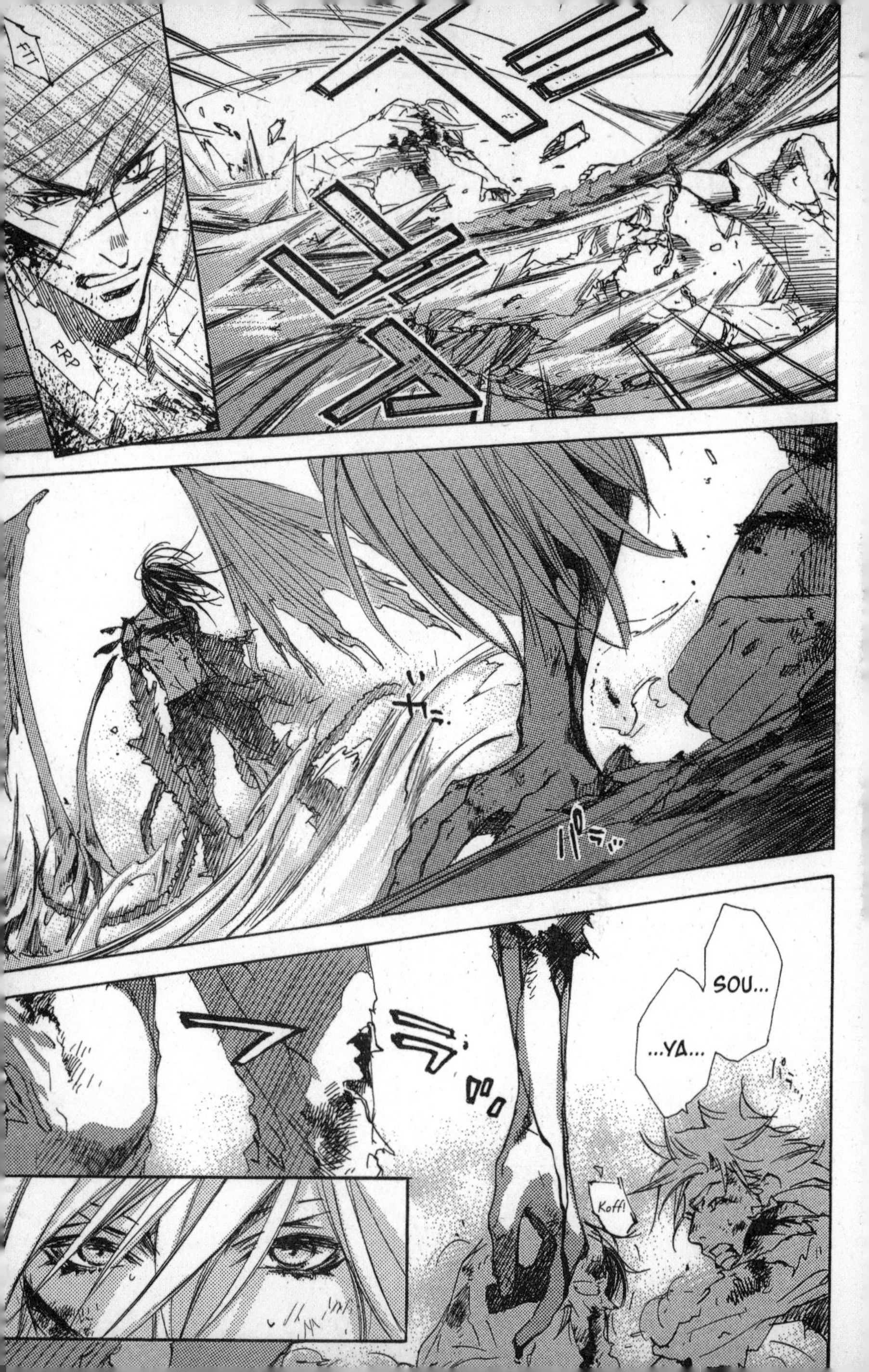
FIT
RRP
SOU...
...YA...
Koff!

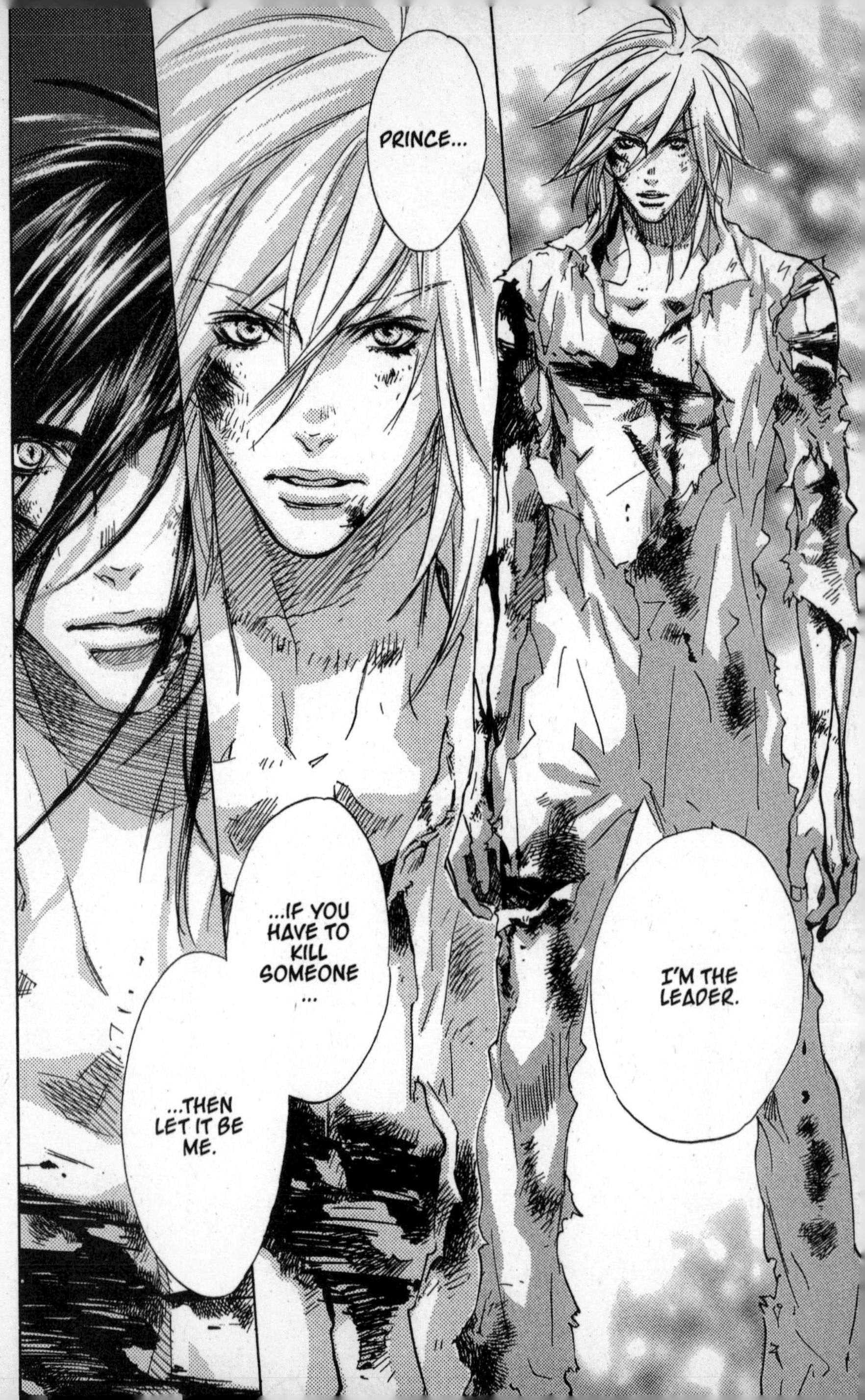
I'M THE LEADER.
PRINCE...
...IF YOU HAVE TO KILL SOMEONE ...
...THEN LET IT BE ME.

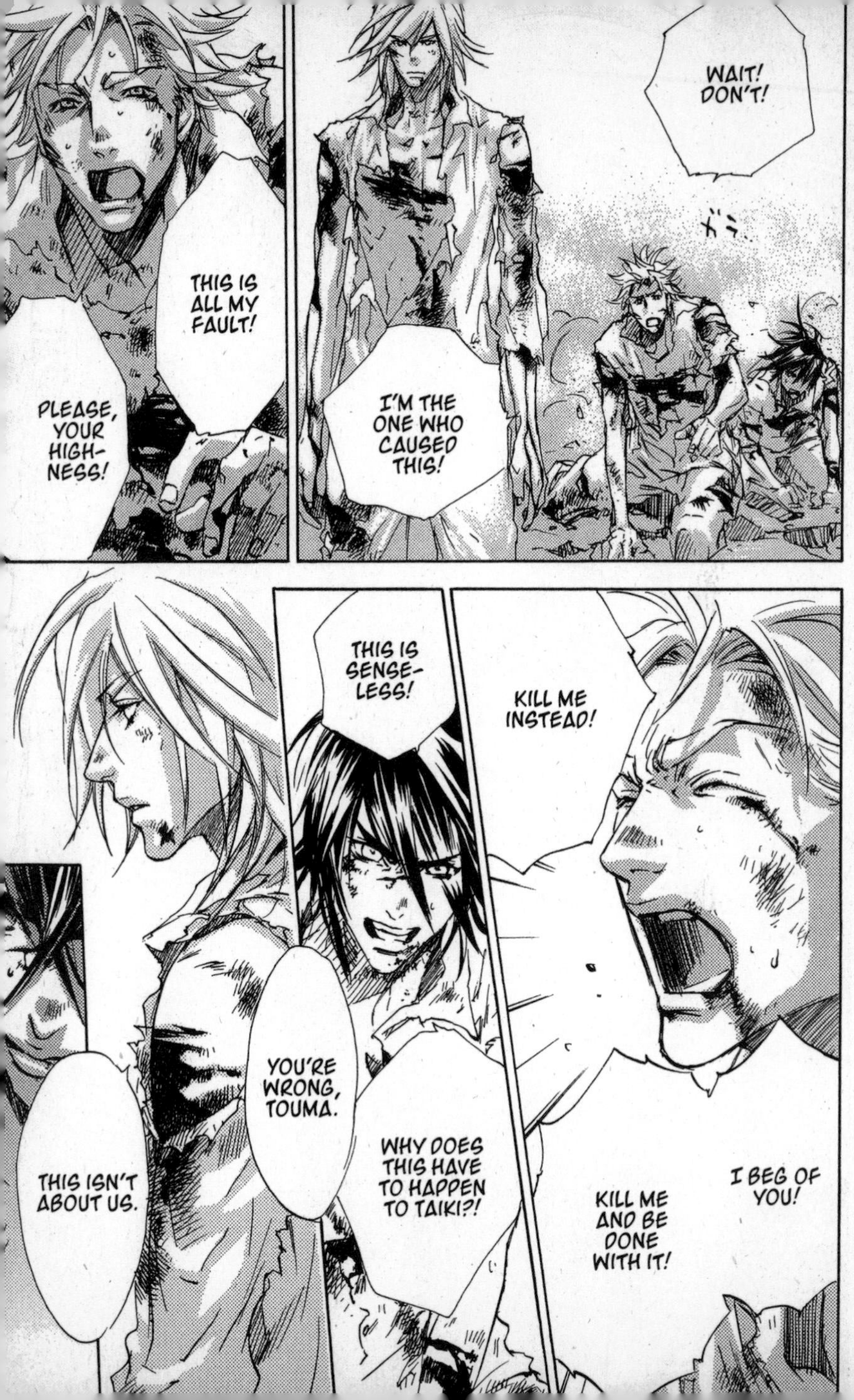
WAIT! DON'T!
ガラ...
I'M THE ONE WHO CAUSED THIS!
THIS IS ALL MY FAULT!
PLEASE, YOUR HIGH-NESS!
KILL ME INSTEAD!
I BEG OF YOU!
KILL ME AND BE DONE WITH IT!
THIS IS SENSE-LESS!
WHY DOES THIS HAVE TO HAPPEN TO TAIKI?!
YOU'RE WRONG, TOUMA.
THIS ISN'T ABOUT US.

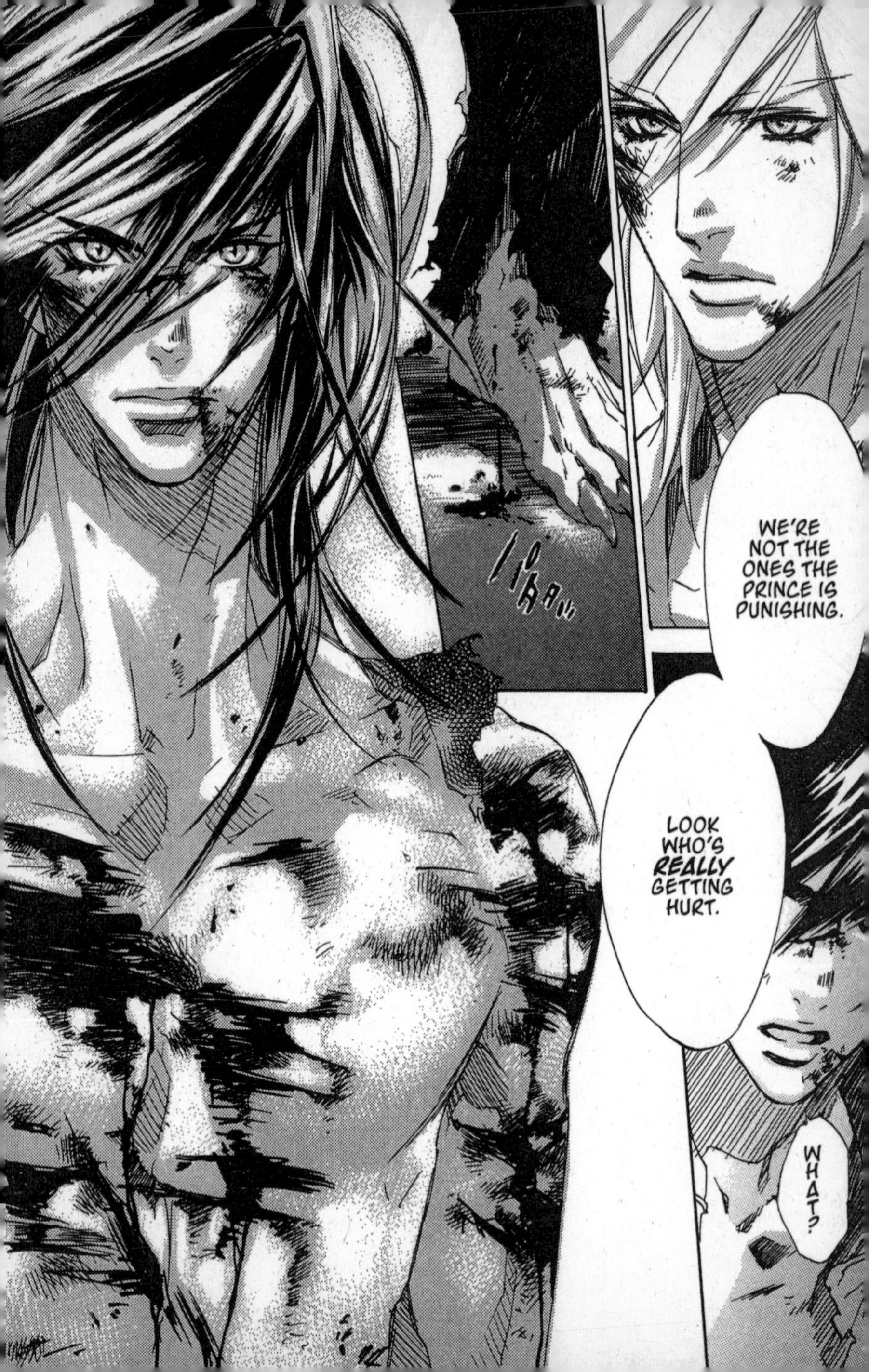
WE'RE NOT THE ONES THE PRINCE IS PUNISHING.
LOOK WHO'S *REALLY* GETTING HURT.
WHAT?

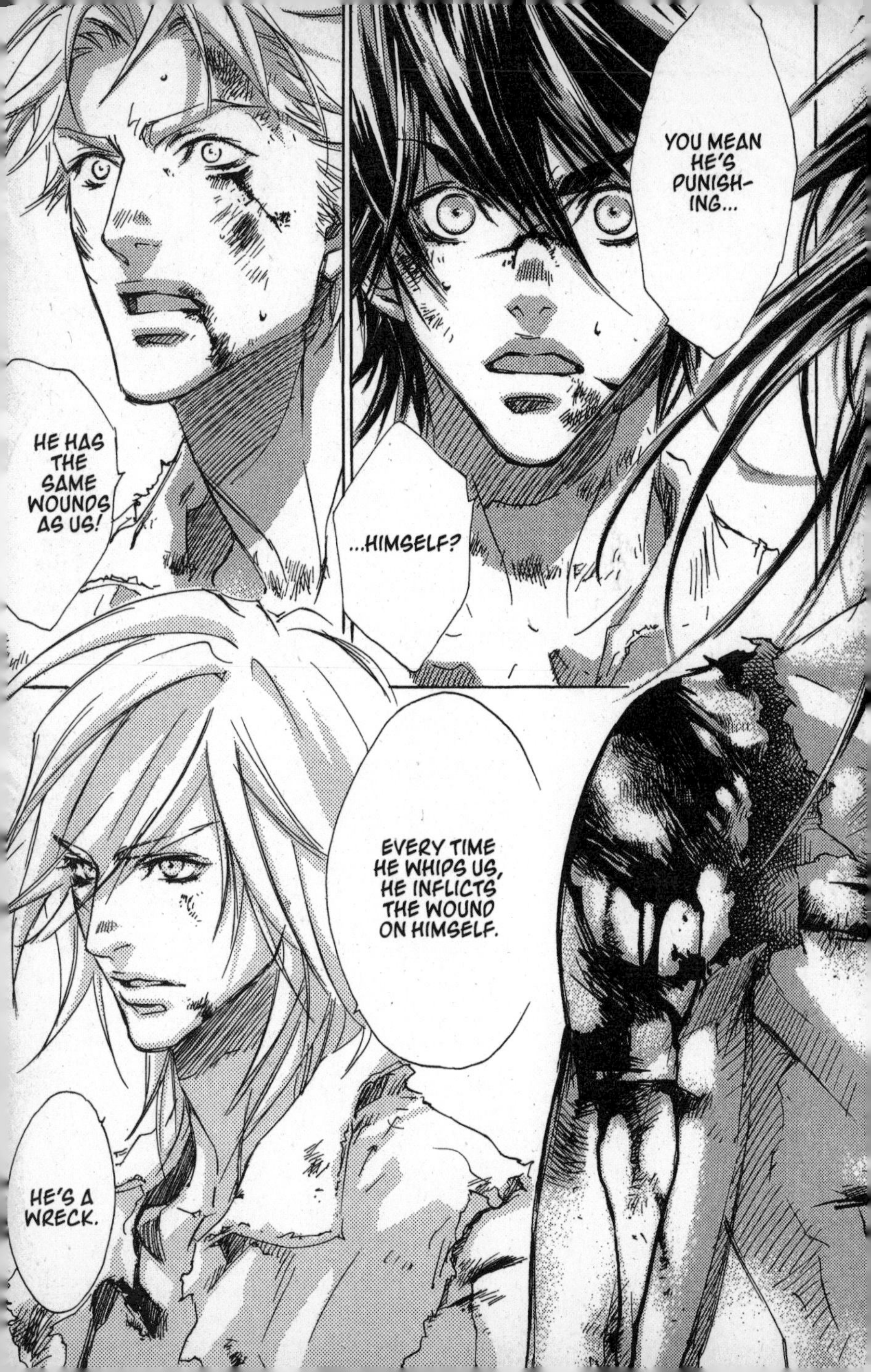
YOU MEAN HE'S PUNISHING...
...HIMSELF?
HE HAS THE SAME WOUNDS AS US!
EVERY TIME HE WHIPS US, HE INFLICTS THE WOUND ON HIMSELF.
HE'S A WRECK.

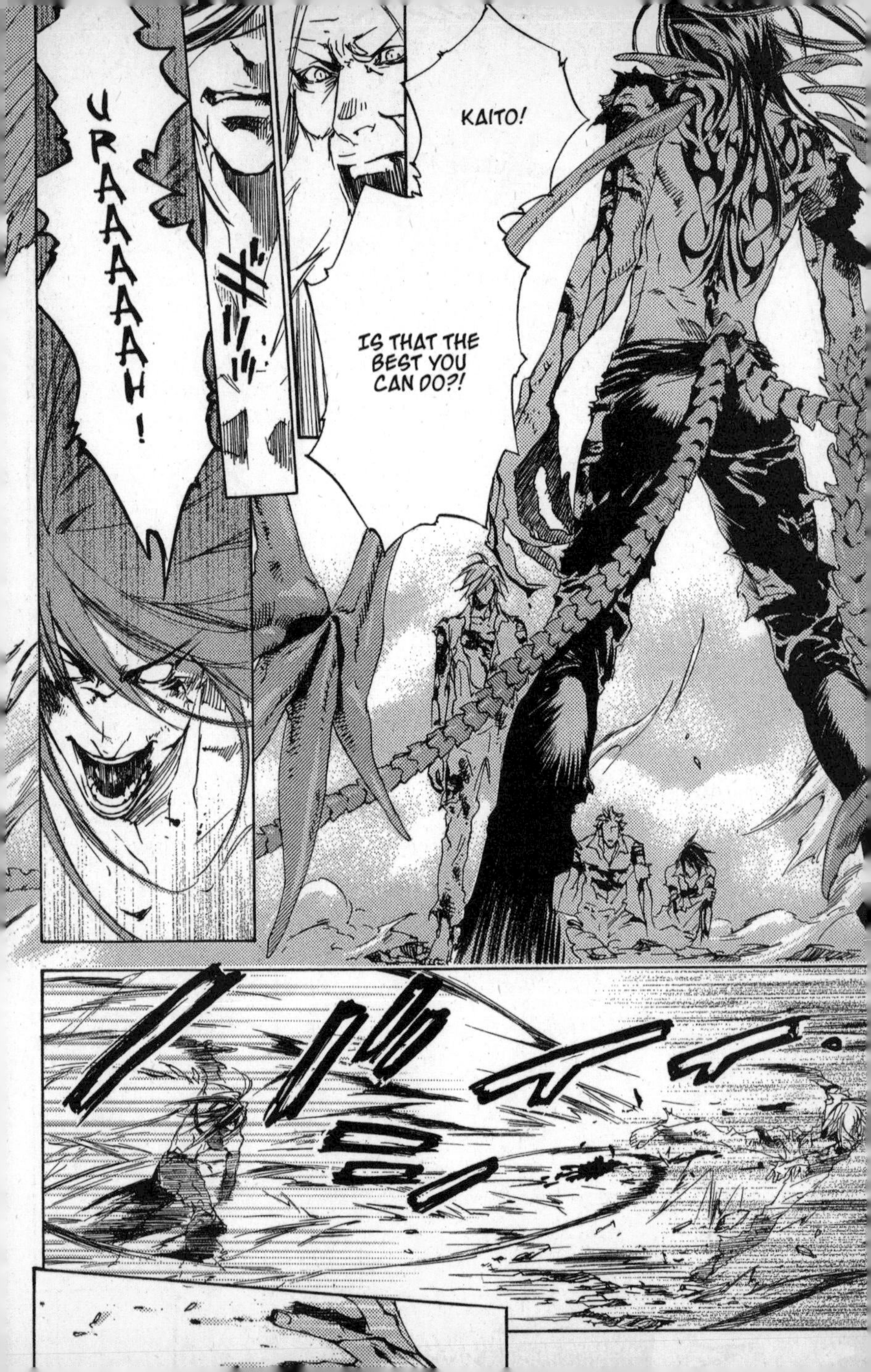
KAITO!
IS THAT THE BEST YOU CAN DO?!
URAAAAAAH!

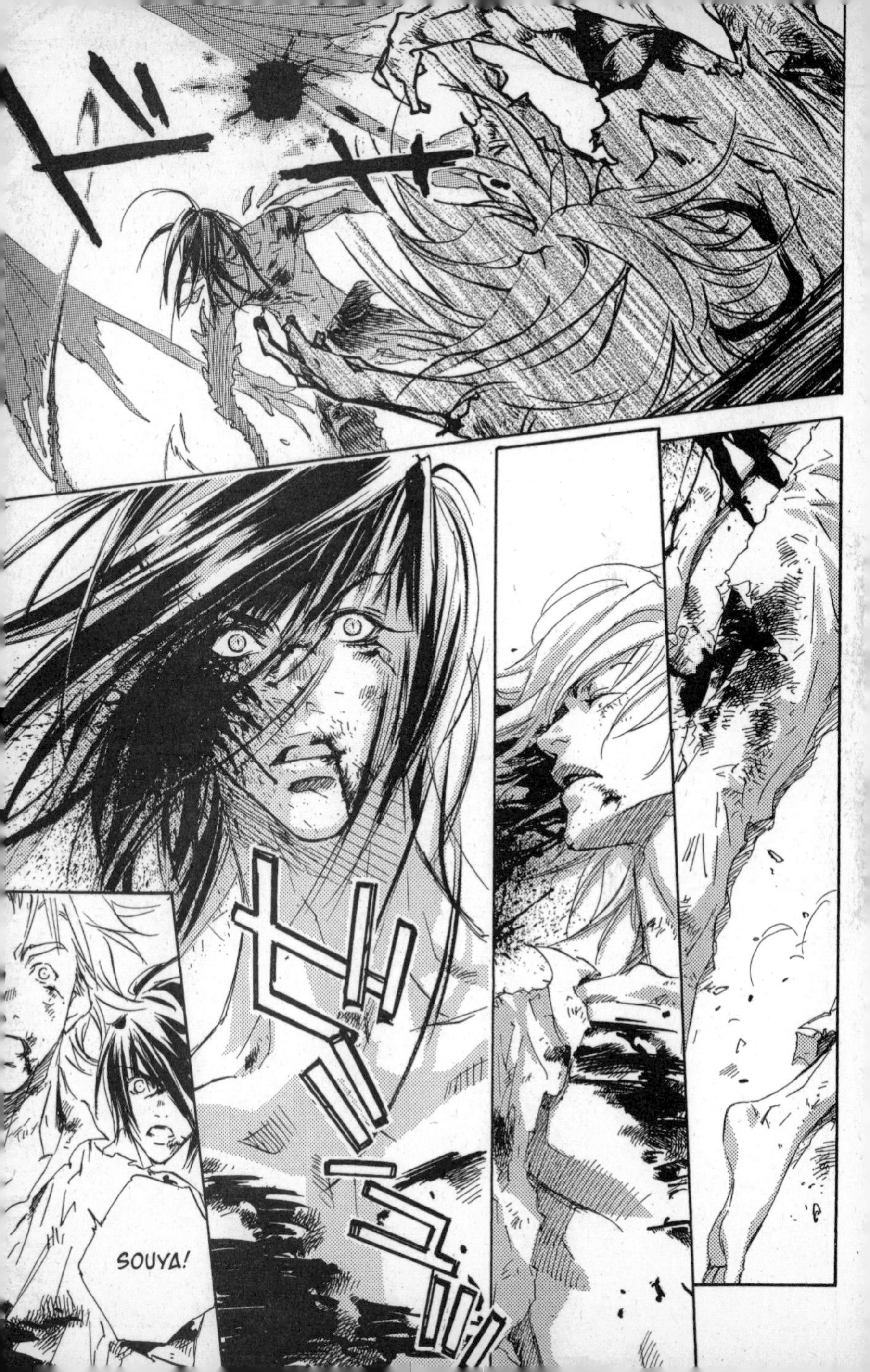
SOUYA!

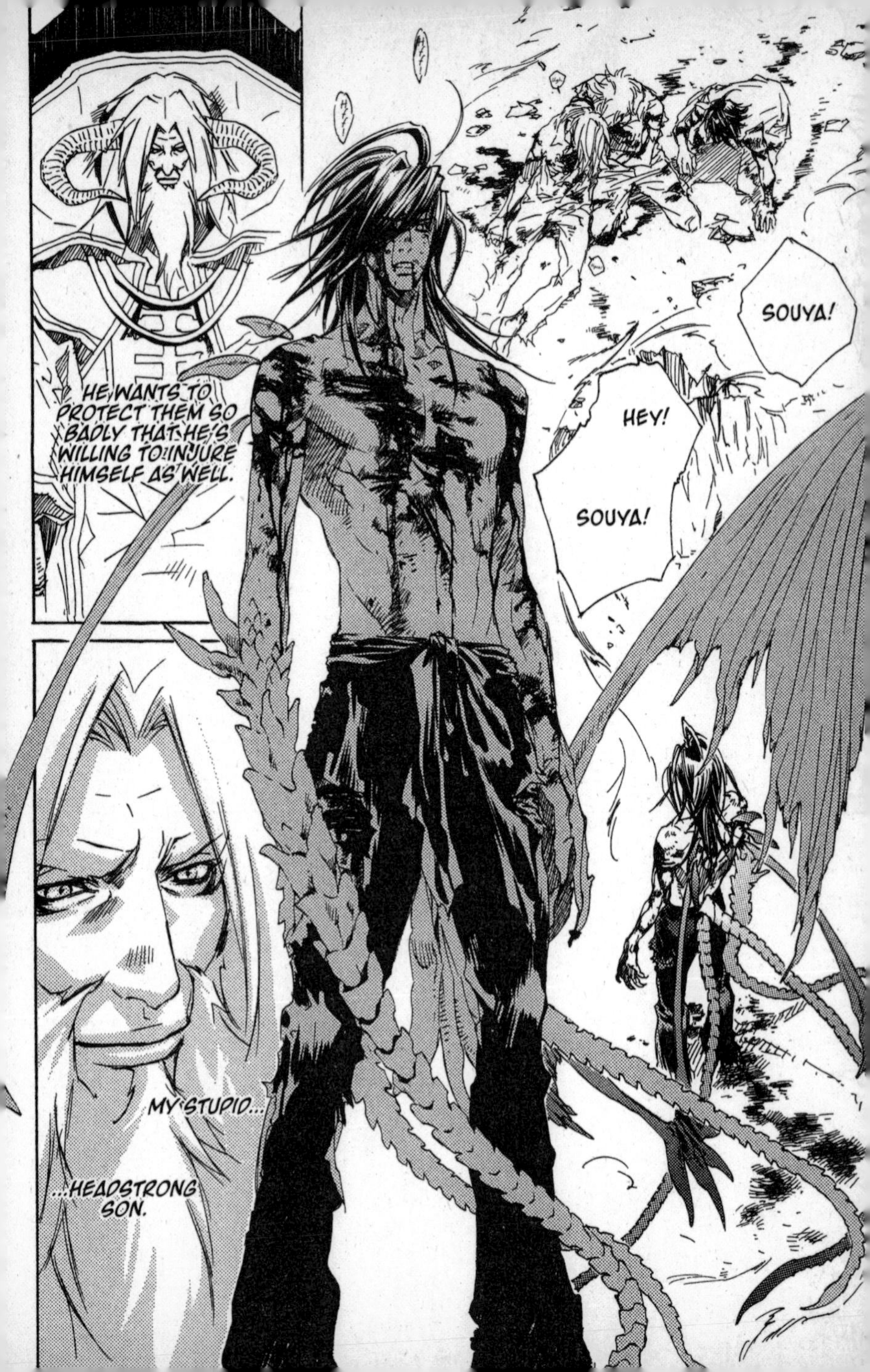
SOUYA!
HEY!
SOUYA!
SOUYA!
HE WANTS TO PROTECT THEM SO BADLY THAT HE'S WILLING TO INJURE HIMSELF AS WELL.
MY STUPID...
...HEADSTRONG SON.

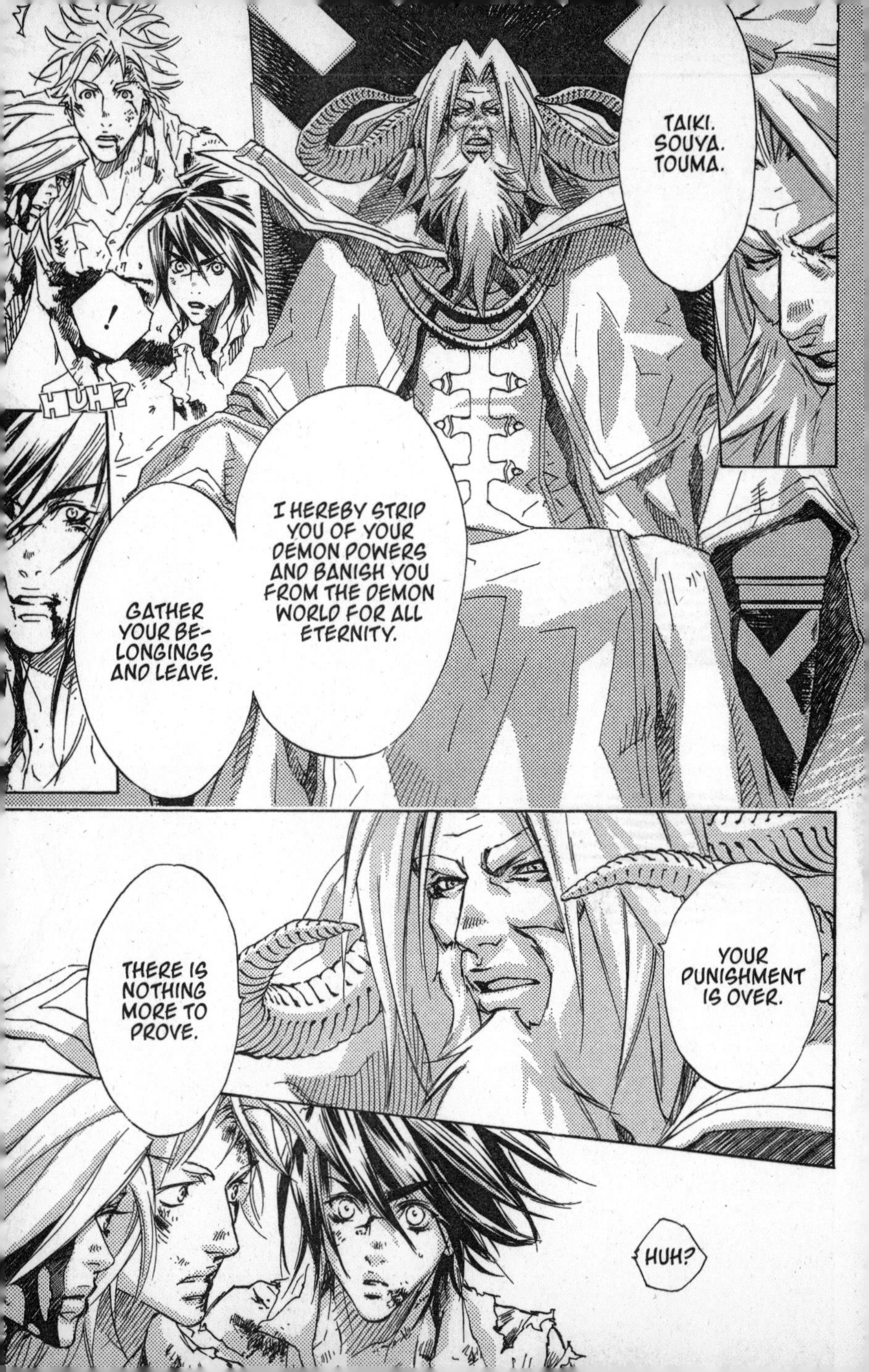
TAIKI. SOUYA. TOUMA.
I HEREBY STRIP YOU OF YOUR DEMON POWERS AND BANISH YOU FROM THE DEMON WORLD FOR ALL ETERNITY.
GATHER YOUR BE-LONGINGS AND LEAVE.
!
HUH?
YOUR PUNISHMENT IS OVER.
THERE IS NOTHING MORE TO PROVE.
HUH?

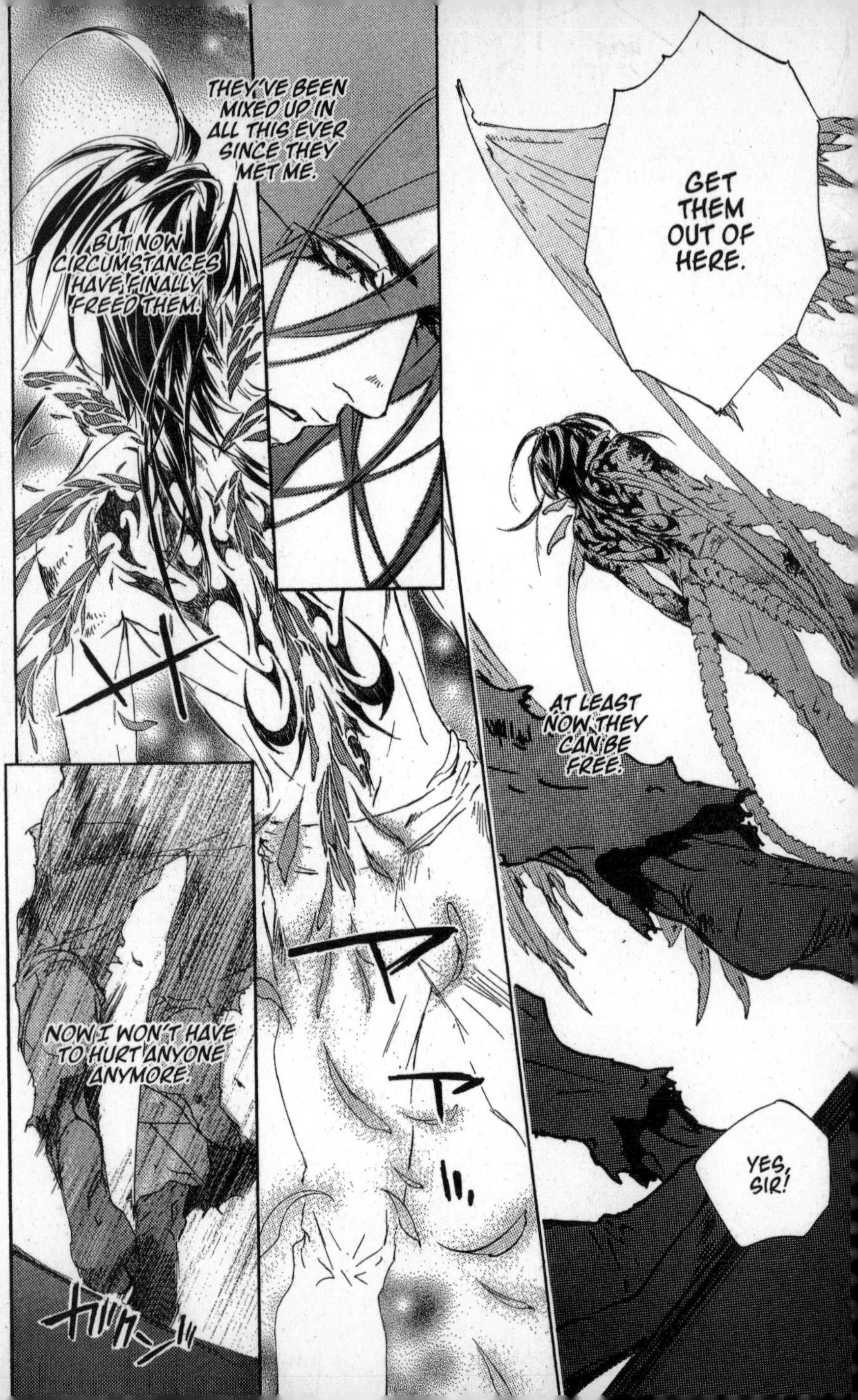
GET THEM OUT OF HERE.
AT LEAST NOW THEY CAN BE FREE.
YES, SIR!
THEY'VE BEEN MIXED UP IN ALL THIS EVER SINCE THEY MET ME.
BUT NOW CIRCUMSTANCES HAVE FINALLY FREED THEM.
NOW I WON'T HAVE TO HURT ANYONE ANYMORE.

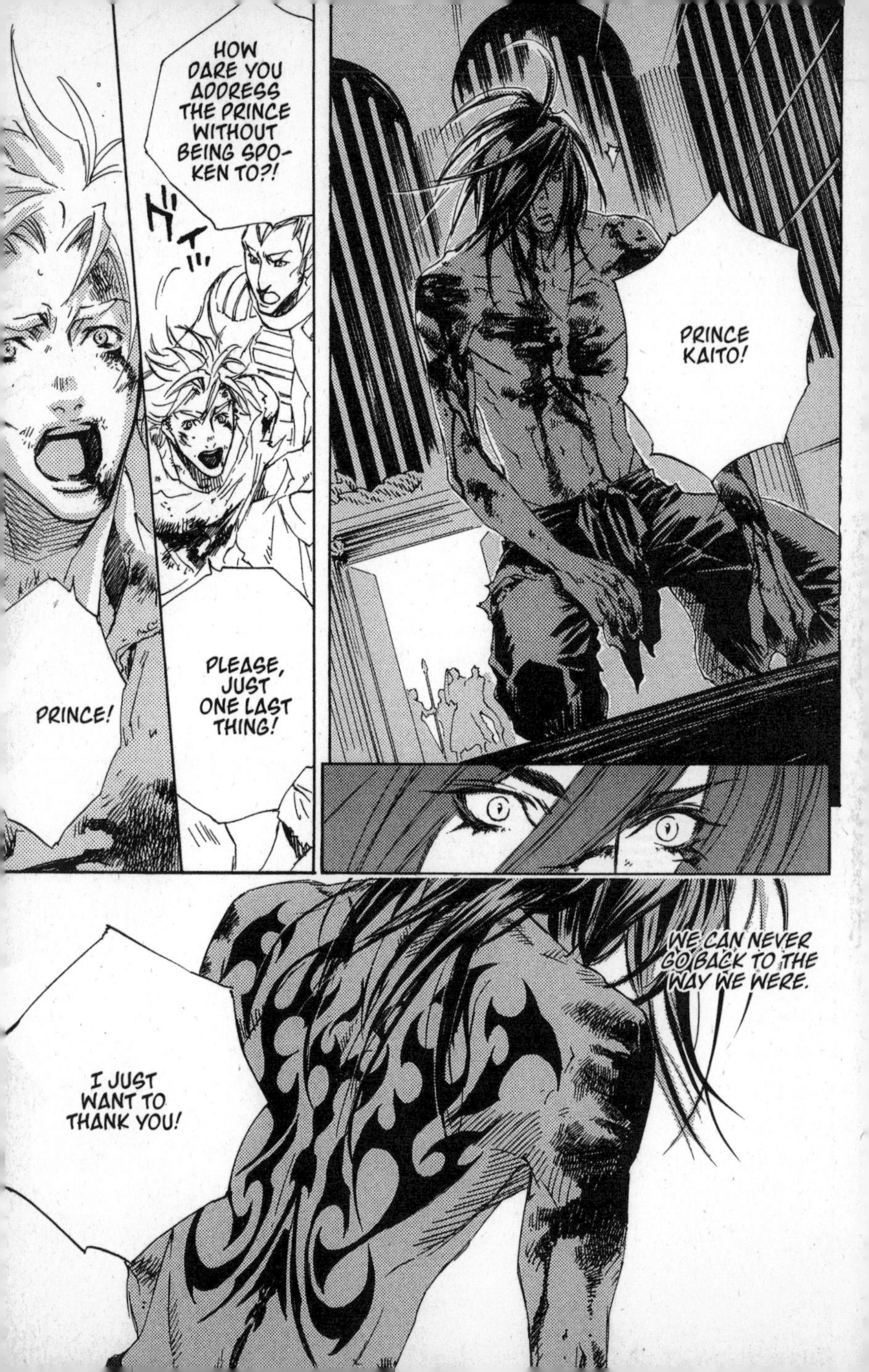
PRINCE KAITO!
HOW DARE YOU ADDRESS THE PRINCE WITHOUT BEING SPO-KEN TO?!
PLEASE, JUST ONE LAST THING!
PRINCE!
WE CAN NEVER GO BACK TO THE WAY WE WERE.
I JUST WANT TO THANK YOU!

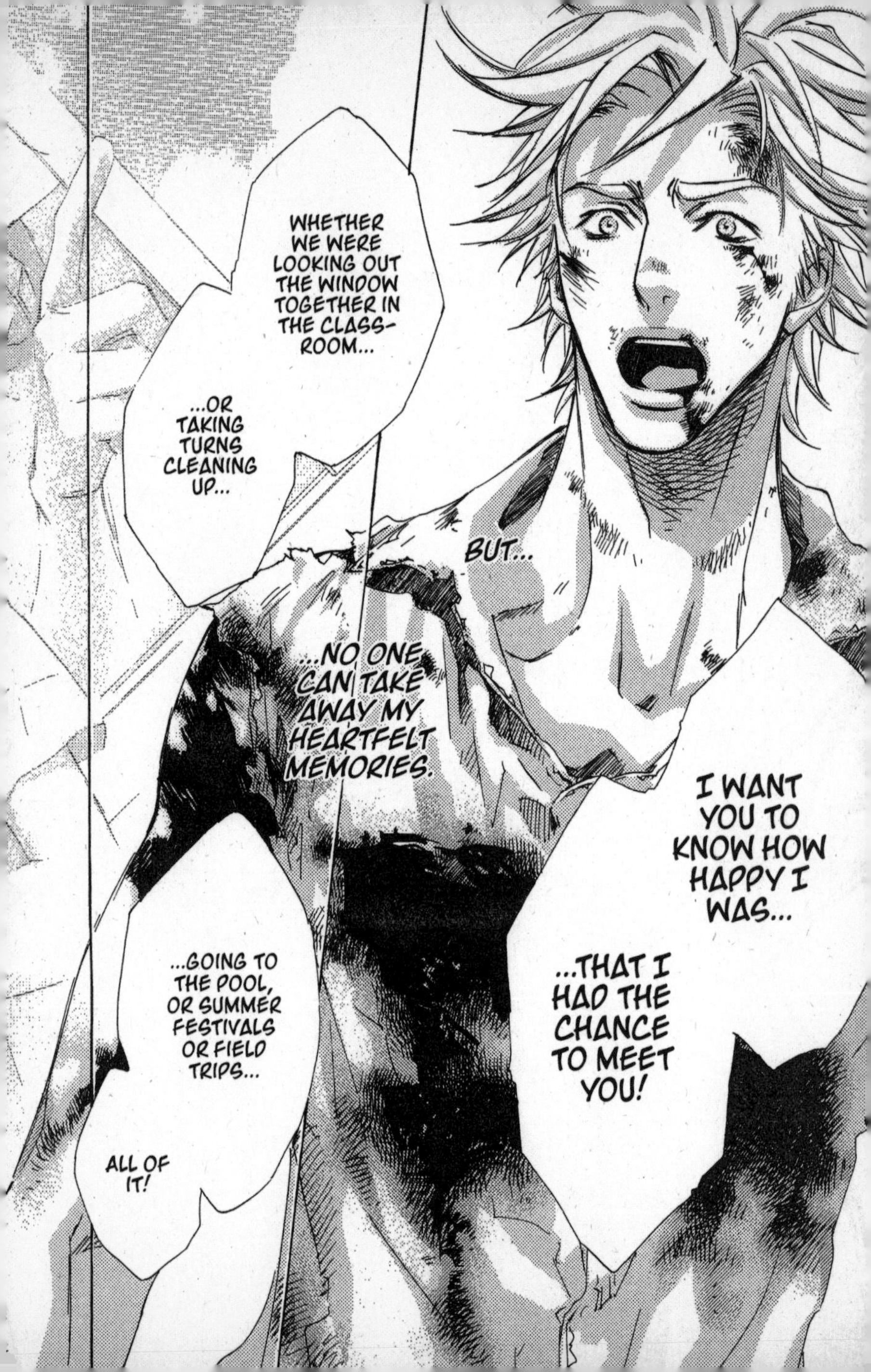
WHETHER WE WERE LOOKING OUT THE WINDOW TOGETHER IN THE CLASS-ROOM...
...OR TAKING TURNS CLEANING UP...
...GOING TO THE POOL, OR SUMMER FESTIVALS OR FIELD TRIPS...
ALL OF IT!
BUT...
...NO ONE CAN TAKE AWAY MY HEARTFELT MEMORIES.
I WANT YOU TO KNOW HOW HAPPY I WAS...
...THAT I HAD THE CHANCE TO MEET YOU!

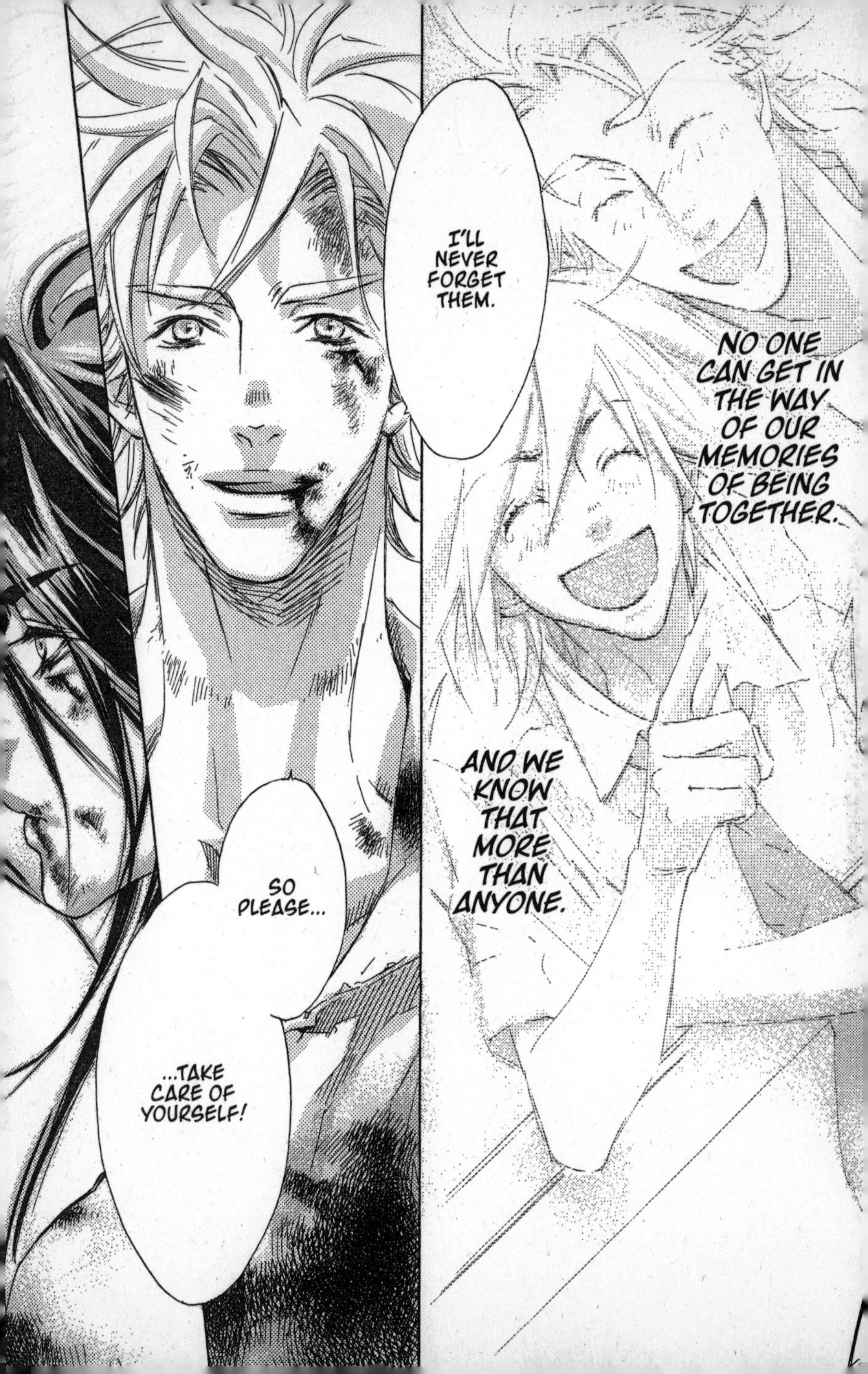
I'LL NEVER FORGET THEM.
NO ONE CAN GET IN THE WAY OF OUR MEMORIES OF BEING TOGETHER.
AND WE KNOW THAT MORE THAN ANYONE.
SO PLEASE...
...TAKE CARE OF YOURSELF!

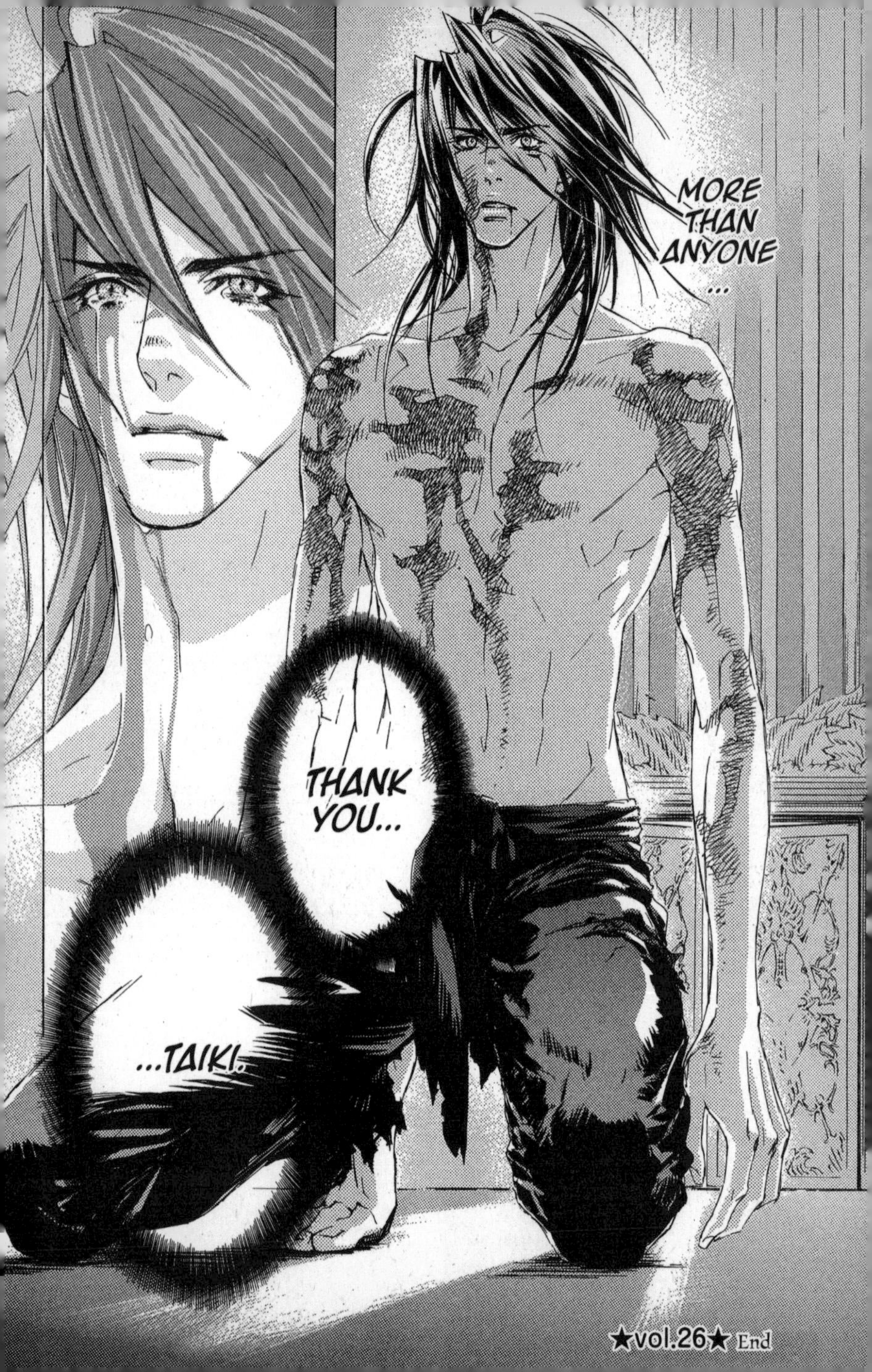
MORE THAN ANYONE ...
THANK YOU...
...TAIKI.
★vol.26★ End

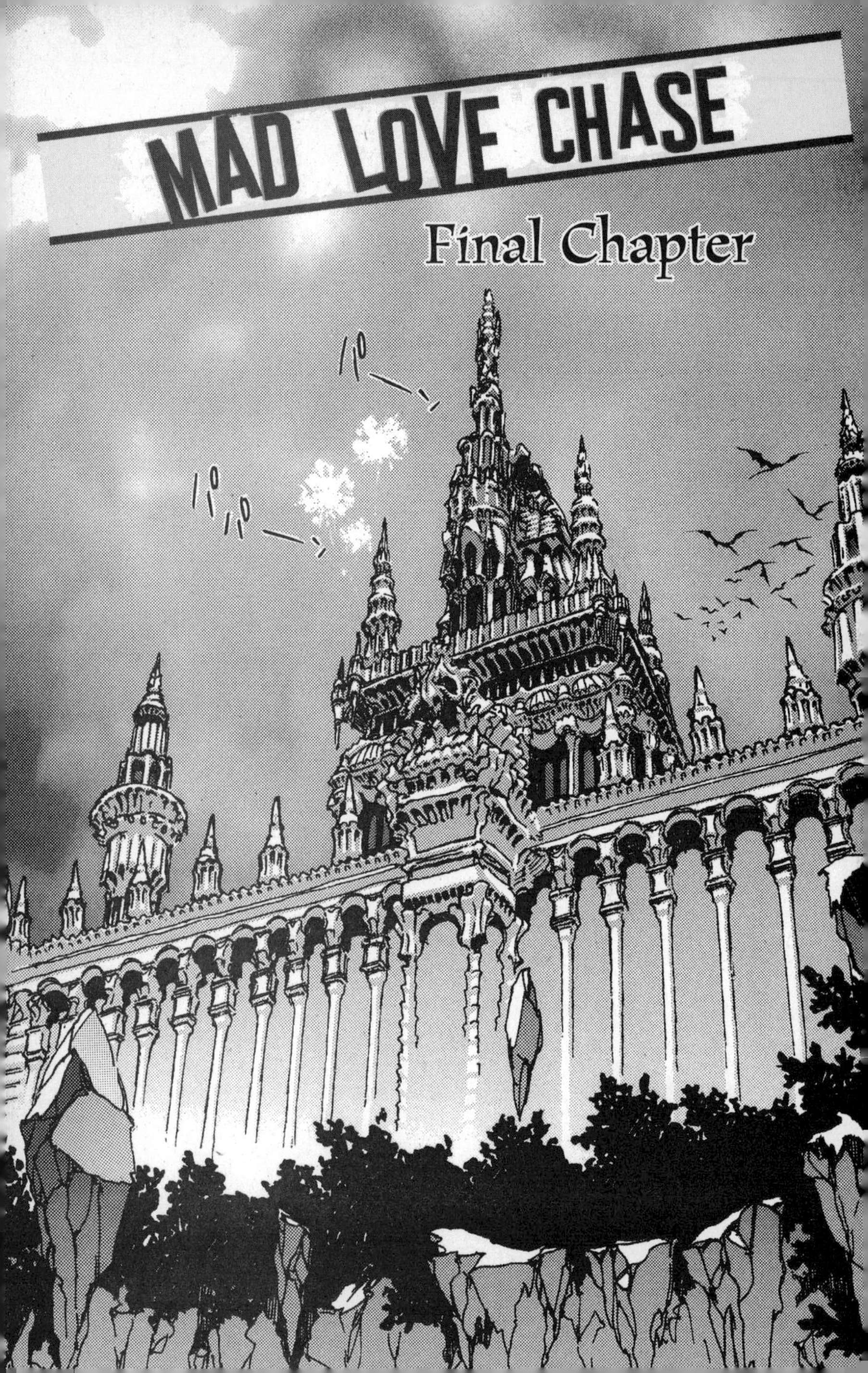
MAD LOVE CHASE
Final Chapter

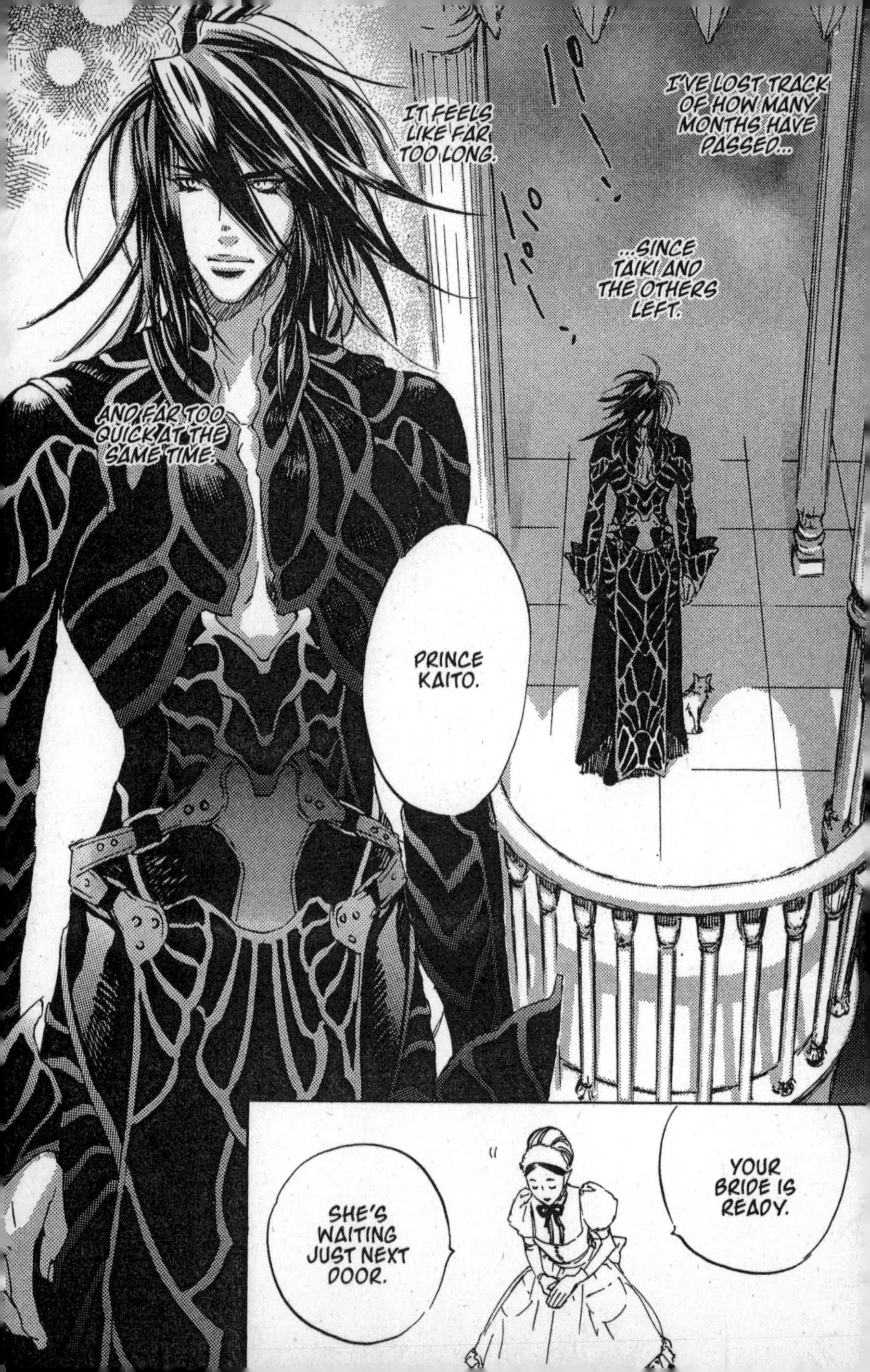
I'VE LOST TRACK OF HOW MANY MONTHS HAVE PASSED...
...SINCE TAIKI AND THE OTHERS LEFT.
IT FEELS LIKE FAR TOO LONG.
AND FAR TOO QUICK AT THE SAME TIME.
PRINCE KAITO.
YOUR BRIDE IS READY.
SHE'S WAITING JUST NEXT DOOR.

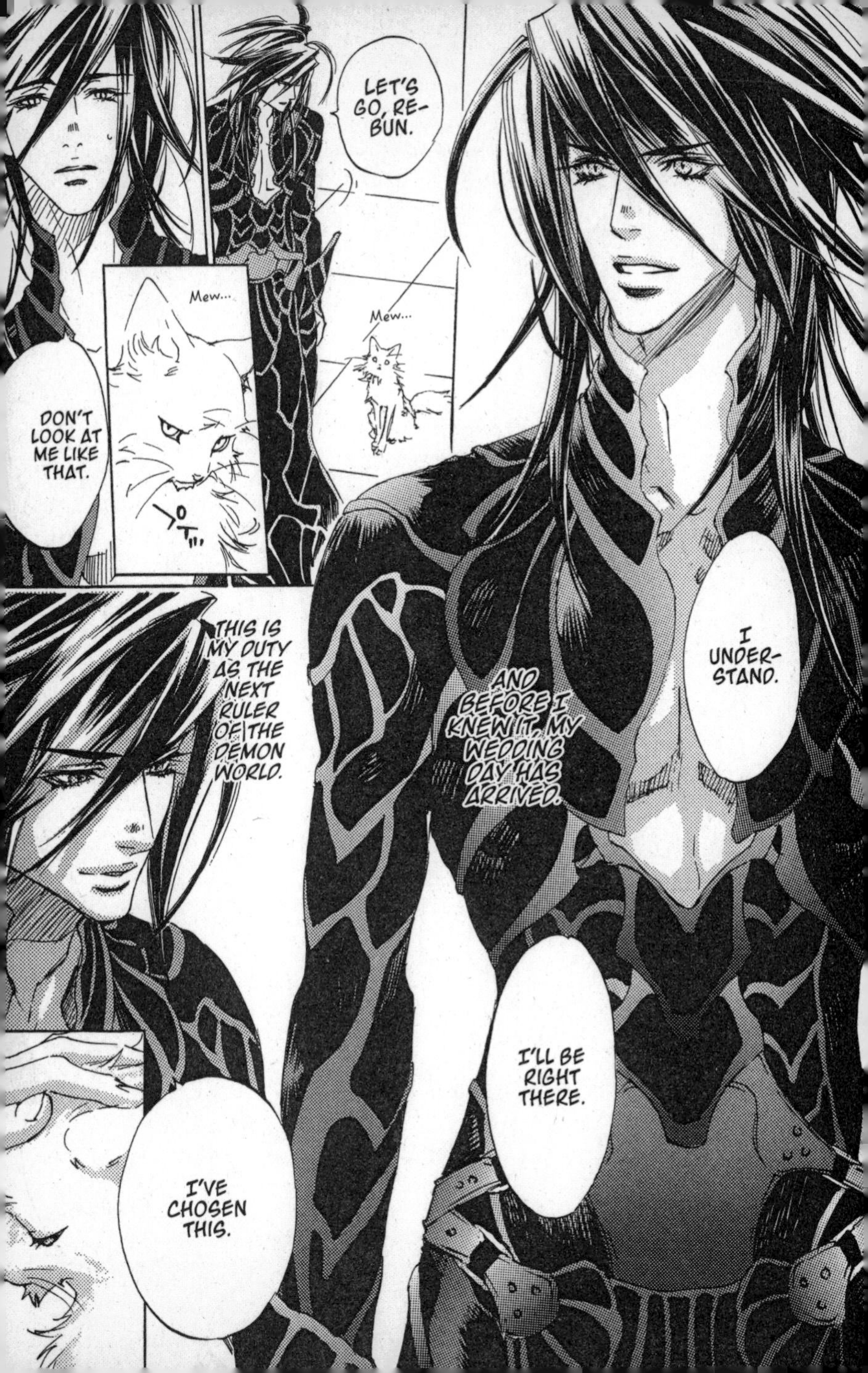
I UNDER-STAND.
AND BEFORE I KNEW IT, MY WEDDING DAY HAS ARRIVED.
I'LL BE RIGHT THERE.
LET'S GO, RE-BUN.
Mew...
Mew...
DON'T LOOK AT ME LIKE THAT.
THIS IS MY DUTY AS THE NEXT RULER OF THE DEMON WORLD.
I'VE CHOSEN THIS.

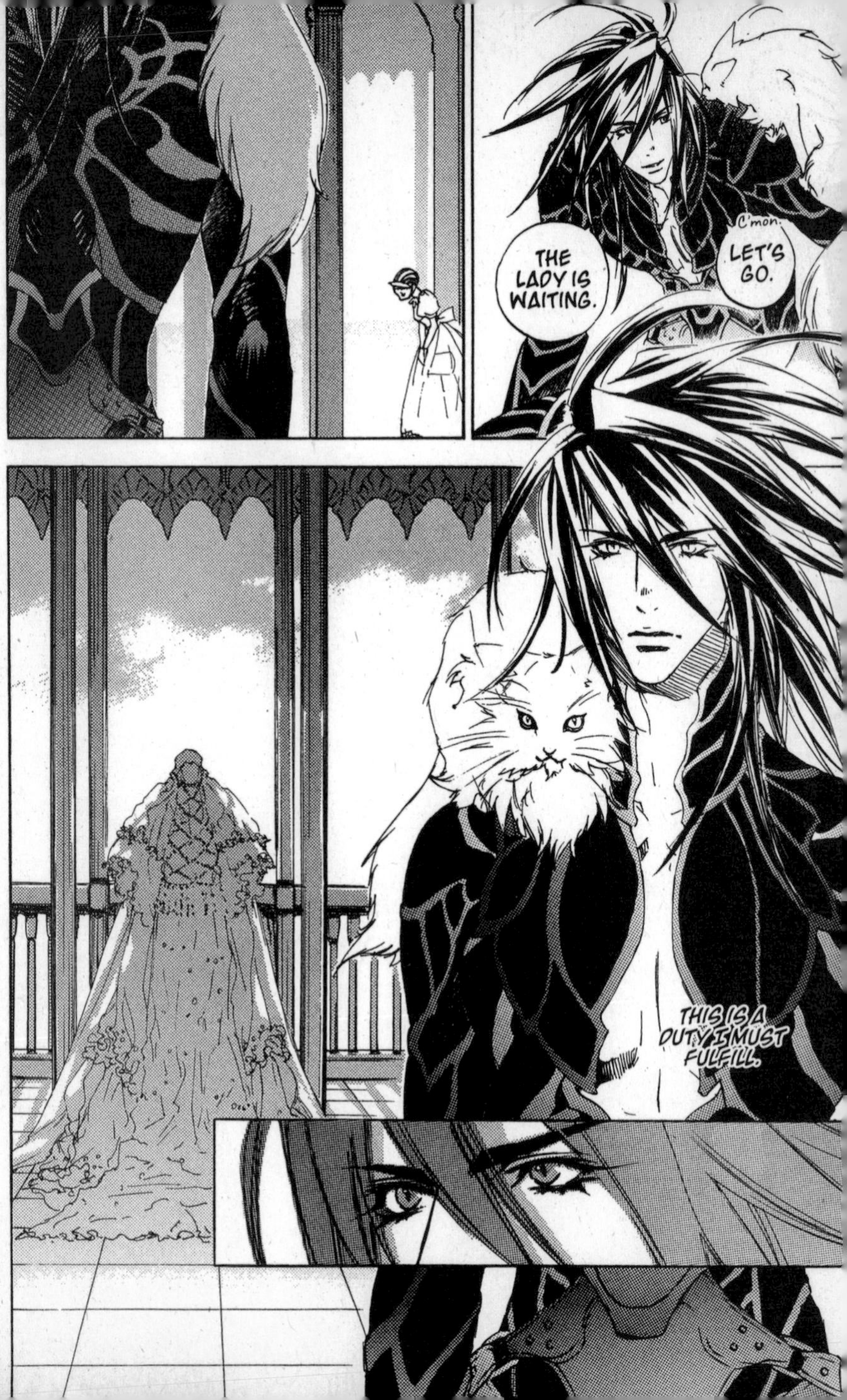
C'mon.
LET'S GO.
THE LADY IS WAITING.
THIS IS A DUTY I MUST FULFILL.

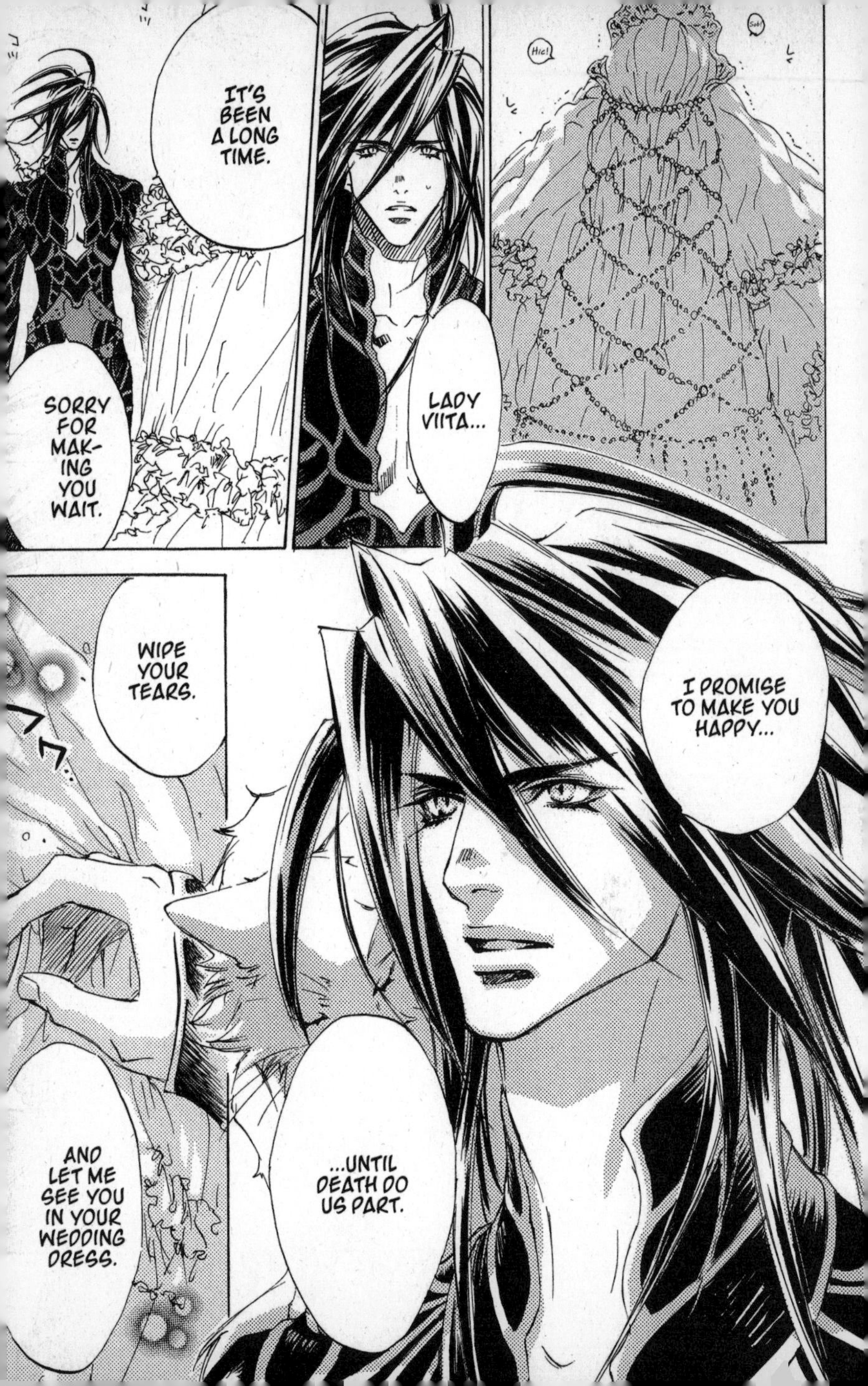
Hic!
Sob!
LADY VIITA...
IT'S BEEN A LONG TIME.
SORRY FOR MAKING YOU WAIT.
I PROMISE TO MAKE YOU HAPPY...
...UNTIL DEATH DO US PART.
WIPE YOUR TEARS.
AND LET ME SEE YOU IN YOUR WEDDING DRESS.

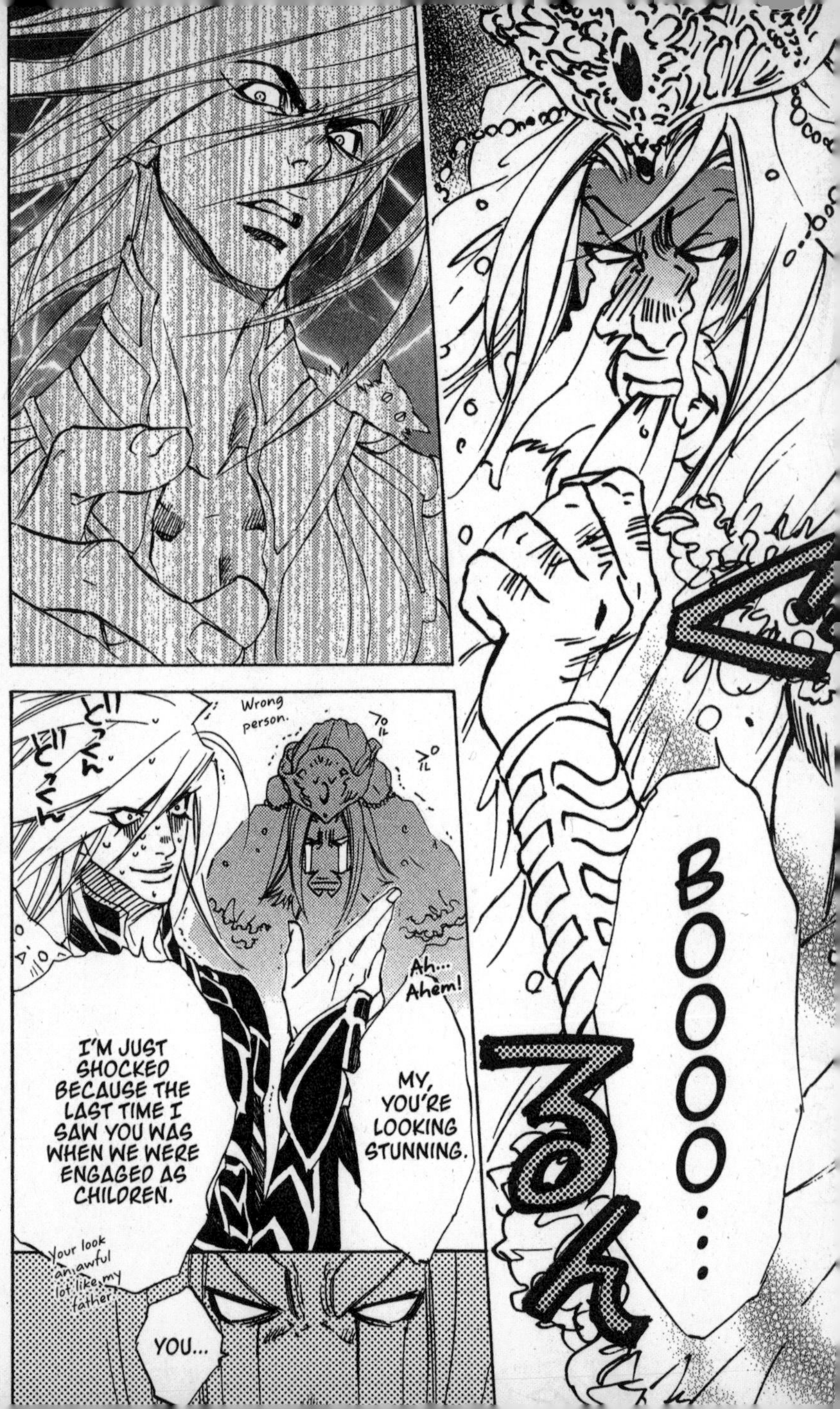
BOOOO...
Wrong person.
Ah... Ahem!
MY, YOU'RE LOOKING STUNNING.
I'M JUST SHOCKED BECAUSE THE LAST TIME I SAW YOU WAS WHEN WE WERE ENGAGED AS CHILDREN.
Your look an awful lot like my father.
YOU...

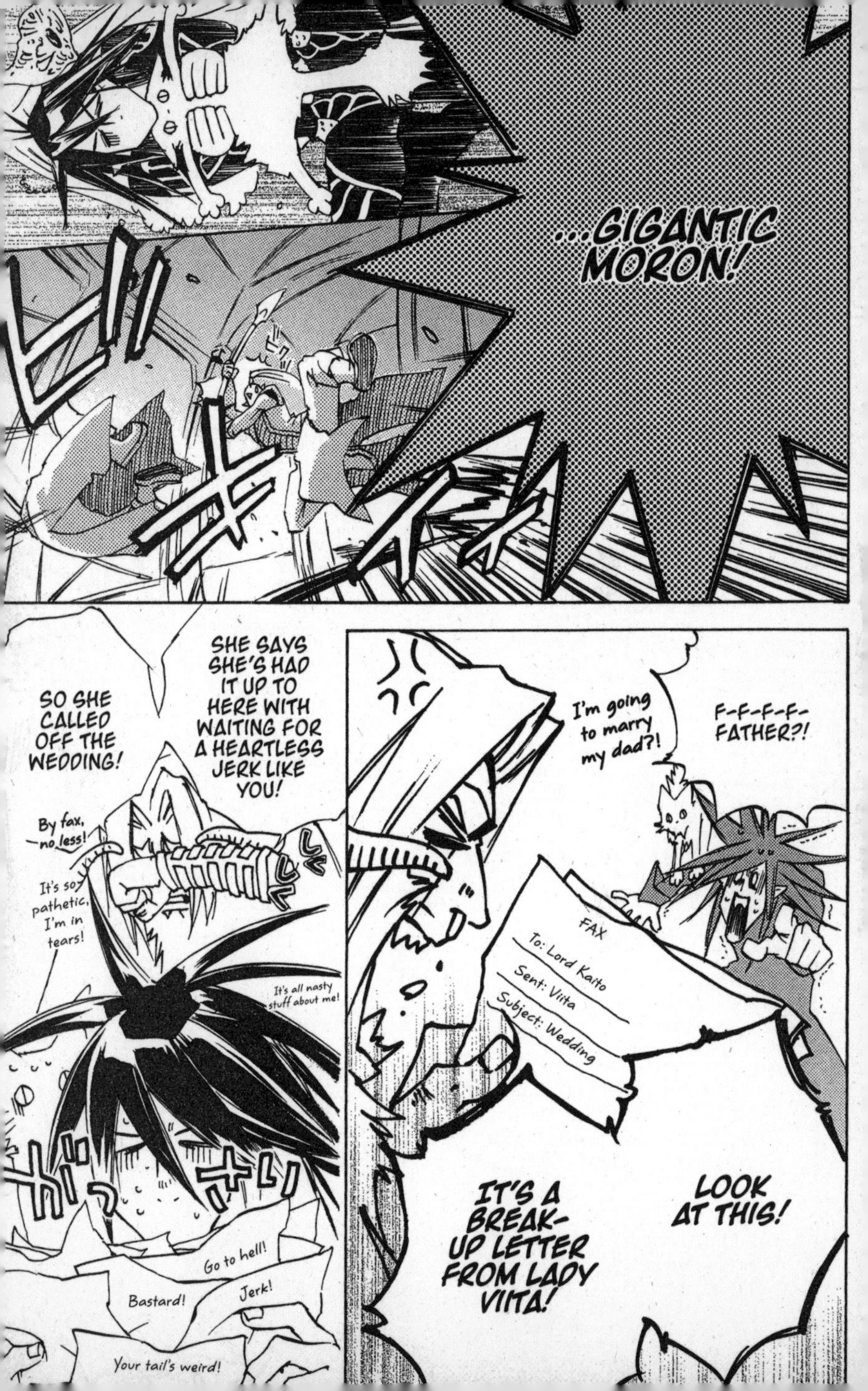

...GIGANTIC MORON!
F-F-F-F-FATHER?!
I'm going to marry my dad?!
LOOK AT THIS!
IT'S A BREAK-UP LETTER FROM LADY VIITA!
FAX
To: Lord Kaito
Sent: Viita
Subject: Wedding
SHE SAYS SHE'S HAD IT UP TO HERE WITH WAITING FOR A HEARTLESS JERK LIKE YOU!
SO SHE CALLED OFF THE WEDDING!
By fax, no less!
It's so pathetic, I'm in tears!
It's all nasty stuff about me!
Go to hell!
Jerk!
Bastard!
Your tail's weird!

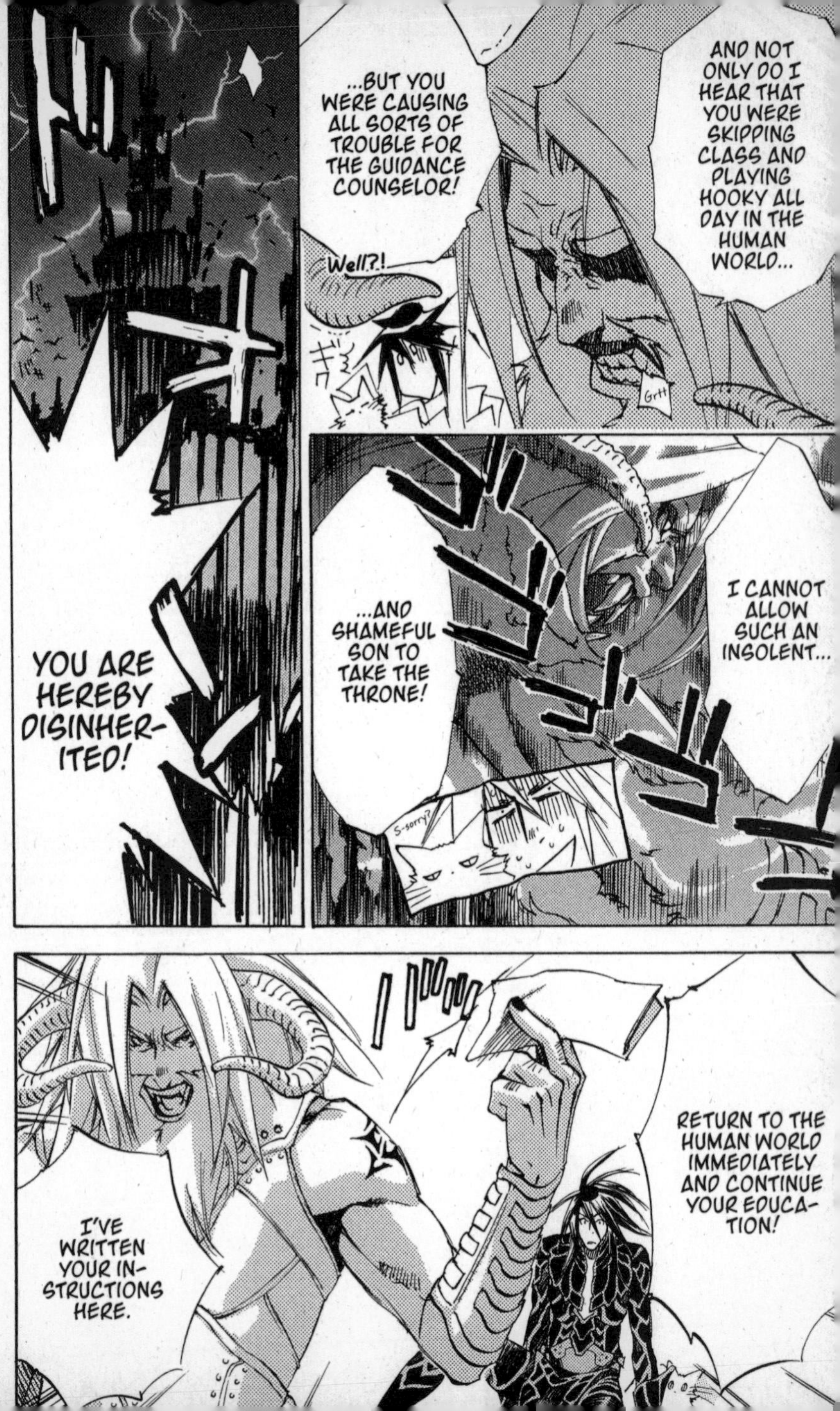
AND NOT ONLY DO I HEAR THAT YOU WERE SKIPPING CLASS AND PLAYING HOOKY ALL DAY IN THE HUMAN WORLD...
...BUT YOU WERE CAUSING ALL SORTS OF TROUBLE FOR THE GUIDANCE COUNSELOR!
Well?!
I CANNOT ALLOW SUCH AN INSOLENT...
...AND SHAMEFUL SON TO TAKE THE THRONE!
S-sorry?
YOU ARE HEREBY DISINHERITED!
RETURN TO THE HUMAN WORLD IMMEDIATELY AND CONTINUE YOUR EDUCATION!
I'VE WRITTEN YOUR INSTRUCTIONS HERE.

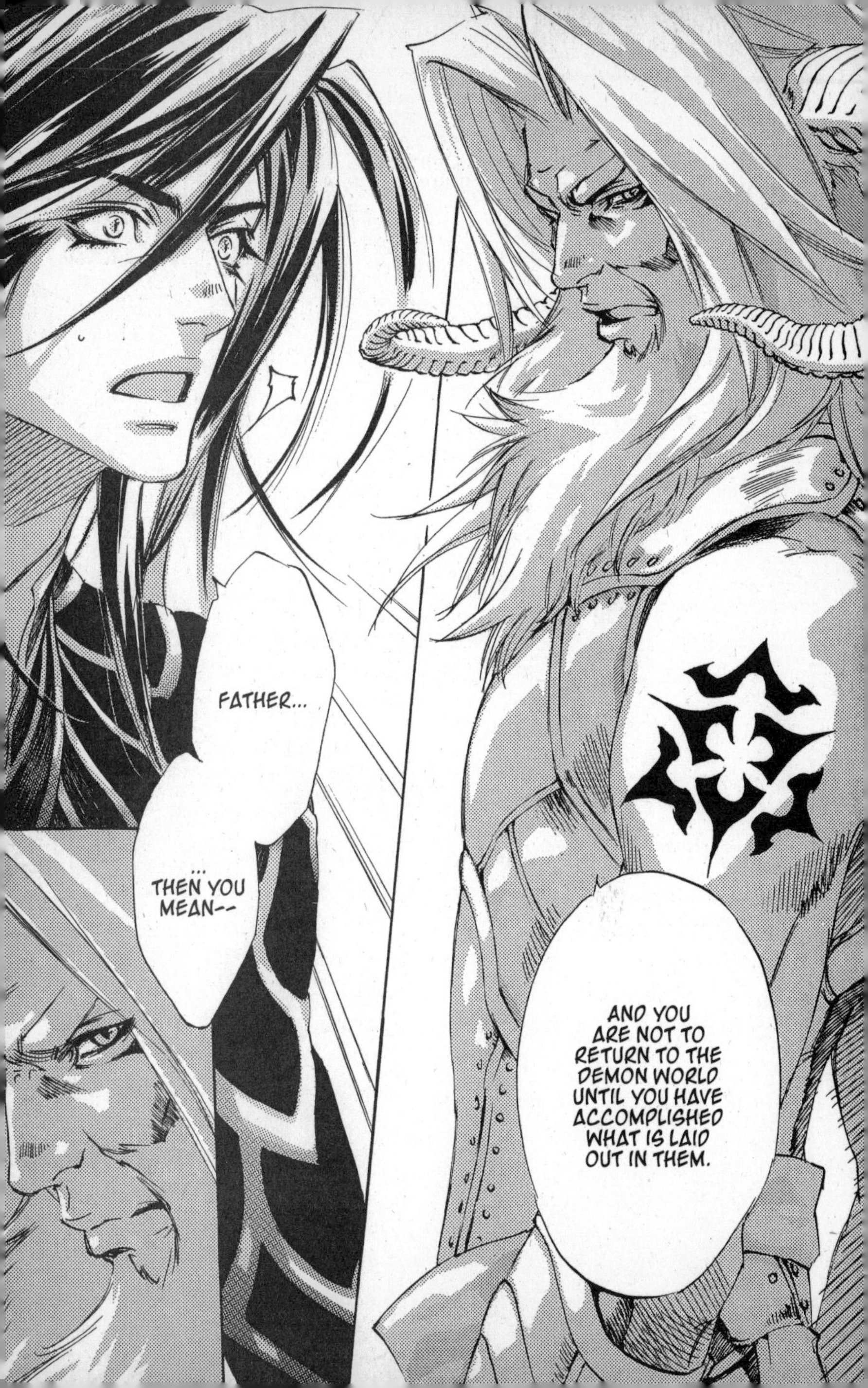

AND YOU ARE NOT TO RETURN TO THE DEMON WORLD UNTIL YOU HAVE ACCOMPLISHED WHAT IS LAID OUT IN THEM.
FATHER...
... THEN YOU MEAN--

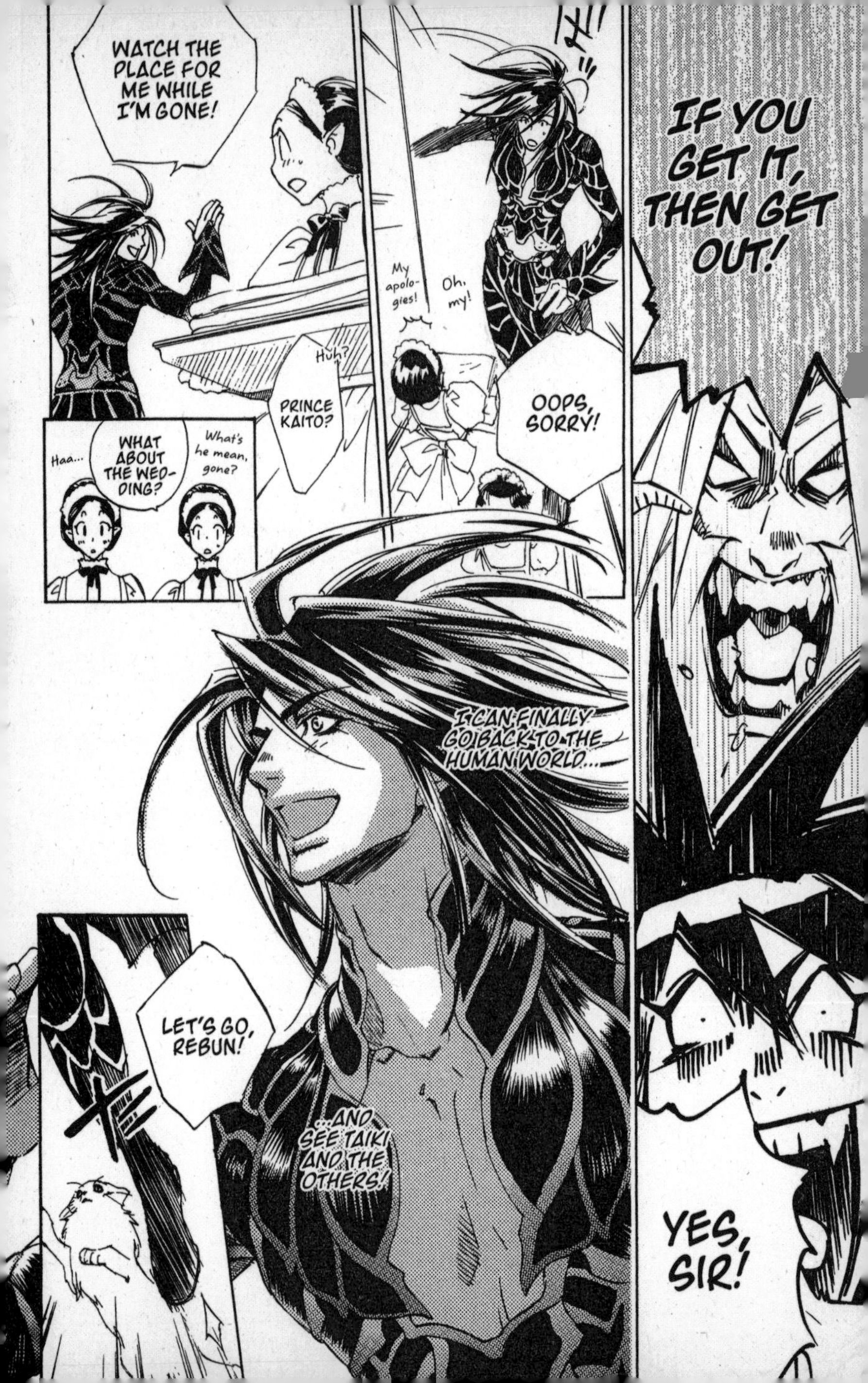
IF YOU GET IT, THEN GET OUT!
YES, SIR!
OOPS, SORRY!
Oh, my!
My apologies!
Huh?
PRINCE KAITO?
WATCH THE PLACE FOR ME WHILE I'M GONE!
What's he mean, gone?
WHAT ABOUT THE WEDDING?
Haa...
I CAN FINALLY GO BACK TO THE HUMAN WORLD...
...AND SEE TAIKI AND THE OTHERS!
LET'S GO, REBUN!

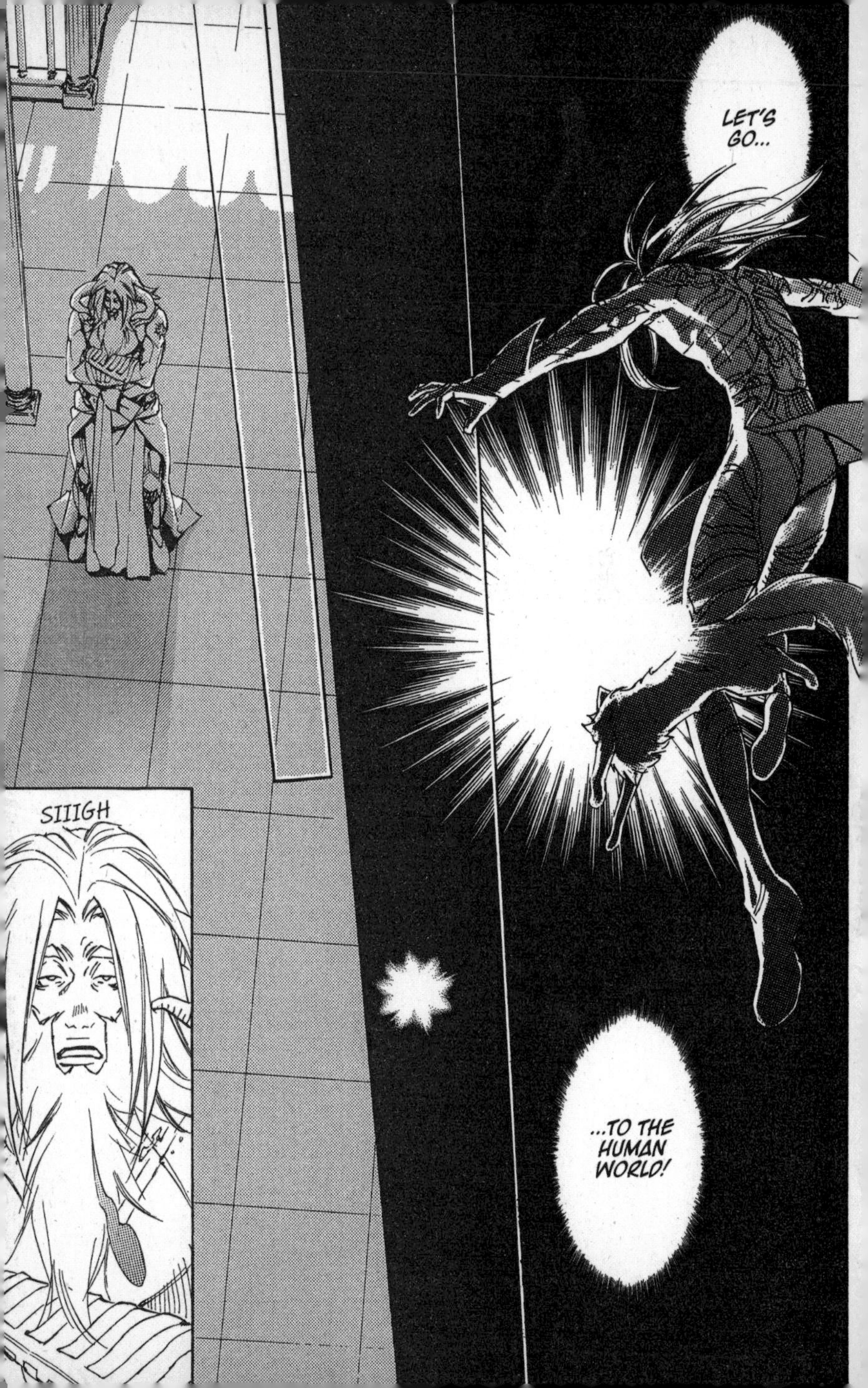
LET'S GO...
...TO THE HUMAN WORLD!
SIIIGH

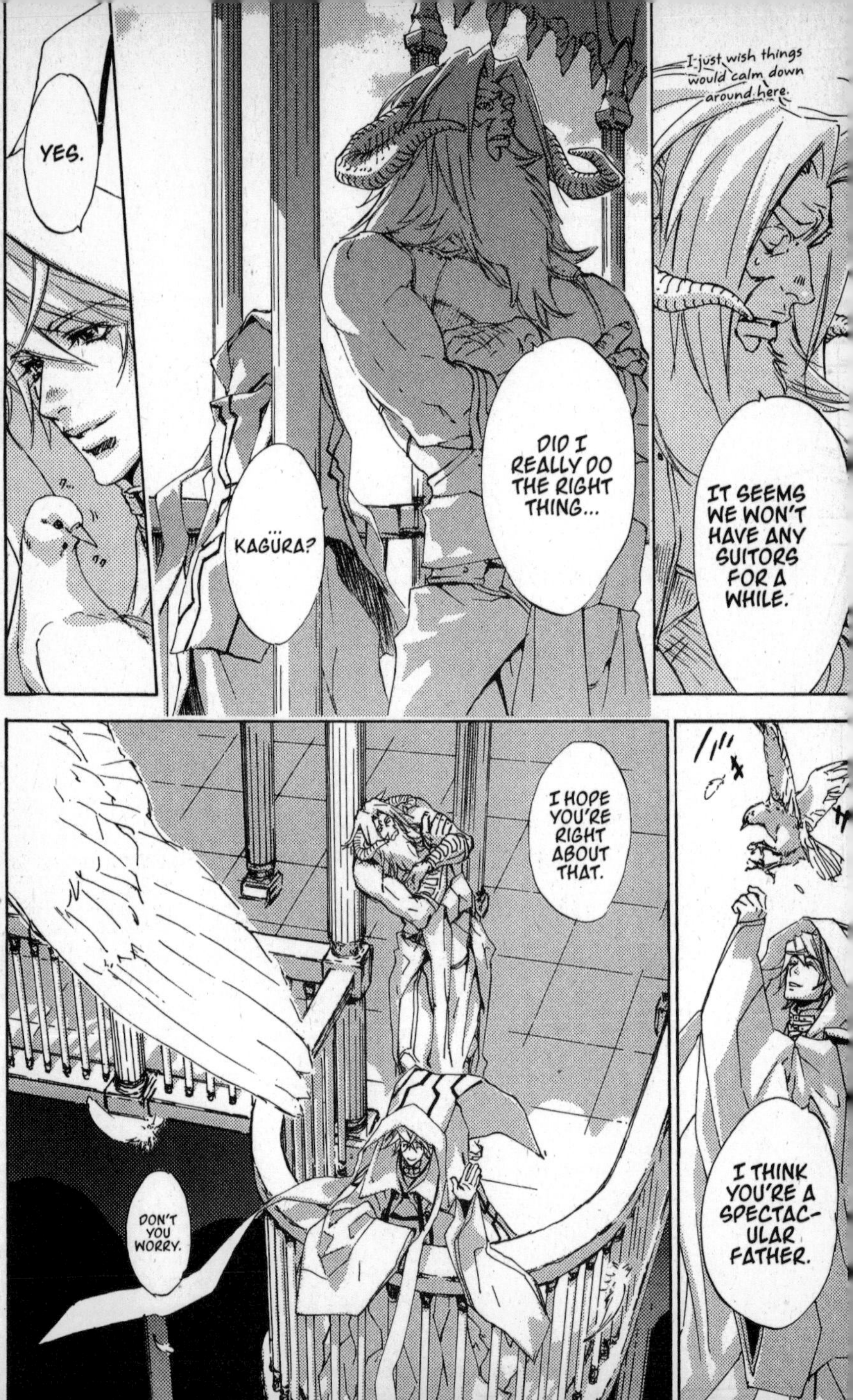

I just wish things would calm down around here.
IT SEEMS WE WON'T HAVE ANY SUITORS FOR A WHILE.
DID I REALLY DO THE RIGHT THING...
KAGÜRA?
YES.
I THINK YOU'RE A SPECTAC-ULAR FATHER.
I HOPE YOU'RE RIGHT ABOUT THAT.
DON'T YOU WORRY.

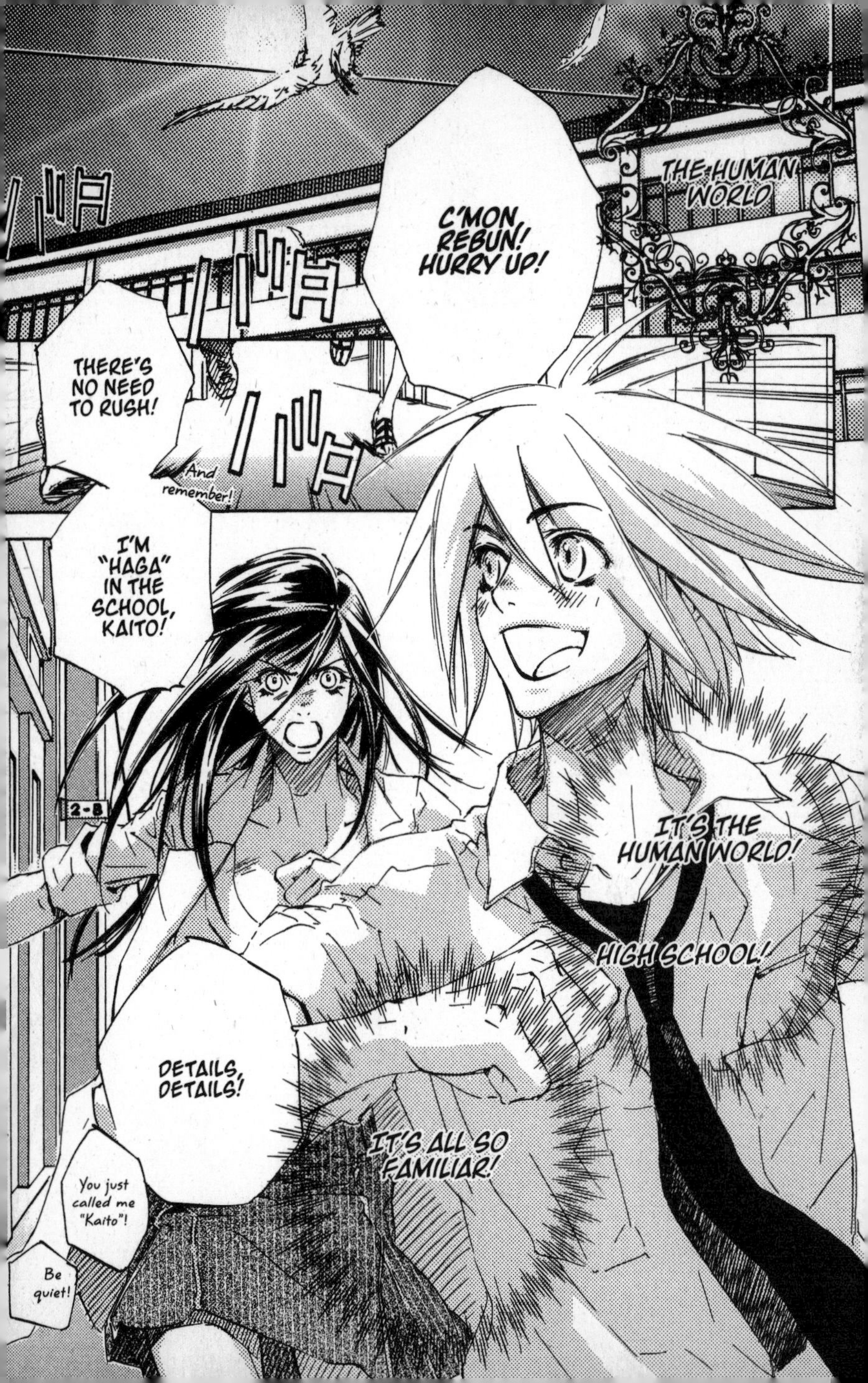
THE HUMAN WORLD
C'MON REBUN! HURRY UP!
THERE'S NO NEED TO RUSH!
And remember!
IT'S THE HUMAN WORLD!
HIGH SCHOOL!
IT'S ALL SO FAMILIAR!
I'M "HAGA" IN THE SCHOOL, KAITO!
2-B
DETAILS, DETAILS!
You just called me "Kaito"!
Be quiet!

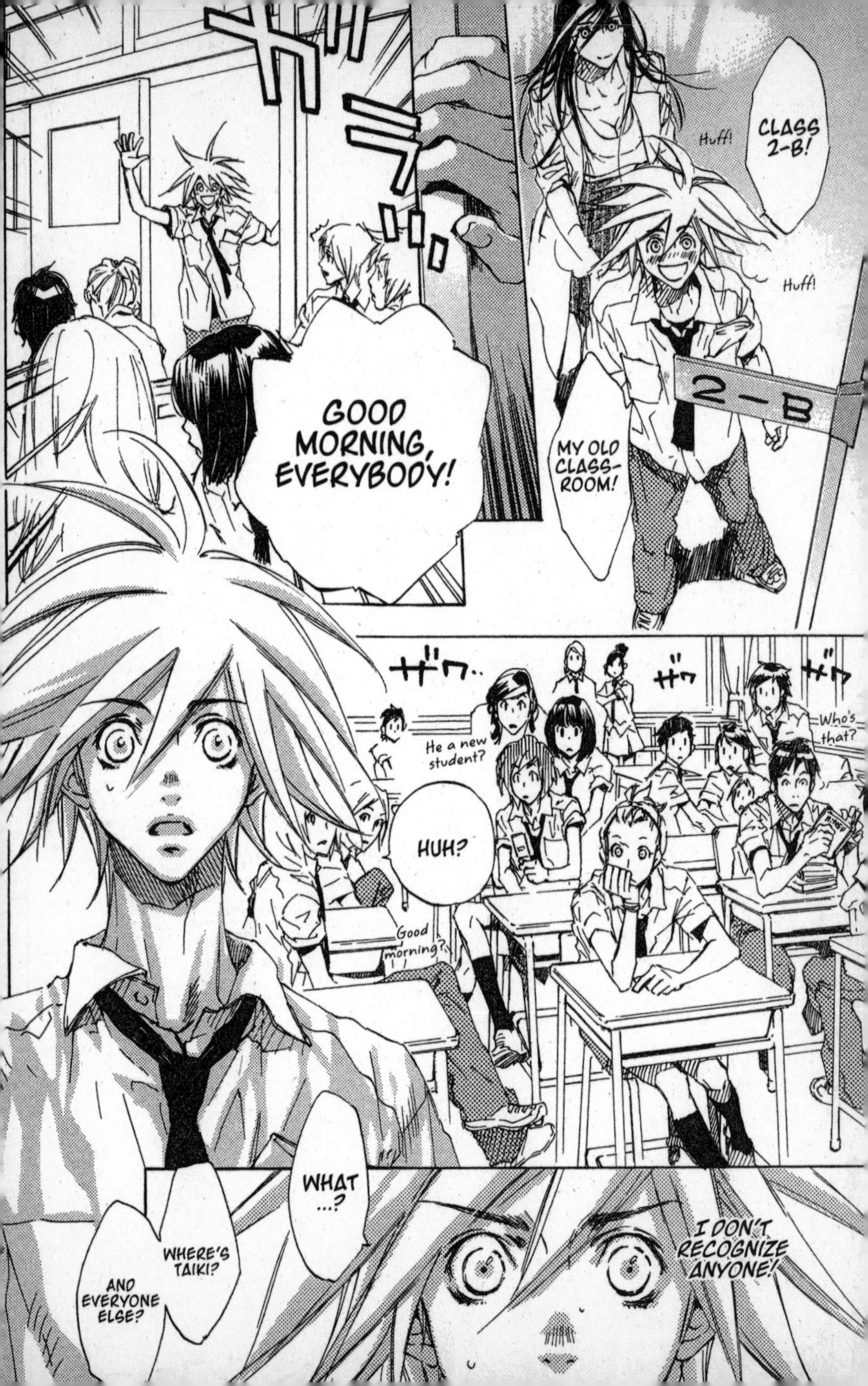
CLASS 2-B!
Huff!
Huff!
MY OLD CLASSROOM!
2-B
GOOD MORNING, EVERYBODY!
ザワ..
ザワ
ザワ
Who's that?
He a new student?
HUH?
Good morning?
I DON'T RECOGNIZE ANYONE!
WHAT ...?
WHERE'S TAIKI?
AND EVERYONE ELSE?

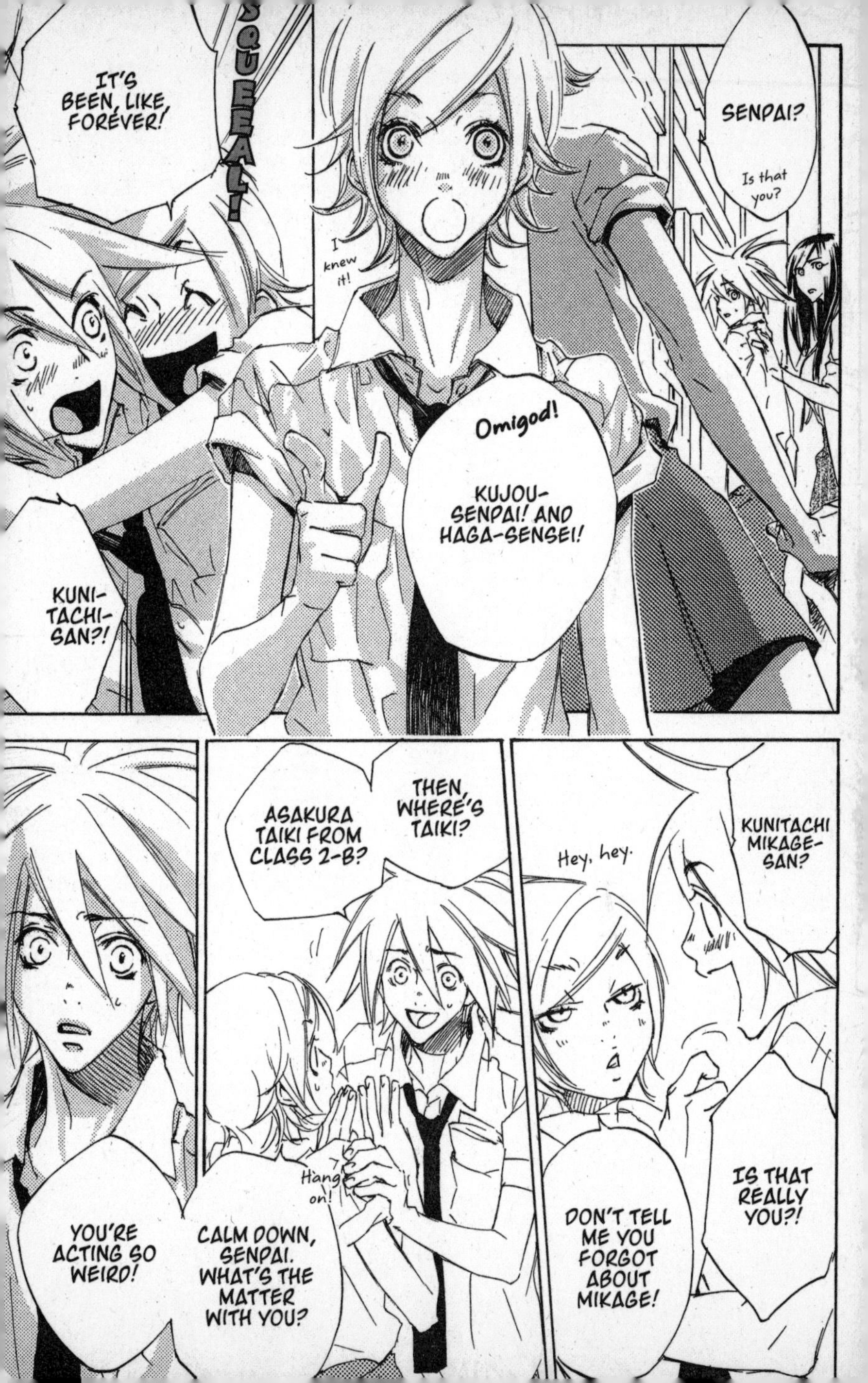
SENPAI?
Is that you?
I knew it!
Omigod!
KUJOU-SENPAI! AND HAGA-SENSEI!
SQUEEEAL!
IT'S BEEN, LIKE FOREVER!
KUNI-TACHI-SAN?!
KUNITACHI MIKAGE-SAN?
Hey, hey.
IS THAT REALLY YOU?!
DON'T TELL ME YOU FORGOT ABOUT MIKAGE!
THEN, WHERE'S TAIKI?
ASAKURA TAIKI FROM CLASS 2-B?
Hang on!
CALM DOWN, SENPAI. WHAT'S THE MATTER WITH YOU?
YOU'RE ACTING SO WEIRD!

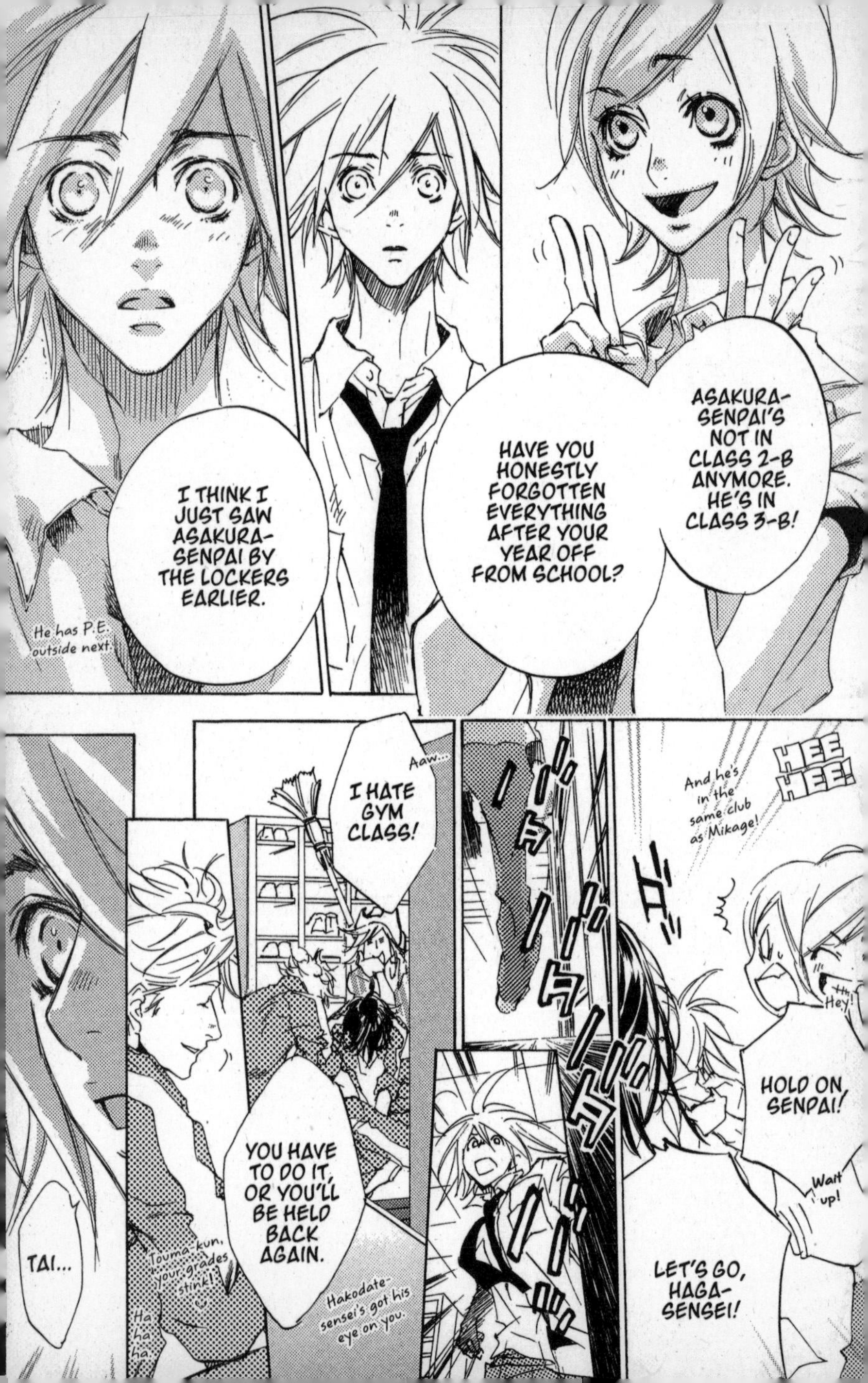
ASAKURA-SENPAI'S NOT IN CLASS 2-B ANYMORE. HE'S IN CLASS 3-B!
HAVE YOU HONESTLY FORGOTTEN EVERYTHING AFTER YOUR YEAR OFF FROM SCHOOL?
I THINK I JUST SAW ASAKURA-SENPAI BY THE LOCKERS EARLIER.
He has P.E. outside next.
HEE HEE!
And he's in the same club as Mikage!
Hey!
HOLD ON, SENPAI!
Wait up!
LET'S GO, HAGA-SENSEI!
Aaw...
I HATE GYM CLASS!
YOU HAVE TO DO IT, OR YOU'LL BE HELD BACK AGAIN.
Touma-kun, your grades stink!
Hakodate-sensei's got his eye on you.
Ha ha ha.
TAI...

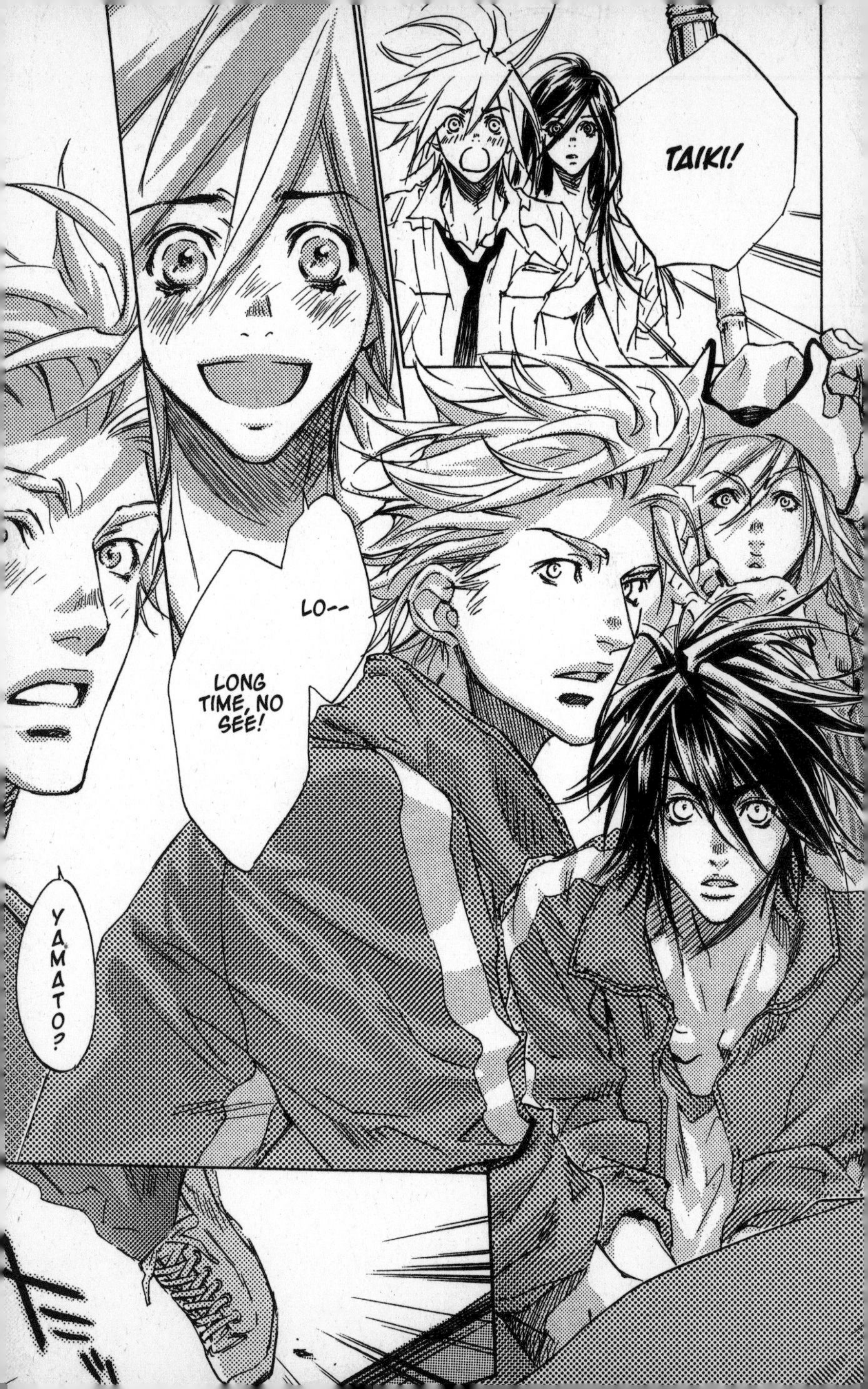
TAIKI!
LO--
LONG TIME, NO SEE!
YAMATO?

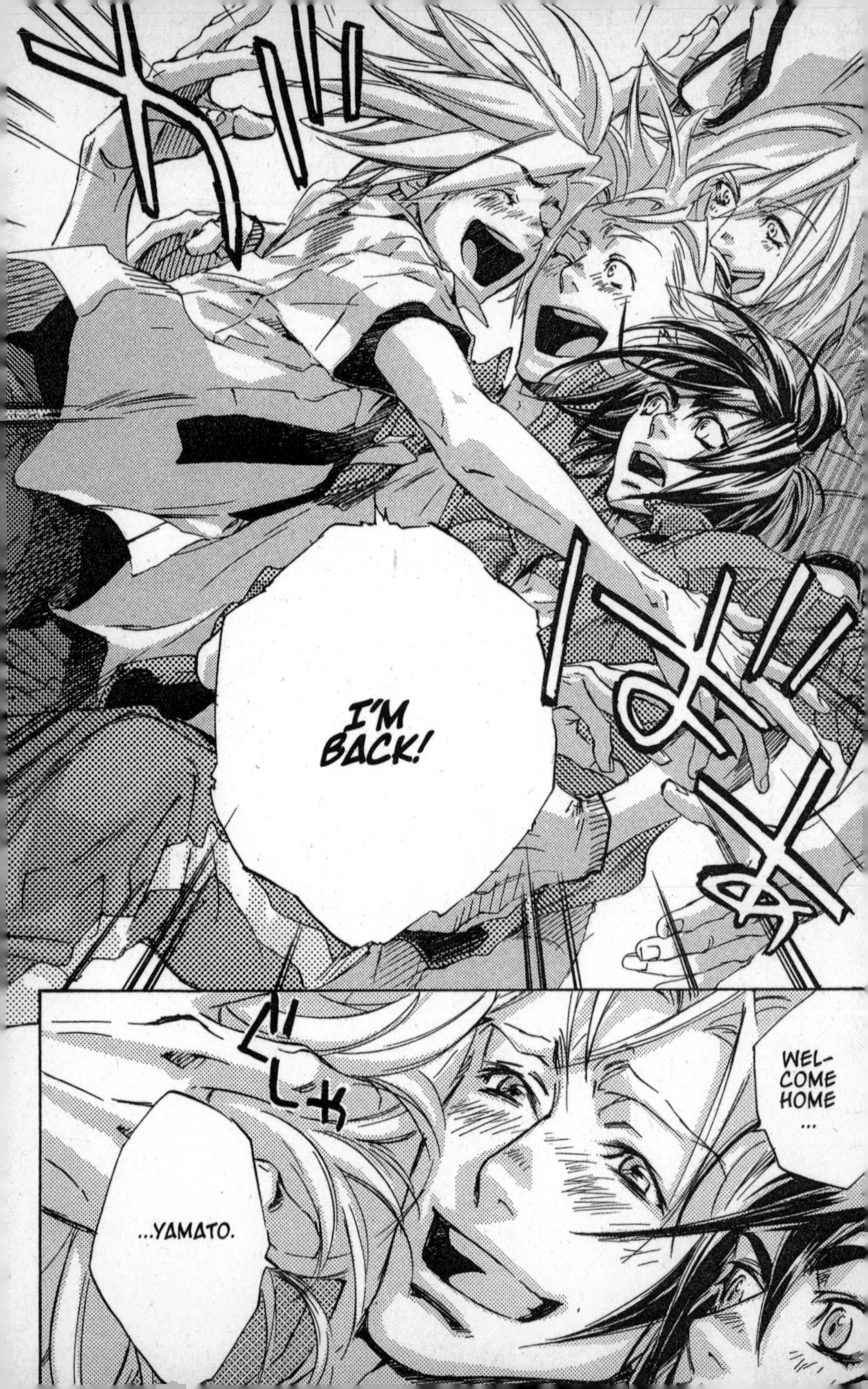
I'M BACK!
WEL-COME HOME ...
...YAMATO.

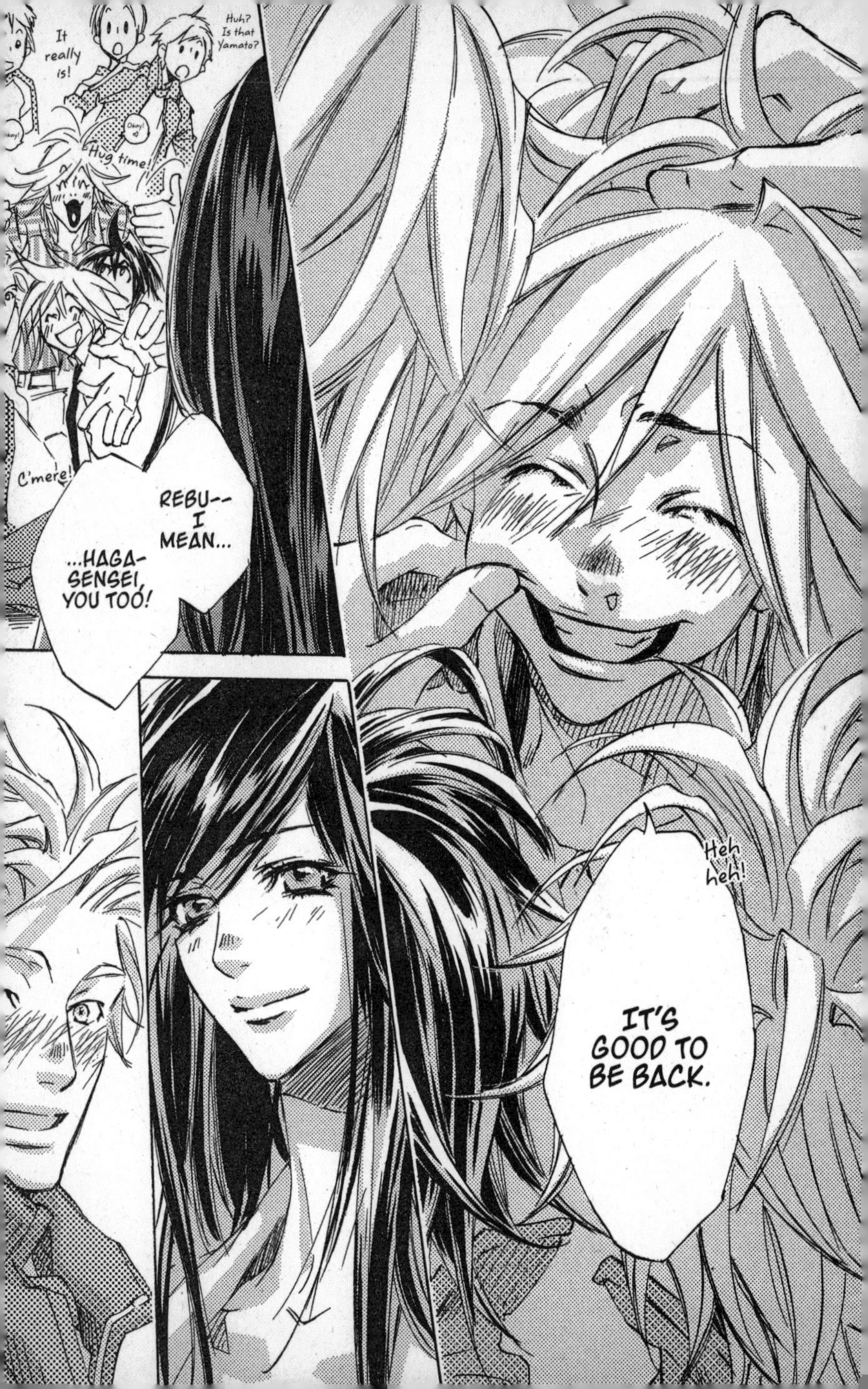
Heh heh!
IT'S GOOD TO BE BACK.
Huh? Is that Yamato?
It really is!
Okay!
Hug time!
C'mere!
REBU-- I MEAN...
...HAGA-SENSEI, YOU TOO!

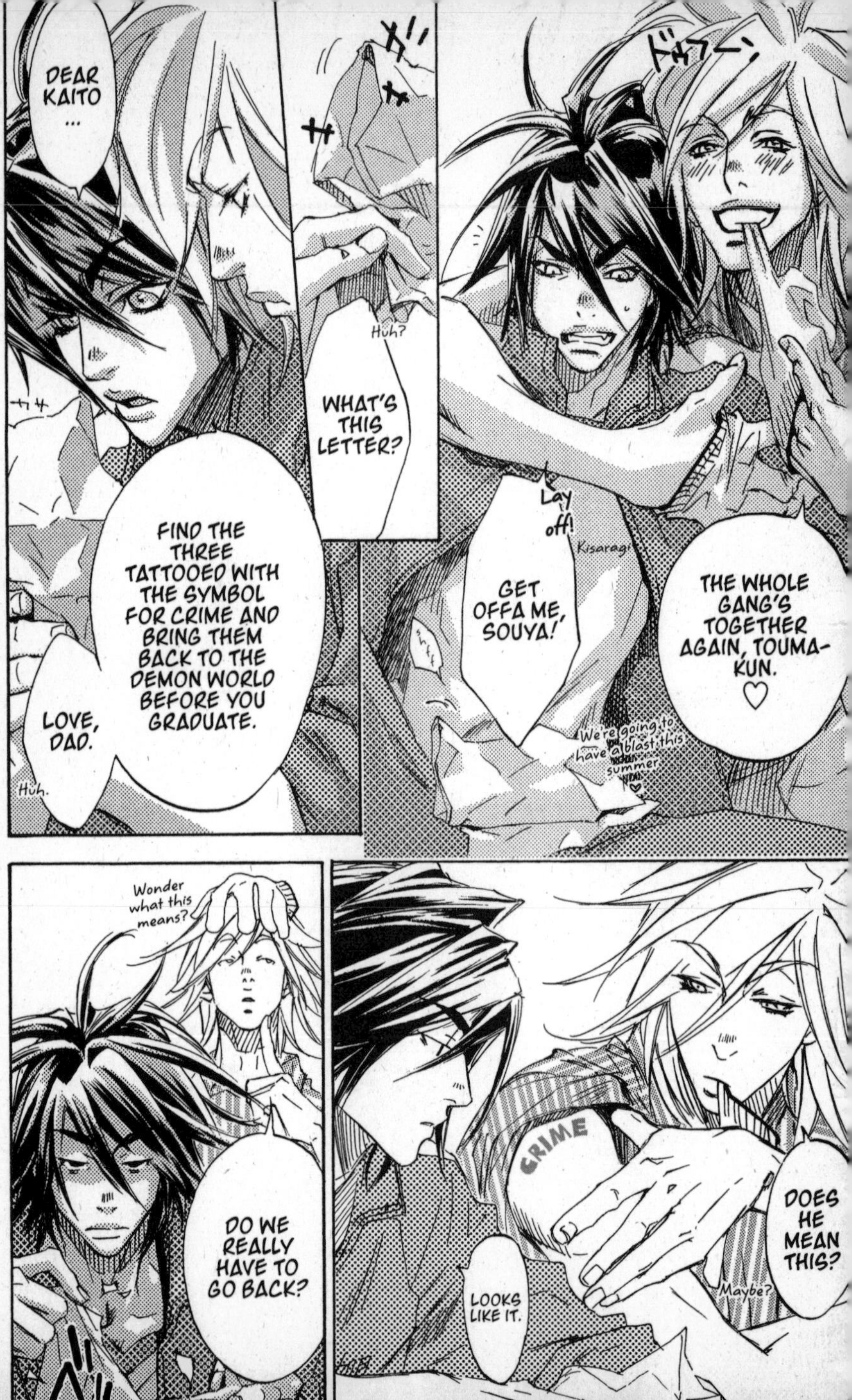
THE WHOLE GANG'S TOGETHER AGAIN, TOUMA-KUN. ♡
We're going to have a blast this summer ♡
Lay off!
Kisaragi
GET OFFA ME, SOUYA!
Huh?
WHAT'S THIS LETTER?
DEAR KAITO ...
FIND THE THREE TATTOOED WITH THE SYMBOL FOR CRIME AND BRING THEM BACK TO THE DEMON WORLD BEFORE YOU GRADUATE.
LOVE, DAD.
Huh.
DOES HE MEAN THIS?
Maybe?
CRIME
LOOKS LIKE IT.
Wonder what this means?
DO WE REALLY HAVE TO GO BACK?

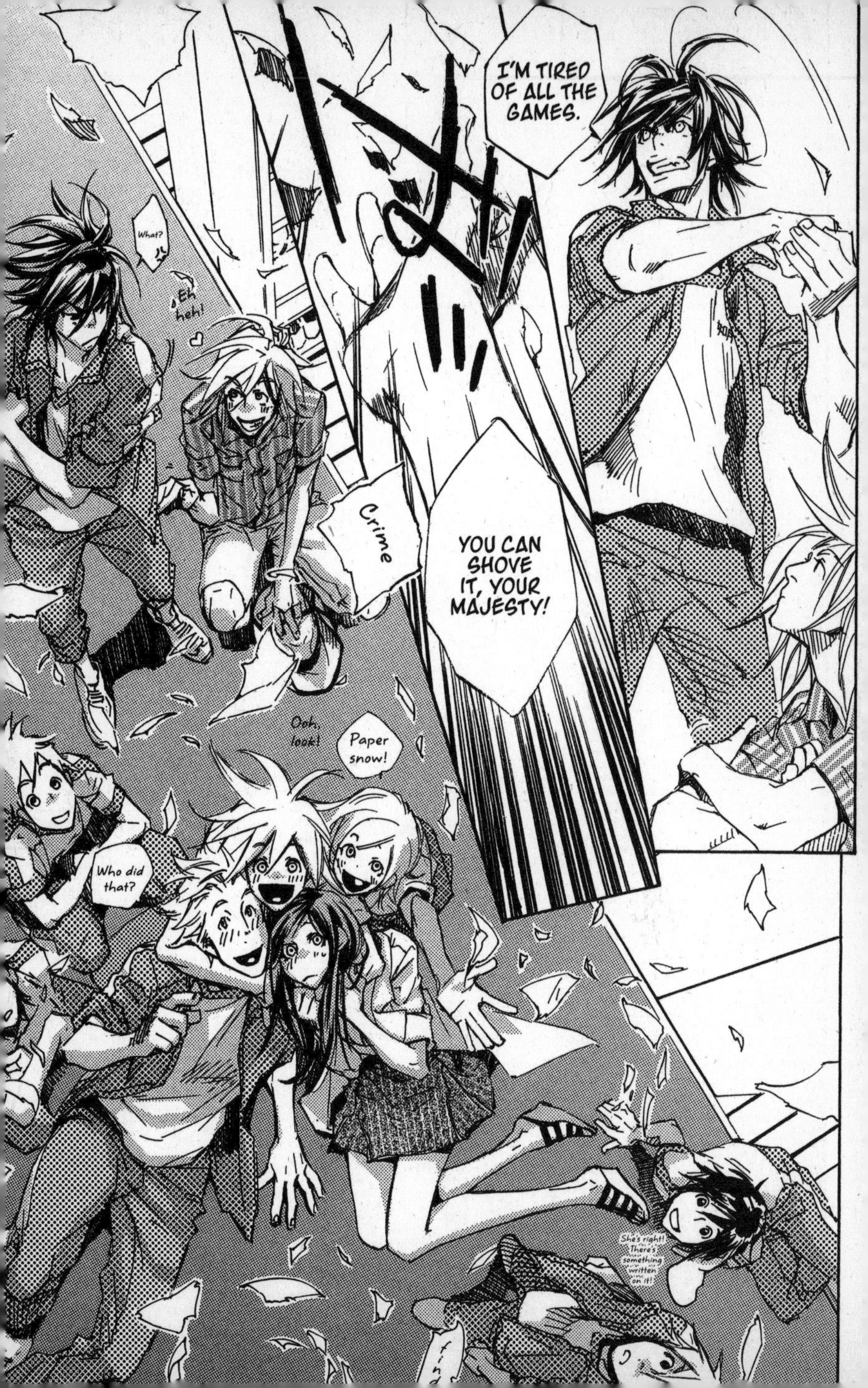
I'M TIRED OF ALL THE GAMES.
YOU CAN SHOVE IT, YOUR MAJESTY!
Crime
What?
Eh heh!
Ooh, look!
Paper snow!
Who did that?
She's right! There's something written on it!

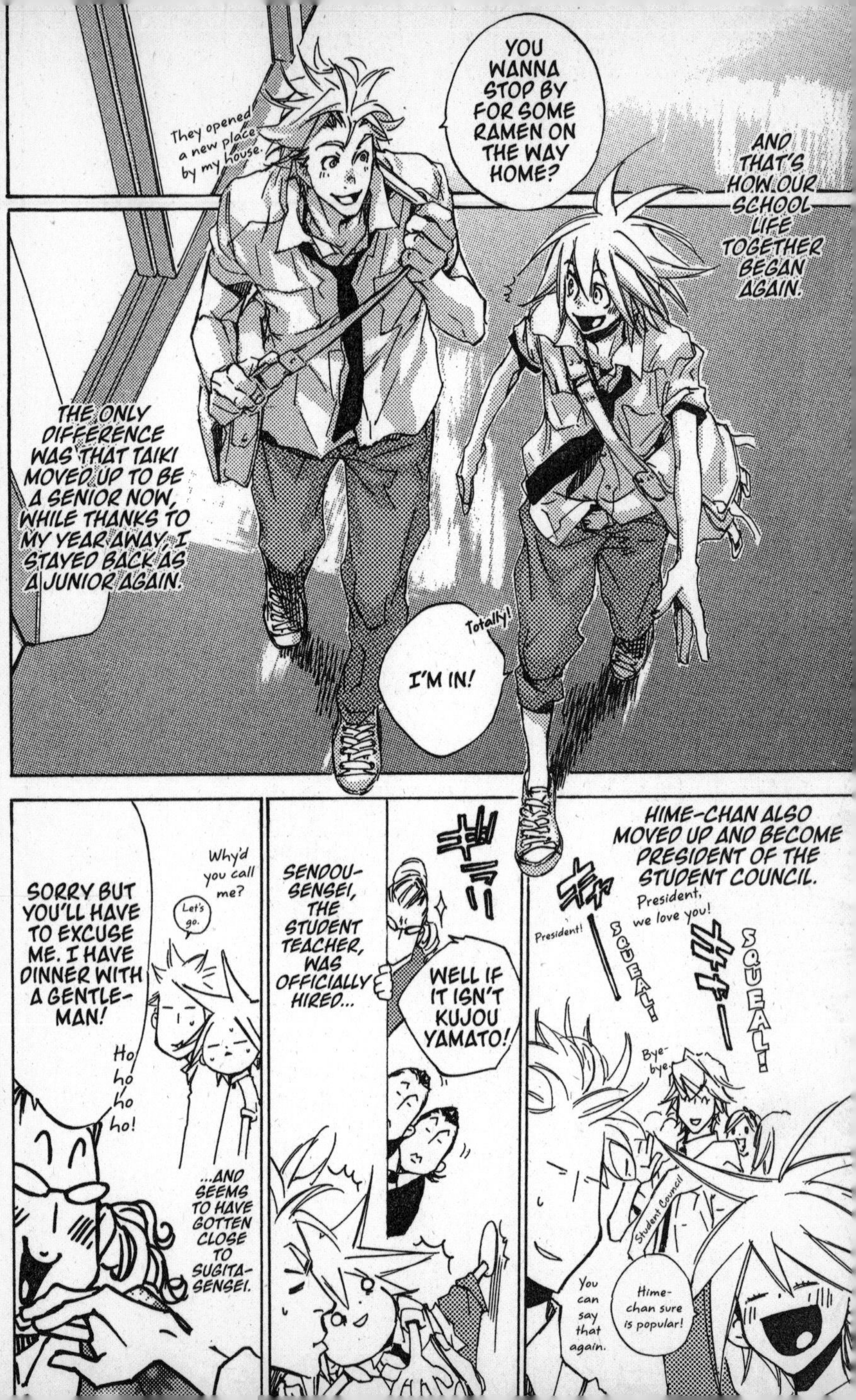
AND THAT'S HOW OUR SCHOOL LIFE TOGETHER BEGAN AGAIN.
YOU WANNA STOP BY FOR SOME RAMEN ON THE WAY HOME?
They opened a new place by my house.
THE ONLY DIFFERENCE WAS THAT TAIKI MOVED UP TO BE A SENIOR NOW, WHILE THANKS TO MY YEAR AWAY, I STAYED BACK AS A JUNIOR AGAIN.
Totally!
I'M IN!
HIME-CHAN ALSO MOVED UP AND BECOME PRESIDENT OF THE STUDENT COUNCIL.
President, we love you!
SQUEAL!
President!
SQUEAL!
Bye-bye.
Student Council
Hime-chan sure is popular!
You can say that again.
SENDOU-SENSEI, THE STUDENT TEACHER, WAS OFFICIALLY HIRED...
WELL IF IT ISN'T KUJOU YAMATO!
Why'd you call me?
Let's go.
SORRY BUT YOU'LL HAVE TO EXCUSE ME. I HAVE DINNER WITH A GENTLEMAN!
Ho ho ho ho!
...AND SEEMS TO HAVE GOTTEN CLOSE TO SUGITA-SENSEI.

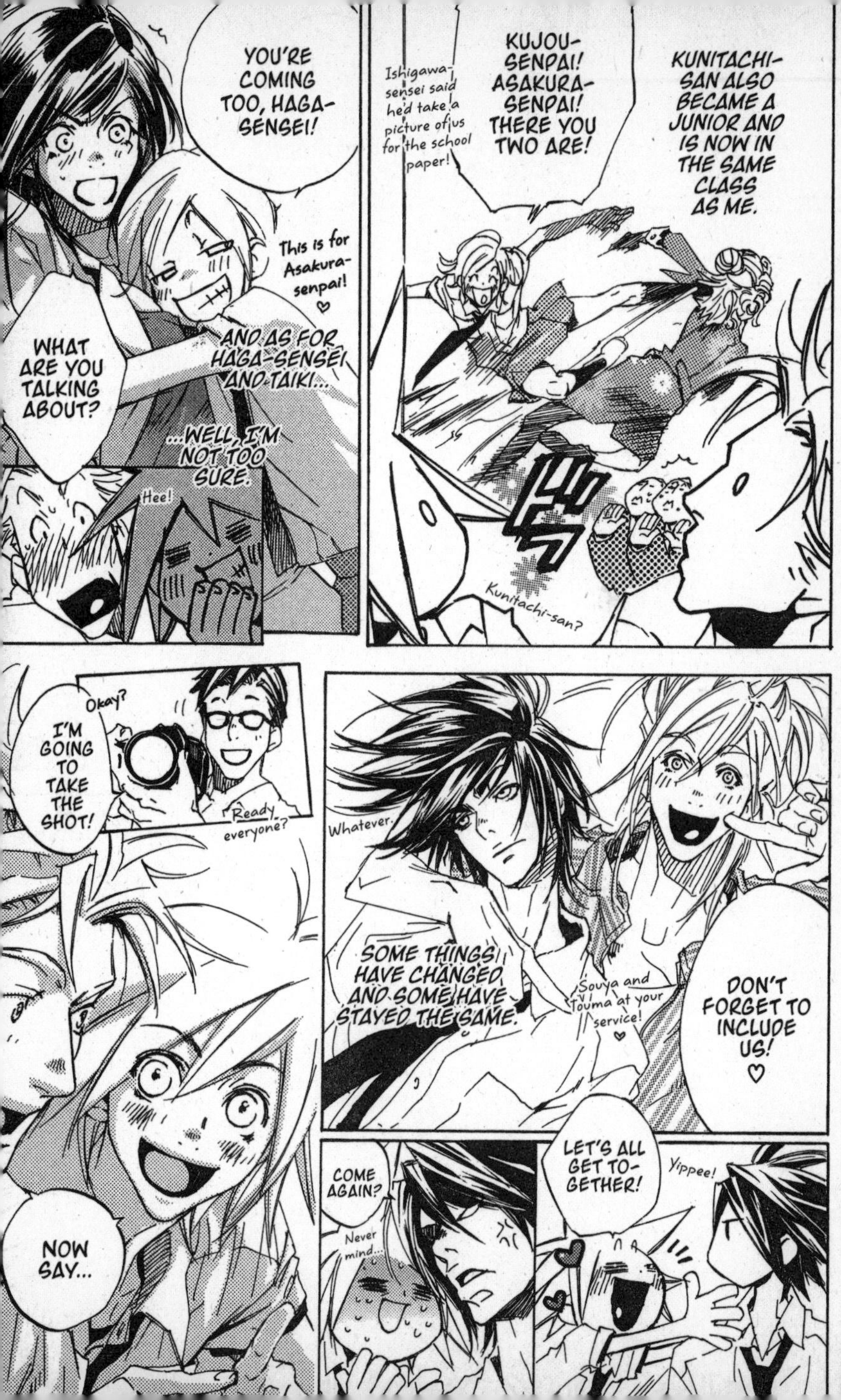
KUNITACHI-SAN ALSO BECAME A JUNIOR AND IS NOW IN THE SAME CLASS AS ME.
KUJOU-SENPAI! ASAKURA-SENPAI! THERE YOU TWO ARE!
Ishigawa-sensei said he'd take a picture of us for the school paper!
Kunitachi-san?
YOU'RE COMING TOO, HAGA-SENSEI!
This is for Asakura-senpai! ♡
AND AS FOR HAGA-SENSEI AND TAIKI...
WHAT ARE YOU TALKING ABOUT?
...WELL, I'M NOT TOO SURE.
Hee!
DON'T FORGET TO INCLUDE US! ♡
Souya and Touma at your service! ♡
Whatever.
SOME THINGS HAVE CHANGED AND SOME HAVE STAYED THE SAME.
LET'S ALL GET TOGETHER!
Yippee!
COME AGAIN?
Never mind...
Okay?
Ready everyone?
I'M GOING TO TAKE THE SHOT!
NOW SAY...

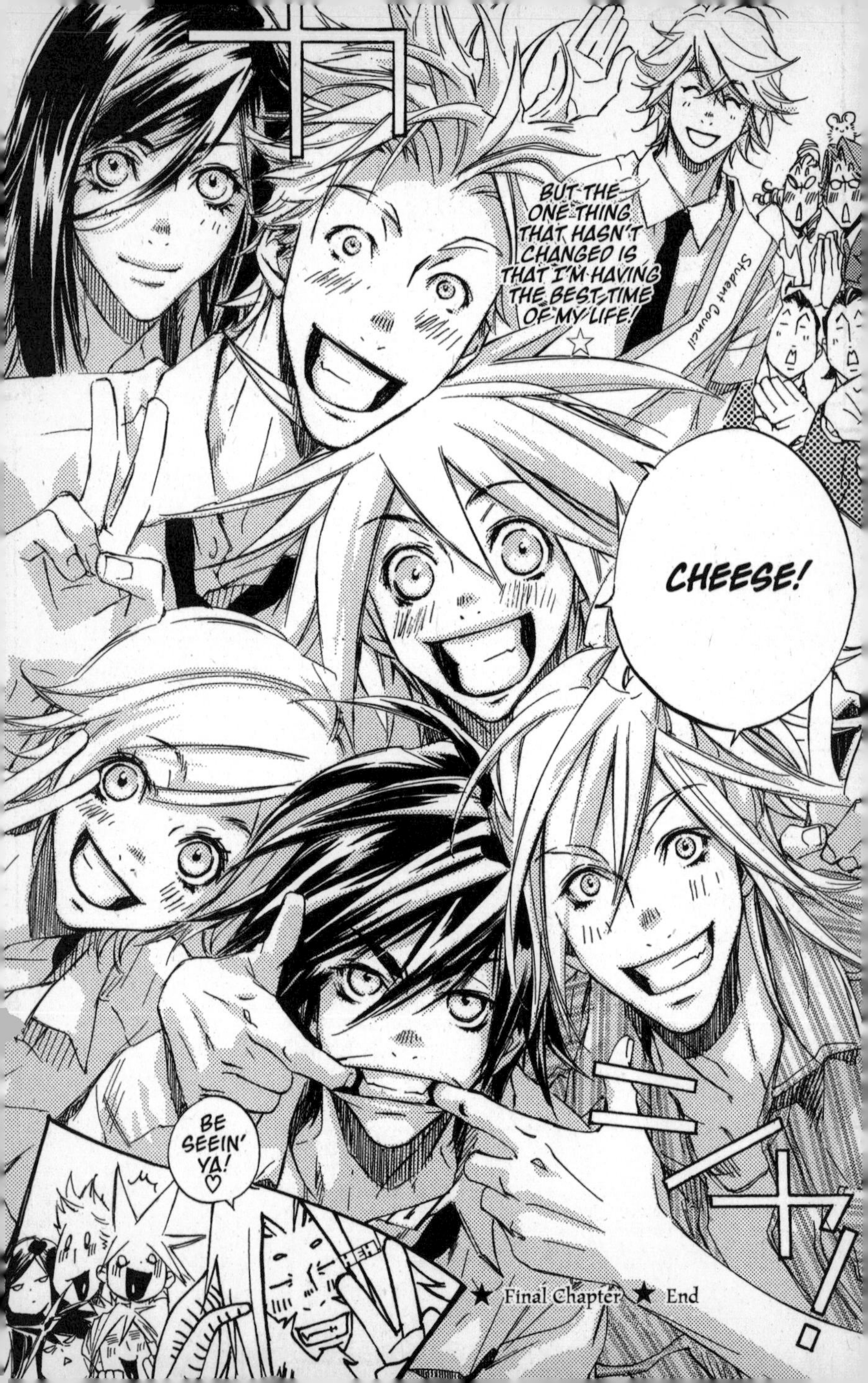
BUT THE ONE THING THAT HASN'T CHANGED IS THAT I'M HAVING THE BEST TIME OF MY LIFE! ☆
Student Council
CHEESE!
BE SEEIN' YA! ♡
★ Final Chapter ★ End

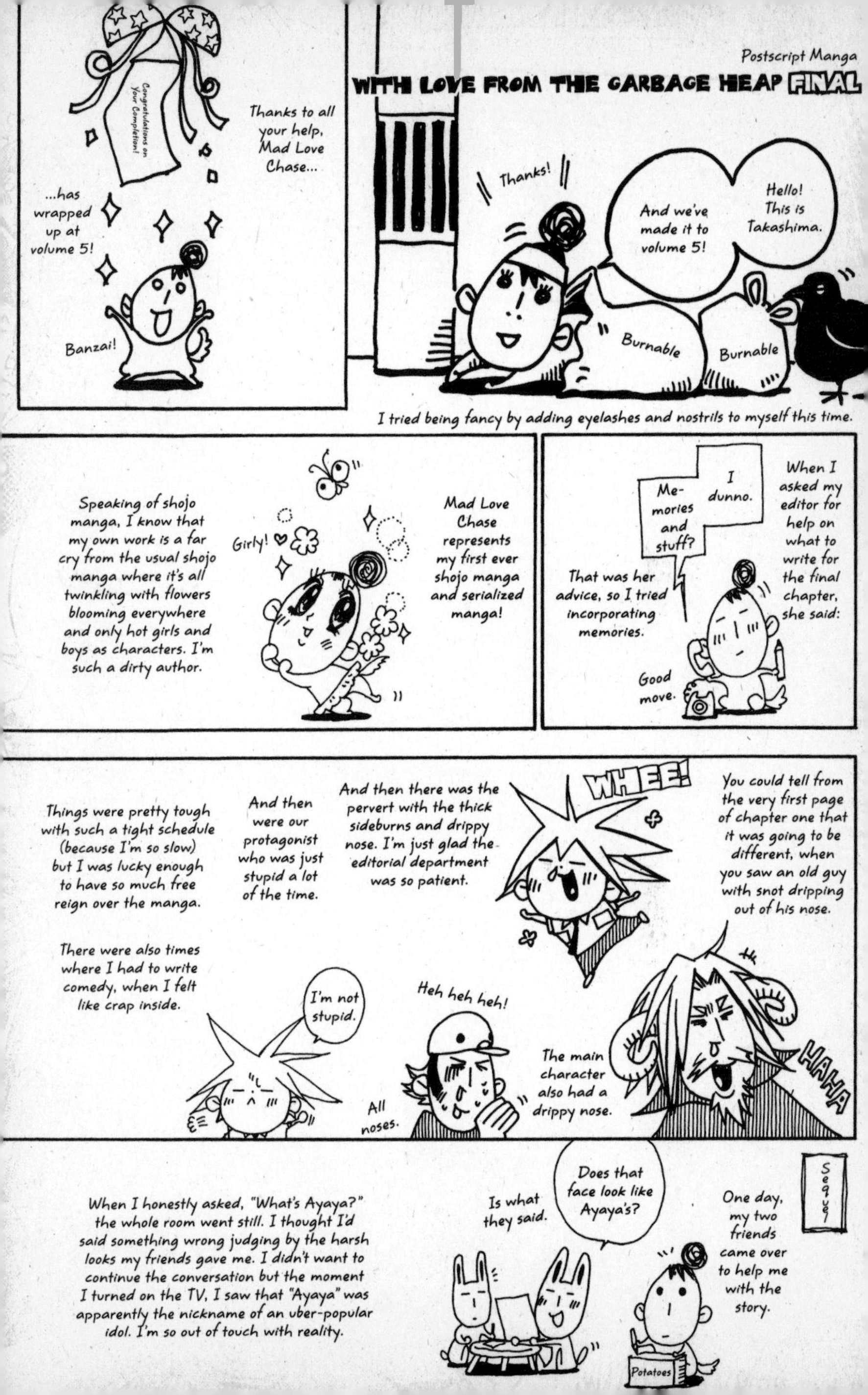

Postscript Manga
WITH LOVE FROM THE GARBAGE HEAP FINAL
Hello! This is Takashima.
And we've made it to volume 5!
Thanks!
Burnable
Burnable
I tried being fancy by adding eyelashes and nostrils to myself this time.
Congratulations on Your Completion!
Thanks to all your help, Mad Love Chase...
...has wrapped up at volume 5!
Banzai!
When I asked my editor for help on what to write for the final chapter, she said:
I dunno.
Me-mories and stuff?
That was her advice, so I tried incorporating memories.
Good move.
Mad Love Chase represents my first ever shojo manga and serialized manga!
Girly!
Speaking of shojo manga, I know that my own work is a far cry from the usual shojo manga where it's all twinkling with flowers blooming everywhere and only hot girls and boys as characters. I'm such a dirty author.
You could tell from the very first page of chapter one that it was going to be different, when you saw an old guy with snot dripping out of his nose.
WHEE!
And then there was the pervert with the thick sideburns and drippy nose. I'm just glad the editorial department was so patient.
And then were our protagonist who was just stupid a lot of the time.
Things were pretty tough with such a tight schedule (because I'm so slow) but I was lucky enough to have so much free reign over the manga.
HAHA
The main character also had a drippy nose.
Heh heh heh!
All noses.
I'm not stupid.
There were also times where I had to write comedy, when I felt like crap inside.
Sequel
One day, my two friends came over to help me with the story.
Does that face look like Ayaya's?
Is what they said.
Potatoes
When I honestly asked, "What's Ayaya?" the whole room went still. I thought I'd said something wrong judging by the harsh looks my friends gave me. I didn't want to continue the conversation but the moment I turned on the TV, I saw that "Ayaya" was apparently the nickname of an uber-popular idol. I'm so out of touch with reality.

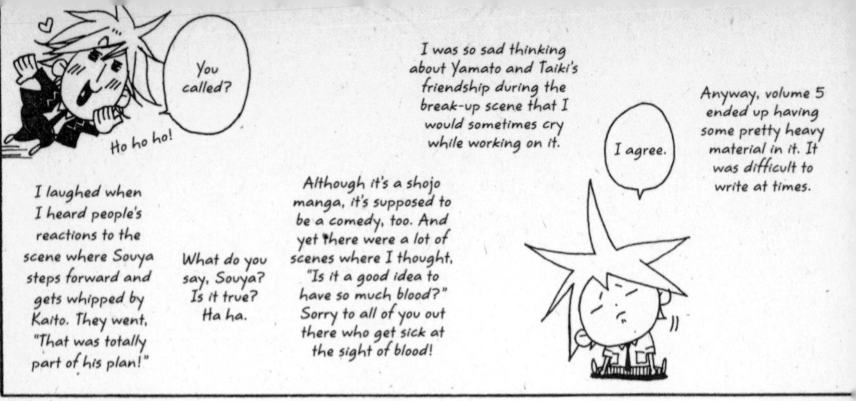
Anyway, volume 5 ended up having some pretty heavy material in it. It was difficult to write at times.
I agree.
I was so sad thinking about Yamato and Taiki's friendship during the break-up scene that I would sometimes cry while working on it.
Although it's a shojo manga, it's supposed to be a comedy, too. And yet there were a lot of scenes where I thought, "Is it a good idea to have so much blood?" Sorry to all of you out there who get sick at the sight of blood!
What do you say, Souya? Is it true? Ha ha.
I laughed when I heard people's reactions to the scene where Souya steps forward and gets whipped by Kaito. They went, "That was totally part of his plan!"
You called?
Ho ho ho!
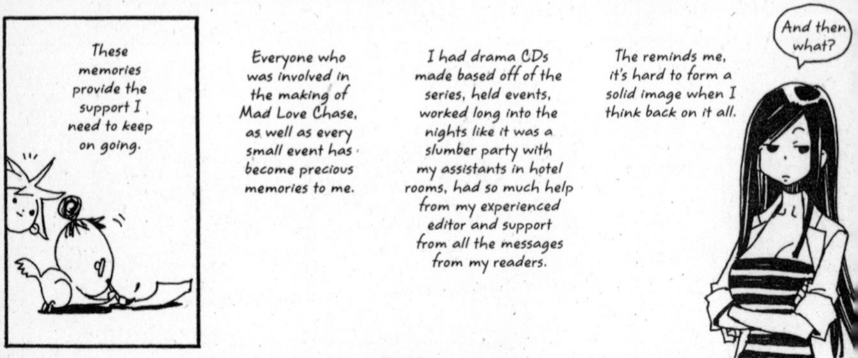
And then what?
The reminds me, it's hard to form a solid image when I think back on it all.
I had drama CDs made based off of the series, held events, worked long into the nights like it was a slumber party with my assistants in hotel rooms, had so much help from my experienced editor and support from all the messages from my readers.
Everyone who was involved in the making of Mad Love Chase, as well as every small event has become precious memories to me.
These memories provide the support I need to keep on going.
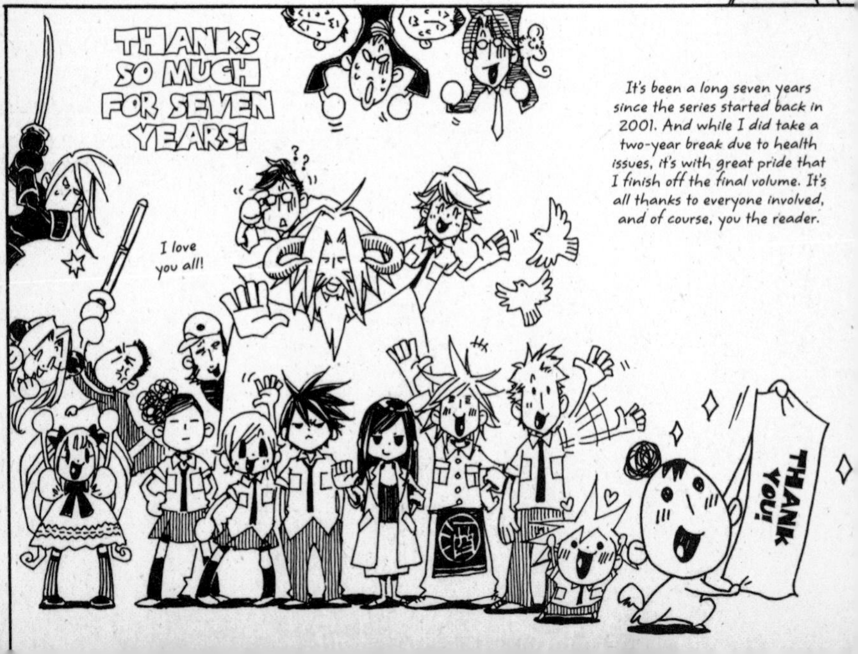
It's been a long seven years since the series started back in 2001. And while I did take a two-year break due to health issues, it's with great pride that I finish off the final volume. It's all thanks to everyone involved, and of course, you the reader.
THANKS SO MUCH FOR SEVEN YEARS!
I love you all!
THANK YOU!

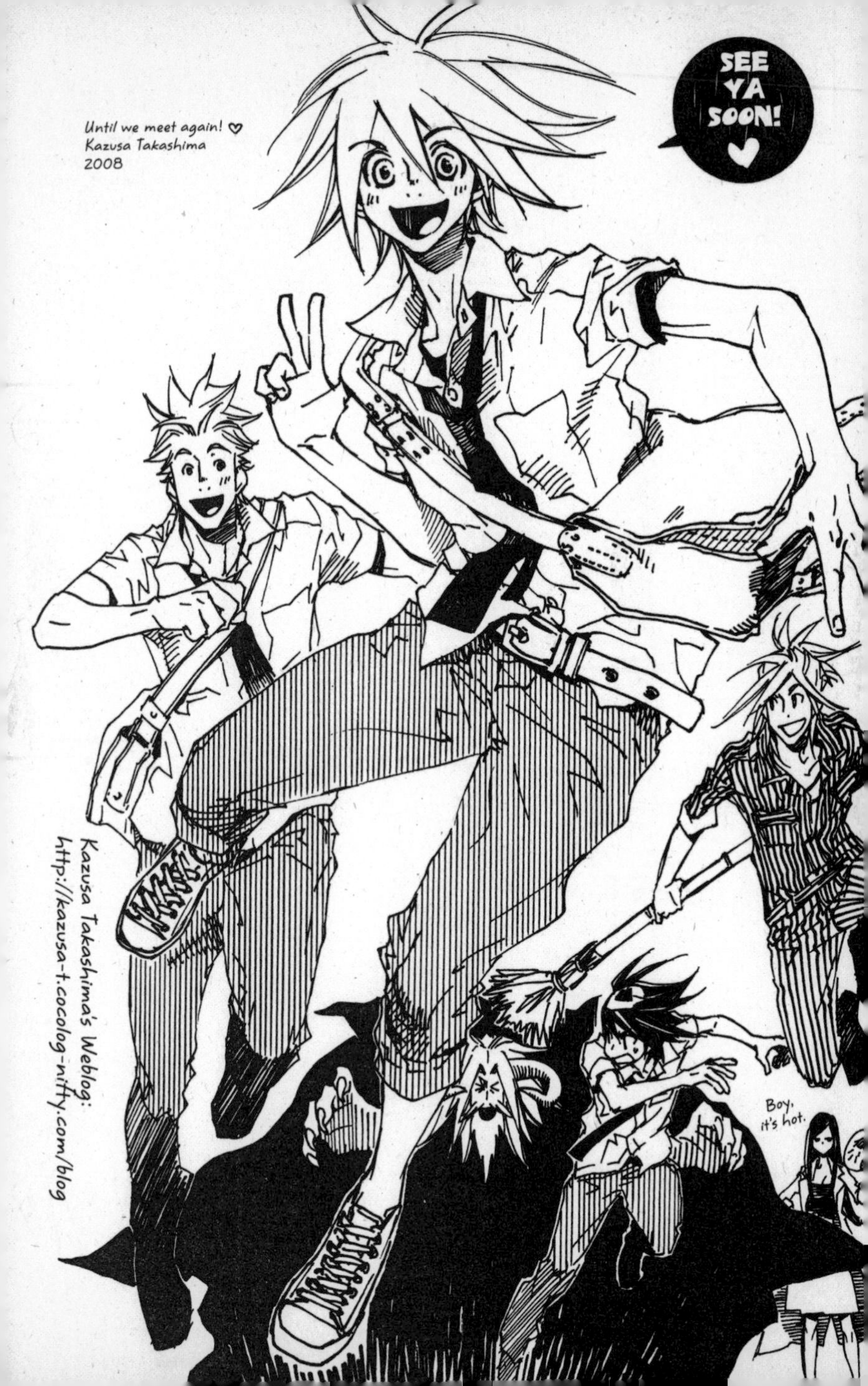
Until we meet again! ♡
Kazusa Takashima
2008
SEE YA SOON! ♥
Kazusa Takashima's Weblog:
http://kazusa-t.cocolog-nifty.com/blog
Boy, it's hot.

DOWNLOAD THE REVOLUTION.

Get the free TOKYOPOP app for manga, anytime, anywhere!

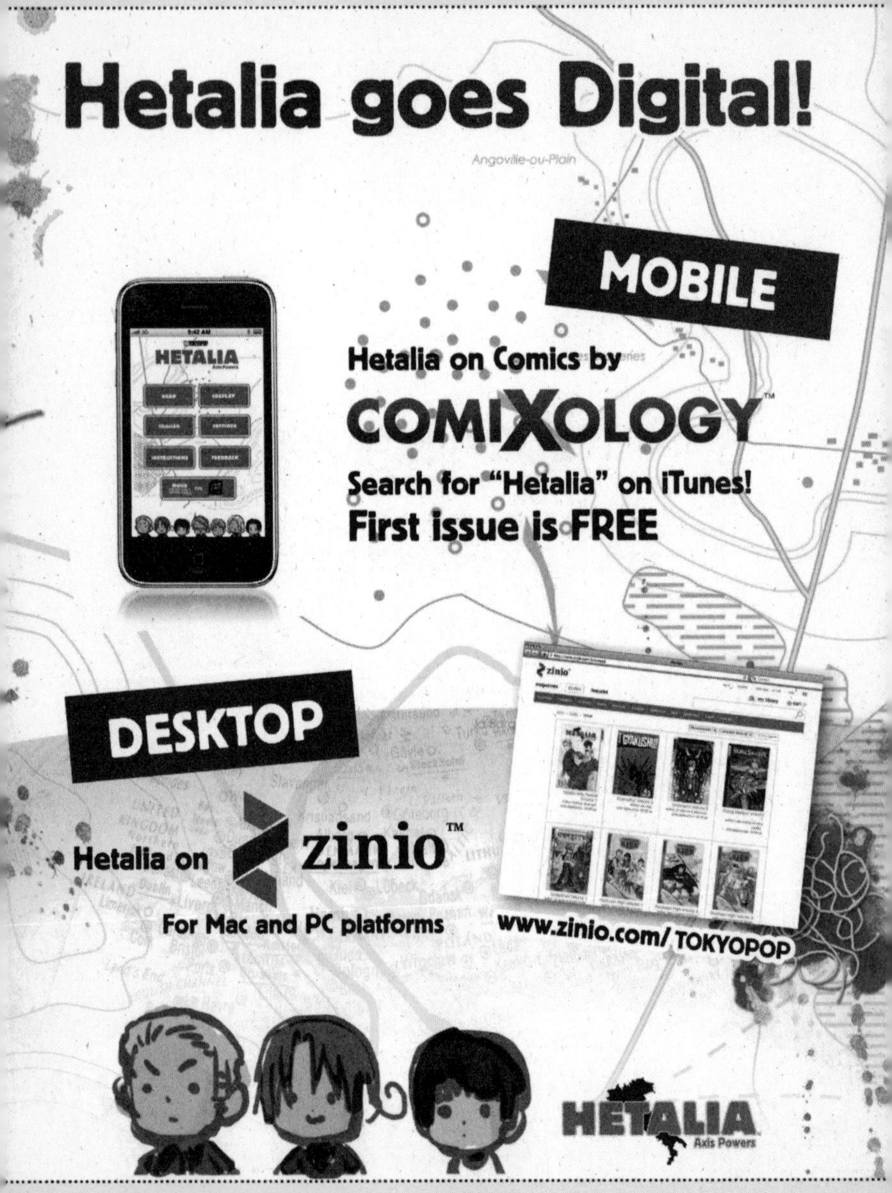
Hetalia goes Digital!
MOBILE
Hetalia on Comics by
COMIXOLOGY™
Search for "Hetalia" on iTunes!
First issue is FREE
DESKTOP
Hetalia on zinio™
For Mac and PC platforms
www.zinio.com/TOKYOPOP
HETALIA
Axis Powers

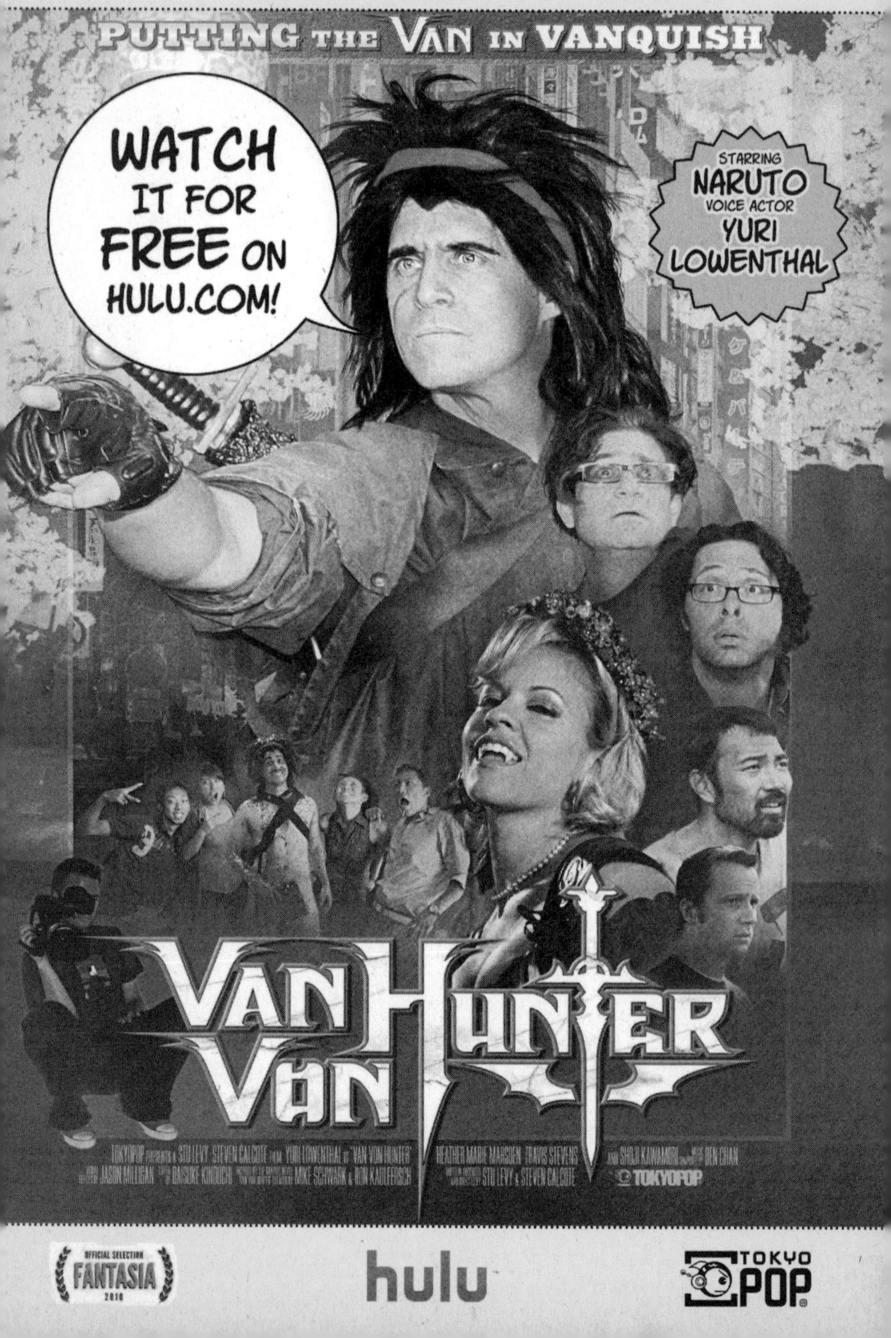
PUTTING THE VAN IN VANQUISH
WATCH IT FOR FREE ON HULU.COM!
STARRING NARUTO VOICE ACTOR YURI LOWENTHAL
VAN VON HUNTER
TOKYOPOP PRESENTS A STU LEVY STEVEN CALCOTE FILM YURI LOWENTHAL "VAN VON HUNTER" HEATHER MARIE MARSDEN TRAVIS STEVENS AND SHOJI KAWAMORI BEN CHAN
JASON MILLIGAN DAISUKE KIMOUCHI MIKE SCHWARK & RON KAULFERSCH STU LEVY & STEVEN CALCOTE
TOKYOPOP
OFFICIAL SELECTION FANTASIA 2010
hulu
TOKYO POP

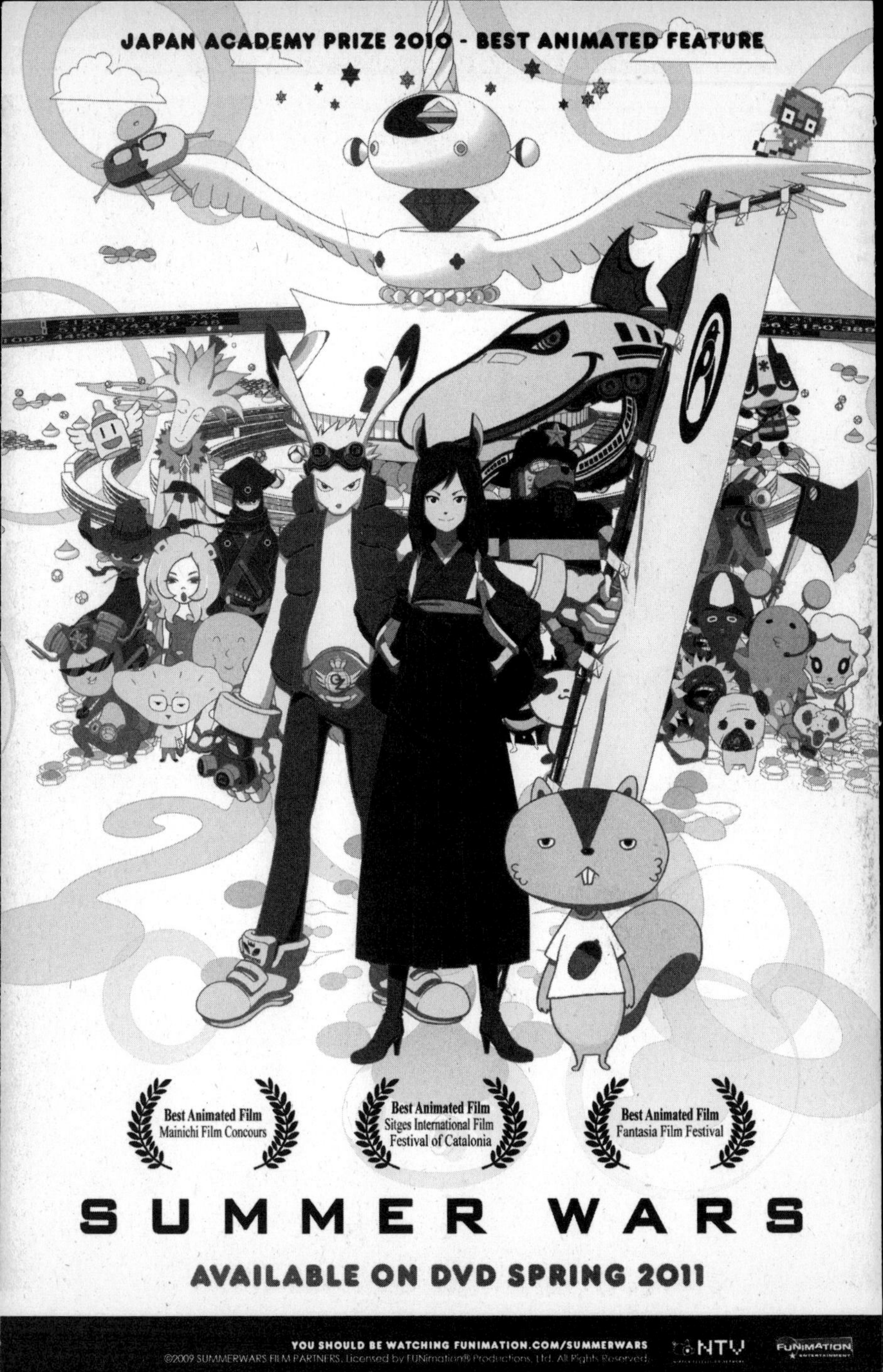
JAPAN ACADEMY PRIZE 2010 - BEST ANIMATED FEATURE
Best Animated Film
Mainichi Film Concours
Best Animated Film
Sitges International Film
Festival of Catalonia
Best Animated Film
Fantasia Film Festival
SUMMER WARS
AVAILABLE ON DVD SPRING 2011
YOU SHOULD BE WATCHING FUNIMATION.COM/SUMMERWARS
©2009 SUMMERWARS FILM PARTNERS. Licensed by FUNimation® Productions, Ltd. All Rights Reserved.
NTV
FUNIMATION

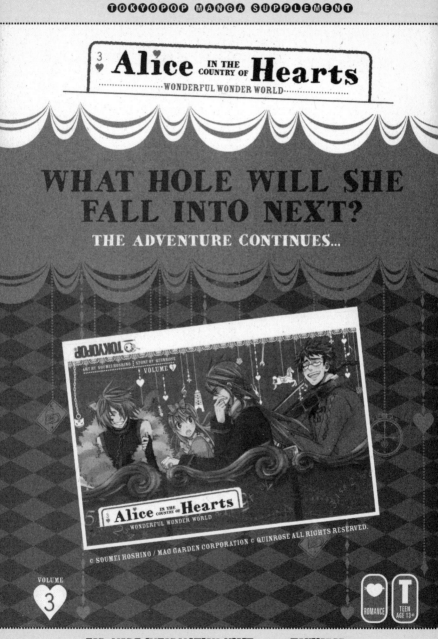

Learn From the Best!

Featuring the artists behind ***Fruits Basket***, ***Vampire Knight***, ***Maid Sama*** and **many more!**

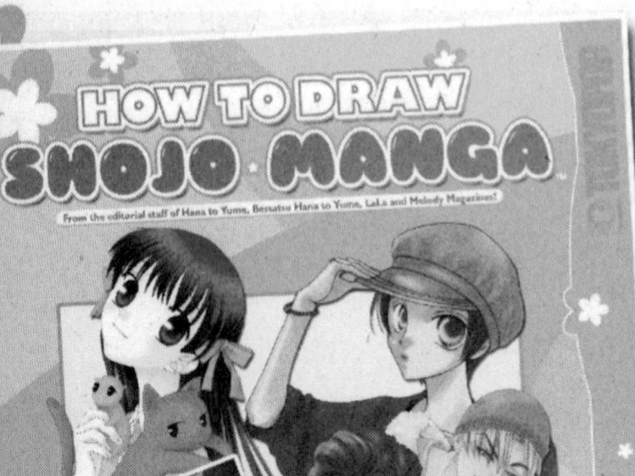
HOW TO DRAW
SHOJO · MANGA
From the editorial staff of Hana to Yume, Bessatsu Hana to Yume, LaLa and Melody Magazines!
Featuring many of the artists behind today's top shojo series!

Wanna draw your own shojo manga but not quite sure where to start? The editors at Hakusensha Publishing, home of such beloved shojo series as *Fruits Basket*, *Vampire Knight*, *Maid Sama* and *Ouran High School Host Club*, have assembled a book jam-packed with useful tips and practical advice to help you develop your skills and go from beginner to ready for the manga big leagues!

Join aspiring artist Ena as she strives to make her big break drawing manga. Aided by her editor, Sasaki, and some of the best shojo artists in Japan, follow along as Ena creates a short story from start to finish, and gets professional feedback along the way. From page layout and pacing to pencils and perspective, this guide covers the basics, and then challenges you to go to the next level! Does Ena (and you!) have what it takes to go pro? Pick up this book and learn from the best!

ROMANCE

T TEEN AGE 13+

FOR MORE INFORMATION VISIT: www.TOKYOPOP.com

NO ONE IS SAFE ANYMORE

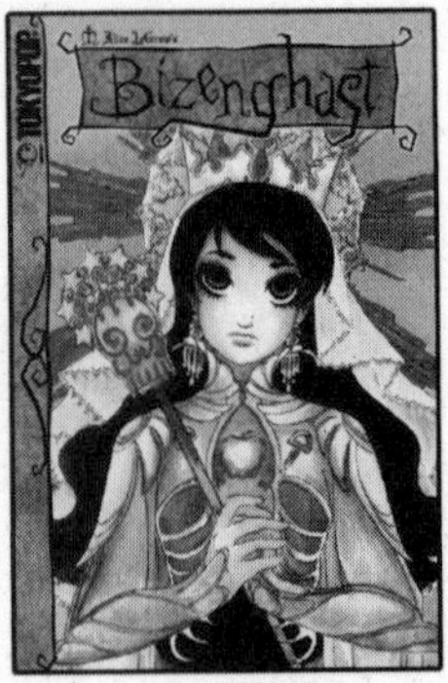
TOKYOPOP
Bizenghast

VOLUME 7

The final battle rages for the lives and souls of the inhabitants of Bizenghast, and no one is safe anymore. Shocking revelations of the town's dark history continue to emerge, and Dinah's struggle will go beyond the borders of the mausoleum...and into some of her worst nightmares...

PREVIEW AT www.TOKYOPOP.com/NoOneIsSafe

Bizenghast

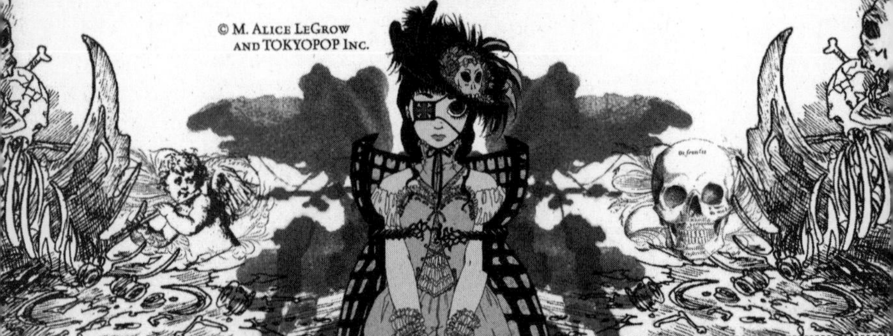

FOR MORE INFORMATION VISIT: www.TOKYOPOP.com

STOP!

This is the back of the book.
You wouldn't want to spoil a great ending!

This book is printed "manga-style," in the authentic Japanese right-to-left format. Since none of the artwork has been flipped or altered, readers get to experience the story just as the creator intended. You've been asking for it, so TOKYOPOP® delivered: authentic, hot-off-the-press, and far more fun!

DIRECTIONS

If this is your first time reading manga-style, here's a quick guide to help you understand how it works.

It's easy... just start in the top right panel and follow the numbers. Have fun, and look for more 100% authentic manga from TOKYOPOP®!